THE CLASSIC THEATRE

Volume Three

Volumes I, II, and IV of THE CLASSIC THEATRE contain:

I: SIX ITALIAN PLAYS

The Mandrake, *Niccolò Machiavelli*
Ruzzante Returns from the Wars, *Angelo Beolco*
The Three Cuckolds, *Anonymous*
The Servant of Two Masters, *Carlo Goldoni*
Mirandolina, *Carlo Goldoni*
The King Stag, *Carlo Gozzi*

II: FIVE GERMAN PLAYS

Egmont, *Johann Wolfgang von Goethe*
Don Carlos, *Friedrich von Schiller*
Mary Stuart, *Friedrich von Schiller*
Penthesilea, *Heinrich von Kleist*
The Prince of Homburg, *Heinrich von Kleist*

IV: SIX FRENCH PLAYS

The Cid, *Pierre Corneille*
The Misanthrope, *Molière*
Phaedra, *Jean Racine*
Turcaret, *Alain-René Lesage*
The False Confessions, *Pierre de Marivaux*
Figaro's Marriage, *Beaumarchais*

THE MODERN THEATRE, Volumes I, II, III, IV, V, VI, edited by Eric Bentley are also available in the Anchor series.

Eric Bentley's four books on the modern theatre are available in paperbacks: *The Playwright as Thinker, In Search of Theatre, The Dramatic Event, What Is Theatre?*

THE
CLASSIC THEATRE

Volume Three

SIX SPANISH PLAYS

Edited by Eric Bentley

DOUBLEDAY ANCHOR BOOKS
DOUBLEDAY & COMPANY, INC.
GARDEN CITY, NEW YORK

Typography by Edward Gorey; cover typography by Leonard Baskin; cover drawing by Gerda With, reproduced, with permission, from *Theater Pictorial: A History of World Theater* by George Altman and others, University of California Press, 1953.

The cover drawing shows the Corral del Principe, Madrid, as it is imagined to have been in the seventeenth century; in a more primitive form, and under the name of Corral de la Pacheca, it had been one of the half dozen original Madrid *corrales*—at first no more than the yards of houses rigged up as theatres.

The Anchor Books edition is the first publication of *The Classic Theatre, Volume III*, edited by Eric Bentley.

Anchor Books edition: 1959

Library of Congress Catalog Card Number 58–12033

CONTENTS

ACKNOWLEDGMENTS

In preparing this volume, the editor was, for various reasons, even more dependent than usual upon the advice and collaboration of others. Particular indebtedness is expressed to the following:

> Mrs. Barbara Bray
> Mrs. Mary Campbell
> Mr. Joaquín Casalduero
> Mr. Jason Epstein
> Miss Rosamond Gilder
> Mr. Claudio Guillén
> Mr. Rob Lyle
> Mr. R. D. F. Pring-Mill
> Miss Violet Serwin
> Mr. Frank Tauritz
> Mr. Eugenio Villicaña
> Mr. Thompson Webb, Jr.

E.B.

FOREWORD

Probably there is no body of World Literature so little known to the world as the classic Spanish drama. This is not entirely the world's fault, for few of the translations are readable, let alone impressive. The only collection of Lope de Vega ever published in English is, it seems, *Four Plays*, in English versions by John Garrett Underhill. I defy anyone to read it through. In the nineteenth century Denis Florence MacCarthy spent many years of his life translating Calderón. In trying to reproduce the sound of the Spanish, he effectively prevented himself from writing English. Edward Fitzgerald had much greater success with Calderón, but went to the other extreme of excessive freedom. For a while the effect must have seemed to be one of brilliance: today one is depressed by the persistent feeling that one is reading Victorian poetry of the second class. In ranging pretty widely over the field of Spanish classics in English, I found most enjoyable a volume entitled *Three Comedies from the Spanish*, published anonymously in London in 1807 and known to be the work of Lord Holland. Unfortunately, Lord Holland did not choose to include a single major play.

What was needed, I thought, was fresh air, such as flooded into the translated Greek drama a generation ago when Cocteau and Yeats applied themselves to it. I got hold of some translations which Roy Campbell had recently made for the B.B.C. Third Programme. *Fuente Ovejuna* and *The Trickster of Seville*, flat and even absurd in the earlier translations I had read, came alive. Campbell was in love with old Spain and was one of the few poets writing English in our day who had a touch of bravado, a vein of bravura. Even qualities I had disliked in certain poems of his own were turned to account in the translations. And he also had a straightforward lyrical gift, invaluable for the rendering of Lope's tenderness and charm. When Roy Campbell came to America for a lecture tour in the autumn of 1955, Jason Epstein and I arranged with him to bring out the B.B.C. translations—plus a couple we ourselves commissioned—in this country.

Campbell was killed, with all the sudden, sprawling violence of Spanish life and literature, some 18 months later. The translations were done, but, as they were not revised, let alone polished and fully prepared for the press, the responsibility devolved upon me of editing manuscripts without being able to consult their author. Should research students ever compare the manuscripts with the texts here published, some of them will wish, I imagine, that I had meddled more, others will conclude that I have already meddled too much. The task being impossible, the solutions found were at best partial and questionable. But in human affairs this is not an unusual situation.

The book remains largely Roy Campbell's, but it is rounded out by a version of one of the few Spanish classics that has received a truly classic translation into English. In the circumstances under which this volume was prepared, I would not have wished to mix Campbell's work with that of other moderns, but I think he would have enjoyed proximity to the Mabbe version of *La Celestina*. "As Greek tragedy," says Moratín, "was composed from the crumbs that fell from Homer's table, so the Spanish drama owed its earliest forms to *La Celestina*." James Mabbe's work, in turn, rendering Rojas in the English of Shakespeare and the King James Bible, stands as a model and a challenge to all subsequent translators of the Spanish classics.

The volumes of the present series represent only a small selection from an enormous repertoire. There will always be a case against the particular selection made, and there will always be a case against the particular translations used. I am very willing to concede that such a volume as the present one is only a beginning, if my critics will grant that it *is* a beginning. "Spanish drama of the golden age" has been a phrase only, referring to we knew not what. If this volume com-

municates something of the spirit of that drama to modern
readers (and, who knows? also to theatre audiences) it will
have succeeded where many worthy efforts in the past have
failed. In any event I shall not be ashamed to have played
even a modest part in the enterprise.

E.B.

CELESTINA

OR THE TRAGI-COMEDY OF CALISTO AND MELIBEA

Fernando de Rojas

*Translated by James Mabbe
and adapted by Eric Bentley*

DRAMATIS PERSONAE

CALISTO, *a young enamoured gentleman*

MELIBEA, *daughter to Pleberio*

PLEBERIO, *father to Melibea*

ALISA, *mother of Melibea*

CELESTINA, *an old bawd*

PARMENO[1]

SEMPRONIO

TRISTAN, *a page*[1] } *servants to Calisto*

SOSIA

CRITO, *a whoremaster*

LUCRECIA, *maid to Pleberio*

ELICIA } *whores*
AREUSA

CENTURIO, *a ruffian*

THE TIME: *about 1500*
THE PLACE: *a city in Spain*

A note on *thou* and *you*. Most readers will be familiar with the distinction between *tu* and *vous* in modern French. It is a useful distinction to keep in mind when reading the seventeenth century English of such a text as the present one, though the English—in this matter as in others—are less consistent and therefore less clear.

---

[1] In the Spanish, the first syllable of Parmeno has an accent. Though this is omitted from the present English version, the name should still be stressed on the first syllable. Tristan, on the other hand, is stressed on the second.

ACT I

A garden

CALISTO. In this, Melibea, I see the greatness of God.

MELIBEA. In what, Calisto?

CALISTO. In endowing thee with so perfect a beauty and in affording me the favour of thy presence—at a place convenient to unsheathe my secret grief. My reward in this is far greater than I have merited by my services to Him. The glorious saints, delighting in the Divine Presence, enjoy no greater pleasure than I, glorified by thy presence!

MELIBEA. Holdest thou this, Calisto, so great a guerdon?

CALISTO. So great that if God should give me a seat above His saints in Heaven, I should not hold it so great.

MELIBEA. I shall give thee a reward answerable to thy deserts if thou persevere in this manner!

CALISTO. O fortunate ears that hear such tidings!

MELIBEA. Unfortunate by the time they hear thy doom! Go, wretch! Begone! My patience cannot endure that a man should presume to speak to me of his delight in illicit love!

CALISTO. I go; but as one against whom adverse Fortune aimeth the extremity of her hate.

CALISTO's house

CALISTO

CALISTO. Sempronio, Sempronio, why Sempronio, I say, where is this accursèd varlet?

Enter SEMPRONIO.

SEMPRONIO. I am here, sir, about your horses.

CALISTO. My horses, you knave, how haps it then that thou comest out of the hall?

SEMPRONIO. The falcon was frisky, and I came in to set him on the perch.

CALISTO. Mischief light upon thee and bring thee (which shortly I hope to see) to a disastrous death! Come, thou unlucky rogue, make ready my bed!

SEMPRONIO. Presently, sir, the bed is ready for you.

CALISTO. Shut the windows, and leave darkness to accompany him whose sad thoughts deserve no light. O death, how welcome art thou to those who outlive their happiness!

SEMPRONIO. What's the matter with you?

CALISTO. Away! Do not speak to me or these hands shall cut off thy days by speedy death!

SEMPRONIO. I will be gone, sir.

CALISTO. The devil go with thee!

SEMPRONIO. There is no reason that he should go with me who stays with you.

He is now outside.

What squint-eyed star hath robbed this gentleman of his wonted mirth—and of his wits? Shall I leave him alone, or shall I go in to him? If I leave him alone, he will kill himself. If I go in, he will kill me. Let him bide alone and bite upon the bit, I care not. Better it is that *he* die whose life is hateful to him than that *I* die when life is pleasing unto me. And say that I should not desire to live save only to see my Elicia, that alone is motive enough to make me look to myself. But admit he should kill himself without any further witness, then must I give account of his life. The safest is to enter.

He goes inside.

CALISTO. Sempronio!

SEMPRONIO. Sir!

CALISTO. Reach me that lute.

SEMPRONIO, *returning.* Sir, here it is.

CALISTO, *singing*.

> Tell me what grief so great can be
> As to equal my misery?

SEMPRONIO. This lute, sir, is out of tune.

CALISTO. How can he tune it, who himself is out of tune? Take this lute and sing me the most doleful ditty thou canst devise.

SEMPRONIO, *singing*.

> Nero from Tarpey doth behold
>> How Rome doth burn all on a flame.
> He hears the cries of young and old
>> Yet is not grievèd at the same.

CALISTO. My fire is far greater and less her pity whom now I speak of.

SEMPRONIO, *aside*. I was not deceived when I said my master had lost his wits.

CALISTO. What's that, Sempronio?

SEMPRONIO. Nothing, sir.

CALISTO. Tell me what thou saidst: be not afraid.

SEMPRONIO. Marry, I said, how can that fire be greater which but tormenteth one man than that which burnt such a multitude?

CALISTO. What difference there is betwixt shadow and substance, so great is the difference betwixt the fire thou speakest of and that which burneth me. If the fire of Purgatory be like unto this, I had rather my soul should go to oblivion with the beasts than by such means share the glory of the saints.

SEMPRONIO, *aside*. Is it not enough to be a fool but you must also be a heretic?

CALISTO. Did I not tell thee thou shouldst speak aloud?

SEMPRONIO. Are you not a Christian?

CALISTO. I am a Melibean: I adore Melibea, I believe in Melibea, and I love Melibea.

SEMPRONIO, *aside*. My master is all Melibea, whose heart, not able to contain her, like a boiling vessel venting its heat, goes bubbling her name in his mouth!

To CALISTO.

Well, now that I know on which foot you halt, I shall heal you.

CALISTO. Thou speakest of matters beyond the moon. It is impossible.

SEMPRONIO, *aside*. As if Love had bent his bow, shot all his arrows only against him!

CALISTO. Sempronio!

SEMPRONIO. Sir?

CALISTO. Do not go away.

SEMPRONIO. This pipe sounds another tune.

CALISTO. What dost thou think of my malady?

SEMPRONIO. That you love Melibea.

CALISTO. And nothing else?

SEMPRONIO. It is misery enough to have a man's will chained to one place only.

CALISTO. Thou wot'st not what constancy is.

SEMPRONIO. Perseverance in ill is not constancy but obstinacy, so they call it in *my* country.

CALISTO. It is a foul fault for a man to belie that which he teacheth to others: for thou thyself takest pleasure in praising thy Elicia.

SEMPRONIO. Do you the good which I say but not the ill which I do.

CALISTO. Why dost thou reprove me?

SEMPRONIO. Because you subject the dignity of a man to the imperfection of a woman.

CALISTO. A woman? O thou blockhead, she's a goddess!

SEMPRONIO. As goddesses were of old. Have you not heard of Pasiphaë who played the wanton with a bull and of Minerva who dallied with a dog?

CALISTO. Tush, they are but fables.

SEMPRONIO. And that of your grandmother and her ape, that's a fable too? Witness your grandfather's knife that killed the villain who did cuckold him!

CALISTO. A pox of this coxcomb!

SEMPRONIO. Have I nettled you, sir? Oh, many women have been virtuous and noble, but, touching the others, who can recount their falsehoods, their tricks, their tradings, their truckings, their lightness, their tears, their mutabilities and impudencies, their dissemblings, their talkativeness, their deceits, their forgetfulness, their unkindness, their ingratitude, their fickleness, their sayings and gainsayings and all in a breath, their windings and turnings, their vainglory, their coyness, their pride, their base submissions, their prattlings, their gluttony, their sluttishness, their witcheries, their cheatings, their gibings, their slanderings, and their bawdry? They observe no mean; they have no reason; nor do they take any heed in what they do. They will privately pleasure him whom afterwards they will openly wrong; and draw him secretly in at their windows whom in the streets they will publicly rail at. They will give you roast meat, and beat you with the spit. They will invite you unto them, and send you packing with a flea in your ear. And, which is the true humour of a woman, whatsoever her will divines, that must be effected and, be it impossible, yet, not effecting it, she straightway censures your want of wit or affection, if not both. O what a plague! What a hell! Nay, what a loathsome thing it is for a man to have to do with them any longer than in the short prick of time that he holds them in his arms!

CALISTO. The more inconveniences thou settest before me, the more I love her. Who taught thee all this?

SEMPRONIO. Why, they themselves, who no sooner uncover their shame than they lose it. Balance thyself aright in the true scale of thine honour. You are a man endued with wisdom, favour, largeness of limbs, force, and agility of body. Fortune hath in so good a measure shared what is hers with you that your inward graces are by your outward the more beautified, and the stars were so propitious at your birth that you are beloved of all.

CALISTO. But not of Melibea. An thou dost glorify my gifts, I will tell thee, Sempronio, compared with Melibea's, they are but as stars to the sun. Do but consider the nobleness of her blood, the great estate she is born into, the excellency of her wit, the splendour of her virtues, her stately carriage, and, lastly, her divine beauty—whereof, I pray thee, give me leave to discourse a little——

SEMPRONIO, *aside*. What lies will my master tell me now?

CALISTO. What's that?

SEMPRONIO. I said I would have you tell me.

CALISTO. I will begin with her hair. Hast thou seen those skeins of fine gold which are spun in Arabia? Her hair is more fine and shines no less. Daintily combed and knit up in knots with curious ribboning, it has the power to transform men into stones.

SEMPRONIO, *aside*. Into asses, rather.

CALISTO. What sayest thou?

SEMPRONIO. That this could not be asses' hair.

CALISTO. Her eyes are quick, the brows prettily arched, her teeth small and white, her lips red and plump. Her breasts are placed at a fitting height, but their rising roundness and the pleasing fashion of her little tender nipples, who is able to figure forth? So distracted is the eye of man when he beholds them. The proportion of those other parts which I could not eye must undoubtedly (judging things unseen by the seen) be incomparably better than that which Paris gave his judgment of.

SEMPRONIO. Have you done, sir?

CALISTO. As briefly as I could.

SEMPRONIO. In that you are a man, I still say you are more worthy than she.

CALISTO. In what?

SEMPRONIO. In that she is imperfect: out of which defect she lusts and longs after yourself or someone less worthy. Did you never read the philosopher who tells you that as matter desires form, so woman desires man?

CALISTO. When shall I see this between me and Melibea?

SEMPRONIO. It is possible that you may, and as possible that, when you come to the full enjoying of her, you may hate her, looking on her with other eyes.

CALISTO. With what eyes?

SEMPRONIO. With clear eyes.

CALISTO. And with what, I pray, do I see now?

SEMPRONIO. With false eyes, like some kind of mirrors, which make little things seem great, and great little. Do not despair. Myself will take this business in hand.

CALISTO. I am proud to hear thee, though hopeless of obtaining my desire.

SEMPRONIO. Nay, I will assure it to you.

CALISTO. Heaven be thy speed! My cloth-of-gold doublet, it is thine, Sempronio. Take it.

SEMPRONIO, *aside*. I thank you for this and for many more to come. If my master clap such spurs to my side, I doubt not that I shall bring her to his bed. Without reward it is impossible to go through with anything.

CALISTO. Tell me, how dost thou think to purchase her pity?

SEMPRONIO. I shall tell you. It is now a good while since, at the lower end of this street, I fell acquainted with an old bearded woman called Celestina, a witch, subtle as the devil, and well-practised in all rogueries, one who has marred and made up again a hundred thousand maidenheads in this city. Such authority she hath, what by her persuasions and devices, that none can escape her. She will move rocks if she list and at her pleasure provoke them to lechery.

CALISTO. O that I might but speak with her!

SEMPRONIO. I will bring her hither. Use her kindly, and whilst I go my ways, study to express your pains as well as, I know, she is able to give you remedy.

CALISTO. O but thou stayest too long!

SEMPRONIO. I am gone. God be with thee.

Exit SEMPRONIO.

CALISTO. And with thee!

He kneels.

Almighty and Everlasting God, Thou who ledst the Three Kings to Bethlehem with Thy star, most humbly I beseech Thee lead my Sempronio, that he may turn my joy to torment and bring me, all unworthy, to the longed-for goal!

CELESTINA'S *house*

CELESTINA, ELICIA, CRITO

CELESTINA. Elicia, what will you give me for my good news?

SEMPRONIO, *outside.* Sempronio is come!

ELICIA. O hush! Peace, peace!

CELESTINA. Why? What's the matter?

ELICIA. Peace, I say, for here is Crito!

CELESTINA. Put him in the little chamber where the besoms be! Quickly, quickly, I say, and tell him a cousin of yours is come!

ELICIA. Crito, come hither quickly, oh, my cousin is come, what shall I do? Come quickly!

CRITO. With all my heart. Do not vex yourself.

Exit CRITO. *Enter* SEMPRONIO.

SEMPRONIO. O my dear mother, I thank my fate that hath given me leave to see you!

CELESTINA. My son, my king, thou hast ravished me with thy presence! Embrace me once more! What? Three whole days and never see us? Elicia, Elicia, wot you who is here?

ELICIA. Who, mother?

CELESTINA. Sempronio, daughter!

ELICIA, *aside.* O how my heart leaps and beats in my body, how it throbs within me!

CELESTINA. Do you see him? I will embrace him; you shall not.

ELICIA, *to* SEMPRONIO. Out, thou accursèd traitor, pox, plagues, and botches consume thee! Die thou by the hands of thine enemies and that for some notorious crime, ay me!

SEMPRONIO. Why, how now, my Elicia, what is it troubles you?

ELICIA. Three days? And in all that time not once come and see me?

SEMPRONIO. Where'er I go, thou goest with me. Where I am,

there art thou. But soft! Methinks I hear somebody's feet above. Who is it?

ELICIA. Who is it? One of my sweethearts!

SEMPRONIO. Nay, like enough.

ELICIA. Nay, it is true, go up and see.

SEMPRONIO. I go.

CELESTINA. Come hither, my son, regard not what she says, for she will tell you a thousand flimflam tales. Come with me and let us talk.

SEMPRONIO. But, I pray, who is that above?

CELESTINA. Would you know who?

SEMPRONIO. I would.

CELESTINA. A wench recommended unto me by a friar.

SEMPRONIO. What friar?

CELESTINA. Well, to save your longing, it is the fat friar.

SEMPRONIO. Alack, poor wench, what a heavy load she is to bear!

CELESTINA. We women must bear all.

SEMPRONIO. Then let me see her.

ELICIA. Wretch! Let your eyes start out of your head and drop down at your feet, for I see it is not one wench that can serve your turn. Go up and see her, but see you come at me no more!

SEMPRONIO. Nay, if this make you so angry, I will neither see her nor any other woman, I will only speak a word with my mother and so bid you adieu.

ELICIA. Go, begone, and stay away three years more if thou wilt!

SEMPRONIO. Mother, put on your mantle, and let us go. By the way I will tell you all.

CELESTINA. Elicia, farewell, make fast the door. Farewell, walls!

Exeunt CELESTINA *and* SEMPRONIO.

A street

CELESTINA, SEMPRONIO

SEMPRONIO. Now, mother, let not your ears go a-woolgathering, for he that is everywhere is nowhere. Listen!

CELESTINA. The friendship which hath taken such deep rooting betwixt thee and me needeth no preambles, no circumlocution, no preparation, no insinuation. Be brief!

SEMPRONIO. Calisto is hot in love with Melibea, and, because he needeth our joint furtherance, let us join together to make some purchase of him. For to take occasion by the foretop, why, it is the rung by which many have climbed to prosperity.

CELESTINA. The winking of an eye is enough for me, for, old as I am, I can see day at a little hole. I tell thee, Sempronio, I am as glad of this news as surgeons of broken heads, and, as they go festering the wounds to endear the sore, so will I delay Calisto's winning of Melibea. For the farther he is from effecting, the fairer will he promise to have it effected.

SEMPRONIO. No more. We are now at the gate, and walls, they say, have ears.

They have come to CALISTO'S *house.*

CELESTINA. Knock!

SEMPRONIO *knocks.*

CALISTO'S *house*

CALISTO, PARMENO, SEMPRONIO, CELESTINA

CALISTO. Parmeno!

PARMENO. Sir?

CALISTO. What a pox, art thou deaf, canst thou not hear?

PARMENO. What would you, sir?

CALISTO. Somebody knocks. Run!

PARMENO, *shouting through a window.* Who's there?

SEMPRONIO, *shouting back.* Open the door for this matronly dame and me.

PARMENO. It is Sempronio and an old bawd. O how she is bedaubed with painting!

CALISTO. Peace, you villain, she is my aunt. Run and open the door.

Aside.

Thinking to keep this matter from Parmeno, I shall have fallen into the displeasure of a woman who hath no less power over my life than God himself.

PARMENO, *who overhears this.* Believe it not. By this title of bawd is she generally known. If she pass along the streets and someone blurts out, "See where's the old bawd," she turns about, nods her head, and answers with a cheerful look. If she pass by where there be dogs, they bark out this name. The frogs that lie in ditches croak no other tune. Your shoemakers sing this song, your combmakers join with them. Your gardeners, your ploughmen, your reapers, your vine-keepers pass away the painfulness of their labors in making her the subject of their discourse, your gamesters never lose but they peal forth her praises—to be short, all things repeat no other name but this. Not one stone that strikes against another but presently noiseth out: "Old whore!"

CALISTO. Dost thou know her?

PARMENO. A great while ago my mother dwelt in her parish and, being entreated by this Celestina, gave me unto her to wait upon her, though now she knows me not.

CALISTO. What service didst thou do her?

PARMENO. I went into the market place and fetched her vict-uals so that, though I continued but a little while with her, yet I remember everything as if it were yesterday. This honest whore, this grave matron forsooth, had at the very end of the city, close by the waterside, a lone house, half

of it fallen down, ill-contrived, and worse furnished. For to
get her living, she had six several trades: she was a laun-
dress, a perfumeress, a former of faces, a mender of cracked
maidenheads, a bawd, and had some smatch of a witch.
Her first trade was a cloak to all the rest, under colour
whereof, being withal a piece of a sempstress, many young
wenches that were servants came to her house to work, some
on smocks, some on other things. Not one of them but
brought either bacon, wheat, flour, or a jar of wine, which
they could steal from their mistresses, making her house
(for she was the receiver) the rendezvous of their roguery.
She was a great friend to your students and pages. To these
she sold the innocent blood of those poor souls who did adventure their virginities, drawn on by the reparation which
she would make them of their lost maidenheads. Nay, she
had access with more secluded virgins and would deal with
these at the time of early mass or the stations of the cross.
Many have I seen of this party enter her house with covered
faces and men behind them, barefoot and disguised, to do
penance for their sins. She professed herself a kind of physician, skilled in the curing of little children. She would go
and fetch flax from one house and put it to spinning in another that she might have freer access unto all. Yet, not-
withstanding her trottings to and fro, she would never miss
mass nor vespers, nor neglect the monasteries: they were the
markets where she made her bargains. And at home she
made perfumes, amber, civet, powders, musk and mosqueta,
confections to clarify the skin, waters to make the face glis-
ter, lip salves, ointments, and a thousand other slibber-
slabbers, some made of the lees of wine, some of daffodils.
She had a trick to refine the skin with juice of lemons, with
turpentine, with the marrow of deer. The oils and greases
which she used would turn your stomach: as of bears,
horses, camels, snakes, cats of the mountain, badgers, hedge-
hogs and others. For the mending of lost maidenheads,
some she holp with little bladders and others she stitched
up with the needle. She had also roots hanging there of sea
onion and ground thistle. With these she did work wonders,
and when the French ambassador came thither, she made
sale of one of her wenches for a virgin three several times.

CALISTO. Parmeno, hold thy hand, we make her stay longer than stands with good manners. Let us go, lest she take it ill. But let me entreat thee, Parmeno, that the envy thou bearest to Sempronio be not an impediment to the remedy whereon my life relieth. I esteem as much of thy counsel as of his labour. As brute beasts do labour more bodily than men, for all this we hold them not in the nature of friends. The like differences do I make between thee and Sempronio, and sign myself unto thee for a friend. But, because, in a case so hard, not only all my good but even my life wholly dependeth, it is needful that I arm myself against all casualties. But let us see her who must work our welfare.

CELESTINA *and* SEMPRONIO *have been eavesdropping.*

SEMPRONIO. Celestina, Parmeno aims unhappily!

CELESTINA. Let me alone with Parmeno; I will bring him like a bird to pick bread from my fist. Thou and I will join together, Parmeno shall make a third, and all of us cheat Calisto.

PARMENO *lets in* CELESTINA *and* SEMPRONIO.

CALISTO. O imaged virtue, hope of my desired end, reliever of my torment, resurrection from my death! I here adore the ground whereon thou treadest!

CELESTINA, *aside to* SEMPRONIO. Can fair words make me fatter? Bid him shut his mouth and open his purse.

PARMENO, *aside.* O unhappy Calisto, kneeling to adore the rottenest piece of whorish earth that ever rubbed her shoulders in the stews! He is fallen into a trap and he will never get out.

CALISTO, *to* SEMPRONIO. What said my mother? She thinks I offer words to excuse my reward?

SEMPRONIO. You have hit the nail on the head, sir.

CALISTO. Come then, bring the keys, I will quickly put her out of that doubt.

Exit CALISTO *with* SEMPRONIO.

CELESTINA. I am very glad, Parmeno, that we have lighted on an opportunity wherein I may make known the singular love I bear to thee and the great interest (though undeservedly) thou hast in me. I say *undeservedly* for not a word you said escaped my ear. And not only that which I hear but even the very secrets of thy heart I pierce with the eyes of my understanding. Parmeno, Calisto is lovesick even to the death. And I would have thee know two conclusions that are infallibly true. The first is that every man must love a woman and every woman love a man. The second is that he who loves must be much troubled with the sweet, superexcellent delight which was ordained by God for the perpetuating of mankind. Now my pearl, my poor silly lad, my pretty little monkey face, come hither, you little whoreson, alack how I pity thy simplicity: thou knowest nothing of the world. But thou hast a harsh voice, and by thy grizzled beard it is easily guessed what manner of man thou art. *Pointing below his belt.*

Is all quiet beneath?

PARMENO. As the tail of a scorpion.

CELESTINA. The sting of a scorpion causeth no swelling, while thine causeth one of nine months' duration!

PARMENO *laughs.*

Laughst thou, pocky rogue?

PARMENO. Nay, mother, I love Calisto, tied thereunto by the fidelity of a servant. I see he is out of the right way, and nothing can befall a man worse than to hunt his desire without hope of a happy end, especially he thinking to recover his game by the vain advice of that beast Sempronio—which is as if he should take the broad end of a spade to dig worms out of a man's hand.

CELESTINA. Knowest thou not, Parmeno, that it is folly to bewail that which cannot be holpen? Thou canst not turn the stream of his passion. Tell me, Parmeno, hath not the like happened to others as well as to him?

PARMENO. But I would not have my master languish and grow sick.

CELESTINA. He is not sick and, were he never so sick, the power to make him whole lies in the hands of this weak old woman.

PARMENO. This weak old whore!

CELESTINA. Now the hangman be thy ghostly father! My pretty villain, how dar'st thou be so bold with me?

PARMENO. Marry, I am Parmeno, son to Alberto thy friend, who lived some little while with thee when thou dweltst by the river.

CELESTINA. Good Lord, art thou Parmeno, Claudina's son?

PARMENO. The very same.

CELESTINA. Now the fire of the pox consume thy bones, for thy mother was an old whore as myself! Come hither unto me, come, I say! Many a cuff on the ear have I given thee in my days and many kisses too! Ah, you little rogue, dost thou remember, sirrah, when thou lay'st at my bed's feet?

PARMENO. Passing well. You would take me up to your pillow and there lie hugging of me, and because you savoured somewhat of old age I would fling and fly from you.

CELESTINA. Out, impudent, are you not ashamed! But, to leave jesting: albeit I have made myself a stranger unto thee, yet thou wast the only cause that drew me hither. My son, thou art not ignorant how thy mother gave thee unto me. Thy father died of the grief he suffered for the uncertainty of thy life. And when the time came to leave this world, he sent for me and told me to enquire after thee and bring thee up as mine own: as soon as thou shouldst come to man's estate, I should uncover unto thee a certain place where he hath left thee more gold than all the revenues paid to thy master Calisto. I have spent much time and money enquiring after thee, and never till three days since heard where you abode. And now, my son, return to reason! Settle thyself some place or other! And where better than where I shall advise thee? Continue here and serve this master—but not with foolish loyalty as hitherto thou hast done. The masters of these times love more themselves than their servants, neither in so doing do they do amiss: the like love ought servants to bear unto themselves. My son Parmeno, thy master is one that befools his servants and wears them out to the very stumps. Get thee some friends in his house (for with him thou must not think to fasten friendship where there is such difference of estate). As for that which I told you of, it shall be safely kept; in the meanwhile it shall be much for thy profit that thou make Sempronio thy friend.

PARMENO. My hair stands on end. I hold thee for my mother, Calisto for my master, I desire riches but would not get them wrongfully!

CELESTINA. Marry, sir, but I would. Right or wrong, so as my house may be raised high enough, I care not.

PARMENO. Well, we are of two contrary minds. I would pass through woods without fear, take my sleep without startings. Contented poverty is safe and secure.

CELESTINA. Heaven be thanked thou hast wealth. But the greater a man's fortune, the less secure, and therefore we must arm ourselves with friends. And where canst thou get a fitter, nearer, and better companion tham Sempronio? O Parmeno, what a life might we lead, even as merry as the day is long! Sempronio loves Elicia, kinswoman to Areusa.

PARMENO. To Areusa?

CELESTINA. Ay, to Areusa.

PARMENO. Areusa, the daughter of Eliso?

CELESTINA. Areusa, the daughter of Eliso.

PARMENO. Is this certain?

CELESTINA. Most certain.

PARMENO. It is marvellous strange.

CELESTINA. Dost thou like her?

PARMENO. Nothing in the world more.

CELESTINA. Thou shalt have her. Man, she is thine, as sure as a club.

PARMENO. Nay, soft, mother, give me leave not to believe thee.

CELESTINA. He is in error that will believe no man!

PARMENO. I dare not be so bold.

CELESTINA. Fainthearted is he that ventureth not for his good!

PARMENO. O Celestina, I have heard that a man should converse with those that may make him better. As for Sempronio, by his example shall I not be won to be virtuous, nor shall he by my company be withdrawn from being vicious.

CELESTINA. There is no wisdom in thy words, for without company there is no pleasure in the possession of anything. Delight is with friends, in things that are sensual, but especially in recounting matters of love, the one to the other. "Let us go by night! Hold thou the ladder! Look, where the cuckold her husband goes! Thus did I kiss her! Thus came we nearer!" Is there any delight in all this without company?

PARMENO. I would not, mother, that you should draw me on as those do who draw men to drink of their heresies, sugaring the cup with sweet poison to catch the wills of the weakminded and blind the eyes of their reason with the powder of sweet-pleasing affection!

CELESTINA. What is reason, you fool? What is affection, you ass? Discretion (which thou hast not) must determine that; and discretion gives the upper hand to prudence; and prudence cannot be had without experience; and experience cannot be found but in old folks, fathers and mothers; and good parents give good counsel, as I do thee, whose life I prefer before mine own.

PARMENO. I am suspicious of this doubtful counsel. I am afraid to venture.

CELESTINA. He that wilfully refuseth counsel shall suddenly come to destruction! And so, Parmeno, I rid myself of thee.
She starts to go.

PARMENO, *to himself.* What I were best to do I know not. I have heard that a man should believe those whose years carry authority. Now what is it she adviseth me unto? To be at peace with Sempronio. And to peace no man should be opposite. I will therefore hearken unto her. Mother, speak anew unto me, for I will receive thy counsel as a kindness. Command me.

CELESTINA. Parmeno, in seeing thee suddenly conform to reason, methinks I behold thy father here before me! What a man he was! But, hush, I hear Calisto coming and thy new friend, Sempronio.

Re-enter CALISTO and SEMPRONIO.

CALISTO, *to CELESTINA.* Receive this poor gift of him who with it offers thee his life.

PARMENO, *aside to SEMPRONIO.* What hath he given her?

SEMPRONIO. A hundred crowns.

PARMENO *laughs.*

Hath my mother talked with thee?

PARMENO. She hath.

SEMPRONIO. How is it then?

PARMENO. As thou wilt. Yet I am still afraid.

SEMPRONIO. I fear me I shall make thee twice as much afraid ere I have done.

CALISTO, *to* CELESTINA. Now, mother, get you home and cheer up your house; then hasten thither and cheer up ours.

CELESTINA. God be with you.

CALISTO. And with you.

Exit CELESTINA.

ACT II

CALISTO'S *house*

CALISTO, SEMPRONIO, PARMENO

CALISTO. Tell me, my masters, the hundred crowns which I gave yonder old beldam, are they well bestowed?

SEMPRONIO. Exceeding well: for better is the use of riches than the possessing of them. And thus, sir, having told you my mind, let me advise that you return to your chamber where I shall talk further with you.

CALISTO. Methinks, Sempronio, it were better that thou shouldst go along with her and hasten her on.

SEMPRONIO. If I leave you thus alone, you will do nothing but sigh, weep, and take on, shutting yourself up in darkness, seeking new means of thoughtful torment, wherein you cannot escape either death or madness. For the avoiding whereof, get some good company about you. The best remedy against love is not to think on love. Kick not against the prick. Feign yourself to be merry, and all shall be well.

CALISTO. Sempronio my friend (for so thy love makes me style thee), since it grieves thee that I should be alone, Parmeno shall stay with me. Parmeno!

PARMENO. I am here, sir.

CALISTO. But I am not, for I did not see thee. Sempronio, ply her hard, I pray thee!

Exit SEMPRONIO.

Now, Parmeno, what thinkest thou? Thou hast opposed thyself to Celestina to draw me to a detestation of her. And I believe thee. Yet had I rather give *her* an hundred crowns than give another five.

PARMENO. It had been better you had employed your liberality on some present for Melibea herself than to cast away your money upon this old bawd—who minds to make you her slave.

CALISTO. How, fool, her slave?

PARMENO. To whom thou tellest thy secret, to him dost thou give thy liberty.

CALISTO. I would fain know this of thee: whether it be not necessary to have a mediator who may go to and fro with my messages until they arrive at *her* ears of whom to have a second audience I hold it impossible?

PARMENO. Marry, sir, one inconvenience is the cause of another and the door that opens unto many.

CALISTO. I understand not thy purpose.

PARMENO. Your losing of your hawk the other day was the cause of your entering the garden where Melibea was; your entering, the cause that you saw her and talked with her; your talk engendered love; your love brought forth pain; and your pain will be the cause of your growing careless of your body, soul, and goods. And that which grieves me most is that you must fall into the hands of this same trot-up-and-down, this maidenhead-monger, this gadding-to-and-fro bawd, who for her villainies in this kind hath been three times tarred and feathered.

CALISTO. Let them tar and feather her the fourth time too. I care not. Thou art not heartsick as I am, Parmeno.

PARMENO. I should but dissemble with you, sir, if I should not tell you that you lost your liberty when you did first imprison your will.

CALISTO. Unmannerly rascal! What remedy Sempronio brings unto me with his feet, the same dost thou put away with thy tongue! Feigning thyself to be faithful, thou art nothing but a lump of earth; a box filled with the dregs of malice; the inn that gives entertainment to envy; not caring so as thou mayest discredit this old woman, be it by right or by wrong. Sempronio did fear his going and thy staying!

PARMENO. My sharp words are better to stifle violent flames than the soft smoothings of soothing Sempronio. These kindle afresh your flames, which shall never leave burning till they have brought you to your grave.

CALISTO. I am in pain and thou readest philosophy to me! Begone, get forth my horse! See he be dressed! I must pass by the house of my Melibea—or rather of my goddess.

PARMENO, *outside*. Holla, boys!

No one stirs.

I must do it myself, and I am glad it is no worse, for I fear, ere long, we shall come to a worse office than to be boys of the spur. Well, let the world slide.

He gets the horse.

How now, you jade, are *you* neighing too? Is not one hot beast enough in the house, or do you too smell Melibea?

CALISTO, *coming out*. When comes this horse?

PARMENO. Here he is. Sosia was not within.

CALISTO. Hold the stirrup. Open the gate a little wider. If Sempronio come in the meanwhile and the old woman with him, will them to stay, for I will return presently.

CALISTO rides away.

PARMENO, *alone*. Go, never to return, and the devil go with you! Celestina and Sempronio will fleece you ere they have done and not leave you one master feather to maintain your flight! Unfortunate that I am to suffer hatred for my truth and receive harm for my service! The world is grown to such a pass that it is good to be bad and bad to be good: I will follow the times and do as other men do. Had I credited Celestina I had not been thus ill-entreated by Calisto. But this shall be a warning to me. Let him destroy, hang, drown, burn himself, and give all that he hath to bawds. I will hold my peace and help to divide the spoil. It is an ancient rule that the best fishing is in troubled waters.

A street

SEMPRONIO, CELESTINA

SEMPRONIO, *to himself.* Look what leisure the old bearded bawd takes! How softly one leg comes drawling after another! Now she has her money, her arms are broken!

To CELESTINA.

Well overtaken, mother, you will not hurt yourself by too much haste.

CELESTINA. How now, son, what news with you?

SEMPRONIO. Our patient knows not what he would have. He will have his cake baked before it be dough, and his meat roasted before it be spitted.

CELESTINA. There is nothing more proper to lovers than impatience, especially these new lovers who fly out without once thinking on the harm which the meat of their desire may, by overgorging, occasion them—and their servants.

SEMPRONIO. Servants? Shall *we* be burned with the sparkles which scatteringly fly forth of Calisto's fire? I had rather see him go to the devil. Upon the first discovery of danger I will not stay with him, no, not an hour. But time will tell me what I shall do, for before his final downfall, like a house that is ready to collapse, he will give some token of his ruin. Every day we see strange accidents. If some should tell you: "Thy father is dead; Granada is taken; Peter is robbed; Inez hath hanged herself," what wouldst thou say, save only that some three days later no wonder will be made of it? All things pass after this manner. Just so will it be with my master's love: the farther it goes on, the more it will slacken. Let us make our profit of him whilst this plea is pending.

CELESTINA. I hold with thee and jump in thy opinion. Yet it is necessary that a good lawyer should follow his client's cause, colour his plea with some show of reason. So shall he not want clients—nor Celestina suitors in cases of love.

SEMPRONIO. Frame it to thine own liking. This is not the first business thou hast taken in hand.

CELESTINA. The first, my son? Few virgins hast thou seen in this city to whom I have not been a broker and holp them to sell their wares. There was not a wench born but I writ her down in my register that I might know how many escaped my net. Can I live by the air? By what do I eat and drink? Find clothes to my back and shoes to my feet? In this city was I born; in it was I bred. He that knows not both my name and my house, thou mayest hold him a mere stranger.

SEMPRONIO. Tell me, mother, what passed betwixt you and Parmeno when I went up with Calisto for the crowns?

CELESTINA. I told him that he should gain more by joining in friendship with us than with all his gay glozings, and that he should not make himself a saint before such an old beaten bitch as myself. I put him in mind of his mother, that he might not set my office at nought, herself having been of the same trade.

SEMPRONIO. Is it long since you first knew her?

CELESTINA. Celestina saw her born and holp to breed her up. His mother and I were nail and flesh, buckle and thong; of her I learned the better part of my trade. Had she lived, I should never have lived to be deceived. She was a faithful friend and good companion. If I brought bread, she would bring meat. If I spread the cloth, she would lay the napkins. She was not foolish, nor proud, as most of your women nowadays are, and I swear she would go barefaced from one end of the city to the other, with her wine jar in her hand, and not one would give her worse word than Mistress Claudina. Everyone would feast her, so great was the affection which they bear her, and she never came home till she had tasted some eight or ten sorts of wine, bearing one pottle in her jar and the other in her belly. Her word was as current as gold: if we found ourselves thirsty, we entered the next tavern and called for a quart of wine, though we had not a penny to pay for it. O Sempronio, were it but cat after kind, and that such were the son as was the mother, assure thyself that thy master should remain without a feather and we without farther care!

SEMPRONIO. How dost thou think to make him thine? He is a crafty subtle fox.

CELESTINA. I will bring him to have Areusa, and make him cocksure ours.

SEMPRONIO. Canst thou do any good upon Melibea? Hast thou any good bough to hang by?

CELESTINA. Melibea is fair; Calisto fond and frank and willing to spend. Money can do anything. It splitteth hard rocks. It passeth over rivers dry-foot . . . This is all I know concerning him and her. Now must I go to Pleberio's house. Sempronio, farewell! For though Melibea stands so high upon her pantofles, yet is she not the first that I have made to stoop. They are all ticklish and skittish, given to wincing and flinging, but, after they are well weighed, they prove good highway jades and travel quietly. You may kill them but never tire them. They curse the cocks because they proclaim it is day; the clocks because they go too fast. They lie prostrate as if they looked after the Pleiades, but when they see the morning star arise, they sigh for sorrow. Above all, note how quickly they change: they endure torment for him whom before they had tormented; they are servants to those whose mistresses they were. If the hinges of their door chance to creak, they anoint them with oil, that they may perform their office without noise. They are enemies of the mean and wholly set upon extremes.

SEMPRONIO. Mother, I understand not these terms.

CELESTINA. A woman either loveth or hated him much of whom she is beloved. If she entertain not his love, she cannot dissemble her hate. And because I know this to be true, it makes me go more merrily to Melibea's house than if I had her fast in my fist already. For I know that, though at the first I must woo her, yet in the end she will be glad to sue to me. Here in this pocket of mine I carry a little parcel of yarn and other trinkets, that I may make my easier entrance, as gorgets, coifs, fringes, nippers, needles, and pins that, whatsoever they call for, I may be ready provided. This bait shall work my acceptance and hold fast the fish

SEMPRONIO. Take heed what you do. Her father is noble and of great power and courage, her mother jealous and furious —and thou no sooner seen but mistrusted. Melibea is the only child to them both, and, she miscarrying, miscarrieth all their happiness, the thought whereof makes me tremble. Seek not to pluck her wings and come back yourself without your plumes!

CELESTINA. As though thou couldst instruct Celestina in her trade! Before ever thou wast born, I did eat bread with crust!

SEMPRONIO. It is the condition of men that what they most desire they think shall never come to pass: I dread both thine and my punishment. But I desire profit: I would that this business might have a good end, not that my master might thereby be rid of his pain, but that I might be rid of my penury.

CELESTINA'S *house*

CELESTINA, SEMPRONIO, ELICIA

ELICIA. Sempronio come! I will score it up, this is news indeed! What, twice in one day?

CELESTINA. Peace, you fool. We have other thoughts to trouble our heads withal. Tell me, is the house clear? Is the wench gone that expected the friar?

ELICIA. Gone? Yes, and another come, since she went, and gone, too.

CELESTINA. Sayest thou so? I hope then she came not in vain?

ELICIA. No, by my fay, for though he came late, yet better late than never, and little need he to rise early, with Heaven to help him!

CELESTINA. Hie you quickly to the top of the house and bring me the oil of serpents which is fastened to the piece of rope that I brought the other night when it rained so fast. Then open my chest where the paintings be and you shall find a paper written with the blood of a bat. Bring it, together with a wing of the dragon whereof yesterday we did cut the claws.

ELICIA, *now upstairs*. It is not here, mother: you never remember where you lay your things.

CELESTINA. Do not feign untruths! Though Sempronio be here be not you proud of it, for he had rather have me for his counsellor than you for his playfellow! Enter into the chamber where my ointments be and there in the skin of a black cat you shall not fail to find it! And bring down the blood of a he-goat and that little piece of his beard which you yourself did cut off!

ELICIA, *down again*. Lo, here it is. I will go up, and take my Sempronio with me.

Exeunt ELICIA *and* SEMPRONIO.

CELESTINA, *alone*. I conjure thee, thou sad god Pluto, Lord of the Infernal Deep, Emperor of the Damned, Captain General of the Fallen Angels, Prince of those three hellish Furies, Tisiphone, Megaera, and Alecto, Administrator of Styx and Dis with their pitchy lakes and litigious chaos, Maintainer of the flying Harpies with the whole rabblement of frightful Hydras, I, Celestina, thy best-known client, conjure thee by these red letters, by the blood of this bird of night wherewith they are charactered, by the weight of the names and signs in this paper, by the fell poison of those vipers whence this oil was extracted, wherewith I anoint this thread of yarn, come presently to wrap thyself therein and never thence depart until Melibea shall buy it of me and in such sort be entangled that the more she shall behold it, the more may her heart be wrought to yield to my request! Open her heart and wound her soul with the love of Calisto and in so extreme a manner that, casting off all shame, she may unbosom herself to me! Do this and I am at thy command to do what thou wilt! But, if thou do not do it, thou shalt forthwith have me thy capital foe and professed enemy. I shall strike with light thy sad and darksome dungeons. I shall cruelly accuse thy continual falsehood. And, lastly, with enchanting terms, I shall curse thy horrible name! I conjure thee again to fulfil my command! Once

twice, thrice! And so, presuming on thy great power, I go
to her with my thread of yarn wherein I verily believe I
carry thyself enwrapped.

A street

CELESTINA

ELESTINA. As I walk, I will weigh what Sempronio feared,
for it may be that, if my intent should be found out by
Melibea's father, it would cost me little less than my life,
either by their tossing me in a blanket or causing me to be
cruelly whipped, so that my sweet meats shall have sour
sauce and my hundred crowns be purchased at too dear a
rate. What shall I do? To go back is not for my profit, and
to go on stands not with my safety. If I should go back,
what will Calisto think—save only that I have revealed this
plot to Pleberio, playing the traitor on both sides that I
might gain by both? And if he do not entertain so hateful
a thought he will rail upon me like a madman saying: "Out,
you old whore, false bawd as thou art, thy promises have
not proved effectual! Thou shalt not want punishment nor
I, despair!" Of two evils it is wise to incline to the lesser, and
therefore I had rather offend Pleberio than displease Calisto.
Well then, I will go. Besides, Fortune friendeth those that
are valiant. Lo, yonder's the gate. Be of good cheer, Celestina, you have seen yourself in greater danger than this! All
divinations are in my favour: of four men that I met by the
way, three were Johns, whereof two were cuckolds. Not a
dog that hath barked at me. I have not seen any bird of
a black feather, neither thrush nor crow. And, which is a
better sign of luck than all these, yonder do I see Lucrecia
standing at Melibea's gate, that is kinswoman to Elicia. It
cannot but go well with us. All is cocksure.

PLEBERIO'S *house*

LUCRECIA, CELESTINA

LUCRECIA. What old witch is this, trailing her tail on the ground? How she sweeps the streets with her gown! What a dust she makes!

CELESTINA, *arriving*. By your leave, sweet beauty.

LUCRECIA. Mother Celestina! You are welcome. I do not remember that I have seen you in these parts this many a day. What wind hath driven you hither?

CELESTINA. Love, my daughter, love and the desire to see my friends and bring commendations from your cousin Elicia as also to see my old and young mistress whom I have not seen since I went from this end of the town.

LUCRECIA. You make me marvel. You were not wont to stir your stumps unless it were for your profit.

CELESTINA. What greater profit would you have, fool, than a person to comply with her desires? Besides, such women as we never want business, especially myself, who, having the breeding of so many men's daughters, go to see if I can sell a little yarn.

LUCRECIA. Did not I tell you so? You never put in a penny but you take out a pound. But, to let that pass, my old mistress hath begun a web: she hath need to buy and you to sell. Come in and stay awhile; you and I will not fall out

LUCRECIA *goes upstairs to her mistresses,* ALISA *and* MELIBEA.

ALISA, *above, to* LUCRECIA. Who is that you talk withal?

LUCRECIA. That old woman forsooth with the scotch on her nose who sometimes dwelt hard by here. Do not you remember her that stood on the pillory for a witch? That sold young wenches wholesale? And that hath marred many marriages by setting man and wife at odds?

ALISA. Go to, you fool, tell me her name.

LUCRECIA. Her name (saving your reverence) is Celestina.

ALISA. Now I call her to mind. Go to, you are a wag. She, poor soul, is come to beg of me. Bid her come up.

LUCRECIA, *to* CELESTINA. Aunt, it is my mistress' pleasure you come up.

CELESTINA *comes up.*

CELESTINA. All blessings abide with you, good lady, and your noble daughter! My many griefs have hindered my visiting your house, but heaven knows the sincerity of my heart. Among my many miseries, good lady, the money in my purse grows daily less, so that I have no better remedy than to sell this little parcel of yarn and, understanding by your maid that you had need thereof, it is wholly at your command.

ALISA. If it be such as will serve my turn, I shall pay you well for it.

CELESTINA. Madam, it is as fine as the hair of your head, equal as the strings of a viol, white as a flake of snow. Look you, lady!

ALISA. Daughter Melibea, I will leave this honest woman with you, for it is now high time to go visit my sister. I have not seen her since yesterday, and her page is come to tell me that her sickness is grown worse.

CELESTINA, *aside.* Now does the devil prepare my stratagem by reinforcing this sickness. Be strong, my friend, stand stiffly to your tackling, for now is the time or never!

ALISA. What sayest thou?

CELESTINA. I say: cursed be the devil that your sister's sickness is grown upon her! But, I pray, what is her sickness?

ALISA. A pain in her side that I fear will cost her her life. Recommend her recovery in your prayers!

CELESTINA. As soon as I go hence, I will hie me to the monastery where I have many devout virgins, all of them my friends, upon whom I will lay the charge.

ALISA. Do you hear me, Melibea? Give our neighbour that which is reason for her yarn. And you, mother, I pray hold me excused.

CELESTINA. God pardon you, madam, and I do.

Exit ALISA; *but* CELESTINA *continues to address her.*

You have left me here with very good company: God grant that she may long enjoy her youth, a time wherein more delights are found than in this old, decayed carcass of mine which is a spittlehouse of diseases, an inn of infirmities, a storehold of melancholy, a friend to brangling and brawling, a poor cabin without one bough of shelter, whereinto it rains on all sides.

MELIBEA. Why do you speak so ill, mother, of that which the whole world desireth to enjoy?

CELESTINA. They desire to live to be old, because, by living to be old, they live. Fain would the hen live, for all her pip. But who is he, lady, that can recount to you the discommodities of old age? Those deep furrows in the face, that change in the hair, that fading of fresh colour, that want of hearing, weakness of sight, hollowness in the eyes, sinking of the jaws, toothlessness of the gums, feebleness of legs, slowness in feeding . . . Besides, madam, when all these miseries come accompanied with poverty, all sorrows to this must stoop and strike sail, for I never knew any worse habit than that of hunger.

MELIBEA. So goes the market as it goes with you! The rich will sing another song.

CELESTINA. There is no way so fair but hath some foul. Renown and rest, glory and quietness run from the rich by by-conduits and gutters of subtlety and deceit, which pipes are never perceived because they are bricked over with well-wrought flatteries. A rich man shall never hear the truth. Besides, he lies open to every man's envy, and you shall scarce find one rich man but will confess that it had been better for him to have been in a middling state. For riches make not a man rich, but busy; not a master, but a steward. More are they that are possessed by riches than they that possess their riches. Every rich man hath a dozen of sons or nephews which desire nothing more than to see him underground.

MELIBEA. Tell me, mother, are you not Celestina that dwelt near the river?

CELESTINA. The very same.

MELIBEA. By my fay, you are an old woman. I did not know you, neither should I, had it not been for that slash over your face. Then were you fair: now wonderfully altered.

CELESTINA. Madam, the day will come when you shall not know your face in a glass! I am not so old as you take me to be: of four daughters my mother had, myself was the youngest. I am grown grey before my time.

MELIBEA. Here, Celestina, take your money and farewell. I have taken pleasure in your discourse. Poor soul, you look as if you had eaten nothing all this day!

CELESTINA. Man shall not live by bread alone, nor woman, especially me, who use to be fasting two days together! My whole life is nothing else but to seek trouble to myself by serving of others! Wherefore I will tell you the cause of my coming. We were all undone if I should return and you not know it.

MELIBEA. Acquaint me with all your wants, good mother.

CELESTINA. *My* wants, madam? Nay, others', as I told you, not mine. For all my poverty, I never wanted a penny to buy me bread, not in all the time of my widowhood. Yet let me tell you that when the good man is missing, all other good is wanting, for ill does the spindle move when the beard does not wag above.

MELIBEA. Ask what thou wilt—be it either for thyself or anybody else.

CELESTINA. Most gracious lady, I come from one whom I left sick to the death, who only with one word which should come from your mouth and be entrusted in my bosom—I verily assure myself it will save his life.

MELIBEA. I have not fully comprehended thy meaning. Who is this sick man?

CELESTINA. You cannot choose, lady, but know a young gentleman in this city whose name is Calisto?

MELIBEA. Enough! I will have thee burned, thou enemy to honesty! Fie upon thee, filth! Lucrecia, send her packing!

CELESTINA. This poor gentleman is at the point of death.

MELIBEA. Dost thou think I do not perceive thy drift? Wouldst thou have me soil mine honour to give life to a madman?

CELESTINA. Had I thought that your ladyship would have made this bad construction of the matter, even your own permission would not have emboldened me to speak of Calisto or any man.

MELIBEA. Let me hear no more of this leaper over walls, this hobgoblin, this nightwalker! This is he who saw me the other day and began to court me as if he had not been well in his wits. Advise him, old woman, that the way to have his sickness leave him is to leave off loving! Other answer of me shall be none, nor hope for any!

CELESTINA, *aside*. Troy held out longer, and many fiercer dames have I tamed in my days. Tush, no storm lasteth long.

MELIBEA. Speak out, I pray! Hast thou anything to say in thy excuse? What canst thou demand of me for such a one as he?

CELESTINA. Marry, a certain prayer to St. Apollonia for the toothache. They say your ladyship knoweth it. Also that admirable girdle of yours which is reported to have touched all the relics in Rome and Jerusalem. The gentleman is at death's door with the toothache, and this was the cause of my coming. But, since it was my ill-hap to receive so harsh an answer, let him continue in his pain!

MELIBEA. If this be what thou wouldst have, why wentst thou about the bush with me?

CELESTINA. My simple understanding made me believe that, though my words had been worse than they were, yet would you not have suspected any evil in them.

MELIBEA. I have heard such tales of thy cunning tricks that I know not whether I may believe thy errand was for this prayer.

CELESTINA. Never let me pray again if you can draw any other thing from me though I were put to a thousand torments!

MELIBEA. Thou dost so confidently plead thy ignorance that thou makest me almost ready to believe thee. I will hold my sentence in suspense. Neither would I have thee wonder that I was moved, for two things in thy discourse were sufficient to make me run out of my wits: first, that thou shouldst name this gentleman who presumed to talk with me, then that thou shouldst entreat me for him. But since no harm was intended, I pardon all that is past. To cure the sick is a holy work.

CELESTINA. Ay, and so sick, madam, that you would not judge him the man which in your anger you have censured him to be! By my fay, the poor gentleman hath no ill meaning in his heart. He is endued with thousands of graces: for bounty he is an Alexander; for strength an Hector; he has the presence of a prince; he is fair in his carriage, sweet in his behaviour, and pleasant in his conversation; nobly descended; a great tilter; Hercules had not his courage, Narcissus was not as fair, as he whom one poor tooth so tormenteth.

MELIBEA. How long hath he had it?

CELESTINA. His beauty, madam? Since his birth, madam. He is some three and twenty, for here stands she who saw him born and took him up from his mother's feet.

MELIBEA. I ask thee how long hath he had the toothache?

CELESTINA. Some eight days, madam. But you would think he had had it a year, he is grown so weak. And the best remedy he hath is to take his viol: when he sings thereto the birds listen unto him with a better will than to that musician of old which made the trees and stones to move: had he been born then, Orpheus had lost his prey.

MELIBEA. How angry I am with myself that thou hast endured the distemperature of my enraged tongue, he being ignorant and thou innocent of any ill! I will forthwith fulfil thy request and give thee my girdle, and, if this will not serve the turn, come secretly for the prayer tomorrow morning, for I have not time to write it before my mother comes home.

LUCRECIA, *aside*. I smell a rat. I like not this: "come secretly tomorrow." I fear me she will part with more than words.

MELIBEA. I pray, mother, say nothing to this gentleman of

what hath passed, lest he should think me cruel, sudden, or dishonest.

LUCRECIA, *aside*. All the world cannot save her now.

CELESTINA. Madam, I marvel you should entertain the least doubt of my service. Well, I will go hence with this girdle as merrily as if I saw his heart leaping for joy that you have graced him with so great a kindness.

MELIBEA. I will do more for your patient than this, if need require.

CELESTINA, *aside*. You *must* do more than this, though perhaps you will scarce thank us for it.

MELIBEA. What's that?

CELESTINA. I say, madam, that we thank you for it.

LUCRECIA, *aside*. Here's cat in the pan. What choplogic have we here?

CELESTINA. Daughter Lucrecia, come hither to me.

Aside to her.

You shall have a powder of me (but tell not your mistress) to sweeten thy breath, which is a little of the strongest.

LUCRECIA. A blessing on you! I have more need of this than of my meat.

CELESTINA. And yet, you fool, you will be prating against me! Hold your peace, for you know not what need you may have of me. Do not exasperate your mistress!

MELIBEA. I cannot abide that anybody should speak in my presence and I not have a part therein. What sayest thou to her, mother?

CELESTINA. I entreated her to temper herself in the time of your anger, putting her in mind of the adage: "A fit of anger is but a flash of lightning."

MELIBEA. I commend this gentleman to your care.

CELESTINA. I will haste to see how he does.

MELIBEA. And God go with thee. As thy coming hither hath not done me good, thy going hither cannot do me harm.

ACT III

A street

CELESTINA

CELESTINA, *alone.* I am much bound unto thee, Devil whom I conjured! Well hast thou kept thy word! Cheer up, Celestina, things are half ended when they are well begun! Be merry, old stinkard, frolic with thyself, old wench, for thou shalt get more by this one suit than by soldering of fifteen cracked maidenheads. (A pox on these long petticoats, how they fold themselves about my legs!) How many have missed that nail which myself have hit on the head! What would these young graduates in my art have done? Perhaps have bolted out some foolish word to Melibea, whereby they would have lost as much by their prattling as I have gained by my silence. Experience makes men artists in their profession, and such an old woman as I, who at every little channel holds up her coats, shall prove a proficient in her trade. O girdle, my pretty girdle, let me hug thee a little! I will make thee bring her to me.

Enter SEMPRONIO.

SEMPRONIO, *aside.* Either mine eyes do not match or that is Celestina. How her skirts trouble her! Who did ever see her walk the streets before with her head hanging in her bosom and her eyes cast down?

To her.

Good mother! Tell me what news you bring. Is it a son or a daughter? Ever since one of the clock I have waited for you.

CELESTINA. Sempronio, my friend, this is no fit place to tell thee, for by communicating myself to many, I should, as it were, deflower my embassage, whose maidenhead I mean to bestow on your master. Go along with me to Calisto, for though you shall have your parcel of the profit, I mind to have all the thanks for my labour.

SEMPRONIO. "Though you shall have your parcel." I tell you plainly, I do not like this word, that I do not. Parcel me no more of your parcels!

CELESTINA. Go to, you fool, be it part or parcel, man, thou shalt have what thou wilt! What is mine is thine! Hang all this trash rather than that thou and I should fall out about dividing the spoil! Yet old folks have more need than young, especially you, who live at full table upon free cost.

SEMPRONIO. There goes more to a man's life than eating and drinking!

CELESTINA. Ay, a hat, or a stonebow to go shooting at birds, aiming with your eye at other birds that take their stand in windows! There is no better bawd than a stonebow. But woe unto her who is to uphold her credit and begins to grow old as I do!

SEMPRONIO, *aside.* It had been better for me to have fled from this viper than to put her in my bosom. But let her gain what she can gain. I will keep my word with her.

CELESTINA. What sayest thou?

SEMPRONIO. You told me you would defer this business, leading my master along in a fool's paradise, and now you run headlong to tell Calisto of all that passed. Know you not that men esteem those things most which are most difficult to achieve?

CELESTINA. A new business requires new counsel, and various accidents, various advice; nor did I think, son Sempronio, that Fortune would have befriended me so soon. I know that my master is liberal and somewhat of a womanish longing and therefore will give more for one day of good news than for a hundred wherein he is pained. Peace, you fool, let me alone with him!

SEMPRONIO. Then tell me what passed, for I long as much to know that lady's answer as my master doth.

CELESTINA. Peace, you fool! What, does your colour change? Come, I prithee, your master will be ready to run mad.

CALISTO's *house*

CALISTO *and* PARMENO, *inside*
SEMPRONIO *and* CELESTINA, *outside*

PARMENO. Master! Master!

CALISTO. What's the matter, fool?

PARMENO. I see Sempronio and Celestina coming. And at every step they make a stop, and where they stand, Sempronio, with the point of his sword, makes lines in the ground.

CALISTO. Thou careless, absurd ass, canst thou descry land and not make to the shore? Dispatch, I say! Unbolt the troublesome door, that this honourable woman may enter, in whose tongue lies my life!

CELESTINA, *to* SEMPRONIO. Dost thou hear him? These words are of another tune than those we heard at our first coming hither. The matter, I see, is amended. Never a word shall I tell him but shall be better to old Celestina than a new petticoat.

CELESTINA *and* SEMPRONIO *go inside.*

CALISTO's *house. Indoors*

On one side, CALISTO *and* CELESTINA
On another, PARMENO *and* SEMPRONIO

CALISTO. Mother! Speak!

CELESTINA. How is it with you, my lord and master? And how can you make this old woman amends, who hath hazarded her life in your service? The very thought whereof empties my veins of all their blood. I would have given my life for less than the price of this old mantle of mine.

PARMENO. Thou art all, I see, for thyself. Thou art like a lettuce that grows between two coleworts: if thou be let alone, thou wilt overtop them. The next I look for is that she beg a kirtle for her mantle. How craftily does she pitch her nets to catch me and my master, seeking to make me faithless and him foolish! Mark her, Sempronio, she will not demand any money of my master, because it is divisible.

SEMPRONIO. Peace, thou despairful fellow, lest Calisto kill thee!

CALISTO. Good mother, either cut off thy discourse, or take this sword and kill me!

PARMENO. He cannot stand. He quivers like one touched with quicksilver. He cannot live long if this fit continue. Every man his mourning weed, and there an end.

CELESTINA. What? Take your sword and kill you? Let your sword kill your enemies. As for me, I will give you life, man, by the good hope I have in her whom you love.

CALISTO. Good hope?

CELESTINA. Ay, good hope, and well may it be called so, since the gates are open for my return: she will sooner receive *me* in this poor tattered kirtle than others in cloth of gold!

PARMENO. Sempronio, sew up this mouth, I can no longer hold.

SEMPRONIO. So she beg her apparel, what's that to thee? I commend her for it.

PARMENO. In one day this old jade would cast off her rugged hairs and get her a new coat—which is more than she could do these fifty years!

SEMPRONIO. Is this all the good she taught thee in breeding you up?

PARMENO. I could be content that she should pill and poll, ask and have, but not cut out all the cloth for her own coat.

SEMPRONIO. It is her fault, I confess. But other vice hath she none. Let her thatch her own house, then afterwards shall she board ours; else had it been better for her she had never known us.

CALISTO. Tell me what she was doing! How gottest thou into the house? How was she apparelled? How did she look on thee?

CELESTINA. With such a look as your fierce bulls use towards those that cast sharp darts against them!

CALISTO. Be these thy good hopes? Death itself could not be half so deadly!

SEMPRONIO. He hath not the patience to stay to hear that which so earnestly he hath desired.

PARMENO. Now, sir, who talks now? Did my master hear you, he would cudgel you!

SEMPRONIO. I offend not him; thou speakest prejudicially of all. Contentious, envious, accursèd caitiff, is this the friendship thou hast contracted with Celestina and me?

CALISTO. All that I have heard are rather tokens of hate than of love. If thou wilt not that I die desperate, certify me briefly whether thy glorious demand had a happy end!

CELESTINA. The greatest glory which is given to the bee (which little creature the discreeter sort ought to imitate) is that whatsoever he toucheth he converteth into a better substance. In like manner hath it befallen me with Melibea: all her sour looks I turned into honey. What did you think Celestina went thither for unless it were to be your shield and buckler and receive upon my mantle all the blows that were struck at you, those revilings and disdainful terms which such as she make show of when they are first sued unto for their love? And why forsooth do they this? To the end that what they give may the better be esteemed. If everyone should say yea as soon as she is asked, there would be no difference between the love of a common whore and an honest damsel that stands upon her honour. And therefore, when they see a man loves them, though they themselves fry in the flames of love, yet they will show a coldness and pour forth words as sharp as vinegar. But because I would have thee take some ease of thy sorrows while I relate all that passed between her and me, know for thy comfort that the end of her discourse was good.

CALISTO. Now my veins recover their lost blood! Now do I find some joy! Sit you down, dear mother, whilst on my knees I give ear to thy sweet answer. Say on, and tell me by what means thou gottest into the house!

CELESTINA. By selling a parcel of thread—by which trick I have taken, in my days, more than thirty such, and some higher women than herself!

CALISTO. Taller, perhaps, but not higher in birth, beauty, discretion, virtue, speech!

PARMENO. Mark how the fool's clock goes: it never strikes under twelve, the finger of his dial is still upon high noon. And, Sempronio, you stand gazing like a wide-mouthed drivelling fool, hearing his fooleries and her lies!

SEMPRONIO. Say they are but fables she tells him, yet, were it only that her discourse is of love, thou oughtst to heed it. Why shouldst thou alone stop thy ears at that to which all the world is willing to hearken?

CELESTINA. When I was about to sell my thread, Melibea' mother was called away. She left Melibea with me to conclude the bargain.

CALISTO. O singular opportunity! O that I had lain hid under thy mantle that I might have heard her speak!

CELESTINA. Under my mantle, sir? Alack, she must needs have seen you through at least thirty holes—should not Fortune give me a better!

PARMENO. I will get me gone. Sempronio, hear you all for me. The fool measures how many steps there be between this and Melibea's house. All his faculties are possessed with her. But he will find that my counsel would have done him more good than the cunning cozenage of Celestina.

CALISTO, *calling to* PARMENO *and* SEMPRONIO. You keep a-tattling and a-prattling there! As you love me, hold your tongues, and you will die with delight, such pleasure will you take in this repetition! Go on, mother, what didst thou do when thou wast left alone with her!

CELESTINA. I was overjoyed!

CALISTO. So is it now with me. But, tell me, wast thou no stricken dumb with this sudden accident?

CELESTINA. No, but grew thereby the bolder, and opened the very bowels of my heart, told her in what pain you lived and how that one word from her would ease you of your torment. But she cut off my words and struck herself a blow on the breast, charging me to cease my prattle and get me out of her sight unless I would her servants should make short work of me, calling me witch, sorceress, bawd, old whore, false baggage, bearded miscreant, mother of mischief . . . Then fell she into swoonings and trances, her hands and fingers being clenched one within another, hurling and rolling her eyes on every side, striking the hard ground with her tender feet, being wounded with that golden shaft which, at the very voicing of your name, had struck her to the heart! I, all this while, stood me still in a corner like a cloth that is shrunk in the wetting, and the more her throbs and pangs were, the more did I laugh in my sleeve, because I knew her yielding would be the sooner and her fall the nearer. Yet must I tell you that, whilst her anger did foam out its froth, I did not suffer my thoughts to run a-woolgathering but took hold on Time's foretop, and found a salve to heal that hurt which myself had made.

ALISTO. I did dream it would come to this but, dear mother, I do not see how thou couldst light upon a fit excuse to cover and colour the suspicion of thy demand.

ELESTINA. I told her your torment was the toothache, and that that which I craved of her was a prayer.

ALISTO. So high a means of help! O cunning creature! Speedy remedy!

To PARMENO *and* SEMPRONIO.

What think you now, my masters? Was ever the like woman born in this world?

ELESTINA. Give me leave to continue, for night draws on, and I would not go home in the dark.

ALISTO. You shall have torches, you shall have pages; make choice of whom you will to accompany you!

ARMENO. For she is young and handsome and may be ravished by the way. Sempronio, thou shalt go with her because she is afraid of the crickets which chirp in the dark.

ALISTO, *to* PARMENO. What's that, my son?

ARMENO. I said that it were meet that I and Sempronio accompany her home, for it is dark.

CALISTO. Well said, Parmeno.

To CELESTINA.

Proceed, good mother: what answer made she for the prayer?

CELESTINA. Marry, that with all her heart I should have it.

CALISTO. How gracious and how great a gift, O God!

CELESTINA. I craved more than this.

CALISTO. What, mother?

CELESTINA. Her girdle which she wore about her, affirming that it would allay your pain because it had touched so many relics.

CALISTO. What said she?

CELESTINA. Reward me for my news, and I will tell.

CALISTO. Take my house and all that is in it or what thou wilt

CELESTINA. Give this poor old woman a mantle, and I will give thee her girdle.

CALISTO. A mantle? Tut, a mantle, a kirtle, all I have!

CELESTINA. A mantle shall content me.

CALISTO. Parmeno, call hither my tailor, and let him cut her mantle and kirtle of fine, pure cloth!

PARMENO, *aside*. I may go hang myself when I have done whilst the old woman with a pox will have every day change of raiment.

CALISTO. Envious wretch, what mumblest thou to thyself? Get thee gone with a murrain! There will as much of the cloth be left to make thee a jerkin.

PARMENO. I said nothing, sir, but that it is too late to have the tailor come tonight.

CALISTO. Then let it alone till tomorrow. Now, mother, I pray let me see this glorious girdle that my afflicted heart may rejoice therein. All my senses have been wounded by her, the eyes in seeing her, the ears in hearing her, the hands in touching her.

CELESTINA. What? You have touched her?

CALISTO. In my sleep.

CELESTINA. Oh, in your dreams?

CALISTO. I have seen her so oft in my dreams, I fear that will happen unto me which befell Alcibiades—he dreamed he saw himself enwrapped in his mistress' mantle, and was the next day murdered.

CELESTINA. Take this girdle and, if death prevent me not, I will deliver into your hands the owner thereof.

CALISTO. O happy girdle, glory of my soul, encircler of so incomparable a creature——

SEMPRONIO. Sir, it is not your rejoicing in this girdle that can make you to enjoy Melibea.

CALISTO. Yet have I not the power to abstain from adoring so great a relic.

CELESTINA. She gave you this for to ease your toothache, not for love.

CALISTO. And the prayer thou hast talked of?

CELESTINA. She hath not given it me yet.

CALISTO. Why not?

CELESTINA. The shortness of time. She willed me to return to-morrow if your pain do not decrease.

CALISTO. Decrease! My pain shall decrease when I see a decrease of her cruelty.

CELESTINA. Sir, she will yield you any help which I shall crave at her hands. Tell me, I pray, if this be not well for the first bout? Well, I will get me home, and have a care, if you walk abroad, that you go muzzled about the cheeks with a cloth that she, seeing you, may not accuse me of falsehood.

CALISTO. I will not stick to clap on four cloths! But passed there nothing more between you? I long to hear the words which flow from so sweet a mouth! How didst thou dare, not knowing her, to be so bold?

CELESTINA. Not knowing her? They were my neighbours four years together. Her mother knows me better than her own hands, and Melibea, too, though now she be grown so great a lady.

PARMENO. Sempronio, a word in your ear.

SEMPRONIO. What's the matter?

PARMENO. Give her a touch on the toe that she may be gone.

CALISTO. Was her like ever born into the world? Did God ever create a better body? If Helen were now alive she would do reverence to this lady for whom I languish!

CELESTINA, *to* SEMPRONIO, *who has approached her*. I understand. But give him leave to run on, for he will fall from his ass, and his journey be at an end.

CALISTO. Nothing could be added to make her fairer! A little fountain water with a comb of ivory is sufficient to make her surpass all other of her sex!

CELESTINA. Sir, give me licence to take my leave of you, for it grows late. And let me have the girdle: I must use it.

CALISTO. Alack, with thee or with this girdle or with both, I would willingly have been accompanied all the dark and tedious night, but there is no perfect happiness in this life. Where be my men? Parmeno, I say!

PARMENO. Here, sir.

CALISTO. Accompany this matron to her house.

CELESTINA. Tomorrow I shall return, not doubting but my mantle and her prayer shall meet here together. Be patient. Settle your thoughts upon other things.

CALISTO. Impossible! It were heresy to forget her for whom alone my life pleaseth me!

A street

PARMENO, CELESTINA

CELESTINA. Parmeno, I ever held thee to be my son and thought thou wouldst have showed thyself more loving to me, but thou gavest me bad payment, even to my face whispering against me in the presence of Calisto. But mark an old woman is a help, a comforter, an inn to give rest to a sound man, a hospital to cure a sick man, a fire in winter, shade in summer, a tavern to eat and drink in. What sayest thou, my pretty fool? I know thou art ashamed of that which thou hast spoken today. Thou canst not say B to a battledore, thou art struck so dumb and dead. And therefore I will not crave any more at thy hands than that which friendship craves of thee, which is: look upon Sempronio. Next under heaven, myself have made him a man. I could wish you would live and love together as brothers and friends. If you will be beloved, you must love, you know: trouts cannot be taken with dry breeches, and if the cat will have fish she must wet her foot.

PARMENO. Mother, I confess the one fault, and offer myself to be ordered by you in all future proceedings, but it is impossible that I should hold friendship with Sempronio. How is it possible to make a contract betwixt two such contrary natures?

CELESTINA. You two are equals; and parity of persons is the main prop of friendship. Take heed, my son: be wise to gain more, for one fortune is gained already. What pains your father took to gain it! But I may not put it into your hands till you lead a more reposed life.

PARMENO. What do you call a reposed life, mother?

CELESTINA. Marry, son, to live of yourself! Not to set thy foot under another man's table, which thou must do unless thou learn to profit of thy service. Out of pity to see thee thus tattered did I beg that mantle of Calisto, thou being without a jerkin. O Parmeno, how happy should I be might I but see thee and Sempronio agree—that you may come to my poor house and each be merry with his wench!

PARMENO. His wench, mother?

CELESTINA. Ay, his wench.

PARMENO. Howbeit I spake against you today, it was not because I thought ill of that which you said, but because, when I told my master the truth, he ill-treated me. Therefore, let us shake hands and use him accordingly. Now I bless the time when you bred me up!

CELESTINA. Son, no more! Mine eyes run over. Thy mother! She was dearer to me than mine own sister. How lusty she was, how quick, how neat, how portly and majestical! Why, she would go you at midnight from churchyard to churchyard seeking for the implements of our trade as if it had been

day! She did not omit Christians, Moors, or Jews: by day
she would watch them and by night she would dig them
out. And one thing I shall tell thee, though I was about to
keep it in: she did pull seven teeth out of a fellow's head
that was hanged with a pair of pincers such as you pull out
stubbed hairs withal, whilst I did pull off his shoes. The
very devils did live in fear of her. She was well known to
them all, as the beggar knows his dish. One devil came
tumbling in upon the neck of another as fast as it pleased
her to call them up, and none durst tell her a lie. Since she
died, I could never attain to the truth of anything!

PARMENO, *aside*. Accursed be this woman with her wordy
phrases!

CELESTINA. What sayest thou, my more than son?

PARMENO. Tell me, when the Justice sent officers to apprehend
you—at which time I was in your house—was there any
acquaintance between you?

CELESTINA. Any acquaintance? Our cases were alike. They took
us, accused us, punished us alike, which was the first punishment we ever had. I wonder that thou shouldst remember it.

PARMENO. True: the worser part of wickedness is the perseverance therein.

CELESTINA, *aside*. He hath pricked me to the quick! But I will
tickle him on the right vein.

PARMENO. What say you?

CELESTINA. Marry, son, that, besides this, your mother was
taken four times alone; and once she was accused for a
witch. She was found one night with certain candles in her
hand, gathering I know not what earth at a crossway, for
which she stood upon a scaffold with a high paper hat
painted full of devils whereon her fault was written, being
brought thither through the streets upon an ass. For all this
she would not give over her old occupation, which I thought
good to tell you, touching that opinion of yours about perseverance. When she was on the scaffold, everyone might
see that she cared not a button for those that stood staring
upon her. Wherein I thought fit to show you that they who

have anything in them fall more easily into error than any
other. Do but weigh what manner of man the poet Virgil
was. And he was hung out of a tower in a wicker basket,
all Rome looking on. Yet was he not the less honoured.

PARMENO. But this was not enjoined by a Justice!

CELESTINA. Peace, you fool, thou art ignorant what a coarse
kind of justice was executed upon thy mother, how wrongfully, by suborning of false witnesses, and by cruel tortures,
they forced her to confess that which was not! But, being a
woman of great spirit, of all this she reckoned not a pin, saying: "If I broke my leg, it was for my good: it made me
better known than I was before!"

PARMENO. Talk of our present business. You promised me I
should have Areusa.

CELESTINA. Let us walk towards her house. This is the least
that I will do for thee.

PARMENO. I was out of hope ever to have her. It is an ill sign
for a man to see his mistress flee and turn the face. This
did much dishearten me.

CELESTINA. Now shalt thou see what power I have over these
wenches! But, hush, here's the door, let us enter with quiet
steps that the neighbours may not hear us. Stay for me at
the stairs' foot whilst I see what I can do.

AREUSA's *house*

AREUSA, CELESTINA

AREUSA. Who's there? That at this time of night comes up to
my chamber?

CELESTINA. One that is more mindful of you than of herself!

AREUSA, *aside.* Now the devil take this old trot!

To CELESTINA.

What news, that you come stealing like a ghost so late? I
was even putting off my clothes to go to bed.

CELESTINA. So soon to roost? Think you ever to be rich if you go to bed so timely? Come, walk a turn or two and talk with me a little.

AREUSA. How cold it is! I will put on my clothes again.

CELESTINA. By my fay shall you not! But if you will go into your bed, do, and *so* shall we talk.

AREUSA. Yes indeed, I have need to do so, for I have felt very ill all this day.

CELESTINA. Cover yourself well, and sink lower, so shall you be warm. How like a siren you look, how fair, how fresh! What sheets, what quilts, what pillows, how white they be! It does me good to touch you!

AREUSA. Nay, do not touch me, it increaseth my pain.

CELESTINA. What pain, pretty chuck? You jest.

AREUSA. A pain which, rising in my breast, swells up to my throat and is ready to stifle me!

CELESTINA. Give me leave to touch you and I will try what I can do, for I know something for this evil—which everyone calls the Mother.

AREUSA. Lay your hand higher—above the stomach.

CELESTINA. So plump, so clear, so fragrant, so dainty a creature! That any sickness should dare to usurp over such an unparalleled beauty! But it is not so. Your disease is self-conceited, and you are to blame if it be so. You should not lose the flower of your youth under six linings of linen. And do not think you were born for nothing, for when you were born, man was born, and when man was born, woman was born. Nothing was created superfluous.

AREUSA. Give me something for my evil, and leave jesting.

CELESTINA. For this common complaint, every strong scent is good, as of partridge feathers, rosemary, and the soles of old shoes, but there is another thing that I ever found to be better, but what it is I will not tell you as you make yourself such a piece of niceness.

AREUSA. As you love me, mother, tell me!

CELESTINA. You understand me. Do not make yourself more fool than you are.

AREUSA. You know that my lover went yesterday with his captain to the wars: would you have me wrong him?

CELESTINA. Great wrong, I promise you!

AREUSA. Yes, for he supplies my wants, loves me, uses me with respect!

CELESTINA. You can never recover by living sole and simple as you now do.

AREUSA. It is late, mother. Tell me, pray, what wind drove you hither?

CELESTINA. Parmeno complains that you refuse to see him. What should be the reason I know not, unless because you know I wish him well. I regard your friends in a kinder fashion.

AREUSA. Aunt, I am beholding to you.

CELESTINA. I must believe works: for words are wind and are sold everywhere for nothing. Love is paid with love, and works with works. Elicia, thy cousin, is kept in my house by Sempronio. Parmeno and he are companions. Both serve the gentleman you wot of and by whom you may gain great good. Do not deny him that, the granting whereof will cost you so little. See how pat all things fall! To tell you truly, I have brought him along. How say you? Shall I call him up?

AREUSA. Heaven forbid! Ay me! I fear he hath heard every word.

CELESTINA. Entertain him friendly, and, if you think fit, let him enjoy you—and you him, and both one another.

AREUSA. Mother, you know to whom I am bound to give an account. If he know I play false, he will kill me. My neighbours are malicious and will acquaint him therewith.

CELESTINA. For this fear of yours myself have already provided: we entered very softly.

AREUSA. Tush, were it but for one night, I would not care: I speak for many other that are to come.

CELESTINA. What? Is this your fashion? An you use these niceties you shall never have a double room but live like a beggar all the days of your life. Did you but see your cousin's wisdom, you would be of another mind. She does all that I will have her do. She will sometimes boast that she hath at one time had one in bed with her, another waiting at the door, and a third sighing for her within the house; and hath given satisfaction to them all. And are you afraid who have but two to deal withal? Can one cock fill all cisterns? One conduit-pipe water all your court? It goes hard with the mouse that hath but one hole to trust to. One swallow makes not a summer. To feed always upon one dish brings a loathing to the stomach. What would you do, daughter, with this number of one? Two is commendable company as you may see in yourself that hath two ears, two feet, and two hands. The more Moors, the better market. Son Parmeno, come up!

AREUSA. I am ready to swoon! Nay fie, mother, I have no acquaintance with him! I am ashamed!

CELESTINA. I will quit you of this shame, and speak for you both, for he is as bashful as you.

Enter PARMENO.

PARMENO. Gentlewoman, heaven preserve your gracious presence!

AREUSA. You are welcome, gentle sir.

CELESTINA, *to* PARMENO. Whither go you now, to sit moping in the corner? Hearken, both of you. Friend Parmeno, you know what I promised you and you, daughter, know what I entreated at your hands.

To AREUSA.

He hath lived in great pain for your sake, and therefore it shall not be amiss that he stay with you here this night.

AREUSA. For my maidenhead's sake, mother, let it not be so!

PARMENO, *aside to* CELESTINA. Offer her all that my father left with you for me.

AREUSA. What doth this gentleman whisper?

CELESTINA. He says that he is glad of your friendship. He also says that he will be a friend to Sempronio and will do what is needful in a business which we have in hand with his master. Is that not true, Parmeno? Have I your promise?

PARMENO. You have, mother.

CELESTINA, *aside*. So, sir rascal, I have thee now, and in good time withal! *Aloud*. Come hither, you clown, you clodpoll, you, I would fain see what thou art worth before I depart. Roll her on this bed!

AREUSA. He will not be so uncivil!

CELESTINA. Dost thou think, daughter, that I know not what thing this is? Did I never see a man and a woman together before? Know I not all their tricks and devices, what they say and what they do?

AREUSA. Rather would I lose an eye than offend thee. Go thou but apart a little, and he may do his will.

CELESTINA. I am not angry, look you, I tell you this against another time. And so good night. I pass my word that you shall rise tomorrow in good health! And this is a brave fellow, a fighting cock that will not lower his crest after three nights of the sport! The doctors of my country were wont to send me such to eat at a time when I had better teeth. The taste is in my mouth to this day. God be with you.

AREUSA. And with you, aunt.

PARMENO. Shall I accompany you home?

CELESTINA. No, marry, it needs not: I am past all danger of ravishing.

Exit CELESTINA.

AREUSA's *house*

PARMENO, AREUSA

PARMENO. It is light in the chamber. It is day.

AREUSA. Sleep, sir, and take your rest, for it is but even now since we lay down. I have scarce shut mine eyes yet and would you have it to be day? Open the window and you shall see.

PARMENO. I saw the light come through the chinks of the door.

Aside.

O what a villain I am! Into how great a fault am I fallen with my master.

To AREUSA.

How late in the day it is!

AREUSA. Late?

PARMENO. Late, late in the day.

AREUSA. Alas, I am not eased of the Mother yet; it pains me still.

PARMENO. What wouldst thou have me do, dear love?

AREUSA. Talk a little—of my indisposition.

PARMENO. What, should we talk yet more? It is now high noon. If I stay longer I shall not be welcome to my master. To-morrow is a new day, and I will come again, and as often afterwards as you please. In the meanwhile, come and dine with us today at Celestina's house.

AREUSA. With all my heart. And farewell. Pull the door after you.

PARMENO. Fare you well.

A street

PARMENO

PARMENO. O singular joy! What man lives that can say he is more fortunate than I, more happy, more successful—that I should enjoy so curious a creature! And no sooner ask than have! If I could brook the old woman's treasons, I would creep upon my knees to do her kindness. How shall I requite her? And to whom shall I impart my joy? For it is true, what the old woman told me: Pleasure not communicated is no pleasure. Yonder is Sempronio at our door.

CALISTO'S *house*

SEMPRONIO, PARMENO

SEMPRONIO. What should be the cause of thy so long stay, unless it were to rub old Celestina's feet as thou wast wont to when little?

PARMENO. O Sempronio, my good friend, do not soil with troubled water the clear liquor of my gladsome thoughts! Embrace me with joy, and I shall tell thee wonders!

SEMPRONIO. Out with it, come! Hast thou seen Melibea?

PARMENO. As though all the world were enclosed in Melibea!

SEMPRONIO. Then we are all in love: Calisto loves Melibea; I love Elicia; and thou, out of mere envy, hast found someone with whom to lose thy little wit.

PARMENO. Do not torment me, Sempronio, with wounding words. Who lives there that sees himself, as I have, raised to the height of my dear Areusa's love? And who, that sees himself more likely to fall from thence than I, being so ill treated of thee? Thou wilt not give me leave to tell thee how much I am thine, what good counsel I received of Celestina and all for thy good and the good of us all. And now that we have our master's and Melibea's game in our hands, now is the time that we must thrive or never!

SEMPRONIO. Thou knowest Areusa, that is cousin to Elicia?

PARMENO. I did enjoy her.

SEMPRONIO. What dost thou call enjoying her? Did she show herself at a window?

PARMENO. I left her in doubt whether she be with child.

SEMPRONIO. The old woman had a finger in this business, had she not?

PARMENO. Her little finger. O brother, what shall I say unto thee of the graces of that wench?

SEMPRONIO. She is cousin to Elicia. But what did she cost thee?

PARMENO. Not anything. So rich an object was never purchased at so low a rate. I have invited her to dinner at Celestina's house. Let us all meet there.

SEMPRONIO. Who?

PARMENO. Thou and she, and the old woman and Elicia.

SEMPRONIO. Now I long to embrace thee! The hatred which I bare thee is turned into love. Let us live like brothers! Let us feast and be merry, for our master will fast for us all!

PARMENO. What does the desperate man?

SEMPRONIO. Lies where thou hast left him last night upon his pallet by his bedside like a man in a trance between sleeping and waking. If I go in to him, he falls a-routing and a-snorting. If I go from him, he either sings or raves. Nor can I comprehend whether the man be in pain or ease.

PARMENO. Did he never call for me? Did he not remember me?

SEMPRONIO. Why should he remember thee? He remembered not himself.

PARMENO. Since things go well, I will send thither our meat. We have wine of Monviedro in the larder, a gammon of bacon, and some dozen dainty chickens which my master's tenants brought the other day and the turtle doves which he willed me to keep against today—I will tell him that they stank and I threw them away. And we will talk with the old woman concerning his love—to his loss and our profit.

SEMPRONIO. Callest thou it love? I verily think he will hardly escape either death or madness.

CALISTO, *in another room.*

> In peril great I love
> And straight of force must die
> Since what desire doth give
> That hope doth me deny.

PARMENO. Our master is a-rhyming, he is turned poet.

SEMPRONIO. The great poet Ovid who never speaks but in verse! Pshaw, he does but talk in his sleep.

CALISTO, *indoors.*

> This pain, this martyrdom,
> O heart, well dost thou prove

Since thou so soon wast won
To Melibea's love.

PARMENO. Did I not tell thee?

CALISTO. Who talks in the hall, ho!

PARMENO. Anon, sir.

PARMENO and SEMPRONIO go in to him.

CALISTO. Is it time to go to bed?

PARMENO. It is, rather, sir, too late to rise.

CALISTO. Is the night past and gone?

PARMENO. Ay, and a good part of the day too.

CALISTO. Give me my clothes. I must go to St. Mary Magdalen's and ask God to direct Celestina and put my remedy into Melibea's heart or else shorten my sorrowful days!

SEMPRONIO. Good sir, leave off these poetical fictions, and eat some conserves that you may keep some life in you.

CALISTO. Sempronio, loyal follower, be it as thou wilt have it, for I assure myself that my life is as dear unto thee as thine own.

SEMPRONIO, *aside to* PARMENO. If thou goest for the conserves, steal a barrel for those thou knowest of.

CALISTO. What sayest thou?

SEMPRONIO. I speak, sir, to Parmeno that he should fetch you a slice of conserves.

PARMENO. Lo, sir, here it is.

He gives it to CALISTO.

SEMPRONIO, *aside to* PARMENO. How fast it goes down! Look, if he do not swallow it whole that he may the sooner have done!

CALISTO. It hath done me good. My sons both, farewell. Go look after the old woman and wait for good news. I will reward your labour.

Exit CALISTO.

PARMENO. The devil and ill fortune follow thee!

CELESTINA's *house*

CELESTINA

CELESTINA, *calling to* SEMPRONIO *and* PARMENO, *who are outside.* Come, amorous youths, come, my pearls of gold! It is time for dinner! You are both welcome.

SEMPRONIO, *to* PARMENO. I wonder what devil taught her all her knaveries.

PARMENO. I will tell you: necessity, poverty, and hunger, than which there are no better tutors in the world.

They enter.

CELESTINA, *calling to* ELICIA *and* AREUSA, *who are upstairs.* Hola, wenches, girls, where be you, you fools? Come down, I say, for here are a couple of gallants who would ravish me!

Enter ELICIA *and* AREUSA.

ELICIA, *to* CELESTINA. You have made my cousin wait three hours, but this same lazy-gut Sempronio was the cause, I warrant you, for all this stay. He has no eyes to look upon me.

SEMPRONIO. He who serves another, sweetheart, is not his own man. Be not angry. Let us sit, and fall to.

ELICIA. You are ready at all times to eat!

SEMPRONIO. Come, we will brawl after dinner. Now let us fall to. Mother Celestina, will it please you to sit first?

CELESTINA. No, first sit you down, my son; here is enough for all. Let everyone take their place as they like and sit next her whom he loves best. As for me, I will sit by this jar of wine and this good goblet, for I can live no longer than while I sit with one of these two. In a cold winter's night you cannot have a better warming pan, for when I toss off two of these little pots, why, I feel not a jot of cold all the night long. With this I fur all my clothes at Christmas. This warms my blood. This makes me look ruddy as a rose. This drives away sorrow better than gold or coral. It adds colour to the discoloured, courage to the coward, diligence to the slothful. It comforts the brain. It expels cold from the stomach. It takes away the stinkingness of the breath. It makes cold constitutions to be potent. It remedies rheums, and cures the toothache. It has but this one fault: it lightens the purse.

SEMPRONIO. Let us eat and talk, aunt, talk and eat, for else we shall not afterward have time to discourse of the love of our lost master and Melibea, lovely, gentle Melibea!

ELICIA. And is Melibea so lovely, is she so gentle as you make her to be? I think my penny to be as good silver as hers!

AREUSA. O sister, hadst thou seen her as I have seen her! All year long she is mewed up at home where she is daubed over with a thousand sluttish slibber-slabbers—all which she must endure for once in a twelvemonth going abroad to be seen. She anoints her face with honey, parched grapes, and crushed figs. It is their riches that make such creatures to be accounted fair, for she has such breasts, being a maid, as if she had been the mother of three children: they are for all the world like two great melons. Her belly I have not seen, but, judging by the rest, I believe it to be as slack and flaggy as a woman of fifty. I know not what Calisto should see in her that he should forsake the love of others whom he may with great ease obtain and far more pleasure enjoy!

SEMPRONIO. It seems to me, sister, that every pedlar praiseth his own wares. Quite the contrary is spoken of her throughout the city.

AREUSA. Nothing is farther from the truth than the opinion of the vulgar. What the vulgar think is vanity! What they speak is falsehood!

SEMPRONIO. It is no marvel if Calisto love Melibea: he is noble, she honourably born.

AREUSA. Noble actions make men noble! Let no man search for virtue in the nobleness of his ancestors!

CELESTINA. Children, as you love me, cease this contentious talk, and you, Elicia, come to the table again, and sit down!

AREUSA. Let him go hang, sister. Sit down—unless you will have me likewise rise from the table!

ELICIA, *sitting*. I would please *thee* in all things, sister.

SEMPRONIO *laughs*.

Now the evil canker consume thee!

CELESTINA. Son, no more, I pray thee. Tell me, how does Calisto? How fell it out that both of you could slip away from him?

PARMENO. He flung from us, fretting and fuming like a madman, his eyes sparkling fire, his mouth venting curses, and now he is gone to St. Mary Magdalen's, vowing never to come home till he hear that you are come with Melibea in your lap. Your mantle and kirtle and my jerkin are cocksure. For the rest, when he will give it to you, I know not.

CELESTINA. Let it come when it will come! Everything makes the heart merry that is gotten without labour, especially coming from where it leaves so small a gap—from a man of that wealth who with the very scraps of his house would make me of a beggar to become rich! Such as he feel it not, they neither see nor hear, being scorched in the fiery flames of love.

SEMPRONIO. Mother, you and I are of a mind. For here is she present who caused me to become another Calisto, desperate in my doings, leaping over walls, putting my life in danger —which I count time well spent since it gained me so fair a jewel!

ELICIA. I assure thee, thy back is no sooner turned but another is with me whom I love better! And he is a properer man than thou and will not anger me as thou dost!

CELESTINA. Son, all this stir is because you commended Melibea. Go to, my masters, enjoy the flower of fresh and lively youth.

> He that will not when he may
> When he would he shall have nay.

I myself repent me of those hours which I lost when I was young and men did love me. For now I am a decayed creature, withered and full of wrinkles, and nobody will look at me. Yet my mind is still the same: I want rather ability than desire. Fall to your flap, my masters, kiss and clip. As for me I have nothing else to do but to look on and please mine eye. It is some comfort to me yet to be a spectator of your sports. Never stand upon nice terms, for, whilst you sit at board, it is lawful to do anything from the girdle upwards. When you are by yourselves, close together at it in a corner, I will not clap a fine on your heads. The king doth not impose any such taxation; and as for these wenches, they will never accuse you of ravishment. God bless you, but it rejoiceth my heart to see you play thus, you rascals! Watch that you overturn not the table there!

A knock at the door.

CELESTINA. Look who it is, daughter.

ELICIA. Either the voice deceives me, or it is my cousin Lucrecia.

CELESTINA. Let her come in, for she understands somewhat of the matter whereof we discoursed, though, being shut up so close at home, she is hindered in the fruition of her friculation and cannot enjoy her youth as others do.

Enter LUCRECIA.

LUCRECIA. Much good to you, aunt, and to all this great meeting.

CELESTINA. So great, daughter? It appears that you have not known me in my prosperity, which is now some twenty years since. He that sees me now, I wonder his heart doth not burst with sorrow. I tell thee, wench, I have seen at this table nine gallant young wenches at a time! Your noblemen old and young, your churchmen of every station from bishop to sexton, were all at my service, and when I came to a church, my foot was no sooner in but I had as many bonnets vailed to me as a duchess. Spying me half a league off, a priest would drop his prayers and ask how did his wench? 'Twas there they would resolve when they should come to my house.

SEMPRONIO. You make my hair stand on end! Would churchmen fall so low?

CELESTINA. Some were very chaste, others took it upon them to maintain me in my profession. This one sends me in partridges, that one a custard, some other a good suckling pig. Poorer priests brought me the offerings from their altars. And now those days are past! I have eaten all my white bread, and know not how to live!

AREUSA. Do not weep, mother. We are come hither to be merry.

CELESTINA. When I call to mind the merry life which then I led, I have cause to weep. I had the world at will, being served, honoured, and sought after of all.

SEMPRONIO. The remembrance of the good time we have had doth profit us nothing. Mother, we will go aloft and solace ourselves, whilst you give this maid her answer.

Only CELESTINA *and* LUCRECIA *remain.*

CELESTINA. What is the cause, daughter Lucrecia, of your happy coming hither?

LUCRECIA. Believe me, I had almost forgot, with thinking of the merry time you talked of! Mistress, I am sent unto you for my lady's girdle. And my lady entreats you to visit her, and that out of hand for she feels very ill. She is heartsick.

CELESTINA. I marvel that so young a gentlewoman should be pained at the heart.

LUCRECIA, *aside.* The subtle old bawd does her tricks, and then afterwards, when one comes for help, it is news to her forsooth. Traitorous hag, thou knowest well enough what she ails.

CELESTINA. What say you?

LUCRECIA. I say: would we were gone and that you would give me the girdle!

CELESTINA. Let us go. I will carry it along with me.

They start out.

MELIBEA, *alone.* O wretch that I am, would it not have been better to have yielded yesterday to Celestina's request and so have contented that gentleman and cured myself than to be thus driven to uncover my heart when haply he will not accept of it, having set his hopes by this on the person of another? And, O my faithful Lucrecia, what wilt *thou* say of me? I know not whether thou hast suspected or no or whether thou art coming even now with that solicitress of my safety. Almighty God, give patience to my wounded heart that I may be able to dissemble my terrible passion! Let not the leaf of my chastity lose its gilding! But how shall I be able to do it? O women, women, why may you not, like men, lay bare your hearts?

LUCRECIA, *outside, to* CELESTINA. Aunt, stay behind this door whilst I go in and see with whom my mistress is talking.

She goes in.

Come in, aunt: she is talking to herself.

MELIBEA. Make fast the door, Lucrecia, and pull down the hanging over it!

CELESTINA, *who has entered.* What is your disease, lady, that you express your torment in maiden blushes?

MELIBEA. Truly, mother, I think there be serpents within that are gnawing on my heart.

CELESTINA, *aside.* It is well! I will be even with you, fool, for your yesterday's anger!

MELIBEA. What's that?

CELESTINA. A great part of health is the desiring of health, but, that I may minister unto you, you must satisfy me in three particulars. First: on which side of your body doth your pain lie most? Second: how long have you had this pain? Third: hath your evil proceeded of any cruel thought which hath taken hold on you? Open the whole truth to your physician as to your confessor.

MELIBEA. My pain is about the heart, its residence near my left pap, but it disperseth itself over every part of my body. Secondly, it hath been so but of late, troubling my sight, changing my countenance, taking away my stomach and my sleep and all my pleasure. Touching the last thing you demanded, I cannot conjecture the cause—neither death of kinsfolk, nor loss of goods, nor any doting dream—save only a kind of alteration caused by your request in the behalf of that gentleman Calisto when you entreated me for the prayer.

CELESTINA. What, madam? Is Calisto so bad a man that but to name him should send forth such poison? Do not believe it. I have another thing in the wind. If your ladyship will give me leave, I will tell you.

MELIBEA. Speak what thou wilt, put thy experience in practice. No remedy is so sharp as my pain. Though it touch mine honour, wrong my reputation, rip and break my flesh, do what thou wilt! If I may find ease, I shall liberally reward thee.

LUCRECIA, *aside*. My mistress has lost her wits. This sorceress hath captivated her will.

CELESTINA, *aside*. A devil is still haunting me: I have escaped Parmeno and fallen upon Lucrecia.

MELIBEA. What is't, mother? What said the wench?

CELESTINA. I cannot tell. But there is not anything more contrary in great cures before stouthearted surgeons than fainting hearts who strike fear into the patient and trouble the surgeon. Therefore, command Lucrecia to be absent.

MELIBEA, *to* LUCRECIA. Get you out! Begone!

LUCRECIA, *aside*. We are all undone.

Exit LUCRECIA.

CELESTINA. Your wound is great and hath need of a sharp

cure. Have patience, for seldom is that cured without pain which in itself is painful: one nail drives out another. Do not conceive hatred, nor give your tongue leave to speak ill of so virtuous a person as Calisto, whom, if you did but know him . . .

MELIBEA. No more of him, for God's sake, you kill me!

CELESTINA. Madam, this is the main point of my cure. There is an invisible needle which you must feel before it come at you and stitch up your wound.

MELIBEA. More pleasing would be it unto me that you would tear my flesh and sinews asunder!

CELESTINA. Without even rending of your garments, your breast was lanced by love. Therefore will I not sunder your flesh to cure the sore.

MELIBEA. How call you this grief?

CELESTINA. Sweet love.

MELIBEA. Tell me, then, what this sweet love may be, for in the very hearing of it named, my heart leaps for joy.

CELESTINA. It is a concealed fire, a pleasing wound, a savoury poison, a sweet hurt, a cheerful torment, and a gentle death.

MELIBEA. According to the contrariety which these names carry, I rest doubtful of my recovery.

CELESTINA. Where God gives a wound, he gives a remedy; as it hurts, so it heals; I know where the flower grows that will free you from this torment.

MELIBEA. How is it called?

CELESTINA. I dare not tell you.

MELIBEA. Speak and spare not.

CELESTINA. Calisto.

MELIBEA *faints.*

If she die in a swoon, they will kill me. Melibea, sweetheart, angel, open your eyes, I say! Lucrecia, run for a jar of water, your lady lies here in a swoon!

MELIBEA, *reviving.* Softly, I pray, do not trouble the house!

CELESTINA. Speak, speak unto me! What will you have me do, my pearl? Whence arose this sudden qualm? I believe my stitches are broken!

MELIBEA. No, it is my honesty that is broken, my bashfulness and shamefulness, which, being my friends, could not absent themselves from my face but they would carry my colour with them, my strength, my speech, my understanding. But now, my faithful secretary, since thou so openly knowest, it is in vain for me to smother it. Thou hast gotten that out of my bosom which I never thought to have uncovered. It is in thy power to do with me what thou wilt.

CELESTINA. Since, madam, you have graced me with so great a confidence, put the managing of this matter into my hands, and you and Calisto shall shortly accomplish your desires.

MELIBEA. Mother and mistress, if thou desirest I should live, so handle the business that I may presently see him.

CELESTINA. See him? You shall both see him and speak with him.

MELIBEA. Speak with him? It is impossible.

CELESTINA. Nothing is impossible to a willing mind.

MELIBEA. Tell me how.

CELESTINA. Marry, within the doors of your house.

MELIBEA. When?

CELESTINA. This night!

MELIBEA. Thou shalt be glorious in mine eyes if thou compass this. But soft: at what hour?

CELESTINA. When the clock strikes twelve.

MELIBEA. Go, begone, my faithful friend, talk with that gentleman and will him to come softly at his appointed hour.

CELESTINA. Your mother is making hitherward already. Farewell.

Exit CELESTINA.

MELIBEA, *to* LUCRECIA, *who has re-entered during the foregoing.* Friend Lucrecia, thou hast seen that I have no power over myself: love hath made me prisoner to this gentleman. I entreat thee to sign what you have seen with the seal of secrecy that I may come to the enjoying of so sweet a love.

LUCRECIA. Since your ladyship hath no other remedy but

either to die or to live, it is meet that you should make choice of the best.

ʟɪsᴀ, *outside, to* ᴄᴇʟᴇsᴛɪɴᴀ. How now, neighbour, what's the matter that you are here thus day by day?

ᴇʟᴇsᴛɪɴᴀ. The thread I sold yesterday lacked a little in weight, and I am come to make it up. God be with you!

ʟɪsᴀ. And with you.

She goes in.

What would this old woman have, daughter?

ᴍᴇʟɪʙᴇᴀ. She would have sold me a little sublimated mercury.

ʟɪsᴀ. Ay marry, I rather believe this than that which the old lewd hag told me. She was afraid I would have been angry with her, and so she popped me in the mouth with a lie. Take heed of her, daughter: she is an old fox and as false as the devil.

ᴜᴄʀᴇᴄɪᴀ, *aside.* My old lady's counsel comes too late.

ʟɪsᴀ. I charge you, daughter, if she come hither any more, give her no manner of welcome. Stand upon your honesty and reputation. Be short with her in your answers, and she will never come at you again, for true virtue is more feared than a sword.

ᴍᴇʟɪʙᴇᴀ. Believe me, madam, she shall never come at me more.

St. Mary Magdalen's

ᴄᴇʟᴇsᴛɪɴᴀ *outside.* ᴄᴀʟɪsᴛᴏ, ᴘᴀʀᴍᴇɴᴏ, sᴇᴍᴘʀᴏɴɪᴏ *inside*

ᴄᴇʟᴇsᴛɪɴᴀ. O thrice-happy day! O joy! But I see Parmeno and Sempronio going into St. Mary Magdalen's. I will after them and if I meet with Calisto we will all along together to his house to demand the reward.

sᴇᴍᴘʀᴏɴɪᴏ, *to* ᴄᴀʟɪsᴛᴏ. Take heed, sir, lest by your long stay you give occasion of talk, for it is commonly spoken amongst the people that he is an hypocrite that is too devout. Uncover not your grief unto strangers since the drum is in the hands who know best how to beat it, and your business in her hands who knows best how to manage it.

CALISTO. Whose hands?

SEMPRONIO. Celestina's.

CELESTINA, *inside*. Who names Celestina? What sayest thou this slave of Calisto's?

CALISTO. Thou joy of the world, ease of my passions, relievere of my pain, speak!

CELESTINA. Sir, let us first go more privately, and, as we wal to your house, I will tell you that which shall make yc glad.

PARMENO, *to* SEMPRONIO. The old woman looks merrily.

SEMPRONIO. Soft, listen what she says.

They leave the church.

CELESTINA. All this day, sir, have I been labouring in you business and have neglected other affairs which did muc concern me. But all is well lost since I have brought you business to so good an end: Melibea is wholly at you service.

CALISTO. What do I hear?

CELESTINA. Nay, she is more at your service than at that her father Pleberio.

CALISTO. Melibea—my mistress? I am *her* servant, I am h slave! She is all my desire, she is my life!

SEMPRONIO. Good sir, you cut off Celestina in the midst of h discourse. It were better you should give her something fe her pains.

CALISTO. Well spoken! Mother, instead of a mantle and kirtl take this little chain, put it about your neck—and go on wit your discourse and my joy!

PARMENO, *aside, to* SEMPRONIO. *Little* chain? Heard you hin Sempronio? I will not give my part thereof for half a ma of gold.

SEMPRONIO. Thou hast two ears and but one tongue: as tho lov'st me, brother, hear and hold your peace.

CELESTINA. Melibea loves you and desires to see you.

CALISTO. You my servants, am I here? Look whether I am awake or not! O God, I beseech Thee this may not prove a dream! Tell me, mother, dost thou make sport with me?

CELESTINA. Whether I jest or no, yourself shall see by going this night to her house as the clock strikes twelve, that you may talk together through the chinks of the door. From her own mouth you shall know my solicitude and her desire.

CALISTO. Can so great a blessing light upon Calisto? No! I am not capable of so great a glory!

CELESTINA. I have heard that it is harder to suffer prosperous than adverse fortune, but it is strange, sir, that you will not consider the time that you have spent in her service, nor the person whom you have made to be your means. Celestina is on your side: for you I would make mountains of craggy rocks to grow plain and smooth.

CALISTO. Did you not tell me that she would come to me of her own accord?

CELESTINA. Upon her very knees.

SEMPRONIO. I fear me it is a trap to catch us all. So men use crooked pins wrapped in bread, poisonous pills rolled in sugar.

PARMENO. The songs of the sirens deceive the simple mariner. Even so with her sudden concession of love she will seize on a whole drove of us and purge her innocency with Calisto's honour and our deaths.

CALISTO. Peace, you suspicious rascals, will you make me believe that angels can do ill?

SEMPRONIO. What, will you still play the heretic?

Aside, to PARMENO.

If the play prove foul, he shall pay for all: we will take to our heels.

CELESTINA. Sir, you are in the right, and these in the wrong. And so I leave you to your joys. If you have further occasion to use me, you shall find me ready.

PARMENO *laughs.*

SEMPRONIO. Why dost thou laugh?

PARMENO. To see what haste the old trot makes. She think
every hour a year till she be clear away with the chain.

SEMPRONIO. What would you have an old bawd do (that uset
to patch up seven virginities at a clap for two pieces o
silver) but make it safe and sure for fear lest he should tak
it from her again after he hath had his desire? But let u
take heed when we come to divide the spoil.

CALISTO. Mother, fare you well, I will lay me down to slee
awhile to redeem the nights past and prepare the better fo
the night to come.

PLEBERIO'S *house*

CALISTO, SEMPRONIO, PARMENO

CALISTO, *with* PARMENO *and* SEMPRONIO. Now it strikes twelv
a good hour.

PARMENO. We are near unto the place.

CALISTO. Go thou, Parmeno, and peep in at the door, to see
that lady be come or no.

PARMENO. Who? I, sir? She may be moved to anger in seein
so many acquainted with that which she secretly desires.

CALISTO. This is sound advice. I will go myself.

He goes to the door.

SEMPRONIO. Be in readiness upon the first alarm to take to th
heels.

PARMENO. I am glad, brother, thou hast advised me to tha
which otherwise, for fear of thee, I should never have done

SEMPRONIO. O my friend, how good it is to live together i
love! Though Celestina should prove good to us in no othe
thing, yet in this hath she done us service.

CALISTO, *at the door.* Mistress, be you there?

LUCRECIA *and* MELIBEA *are on the other side of the door.*

LUCRECIA, *going a little nearer.* Who speaks?

CALISTO. He that comes at your command.

MELIBEA. Go a little aside, Lucrecia. Sir, who willed you to come?

CALISTO. She whom I may not merit to serve.

MELIBEA. You have already received her answer. I know not what more you can get of my life than what I then made known.

CALISTO. Miserable Calisto, how hast thou been mocked! Cozening Celestina, why didst thou falsify this lady's message? Didst thou not say she would be favourable? Miserable that I am, whom shall I trust? In whom shall I find any faith? Where is truth to be had? Where the faithful friend?

MELIBEA. Now cease, good sir, your just complaints. Thou weepest out of grief, judging me cruel; I weep out of joy, seeing thee faithful.

CALISTO. O my heart's joy, what tongue can be sufficient to give thee thanks? I stand amazed!

MELIBEA. My heart hath not one moment been absent from thee. As soon as that woman returned thy sweet name to my remembrance, I appointed our meeting at this place and time. Dispose of my person according to thy pleasure.

CALISTO. These doors debar us of our joy!

MELIBEA. I curse these locks and bars as also mine own weak strength!

CALISTO. O troublesome and sport-hindering doors! Give me leave, sweet lady, to call my servants and break them open!

PARMENO, *to* SEMPRONIO. Hearest thou what he says? We shall run into a peck of troubles!

SEMPRONIO. Peace! She will not consent.

MELIBEA. If you break down these cruel doors, though haply we should not presently be heard, yet tomorrow there would arise a terrible suspicion in my father's house, which, in the turning of a hand, would be noised through the whole city.

SEMPRONIO. We are far enough off. Upon the very first noise, we will take to our heels.

PARMENO. Well spoken! Let us shun death, for we are young, and not to desire to die nor to kill is not cowardice but natural goodness. I stand sideling, my legs apart, my left foot foremost, the skirts of my cassock tucked under my girdle, my buckler close to my arm. I believe I should outrun the swiftest buck.

SEMPRONIO. I have bound my sword and buckler together that they may not fall when I run. Hark! Hearest, thou, Parmeno? Away! Begone! Make toward Celestina's house that we may not be cut off on our way to our own!

They run.

PARMENO. Fly, fly, you run too slowly! Throw away thy buckler and all.

SEMPRONIO. Have they killed our master?

PARMENO. I know not. Say nothing to me. Run and hold your peace! He is the least of my care.

SEMPRONIO. Parmeno! Turn and be still! It is nothing but the watch!

PARMENO, *stopping.* They have not left me one drop of blood in my body. Never was I in the like fear.

SEMPRONIO. Turn back, for it is the watch, that's certain.

They turn back.

MELIBEA, *to* CALISTO. What noise is that?

CALISTO. It should be my men who disarm as many as pass by.

MELIBEA. Are they many that you brought?

CALISTO. No more than two, but should half a dozen set upon them, they would not be long in disarming them, they are such true and approved metal. Were it not for thy honour, they would have broken these doors in pieces and, had we been heard, have freed thyself and me from thy father's servants.

PARMENO, *to* CALISTO. Sist, sist, hear you, sir? Begone, for here is a great company with torches. Unless you make haste you will be seen and known.

CALISTO. Believe me, lady, the fear of death would not work so much upon me as the fear of thy honour doth. I take my leave. My next coming, as thou hast ordered it, shall be by the garden.

MELIBEA. Be it so. And happiness go with thee.

PLEBERIO *and* ALISA, *in another room.*

PLEBERIO. Wife, are you asleep?

ALISA. No, sir.

PLEBERIO. Do not you hear some noise in your daughter's chamber?

ALISA. Marry do I. Melibea!

PLEBERIO. I will call louder. Melibea!

MELIBEA. Sir?

PLEBERIO. Who stirs?

MELIBEA. Lucrecia, sir, who went forth to fetch some water.

PLEBERIO. Sleep again, daughter, I thought it had been something else.

LUCRECIA, *to* MELIBEA. A little noise can wake them. Methought they spoke fearfully.

CALISTO's *house*

CALISTO, SEMPRONIO, PARMENO

CALISTO. Tell me, Parmeno, what dost thou think of the old woman whom thou didst dispraise? What could we have done without her?

PARMENO. I advised you as I thought best, but now I see Celestina is changed from what she was.

CALISTO. Didst thou hear what passed between me and my mistress? What did you do all that while? Were you not afraid?

SEMPRONIO. Of what? All the world could not make us afraid!

CALISTO. Took you not a little nap?

SEMPRONIO. I did not so much as sit down but watched as diligently as a cat for a mouse. And Parmeno, he was as glad when he spied the torches coming as a wolf when he spies a flock of sheep.

CALISTO. It is natural in him to be valiant: the fox, though he may change his hair, cannot change his nature. My sons, I am much bound unto you; pray to heaven for success, and doubt not but I will reward your service. Good night.

Exit CALISTO.

PARMENO. Shall we go sleep, Sempronio? Or break our fast?

SEMPRONIO. Ere it be day I will get me to Celestina's house and see if I can recover my part in the chain. She is crafty and I will not give her time to invent some trick and cozen us of our shares.

PARMENO. Let us go together, and, if she stand upon points, let us put her into such a fear that she will betray herself. For money goes beyond all friendship.

They go.

CELESTINA'S *house*

CELESTINA, SEMPRONIO, PARMENO

SEMPRONIO, *outside, to* PARMENO. Her bed is hard by this little window.

He knocks.

CELESTINA, *inside*. Who knocks?

SEMPRONIO. Celestina, open the door, your sons be here.

CELESTINA. I have no sons that be abroad at this time of night.

SEMPRONIO. It is Parmeno and Sempronio.

CELESTINA. Ye mad lads, you wanton wags, enter, enter!

They enter.

How chance you come so early? It is but break of day. How goes the world? Calisto's hopes, are they alive or dead? How stands it with him?

SEMPRONIO. How, mother? Had it not been for us, his soul ere this had gone seeking its eternal rest.

CELESTINA. Have you been in such danger? How was it, I pray?

PARMENO. Provide something for his and my breakfast. When we have eaten, our choler will be somewhat allayed.

CELESTINA. The pox canker my carcass to death, but thou lookest so fierce and ghastly! Sempronio, what hath befallen you?

SEMPRONIO. Mother, I have brought hither my arms all broken and battered, my sword like a saw, my casque dented in with blows. My master shall this night have access to his mistress' garden, but to furnish myself anew I know not where to have one penny.

CELESTINA. Go to your master for it!

SEMPRONIO. He for his part hath done enough. He hath given us a hundred crowns in gold. He hath given us a chain.

CELESTINA. Art thou well in thy wits, Sempronio? What has thy remuneration to do with my reward? As soon as I came home, I gave the chain to this fool Elicia that she might look upon it. She for her life cannot call to mind what she hath done with it, and all this livelong night neither she nor I have slept a wink for grief thereof. At the time that we missed it came in some friends of mine, and I am afraid lest they have taken it away with them. But now, my sons, that I may speak home to the point: if your master gave me anything, what he gave me is mine. I have twice endangered my life for it. More blades have I blunted in his service than you both. More hose and shoes have I worn out. And, my sons, all this costs me good money, besides my skill which I got not warming my tail over the fire. I get *my* living by trade and travail; you yours with recreation and delight; and therefore are you not to expect equal recompense. But because I will deal kindly with you, if my chain be found, I will give each of you a pair of scarlet breeches, which is the comeliest habit that young men can wear. If this will not content you, to your own harm be it!

SEMPRONIO. How doth penury increase with plenty! How often did this old woman say that I should have all the profit that should grow from this business!

PARMENO. Let her give thee that which she promised or let us take it from her!

CELESTINA. I perceive on which foot you halt. Because you think I will make you captives to Elicia and Areusa and provide you no fresh ware, you quarrel thus with me for money! Be still, my boys, she who could help you with these will not stick to furnish you with half a score of handsome wenches apiece!

SEMPRONIO. You talk of chalk and we of cheese. Lay aside these tricks, and give us two parts of that which you received of Calisto. We know you too well.

CELESTINA. I am an old woman of God's making, no worse than other women are. I live by my occupation as other women do. For the life I lead, whether it be good or bad, heaven knows my heart. And do not think to misuse me, for there is justice for all. And you, Parmeno, do not think that I am thy slave because thou knowest my life past and all that passed betwixt me and that unfortunate mother of thine, for she also was wont to use me on this fashion when she was disposed to play her pranks.

PARMENO. Do not hit me in the teeth with memorials of my mother unless thou meanest I should send thee unto her!

CELESTINA. Elicia, Elicia, come down quickly and bring my mantle! I will hie me to the Justice and there rail at you like a madwoman! What do you mean, to menace me in my own house, an old woman of sixty years of age? Go and wreak your anger upon men!

SEMPRONIO. Thou covetous old crib that art ready to die with the thirst of gold, cannot a third part of the gain content thee?

CELESTINA. Out of my house in the devil's name, you and your companion with you! A pox on you both!

SEMPRONIO. Cry, bawl, make a noise, we care not. Either look to perform your promise or end your days.

ELICIA, *who has come downstairs*. Hold him, Parmeno, for fear the fool *should* kill her in his madness!

CELESTINA. Justice! Neighbours, help! Murder! Here be ruffians that will murder me!

SEMPRONIO. Ruffians, you whore? Ruffians, you bawd? Sorceress! Witch! I shall send thee post to hell!

He stabs her.

CELESTINA. Ay me, I am slain. Confession, confession!

PARMENO. Be brief with her, lest the neighbours chance to hear! Kill her, kill her!

CELESTINA *moans and dies.*

ELICIA. My mother is dead, and with her my happiness. The extremity of justice fall upon you!

SEMPRONIO. Fly, fly, Parmeno, the people begin to flock hither. See, see, yonder comes the watch!

PARMENO. There is no means of escape. They have made good the door.

SEMPRONIO. Let us leap out at these windows and die rather than fall into the hands of justice.

PARMENO. Leap then! I will follow.

They leap through a high window.

CALISTO's *house*

CALISTO

CALISTO. O how daintily have I slept! Contentment and quietude have proceeded from my joy. What happiness do I now possess! O my sweet lady and dearest love, what dost thou think on now? Thinkst thou on me, Melibea, or somebody else? O most fortunate Calisto, if only it be true and no dream! Now I remember, my two servants waited on me: if they shall affirm it be no dream I am bound to believe it. Tristan!

Enter TRISTAN.

TRISTAN. Sir?

CALISTO. Call hither Sempronio and Parmeno.

TRISTAN. I shall, sir.

Exit TRISTAN.

CALISTO, *singing.*

> Now sleep and take thy rest,
> Once griev'd and painèd wight,
> Since she now loves thee best
> Who is thy heart's delight.
> Let joy be thy soul's guest
> And care be banished quite
> Since she hath thee exprest
> To be her favourite.

TRISTAN, *returning.* There is not so much as a boy in the house.

CALISTO. Open the windows and see whether it be day.

TRISTAN. Sir, it is broad day.

CALISTO. Go again, and see if thou canst find them; and wake me not till it be dinner time.

TRISTAN, *going.* I will go down and stand at the door that my master may take out his full sleep. But what outcry do I hear in the market place? Yonder comes Sosia, my master's footboy: he will tell me. Look how the rogue comes pulling and tearing of his hair! What's the matter, Sosia?

Enter SOSIA.

SOSIA. Misfortune! Dishonour! O unhappy young men!

TRISTAN. What's the matter?

SOSIA. Sempronio and Parmeno!

TRISTAN. What of them?

SOSIA. They lie slain in the street!

TRISTAN. Is it true? Let us haste with these tidings to our master!

They go to CALISTO's *room.*

SOSIA. Master! Master!

CALISTO. Did I not will you I should not be wakened?

SOSIA. Sempronio and Parmeno lie beheaded in the market place as public malefactors!

CALISTO. Heaven help me! But I know not whether I may believe this news. Didst thou see them?

SOSIA. I saw them, sir.

CALISTO. Take heed what thou sayest, for this night they were with me.

SOSIA. But rose too early to their deaths.

CALISTO. My loyal servants! My chiefest followers! For pity's sake, Sosia, what was the cause of their deaths?

SOSIA. The cause, sir, was published by the common hangman who delivered with a loud voice: "Justice hath commanded that these murderers be put to death."

CALISTO. Who was it they slew? Who might it be? It is not four hours since they left me. What was he for a man?

SOSIA. It was a woman, sir, one whom they call Celestina.

CALISTO. What's that?

SOSIA. That which you heard me tell you, sir.

CALISTO. If this be true, kill thou me too. For sure there is more ill behind if that Celestina be slain, that hath the slash over her face.

SOSIA. It is the very same, sir, for I saw her stretched out in her own house, and her maid weeping by her, having received in her body above thirty several wounds.

CALISTO. Spake they unto thee?

SOSIA. That they might not fall into the hands of the watch, they leapt out of a high window. One had his brains beaten out. The other had both his arms broken and his face so sorely bruised that it was all of a gore-blood. When their heads were chopped off, I think, they scarce felt what harm was done them.

CALISTO. O mine honour, my reputation, how dost thou go from table to table, from mouth to mouth! O my secret actions, how openly will you walk through every street! Tell me, Sosia, what was the cause they killed her?

SOSIA. The maid who sat weeping over her made known the cause to as many as would hear it, saying that they slew her because she would not let them share in that chain of gold which you had lately given her.

CALISTO. O Fortune, how hast thou beaten me! And yet by adversities the heart is proved, whether it be of oak or elder. Come what will come, I will accomplish her desire for whose sake all this hath happened. For it is better to pursue the glory which I expect than the loss of those that are dead; they would have been slain at some other time, if not now. And the old woman was wicked and false; this was a judgment of God upon her. Sosia and Tristan shall accompany me, and carry ladders, for the walls are high.

PLEBERIO's *garden*

MELIBEA, LUCRECIA, SOSIA, TRISTAN, CALISTO

MELIBEA. The gentleman stays long. Tell me, Lucrecia, will he come or no?

LUCRECIA. I conceive, madam, he hath some just cause of stay.

MELIBEA. I am afraid lest some misfortune may befall him as he is on his way. Hark! What steps are those?

SOSIA, *on the other side of the wall.* Set the ladder here, Tristan.

CALISTO. I will in alone, for I hear my mistress.

CALISTO *climbs into the garden.*

MELIBEA. Take heed, my dear lord, how you leap, I shall swoon in seeing it. Take more leisure in coming down the ladder!

CALISTO. My lady and my glory! I embrace and hug thee in mine arms! A turbation of pleasure seizeth on my person!

MELIBEA. My lord, rejoice in that wherein I rejoice: which is to view and touch thee. But do not ask that which, being taken away, is not in thy power to restore.

CALISTO. Dear lady, it is not in any man that is a man to forbear in such a case; much less in me, having swum through this sea of thy desire and mine own. After so many travails, will you deny me entrance to the sweet haven where I may find some ease of all my sorrows?

MELIBEA. Content yourself in the enjoying of this outwardness!

Do not rob me of the greatest jewel which nature hath enriched me with!

CALISTO. Madam, what mean you? Pardon, sweet lady, these my impudent hands if too presumptuously they press upon you! Though once they never thought to touch thy garments, they now have leave to lay themselves with gentle palm on thy dainty body, this white, soft, delicate flesh.

MELIBEA. Lucrecia, go aside a little.

CALISTO. And why, madam? I should be proud to have such witnesses of my glory.

MELIBEA. So would not I, when I do amiss.

LUCRECIA *goes aside.*

Passage of time.

SOSIA, *on the other side of the wall.* Tristan, thou hear'st how the gear goes?

TRISTAN. I hold my master the happiest man that lives and, though I am but a boy, methinks I could give as good an account of such a business as my master!

SOSIA. To such a jewel who would not reach out his hand? And he hath paid well for it: a couple of his servants served to make sauce for this his love.

MELIBEA. O my lord, how couldst thou find in thy heart that I should lose the name and crown of a virgin for so momentary a pleasure? O my poor mother, if thou knewest this, how cruel a butcher of thyself and me wouldst thou become! O my honoured father, how have I wronged thy reputation and given place to the undoing of thy house! Traitor to myself, why did I not foresee the error which would ensue by thy entrance, Calisto?

SOSIA, *as before.* What's done cannot be undone. You should have sung this song before.

The clock strikes three.

CALISTO. Methinks we have not been here above an hour, and now the clock strikes three.

MELIBEA. My lord, for God's love, now that I am thy mistress, deny me not thy sight. And let thy coming be ever at this secret place and at the selfsame hour. Farewell, my lord. Thou wilt not be seen, for it is dark, nor I heard, for i is not yet day.

CALISTO *goes to the wall.*

CALISTO. Bring hither the ladder.

SOSIA. Sir, it is ready.

CALISTO *descends.*

ACT V

Several weeks later. CALISTO's *house*

SOSIA, TRISTAN

SOSIA. What thinkest thou of Calisto?

TRISTAN. On the one side he is oppressed with sadness for Sempronio and Parmeno, and on the other side transported with the gladsome delight which he hath enjoyed these nights with his Melibea. And where two such strong and contrary passions meet, thou knowest with what violence they will work upon a feeble subject.

SOSIA. Dost thou think he feels grief for those that are dead? If she did not grieve more whom I see here out of the window go along the street, she would not wear a veil of such a colour.

TRISTAN. Who is that, brother?

SOSIA. Seest thou that mournful maid which wipes the tears from her eyes? That is Elicia, Celestina's servant and Sempronio's friend, and in the house you see her entering there dwells a lovely woman. She is half-courtesan, yet happy is he that can win her. Her name is Areusa, for whose sake poor Parmeno endured many a miserable night. And she, poor soul, is nothing pleased with his death.

AREUSA'S *house*

AREUSA, ELICIA

AREUSA. O my Parmeno, how doth thy death torment me!

ELICIA. Great sorrow, great loss! That which I show is but li
tle to that which I feel! My heart is blacker than m
mantle, my bowels than my veil!

She breaks down, sobbing.

AREUSA. But, being that this ill-success hath ensued and, b
ing that their lives cannot be restored by tears, do not, siste
vex thyself in weeping out thine eyes. I grieve as much, an
yet thou seest with what patience I pass it over.

ELICIA. Wretch that I am, I am ready to run out of my wit
Whither shall I go? I have lost money, meat, drink, an
clothes! I have lost my friend! And that which grieves n
most is to see that this villain Calisto, who hath no sen:
nor feeling of his servants' death, goes every night to vis
his filth Melibea, feasting and solacing himself in her con
pany, whilst she grows proud, glorying to see so much bloc
sacrificed for her!

AREUSA. If this be so, of whom can we revenge ourselves be
ter? He that hath eaten the meat, let him pay for it . .
There is a ruffian, one Centurio, who even now went fro
me sad and heavy, for that I would not impose any servi
upon him. If this villain prove not a worse executioner f
Calisto than Sempronio was for Celestina, never trust n
more. Now tell me, cousin, how this business goes.

ELICIA. Sosia, Calisto's groom, accompanies him . . .

AREUSA. Enough! Send hither this Sosia. I will take him
hand.

Passage of time.

A knock on the door.

Who is't that knocks?

SOSIA, *outside*. Sosia.

AREUSA, *to* ELICIA. Hide yourself, sister, behind these hangings, and thou shalt see how I will puff him up.

Enter SOSIA.

My Sosia! My inward friend—whom I have longed to know—though perhaps he knew it not! I will hug thee in mine arms, for I see report comes short and there are more virtues in thee than I have been told of. How thou dost resemble my unfortunate Parmeno! Tell me, gentle sir, did you ever know me before?

SOSIA. The fame, gentlewoman, of your graces flies with so swift a wing that you need not marvel if you be of more known than knowing.

ELICIA, *aside*. To see how the silly fellow exceeds himself! He that hath seen him go to water his horses, riding without a saddle, with his naked legs hanging down beneath his canvas frock, and should now see him, thus handsome and well-suited, why, he would crow like a cockerel!

AREUSA. False and deceitful praises are common among men but, Sosia, that thereby thou shouldst think to gain my love is needless, for thou hast gained it already. There are two things, Sosia, which caused me to send unto thee. What they are I will leave to thyself to relate.

SOSIA. Answer for me your own questions: I shall confirm whatever you propound.

AREUSA. First, then, did I send for thee that I might give thee to understand how much I love thee; secondly, that I may admonish thee not to tell thy secrets to any, for thou seest what befell Parmeno and Sempronio. There came one unto me and said thou hadst told him of the love betwixt Calisto and Melibea and how thou goest along with Calisto night by night. Take heed, sir, and do not think thy friend will keep thy secret when thyself cannot keep it. When thou goest to that lady's house, make no noise, for some have told me that thou canst not contain thyself.

SOSIA. O what busybodies be they who abuse your ears with such tales! And some others, perhaps, because they see me go a-nights, when the moon shines, to water my horses, whistling and singing, conceive an evil suspicion, and of this suspicion make certainties. Nor is Calisto so foolish that he should go about such a business but that he will first be sure that all is quiet. And less are you to suppose that he goeth every night unto her: such a duty will not endure a daily visitation!

AREUSA. If you love me then, my dear, that I may accuse these busybodies to their faces, acquaint me with the days you determine to go thither.

SOSIA. Mistress, this very night, when the clock shall strike twelve, they have appointed to meet in the garden.

AREUSA. On which side of the garden, my sweetheart—that I may contradict these babblers?

SOSIA. By the street where the fat hostess dwells, just on the back side of her house.

AREUSA. Brother Sosia, this shall suffice, and so a good speed of thee, for I have other business to despatch.

SOSIA. Courteous sweet mistress, your own best wishes attend you.

Exit SOSIA. ELICIA *comes out.*

AREUSA. Now that we have squeezed this orange, I think it not amiss to call hither that dog's face Centurio.

Passage of time.

Enter CENTURIO.

CENTURIO. Command me, mistress, in such things as I know: to kill this or that man; to cut off a leg or an arm; to slash any woman over the face that shall stand in competition with thee. Such trifles shall be no sooner said than done.

AREUSA. I take you at your word. Revenge me upon a gentleman called Calisto, who hath wronged me and my cousin.

CENTURIO. Incontinently! But hath he received confession?

AREUSA. His soul is no charge of thine.

CENTURIO. Then let us send him to dine in hell without confession!

AREUSA. Fail me not, I advise you. This night, if you will, you may take him napping.

CENTURIO. No more! I apprehend your meaning! But tell me, how many accompany him?

AREUSA. Only two, and those, young fellows.

CENTURIO. This is too poor a pittance. My sword will have but a short supper: it would fare better at some other time.

AREUSA. I must not be fed with delays: I would see whether sayings and doings eat together at your table.

CENTURIO. If my sword should tell you the deeds it hath done it would want time to utter them. What peoples church-yards but my sword? Who makes surgeons rich but my sword? Who slices the helmets of Calatayud? Who shreds the casks of Almazan? For this blade the name of Centurio was given to my grandfather!

AREUSA. We would not have to do with your pedigree. Resolve suddenly if you will do that I spake to you of.

CENTURIO. Make your own choice what death you will have him die! For I can show you a bead-roll wherein are set down some seven hundred and seventy sorts of deaths, which, when you have seen, you may choose that which likes you best.

ELICIA. He is too bloody for this business, Areusa!

AREUSA. Sister, hold your peace.

CENTURIO. Some I use like sieves, pricking them full of holes with my poniard! Some I cut in a large size, giving them a mortal wound, a fearful *stoccado!* And now and then I use my cudgel or *bastinado* that my sword may keep holiday!

ELICIA. Bastinado him, I pray you, for I would have him beaten but not slain!

AREUSA. Sister, let Melibea weep as you have done. Centurio, so long as you revenge us on him, any way shall content us.

CENTURIO. Unless he take to his heels, he is going to hell, I warrant you! I will give him his passport!

AREUSA. God direct thy hand! And so, farewell.

CENTURIO *goes outside.*

CENTURIO. Now, O headstrong whores, will I think how I may excuse myself of my promise, and in such sort, too, that they may be persuaded that I used all possible diligence to execute their desire. I will feign myself sick. But then they will be at me again when I am well. I will say I have forced

this Calisto to fly. But then they will ask who was with him
and by what marks I knew them. And so the fat is in the
fire. What counsel shall I take that may comply with mine
own safety and their desire? I will send for lame Thraso and
his companions, and tell them to go and make a clattering
with their swords and bucklers in manner of a fray. This is
a sure course and no other hurt can follow save to make
this Calisto get him home to bed.

PLEBERIO's *garden*

CALISTO, SOSIA, TRISTAN, LUCRECIA, MELIBEA

CALISTO, *outside, to* SOSIA *and* TRISTAN. Set up the ladder, and
see you make no noise, for I hear my mistress' tongue.
will get me to the top of the wall, and there stand awhile
to see if I can hear any token of her love to me.
He does so.

MELIBEA, *inside the garden.* Sing on, Lucrecia, sing on, till my
lord come, and let us go aside into this green walk that they
that pass by may not hear.

LUCRECIA.

> Sweet is the fount, the place,
> I drank at, being dry;
> More sweet Calisto's face
> In Melibea's eye.
> And though that it be night,
> His sight my heart will cheer,
> And when he down shall light
> O how I'll clip my dear!
> The wolf for joy doth leap
> To see the lambkins move,
> The kid joys in the teat
> And thou joy'st in thy love.
> Never was loving wight
> Of's friend desirèd so;
> Ne'er walks of more delight
> Nor nights more free from woe.

MELIBEA. Methinks I see that which thou singest. It is as if
   he stood before me. Go on: I will bear a part with thee.
LUCRECIA *and* MELIBEA.

> Sweet trees who shade this mould
> Of earth, your heads down bend
> When you those eyes behold
> Of my best-lovèd friend.
> Fair stars whose bright appear
> Both beautify the sky,
> Why wake ye not my dear
> If he asleeping lie?

MELIBEA, *alone.*

> You birds whose warblings prove
> Aurora draweth near,
> Go fly and tell my love
> That I expect him here.
> The night doth posting move
> Yet comes he not again.
> God grant some other love
> Do not my love detain!

CALISTO. The sweetness of her voice hath ravished me! Dear
   lady and glory of my life, if thou lovest me, give not over
   thy singing!

MELIBEA. My desire of thee was that which made me air my
   notes; now that thou art come, that desire disappears.

CALISTO. O interrupted melody, short-timed pleasure!

MELIBEA. The whole garden delights in thy coming! Look on
   the moon, how bright she shines! Look on the clouds, how
   speedily they rack away! Hark to the fountain, how sweet
   a murmur! Hark to the cypresses, how one bough makes
   peace with another! Behold these silent shades, how dark
   they are, for the concealing of our sports!

LUCRECIA *makes as if to embrace* CALISTO.

Lucrecia, art thou mad with pleasure? Touch not my love!
LUCRECIA *withdraws to one side.*

CALISTO. My sweet mistress! My life's happiness!
He takes her in his arms.

MELIBEA. Sir, as thou art the pattern of all courtesy, if thou wouldst learn if my dress be of silk or wool, why dost thou lay hands upon my petticoats, which assuredly are of linen?

CALISTO. He, madam, that wisheth to eat the bird first removes the feathers!

LUCRECIA, *aside.* Here's a life indeed. I feel myself melt like snow beneath the sun.

MELIBEA. Shall I send Lucrecia to fetch you sweetmeats?

CALISTO. No sweetmeats for me save this thy body! Wish rather that I should not let slip the least moment in enjoying such a treasure!

LUCRECIA, *aside.* My head aches with hearing, and yet their lips ache not with kissing. Sure, they will make me gnaw the finger of my glove to pieces!

A clattering outside.

SOSIA, *outside.* Out you ruffians! Out you rogues!

CALISTO. Madam, that is Sosia's voice, suffer me to see that they do not kill him, for there is nobody with him but a little page.

SOSIA. Yea? Are you come again? I shall fleece you, you rascals!

CALISTO. Lady, if you love me, let me go. The ladder stands ready.

He leaves her.

MELIBEA. Why dost thou go so furiously and fast to hazard thy life amongst thou knowest not whom? Lucrecia, come quickly, for Calisto is gone to thrust himself into a quarrel.

CALISTO *climbs the wall.*

TRISTAN. Stay, sir! They are gone! It is nobody but lame Thraso and his companions that made a noise as they passed by. Take heed, sir! Hold fast by the ladder lest you fall!

CALISTO *falls from the top of the wall.*

CALISTO. Our Lady help me! I am dead! Confession!

TRISTAN. Sosia! Our master is fallen from the ladder! He neither speaks nor wags!

SOSIA, *bending over* CALISTO's *body.* Master! Master! Do you hear, sir? Let us call a little at this other door. He hears on neither ear. He is as dead as a doornail. There is no more life in him than in my grandfather who died some hundred years since.

LUCRECIA. Hark, hark, madam, what mischance is this?

TRISTAN. My master, my master is dead! He is fallen headlong down. Dead and without confession! Help, Sosia, help to gather up these brains that lie scattered among the stones! Let us put them back in his head!

MELIBEA. What is this? Help me, Lucrecia, to get up this wall that I may see my sorrow! Is all my joy turned to smoke?

LUCRECIA. What's the matter, Tristan, why dost thou weep so?

TRISTAN. My master Calisto hath fallen from the ladder and is dead. His head is in three pieces. He perished without confession. Bear this sad message to his new mistress that she never more expect him. Sosia, take up his feet and let us carry his body hence that he may not suffer dishonour in this place.

They do so.

MELIBEA. So soon to see my sorrows come upon me!

LUCRECIA. Tear not your face, madam, rend not your hair! Out alas! Arise from the ground! Let not your father find you in so suspicious a place!

MELIBEA. My time is come. I am a dead woman. That I should let thee go! Ungrateful mortals, we never know our happiness until we want it!

LUCRECIA. Let us into your chamber. Lay you down on your bed, and I will call your father. We will feign illness, since to hide this it is impossible.

PLEBERIO'S *house*

PLEBERIO, LUCRECIA, *in* PLEBERIO'S *room.* MELIBEA *in her own room*

PLEBERIO. What sudden sickness hath seized upon her, that I cannot have the leisure to put on my clothes?

LUCRECIA. I know not, sir. But if you will see her alive, come quickly.

They go to MELIBEA's *room.*

PLEBERIO. Lift up the hangings, open this window, that I may take a full view of her. Daughter, speak unto me, open thy gladsome eyes!

MELIBEA. Ay me!

PLEBERIO. Thy mother, when she heard thou wast ill, fell into a swoon. Tell me, sweet soul, the cause of thy sorrow.

MELIBEA. Before you can cure it, you must take out my heart, for the malady lies in the most secret place thereof.

PLEBERIO. Youth should be an enemy to care, and a friend to mirth. Rise then, and let us take some fresh air by the riverside. Do not cast thyself away!

MELIBEA. Let us go whither you please, and, if it stand with your liking, to the top of the tower, from whence I may enjoy the sight of the ships that pass to and fro.

PLEBERIO. Let us go, and take Lucrecia with us.

MELIBEA. Father, I pray, cause some musical instrument to be sent unto me. Delightful harmony will mitigate my sorrow.

PLEBERIO. I will go myself and will it to be provided.

Exit PLEBERIO. MELIBEA *and* LUCRECIA *go to the top of the tower.*

MELIBEA. Friend Lucrecia, this place is high. I am loth to lose my father's company. Step down and entreat him to come to the foot of this tower, for I have a word or two to tell him that he should deliver to my mother.

LUCRECIA. I go, madam.

Exit LUCRECIA.

MELIBEA. All have left me, I am now alone. The manner of my death falls pat to my mind; it is some ease unto me that Calisto and I shall meet again so soon. I will make fast the door that nobody may stop me on my journey to him. Things have fallen out luckily. I have time to recount to my father Pleberio the cause of this my short and sudden end. I shall much wrong his silver hairs and shall work great woe unto him by this my error, leaving him in desolation all the days of his life; but it is not in my power to do otherwise. Thou, O God, who art witness of my words, Thou seest the small power that I have over my passion! My senses are taken with the love of the deceased gentleman who hath deprived me of the love which I bear to my living parents.

PLEBERIO *comes to the foot of the tower.*

PLEBERIO. Daughter Melibea, shall I come up to you?

MELIBEA. No, Father, you shall see the death of your only daughter. Hear the last words that ever I shall speak. I am sure you hear the lamentation throughout the city: the ringing of bells, the scriking and crying of people, the howling and barking of dogs, the noise and clattering of armours. Of all this have I been the cause. Even this day I have clothed the knights of this city in mourning. I have left servants destitute of a master. And because you stand amazed at the sound of my crimes I will open the business unto you. It is now many days, dear father, since a gentleman called Calisto, whom you knew, did pine away for my love. (As for his virtues, they were generally known.) So great was his love-torment that he was driven to reveal his passion to a crafty woman named Celestina, which Celestina drew my secret from my bosom and made the match between us. Overcome with the love of Calisto, I gave him entrance to your house; he scaled your walls with ladders, brake into your garden, and took the flower of my virginity. Almost a month have we lived in this delightful error of love. And when he came last night unto me, e'en just about the time that he should have returned home, as Fortune would have it, the walls being high, the night dark, the ladder light and weak, his servants unacquainted with that kind of service, he going down hastily to see a fray in the street, being in choler, making more haste than good speed, not eyeing well his steps, he set his foot quite beside the rungs, and so fell down. With that unfortunate fall, he pitched upon his head and had his brains dashed in pieces against the stones of the street. Thus did the Destinies cut off his thread, cut off my hope, cut off my glory. What cruelty were it now in me that I should live all the days of

my life! His death inviteth mine. Inviteth? Nay, enforceth.
It teacheth that I also should fall headlong down that I
may imitate him in all things. Calisto, I come! My best-
beloved father, I beseech you that our obsequies be solem-
nized together and that we may both be interred in one
tomb. Recommend me to my most dear mother, and inform
her of the doleful occasion of my death. I am glad with all
my heart that she is not here with you. I sorrow much for
myself, more for you, but most for her. God be with you
and her. To Him I offer up my soul. Do you cover up this
body that now cometh down.

She throws herself from the tower.

PLEBERIO's *house*

PLEBERIO, ALISA

ALISA. Pleberio, my lord, why do you weep?

PLEBERIO. Our solace is in the suds, our joy is turned into
annoy, let us no longer desire to live! Behold her whom
thou broughtest forth and I begot—broken to pieces! O my
dear wife, rise up, and if any life be left in thee, spend it
with me in tears and lamentation! Hard heart of a father,
why dost thou not burst to see thyself bereavèd of thy heir?
For whom didst thou build those turrets, for whom planted
trees, for whom wrought ships? O variable Fortune, stew-
ardess of temporal happiness, why didst thou not execute
thy cruel anger against me? Thou mightest, O Fortune,
fluctuant as thou art, have given me a sorrowful youth and
a mirthful age, neither have therein perverted order. O
World, World, in my more tender years I thought thou
wast ruled by reason, but now thou seemest unto me a
labyrinth of errors; an habitation of wild beasts; a dance
full of changes; a fen full of mire; a steep and craggy
mountain; a meadow full of snakes; a garden pleasant to
look at but without fruit. O thou false World! Thou dost

put out our eyes and then to make amends anointest the
place with oil; after thou hast done us harm, thou givest
us cold comfort, saying that it is some ease to the miserable
to have companions in misery. But I, alas, disconsolate old
man, stand all alone. I am singular in sorrow; no misfortune
is like unto mine. What remedy now, thou flattering World,
wilt thou afford my age? Who shall cherish me, who with
gentle usage shall cocker my decaying years? O Love, Love,
what end have thy servants had? As also that false bawd
Celestina who died by the hands of the faithfullest companions that ever she lighted upon! They lost their heads;
Calisto, he brake his neck; and my daughter——! Some, O
Love, have called thee a god, but I would have such fools
consider—it savours not of a deity to murder those that
follow him. Thou enemy to all reason! Thy fire is of lightning which scorches unto death! The sticks which thy
flames consume are the souls and lives of numberless human creatures, not Christians only, but Gentiles and Jews.
What service did Paris do thee? What Helena? What
Clytemnestra? What Aegisthus? And all the World knows
how it went with them. I complain of the World because
I was bred up in it. For had not the World given me life, I
had not therein begot Melibea. Not being begot, she had
not been born. Not being born, I had not loved her. And
not loving her, I should not have mourned, as now I do. O
my bruised daughter, why hast thou left me comfortless and
all alone in this vale of tears?

THE SIEGE OF NUMANTIA

Miguel de Cervantes

English Version by Roy Campbell

When the Roman Senate resolved to destroy Carthage—"Delenda est Carthago!"—the general to whom the operation was entrusted was Scipio, thereupon surnamed Africanus. A second surname—Numantinus—was accorded him by the Senate when in the year 134 B.C. he wrought the downfall of Numantia in Spain.

E.B.

DRAMATIS PERSONAE

SCIPIO
JUGURTHA
CAIUS MARIUS
QUINTUS FABIUS
} *Romans*

CAIUS, *Roman soldier*

TWO NUMANTINES, *ambassadors*

FOUR ROMAN SOLDIERS

SPAIN

THE RIVER DUERO, CALLED ALSO THE DOURO

THREE BOYS REPRESENTING TRIBUTARY STREAMS

THEOGENES
CARAVINO
} *Numantines*

TWO NUMANTINE GOVERNORS

MARQUINO, *a Numantine magician*

MARANDRO
LEONICIO
} *Numantines*

TWO NUMANTINE PRIESTS

A NUMANTINE PAGE

SIX NUMANTINE PAGES

A NUMANTINE MAN

MILBIO, *a Numantine*

A DEVIL

A CORPSE

FOUR NUMANTINE WOMEN

LIRA, *a maiden*

TWO NUMANTINE CITIZENS

A NUMANTINE WOMAN

HER SON

A BOY, LIRA'S BROTHER

A NUMANTINE SOLDIER

WAR

PESTILENCE

HUNGER

WIFE OF THEOGENES

HIS SON

ANOTHER SON, AND A DAUGHTER, OF THEOGENES

SERVIUS, *a boy*

BARIATUS, *a boy, who throws himself from a tower*

A NUMANTINE

ERMILIUS, *a Roman soldier*

LIMPIUS, *a Roman soldier*

FAME, *personified*

ACT I

Enter SCIPIO, JUGURTHA, CAIUS MARIUS, QUINTUS FABIUS, *the brother of* SCIPIO, *and other Romans.*

SCIPIO. This difficult and heavy task with which
The Roman Senate charged me weighs me down
And wearies me till my attention almost
Becomes unhinged. Who would not long to finish
The course of such a long and monstrous war
That cost so many Roman lives? Alas!
Who would not tremble, having to renew it?

JUGURTHA. Why, Scipio, you yourself! For you contain
Both luck and peerless valour in your person,
And both will make your victory secure.

SCIPIO. Force, when applied with prudent moderation,
Humbles the steepest mountains to the earth,
But, when it's fiercely plied with a mad hand,
Trenches the smoothest plains to rugged wastes.
From what I see, it seems there's no repressing
The frenzy of our present army here,
Which, careless both of glory and of spoils,
Lies drunk in burning lust. Here's what I plan,
This is my only wish: to turn our troops
To new and better conduct and, by mending
That which is friendly to us first, the sooner
To subjugate our enemy. Ho! Marius!

CAIUS MARIUS. My lord?

SCIPIO.   Give orders for a general muster
Of the whole army without more delay
Or hindrance. Everybody on parade
Together must immediately appear.
I have a short harangue to give the troops.

CAIUS MARIUS. At once, sir!

SCIPIO.   It is right that they should know
My new designs and their past errors. Go!

Exit CAIUS MARIUS.

JUGURTHA. Sir, I can tell you there's no soldier here
    Who does not love you or who does not fear
    You too, because your matchless valour's known
    From the far south up to the Boreal zone.
    Not one of them, but with fierce, daring zeal
    Will serve you once he hears the trumpet peal
    And eagerly looks forward to the day
    Fabulous deeds of valour to display.

SCIPIO. But first we need to bridle and to quiet
    The vice that seems amongst them to run riot.
    While *that* disgrace continues, to their shame,
    How can they hope to win a glorious name?
    If this most harmful plague is left unchecked
    To root its burning flame and to infect
    The camp—then Vice will work us far more harms
    Than could the fiercest enemy in arms.

*The fall-in for the muster is sounded: and these orders are
heard off-stage:*

    "Our general orders every soldier here
    Upon the main parade-ground to appear,
    This instant, fully armed. Whoever's missed
    Will have his name struck from the army-list."

JUGURTHA. I do not doubt but that with a strong bit
    This evil must be curbed, and that it's fit
    The soldier should be jerked on the short rein
    When justice is a name he takes in vain.
    An army's strength is bloodsucked from within
    When not supported by just discipline
    In spite of all the squadrons that it brags
    And the display of many-coloured flags.

*Soldiers enter and fall in on parade. They are equipped in
the ancient style, without arquebuses.* SCIPIO *gets on a boul-
der, which should be handy nearby, and harangues the
troops.*

SCIPIO. From your fierce mien, and from your sprightly show,
    Comrades, that you are Romans, well I know—
    Romans both strong and lusty for the fight—
    But in your hands so delicate and white,
    And in that pink that's on your faces written,

Why, anyone would think you reared in Britain,
Or that by Flemish sires you'd been begot!
Now, comrades! your joint negligence in not
Heeding what most concerned your good revives
A fallen enemy to seek your lives,
Despising both your prowess and your fame.
For you are Romans, now, only in name.
My sons! does it seem good in your opinion
That the whole world should bend to the dominion
Of Rome, but that you here in Spain, of all
Her subjects, would precipitate her fall?
What a strange flabbiness has laid you low,
A flabbiness, which, in my mind, I know
Is due to Indolence—that deadly foe
To martial strength! Soft Venus does not mate
With Mars, for whole months to cohabitate:
She studies fleeting pleasures, he—the foe,
Conning the art of havoc, blow for blow.
The Cyprian goddess from the camp of Rome
Must leave her quarters, and set out for home.
Her son must leave the barracks, too, who thinks
Of nothing more than banquetings and drinks.
Do you think that mere spears and helms alone
Can raze these mighty battlements of stone?
Or that mere numbers, joined in arms, can crush
And trample down a fortress in one rush?
If no attempt at prudence has been made,
And all things with due foresight are not weighed,
Small profit from vast multitudes can stem,
And far less, from vast armaments, than them.
Now: if in martial unity we stand
It matters not how small may be the band,
You'll see it shine in glory like the sun,
And all its fights will certainly be won;
But if in flabby slothfulness it lies,
Though it should dwarf the whole world with its size,
One moment will suffice to rout it, if
The hand is disciplined, the chest is stiff.
Shame on you, lusty fellows! Shame, I say!
That to our grief, with arrogant display,

A few surrounded Spaniards, in this wall,
Can keep Numantia's eyrie from us all.
Sixteen long tedious years, and more, have passed
Since they have waged us war, up to the last
Holding the vantage still, our ranks dismaying,
And tens of thousands of our kinsmen slaying.
Conquer yourselves! Conquered by vice, you wallow
In base effeminate lust, lewdly to follow
Venus and Bacchus with their trivial charms—
And never reach a hand to take up arms!
Run off, then! If you don't run mad with pain
To see this little country-town of Spain
Defy Rome's might, her own and sole defender,
Offensive most when nearest to surrender!
I'll have your filthy strumpets, at the double,
Run out of camp—the cause of all this trouble!
No man must have more than one eating-bowl.
Your beds, whereon with whores you loved to roll,
Must all be broken up. Let none be found!
And all must sleep on straw, strewn on the ground.
The only perfumes that I will not bar,
Throughout the camp, are those of pitch and tar.
No kitchen pots and pans to fatten greed!
You'll have one mess-can each from which to feed,
For it ill suits with warlike strain and strife
To lead a lounging, plutocratic life.
I'll have no other luxury or scent
Until Numantia to our heel has bent
Than sweat. Men! Let it not appear to you
That you have a rough pathway to pursue
In these just orders! They are what you need
To crown your task, your victory to speed!
It will be difficult at first, I know,
To change your habits at a single blow,
But, if you do not, then this chronic war,
More than it drags behind, will stretch before!
'Twixt wine and dalliance, in soft beds to sport
Suits ill with strenuous Mars. A different sort
Of gear he seeks. He walks in different ways
With different arms his standard to upraise.

I am so sure that, in the end, you'll show
Yourselves true Romans that I now appraise
This beetling wall as naught, which by a foe
Of base, barbarian rebels is defended,
And if your hands can match the zeal you show,
My own to pay you well will be extended,
And with my tongue I'll praise you. Now you know!
The soldiers look at each other, making signs to one of them,
CAIUS, *to answer for them.*

CAIUS. If with attentive eyes you have observed
The changing countenances that surround you
As they were moved by your brief argument,
You've seen how they lost colour, were confused,
And showed the shame and fear that now afflicts
And punishes us all—shame to behold
To what a level they have been reduced
By their own guilt, and that, when chid by you,
They could not find the least excuse to offer
And fear at having made such fatal errors
And having sunk into such drowsy sloth
That they would rather die than do their duty.
But there is still both time and place to spare
For them to make the recompense they owe,
And that's a reason why their grave offences
Should vex you less. Because, from this day on,
With gay and ready zeal, the least of them
Will think of naught but, in your loyal service,
To sacrifice his honour, home, and life.
Accept, my lord, the offer of their saner
And better resolutions, and consider
That in the end they're Romans after all,
In whom there never lacks true, manly fire.
Raise your right hands above your heads, you others,
To show that you approve my vote!

FIRST SOLDIER.   In all
You said, we here confirm you!

SECOND SOLDIER.   And we swear it!

ALL. We swear it: yes!

SCIPIO.   My confidence grows greater

From this day forth, supported by your offer.
For now a new fire kindles in your hearts
With this new change to your old way of life.
I hope the wind will not bear off your vows,
And that you'll make them truthful with your lances.
For my own vows to blossom forth as true,
Yours must as well. It all depends on you.

FIRST SOLDIER. With a safe conduct, two Numantines here
Have come upon an embassy to Scipio.

SCIPIO. Why don't they come? What keeps them?

SOLDIER.   Your permission
Is what they crave.

SCIPIO.   If they're ambassadors
It's theirs already.

SOLDIER.   They're ambassadors.

SCIPIO. Well, let them in then, for, although dissembled,
The enemy will still betray some glint
Of truth. Yes, though he covers it with skill,
You'll always find a little chink through which
You'll get a glimpse of what is wrong with him.
To give an audience to one's enemy
Has always done more good than harm. Experience
In things of war has taught me what I say,
And one acquires sure knowledge in this way.

Enter TWO NUMANTINE AMBASSADORS.

FIRST NUMANTINE. Well, thanks to the safe-conduct that you
    grant
Out of the bounty of your regal greatness,
I'll start upon the reason for our mission.
Numantia, of which I am a burgess,
Illustrious general! has sent me to you,
Being the strongest general of Rome
Whom night has ever hid or daylight seen,
To ask of you, my lord, a friendly hand
To signify an end to all this fierce
And vicious strife that for so many years
Has been so harmful to yourselves and us.
Numantia says that never from the laws
And statutes of the Roman Senate will she

Depart as long as we have not to suffer
Beneath the lawless and insufferable
Weight of one consul's rule after another.
They, with their cruel laws and vicious greed,
Placed such a heavy yoke upon our necks,
We were compelled to shake it off by force.
All through the long duration of this war
We have not found a general till now
Whom we could trust enough to treat of peace.
However, now that Fate has steered our ship
To a good harbour, we have reefed our sails,
And wish at last to come to some agreement.
Do not imagine we were brought by fear
To ask for peace in such an urgent way,
Because a long experience has proved
The stubborn strength and valour of Numantia.
Your virtue and your bravery are the bait
That tempted us and showed how we would gain
If we could count upon you as our friend
And lord. That is the reason why we came.
Answer us now, my lord, what is your pleasure?

SCIPIO. You show these signs of penitence too late.
Your friendship gives me little satisfaction.
Once more go exercise your strong right hand
Because I wish to see what mine can do.
Perhaps Fate has entrusted to its grasp
Our glory and your burial. For the shame
Of these long years, it is small recompense
To sue for peace. Go carry on the war!
And let the valiant ranks be formed once more.

FIRST NUMANTINE. False confidence brings after it a thousand
Deceptions. Study well what you decide,
My lord, since this hard arrogance you show
Strengthens our hands to deal you blow for blow.
And since you grudge that peace which our good will
Demands, our cause will be the juster still,
And long before you tread Numantia's earth
You'll learn what the indignant strength is worth
Of those who, though your foes, to make amends,
Have sought to be your vassals and your friends.

SCIPIO. Have you got more to say?

THE NUMANTINES.   No, but we've more
   To do, since you, my lord, will have it so.
   Not to accept the friendship that we bring
   Ill suits the person that you are. But now
   We'll have to show you what we can perform,
   And you, for your part, show what you can do,
   Since it's another thing to ask for peace
   Than through the armoured ranks to burst in storm.

SCIPIO. That's true. And now, to show you whether I
   Know how to treat of peace or speak of war,
   Learn this: I do not want you for my friends,
   Nor of your country can I pay the score.
   With that, you can return back home once more.

NUMANTINES. So that's your will, my lord?

SCIPIO.   I've told you. Yes.

SECOND NUMANTINE. From words to deeds! Numantines love
   the battle!

   Exeunt NUMANTINES.

QUINTUS FABIUS. Past carelessness on our part caused them thus
   To speak to us, but now the time has come
   When you shall see your glory or your death!

SCIPIO. Vain boasting ill becomes strong, valiant breasts.
   Temper your threats, my Fabius, hold your tongue,
   And keep your courage for the hour of battle!
   And yet I think I can prevent that any
   Numantines come to grips with us, and hope
   To find another way to conquer them
   Which is more profitable, to my mind.
   It will humiliate their pride, astound them,
   And make them turn their fury on themselves.
   I think we'll dig a deep ditch round the town
   And with insufferable famine finish
   Them off. I do not wish the wasted blood
   Of any other Romans to discolour
   This ground again. Enough blood has been shed
   By these cursed Spaniards, in this long, hard war.
   Now let us all exert our hands in breaking

And digging this hard earth. Let friends by friends
Be covered with the dust they raise, no longer
Covered with blood by enemies. None here
Will be excused this task, however high
His rank. Let the Centurion, with the ranker,
Labour alike. I too will ply this heavy
Pick-axe, and easily break up the soil.
Do all of you likewise! To see me work,
All should be satisfied. Let no one shirk!

QUINTUS FABIUS. My valiant lord and brother, you have shown
    us
Your prudence in this labour. It would be
An obvious error and a reckless show
Of folly to contend with the mad rage
Of those poor, luckless desperados there.
Far better wall them up and sap the roots
Of their mad vigour. They can be walled round
On every side, save only by the river.

SCIPIO. To work, then! and may my new plan turn out
Better than the old method. If at last
Heaven should deign to favour me, all Spain
Will then be subject to the Roman Senate:
We've but to humble this mad people's pride.

Exeunt omnes.

SPAIN *enters, crowned with towers and bearing in her hand
a castle (which signifies Spain).*

SPAIN. Lofty, serene, and spacious Heaven above!
Who with your starry influence and love
Enrich the greater part of this, my earth,
And over all the rest exalt its worth,
Be moved to pity by my bitter grief,
You, who to the afflicted bring belief,
O favour me in this, my so-great pain,
Who am the lonely and unlucky Spain!
Let it suffice that once you set on fire
My tender limbs and burned me up entire,
Then through my entrails to the sun displayed
The kingdom of the damned. 'Twas you that made
A thousand tyrants rich with what I paid.

To the Phoenicians and the Greeks you gave me,
Either that your will had to be obeyed,
Or that from my own sins I could not save me.
Must each strange nation in its turn enslave me,
So that, not for the briefest time at least,
My flags to Liberty may be released?
Fierce punishments upon us all do rain
But while all suffer greatest is my pain,
For my courageous sons with one another
Are still at strife and brother envies brother.
While separate schemes and contradicting plans
Upset all unity and split the clans,
Never within one aim can coincide
One man's opinion with another man's;
And all their fury does is to divide
When most they need to battle side by side.
It's thus, with inward discord they invite
Barbarians of voracious appetite,
In search of spoil, to plunder right and left
Till of my riches I am all bereft.
Numantia only had the brave resilience
To draw the sword and flash it with such brilliance.
She only raised her face out of the mud
To suckle Liberty with her own blood,
Belovèd Liberty, her child and heir!
And yet I feel the end is coming there,
Where she will end her life, but not her fame,
And, like a Phoenix, be renewed by flame.
These dreaded Romans by a myriad ways
Rather than front the clansmen face to face,
Although the latter are so few, refuse
Anything else than stratagem and ruse.
Oh, that their subtle webs could be undone,
And all the cunning intrigues they have spun,
That just this one small city could be saved
Because of all the perils she has braved!
But now, alas! the enemy surround,
Not only with their arms the walls that bound
Her limits, but a ditch that hems her hopes
Both from the plain and the surrounding slopes,

And only by the swift Duero's side
This all-encircling stratagem's defied.
The sad Numantines in their walls they hem,
Whence no escape, nor entrance into them:
From all assault they're free, and fear no harm,
Yet cannot reach the foe with their strong arm,
And so I claim for them, in one fierce breath,
Either an open war or speedy death.
And since it's only where the Duero runs
There can come aid or access to my sons,
Whose home's their gaol, I'll ask the grand, proud river
How it were best my people to deliver.
O kindly Duero! in your winding quest,
Who water so much of my ample breast,
So may you ever coil your swirling tides
On golden shingles such as Tagus rides,
So may each fugitive and free wood-nymph
Come with her loveliness to grace the lymph
Of your clear mirrors—though you have to leave
Your joys awhile—O hear me, as I grieve!
I beg you to delay no more, but take
Vengeance upon these Romans for the sake
Of the Numantines in their parlous state.
With endless floods rush headlong down in spate!

Enter the river DUERO, *with three other tributaries repre-*
sented by three boys, dressed as if they were the streams
that join the Duero near Soria (which was called Numantia
in those times) in willows and white poplar leaves.

DUERO. Dear Mother Spain, long have I heard your cry,
And, if I have been tardy to reply,
It is that I have sought, but sought in vain
Some remedy to help you in your pain.
The fatal, sad, black day at length will come!
The stars say that Numantia must succumb.
See Obron, Minuesa, and Tera, here,
Who've swelled my current with their waters clear
To such a height that it has burst its sides:
But with no greater heed of my swelled tides
Than had I been a rill (a thing you never,

Spain, have beheld!) they've spanned my mighty river
With dykes and floating towers. But now I've ended
The worst that Fortune, harsh and adamantine,
Has to inflict upon the doomed Numantine.
Let this console your sorrow: that the splendid
Exploits of the Numantines will not fade
Or wither in oblivion's dusky shade,
But live to be a wonder to all ages!
And since the dire, ferocious Roman rages
Lording it over your dear fertile ground,
The time will come when fate will swivel round
Their two Protean destinies: the Roman
Will be oppressed by his now prostrate foeman.
To the remotest countries will arrive
The folk that on your gentle breast survive.
After they've bent the Romans to their yoke,
Goths[1] they will be, a handsome, comely folk
Whose deeds will fill the whole world with their story.
Here on your breast they'll settle down in glory,
And drink new vigour for new deeds of daring.
These injuries of which you're now despairing
Will be avenged in the great havoc done
To Rome, in times to come, by the fierce Hun,
Attila, whom the world will hold in awe,
For his brave sons and other strangers yet
Even into the Vatican will get,
The pilot of the sacred ship to fright
To foreign lands, an exile, taking flight.
That time will also come when, as the Lord
Of Rome, the Spaniard will uphold his sword
Over the Roman's neck, bent in submission,
Who scarce can breathe except by his permission.
Then the great Alban, dealing blood and fire,
Shall cause the Spanish army to retire,

[1] The allusions in the lines that follow are: Goths, who were in
Spain from the fall of Rome (fifth century A.D.) till the arrival of
the Moors (eighth century). Pilot of the sacred ship, Pope Clement
VII, who had to flee Rome when it was sacked in 1527. The great
Alban, the Duke of Alva (later to be the villain of Schiller's *Don
Carlos*). Philip II reigned from 1556 to 1598. Portugal was incor-
porated in Spain in 1580. [E.B.]

Short, not of courage, but of men and horses,
Since, with them both, he will increase his forces;
And when you reach the peak of your renown
The Maker of the earth and sky above,
Through that Viceroy who represents his crown,
Will give your kings a name of joy and love,
Calling them *Catholic*, with all that own
Rule and allegiance on the Gothic throne.
But he whose hand will raise to greatest height
Your honour, and the general delight,
Making the valour and the name of Spain
Above all other countries show most plain,
Will be a king, whose strong and sane desire
To high and lofty exploits will aspire.
He will be called, by name, Philip the Second,
And nearly all the world as his be reckoned.
Beneath his happy empire he'll combine
Your separate kingdoms, hitherto close-shut,
And in his coat of arms quarter the sign
Of famous Portugal which will be cut
From them, only to be restored again
To famed Castile, and make a part of Spain.
What envy, dear-loved Spain, a thousand lands
Will feel for the sharp sword-thrust of your hands
And your triumphant banners shadowing
The world! Let this some consolation bring
At the sad pass which now you well may mourn!
For we cannot avert the judgment dire
That is already passed and must be borne:
It marks Numantia for her own red pyre.

SPAIN. Your arguments alleviate in part,
    Great Duero, the affliction of my heart,
    Simply because I trust there's no deception
    In what you prophesy.

DUERO.   Without exception,
    Though long in coming, Spain, you may be sure
    That in the end your triumph is secure.
    Farewell! I have a tryst with Neptune's daughters.

SPAIN. May heaven swell your clear, sweet-tasting waters!

ACT II

THEOGENES *and* CARAVINO *enter, with four other* NUMAN-
TINES, *and* MARQUINO, *the magician. They sit down.*

THEOGENES. To me it seems, you vigorous, grown men,
That dismal omens and contrary fates
Combine their influences to our harm
Because our strength is being sapped within us.
The Romans hold us shut in on all sides
With craven hands destroying us inchmeal.
We cannot seek revenge, nor perish killing,
Nor, without wings, can we escape from here.
Not only are they likely to subdue us,
Whom we have put to rout so many times,
But fellow Spaniards join in league with them
To cut our throats. Oh, may the heavens prevent
And with their lightnings strike the fickle feet
Of friends who run to help the enemy
To harm their fellow countrymen! Now think
If you can find some remedy to save us
From this sad quandary, because this long,
Laborious siege now threatens to become
Our funeral. The deep wide trench forbids
That we should put things to the test of arms
And hazard an attack, though strength of arms
Can often burst through such impediments.

CARAVINO. If only it pleased Jupiter supreme
That our young men alone might reach the full
Strength of the cruel Roman army, then
Despising death, they'd open up a road
To safety for the whole Numantine people,
But, since within these limits we're confined
Like women kept inside the house, let's do
The most we can to show our daring spirit
By challenging our foes to single combat
So that, grown weary of this tedious siege,
We put an end to it, each for himself.

Or, if this remedy proves unsuccessful
In the just measure we expect of it,
There is another path for us to try
Though it is more laborious: by night,
All in one mass, to storm the wall and ditch
That hold us from the foe that lurks beyond them
And rush through to our countrymen for help.

FIRST NUMANTINE. Or through that ditch, or through the gates
  of death,
We have to make an opening for our lives.
Insufferable is the pain of death
If it comes on us when we're most alive,
Yet death's a cure for miseries, when they
Grow with our lives, and all the better, when
It comes with honour, as befits brave men.

SECOND NUMANTINE. With what more honour can our souls
  and bodies
Be parted than by falling on the Romans
To prove the prowess of our strong right hands?
Let any one who wishes to, remain
Here in the city, if he feels afraid.
I find it far more welcome to lie dead
In the closed ditch or in the open field.

THIRD NUMANTINE. This cursèd and insufferable famine
Forces me to agree with all you say
However hazardous and hard it be.
By dying we escape from ignominy.
Let him who does not wish to die of hunger
Plunge down here in the ditch with me, and hack,
To his delivery, a gory track!

FOURTH NUMANTINE. Before you undertake so great a peril
As that which you've resolved, it seems to me
That our fierce enemy should first be summoned
And asked to give permission for one Roman
And one Numantine to have single combat.
The death of one of them will be the verdict,
Thus finishing our differences for good.
The Romans are so proud they must accept,
And if they only do as I expect,

There'll be a speedy end to all our troubles,
Because there's one Numantine with us here
Whose valour and whose strength convince me quite
He'd kill any three Romans in one fight.
Also we should elicit from Marquino,
Who is so famous for his auguries,
What star, what planet, or what constellation
Portends our death or else a glorious ending.
We also should find out if he can tell us
If from this doubtful and oppressive siege
We shall emerge the victors or the conquered.
Next (the first duty that must be performed),
We'll make a solemn sacrifice to Jove
From whom we are entitled to expect
Better rewards than we enjoy today.
Next, our inveterate vices must be cured;
Perhaps our grudging fate would then relent
And to our final happiness consent.
To die? Why, there is always time to die
For any one who's desperate to try.
We'll always be in time for our last breath
With daring hearts to die a hero's death.
But that such time may not be passed in vain
Consider what I've striven to make plain,
And, if you do not find it stands the test,
Let someone else advise us what is best.

MARQUINO. The logic of your reasonings I approve.
Let sacrifices and oblations be
Made to the gods. Then we must launch the challenge.
I shall not lose a chance to show my science
And power. Into the future I shall enter,
And draw what's good or bad from its dark centre.

THEOGENES. I offer myself here to you, who well
May trust in my endeavour, as you know,
To go out and perform the duty offered,
If by good luck, the challenge proves effective.

CARAVINO. Your spotless valour merits greater honours.
Your powers to tasks more difficult than this
Should be devoted, since you are, yourself,

In all things, so much better than the best.
And since you occupy the foremost place
In honour and in valour, with just cause,
And since I come far after you in value,
I wish to be the herald of this joust.

FIRST NUMANTINE. And now, with all my people, I prefer
To do what's pleasing most to Jupiter:
Sacrifice and oblation give delight
To him, if in our hearts we are contrite.

SECOND NUMANTINE. Come, hasten to perform all we proposed
Before this curst, pestiferous hunger slays us,
That Heaven for our death may quash the sentence,
To mercy moved by our sincere repentance!
Exeunt.

Enter MARANDRO *and* LEONICIO, NUMANTINES.

LEONICIO. Whither away, Marandro?

MARANDRO.   If I don't
Know of my own accord, it's very little
You will find out.

LEONICIO.   Your amorous sentiments
Have left you without reason.

MARANDRO.   Tell me rather
That, since I felt them, my wits have increased.

LEONICIO. It has been proved of old that everyone
Who loves, loves to his own discomfiture—
That's the most rational conclusion proved.

MARANDRO. What you have said is tinged with wit and malice.

LEONICIO. You understand my wit, but your stupidity
Is beyond me.

MARANDRO.   It's stupid—to love well?

LEONICIO. Love must be kept within the bounds of reason.
Whom you love, when and how, that is what counts.

MARANDRO. You wish to lay down laws to love?

LEONICIO.   One's reason
Can lay them down.

MARANDRO.   Such laws are rational,
No doubt, but do not daze me with their beauty.

LEONICIO. In love's mad game, reason has got no place.

MARANDRO. Yet love does not oppose our reason though
Sometimes it deviates from it.

LEONICIO.   And so
You think it doesn't go against the reason
That soldiers so exemplary as you
Should dote with love at such a time as this?
When you should be upon your knees to Mars
Begging his favour, all that you can do
Is worship Love, who deals out milksop pleasures.
You see your country half consumed, and by
Her enemies shut in, yet tricked and fooled
By Love, you must forget her altogether?

MARANDRO. My heart burns in me at your senseless speech.
Has loving ever made a man a coward?
Have I deserted yet my post as sentry
To go and see my girl? Or do I lie
Asleep in bed while my commander watches?
Have you yet seen me falter in my duty
For any vain delight or vicious purpose?
Nay, all the less for being so in love!
And if you cannot state a single instance
What have I to excuse? Why blame me so
Because I am enamoured? If I'm shy
Of conversation and preoccupied,
Put your own hand into your heart, and you
Will see I have good reason to be so.
Do you not know how many years my heart's
Been lost to Lira? And do you not know
The time has come to end our suffering
Because her father had arranged our marriage
And she had found acceptance with my own?
You also know that, at this joyful juncture,
Came this fierce strife by which my glorious hopes
Were slain, and so the wedding was deferred
Till after the cessation of the war
Because our country's now no place for feasts
And happiness, and you can see what small
Hope I can have of my delight since now

Victory flies upon the foeman's lance.
We're hunger-stricken, hopeless of a cure.
We're few and prisoners of the wall and dyke,
And all my hopes are scattered to the winds.
That's why I am so sad and discontented.

LEONICIO. Marandro, calm your stormy breast. Return
To the gay vigour you were wont to show.
Perhaps in other ways our luck will turn,
And sovereign Jupiter may find a path
By which to free Numantia from the Romans,
And then in sweetest peace you may enjoy
Your bride and temper the fierce fire of love.
Today Numantia makes sacrifices
To the great thundering Jupiter above:
O Jupiter! look on our plight with love!

They go to the side and TWO NUMANTINES *enter, dressed as
priests of ancient times, pulling in a big ram by its horns:
the ram is crowned with olive and other flowers. There now
follow a* PAGE *with a font of silver and a towel; another
with a jug of water; two more with jars of wine; another
with another font of silver and some incense; others with
fire and wood for fuel. Another* PAGE *lays a table with a
table-cover on which the rest place everything they are carrying. They are all dressed in the Numantine costume. Then
one of the* PRIESTS *leaves the ram in the hands of the other,
begins to speak while* THEOGENES *enters with a crowd of
Numantines.*

FIRST PRIEST. Sure omens of disaster have appeared
Along the way we came, and my white hair
Stands stiff with fright.

SECOND PRIEST.   If I am not a bad
Diviner, we shall never come off well
Out of this plight. Ah! poor Numantine people!

FIRST PRIEST. Let's carry out the rite with all the haste
These dismal presages require of us.
Come, friends, and put a table over here.

SECOND PRIEST. The wine, water, and incense that you bring
Place on the table here, and then go back,
Repenting all the evil you have done.

A spirit cleansed and a sincere good will
Is far the best oblation you can offer.

FIRST PRIEST. The fire must not be kindled on the ground.
Here comes a brazier for it, as religion
And reverence require.

SECOND PRIEST.   Now wash your hands
And clean your neck. Here, bring the water, here!
Will not the fire light?

A NUMANTINE.   Nobody can light it,
My lords.

SECOND PRIEST. O Jupiter, what woe does Fate
Intend to wreak upon us, that the fire
Refuses to be kindled on the torch?

A NUMANTINE. It seems, my lord, at last to come to life.

SECOND PRIEST. Leave it alone and go. Oh, dim, weak flame
What grief I suffer to behold your light!
See how the smoke towards the setting sun
Goes trailing, while the sickly yellow flame
Points to the east. Unhappy sign of woe!
Disastrous portent of our overthrow!

FIRST PRIEST. Although the Romans get the victory
Through our destruction, yet the smoke will turn
To live flames, and our death and glory burn
Forever!

SECOND PRIEST. Then bedew the sacred fire
With wine, and let the incense now be lit!

He sprinkles the fire all round with wine, then throws incense into it.

To the advantage of Numantia's people,
Great Jupiter, reverse and make propitious
The force of their grim fate, and, as this fire
Forces the sacred incense to aspire,
So may the Romans' efforts end in smoke!
And grant (Eternal and Almighty Sire!)
That all Rome's luck and glory be reversed,
For so You can perform it, well I know!
May Heaven hold their cruel strength at bay

As we this victim we're about to slay,
And, like this victim, may it be laid low!

FIRST PRIEST. The omen answers ill. We cannot give
The slightest hope that our unhappy people
May flee from the dread quandary we're in.

*A sound of thunder under the stage made by rolling a tub
full of stores. A rocket is fired.*

SECOND PRIEST. Did you not hear a sound? Did you not see
The fiery thunderbolt fly past us then?
It is a sure presage of all I said.

FIRST PRIEST. I am confounded and I shake with fear!
What ghastly omens! From them I divine
A most disastrous ending to us all.
Do you not see that foul and angry squadron
Of ugly eagles fighting other birds
And wheeling round, embattled, in the sky?

SECOND PRIEST. See! they devote their cruel strength to
rounding
The other birds into a narrow space,
And, by their skill and cunning, hem them in.

FIRST PRIEST. I curse that omen. I can never praise it.
Imperial eagles are the conquerors?
Farewell, Numantia, then! Your end is nigh.

SECOND PRIEST. Eagles, depart! Announcers of disaster!
For from your augury I can divine
Our hours are numbered.

FIRST PRIEST.   But in spite of all
I'll sacrifice this innocent young ram
So to make less the gods' tremendous ire.

SECOND PRIEST. O mighty Pluto, on whom Fate bestowed
The kingdom of the dark for your abode
And made commander of the realms infernal,
So may the peace and comfort be eternal
Which you derive from loving Ceres' daughter,
And so you may be prosperous in all things
Look upon this sad people, doomed to slaughter,
Who now invoke you! King of shady kings,
Close the great crater at the mouth of hell
From whence emerge the Furies fierce and fell,

The three grim sisters who have wrought our woe,
And make their dire designs as vain, as though
They were these hairs that to the winds I throw.

He pulls some wool from the ram and scatters it in the air.

FIRST PRIEST. With a pure thought and spirit cleansed of sin
Just as I plunge and stain my knife within
This ram's pure blood, so may Numantia stain
Her hard earth with the blood of Romans slain,
And prove a mighty grave to whelm them in!

A DEVIL emerges to the waist from a hole in the stage. He seizes the ram and carries it off. All kinds of fireworks and rockets go off.

SECOND PRIEST. But who has reft the victim from my hands?
Ye gods, what's this? What monstrous prodigies
Are these we see? Have our laments not touched
Your hearts, though coming from a tribe afflicted
And full of tears? Have our harped hymns not softened
Your hearts? No! they have hardened them the more
To judge from all these signs of cruel wrath.
The remedies of life are fatal to us:
Neglect of prayer would profit us far more.
Our good is alien, but our ills are native.

A NUMANTINE. Now that the heavens have given out the sentence
Of our most grievous, miserable end,
And do not wish to grant us any mercy,
We'll grieve in such a way for our misfortune
That future ages never will forget.

THEOGENES. Now let Marquino make the final trial
Of his vast science, to find out the sum
Of all the evils that disastrous Fate
Promises us, turning our smiles to tears.

All exeunt, and only MARANDRO and LEONICIO remain.

MARANDRO. Say, Leonicio, does it seem to you
There's any remedy for our misfortunes
That heaven can afford us? My bad luck
Can only finish when this war is finished
And when the earth becomes my sepulchre.

LEONICIO. Marandro, to a proper soldier, omens
   Should give no pain, because he woos good luck
   With strenuous effort and mistrusts the vain
   Appearances of things from the outside
   Which should not make him lose his common sense.
   Your arm's your lucky star or else your doom.
   Your valour is the talisman in which
   To trust. But if you wish to chase illusions
   And put that sort of thing to further trial,
   Marquino manages it better far
   Than any one who deals in things like that,
   And if you want to know if good or bad
   Will be the net result of all our trouble,
   You'll know quite soon. I think I see him coming—
   But in what strange, extravagant attire!

Here enter MARQUINO *in a huge robe of glazed buckram with a black wig and bare feet. At his belt are hung three flasks or phials of water—one black, the second clear, and the third dyed with saffron. He has a lance in one hand, stained black; and, in his other hand, a book. Another man comes along with him,* MILBIO *by name.* MARANDRO *and* LEONICIO *go to one side.*

MARQUINO. Where, Milbio, did they bury this young man?

MILBIO. Here in this tomb.

MARQUINO.   You're sure you're not mistaken?

MILBIO. No! with that sprig of ivy that you see
   I marked it, when they buried him with tears.

MARQUINO. What did he die of?

MILBIO.   Of almighty Famine—
   That cruel sapping pest, born out of hell!

MARQUINO. You're sure it was no wound that cut his thread?
   No cancer is the reason why he's dead?
   I ask you this because I need whole flesh
   To waken and resuscitate afresh.

MILBIO. It's only three hours that I brought him here
   To give him his last rest and burial.
   He died of hunger only, never fear,
   As I declare once more.

MARQUINO.   That's to the good.
Propitious signs favour me at this juncture
From their dark realm to call fierce evil spirits.
Now give attentive hearing to my verse,
You ministers to souls that are perverse!
May luck and fortune bless you! And obey,
Even if you be unwilling, what I say
Upon this dire occasion! No delay!
Do not wait for compulsion harder still.
I wish the body buried in this clay
With its own spirit and new life to thrill
Even though Charon tries to bar the way.
Upon the further bank of the black river,
Though it be hidden in the triple throat
Of Cerberus, I charge you to deliver
His spirit back into this world up here
Soon to return unto your darker sphere.
Since he *must* come, let him bring information
Of this harsh, bitter siege's termination.
Let him hide nought from me, unhappy youth,
But give to me the clear, cold, naked truth.
Let him not speak in riddles to bemuse me
Nor with vague ambiguities confuse me.
Send him at once! Come! Do you dare refuse me,
False ministers? What more do you await?
You will not move the tombstone's massive weight?
How have you dared to make no sign as yet?
A stronger conjuration must I set
Upon you all to soften your hard hearts,
Exerting greater powers in these dark arts?
Crapulous liars! sentenced to the fire,
You know I've but to speak a little higher
To double your fierce rage and torments dire.
Say, you! the faithless husband of a wife
Who for six months of each year of her life
Horns you with countless antlers without doubt—
Why have you dared my dread commands to flout?
This iron, splashed with dew, will search you out,
Which, never having touched the ground this May,
Wounding this stone, will prove that what I say

Is in dead earnest, not in idle play!

With the clear water from one flask he bedews the point
of his lance and strikes the floor of the stage, beneath which
rockets and crackers and squibs resound with thunder.

You see, *canaille!* that even from the clear
Water you catch a cruel pang of fear.
What sounds are these, accursèd souls, who though
You've not come yet, were shifted by the blow?
What's this? You'd still delay? Where do you hide?
Are all my threats and menaces defied?
I'll threaten you no more, nor give you quarter,
But with these deadly drops of coal-black water
I'll give just punishment for your delay
And now you'll have a heavy debt to pay!
O water from the fatal black lagoon,
Drawn on a dark, sad night without a moon,
By the great power that lives in you alone,
Against whose power no other power is known,
Now the whole race of devils dire (and thee
Who first became a serpent in the tree!)
I conjure, I constrain you to obey
And all come flying here without delay!

He sprinkles the tomb with black water and it opens.

Unhappy youth! Come out! Return to see
The sun serene and clear! Leave that dark region
Where you need never hope to see a day
Of peace and comfort! Give me, since you can,
The whole relation of what you have learned
In the abyss—what you were sent to say,
And more, if it concerns us, and you can.

The CORPSE *slowly appears in its shroud and goes on gradu-*
ally emerging till in the end, when it has finally come out,
it collapses on the stage.

What's this? No answer? Have you not revived?
What? Have you tasted death a second time?
Then I will cause your pain to wake you up
And you will soon address me with a will!
Since you are of my tribe, come, don't be backward
In speaking and replying. If you're silent,

It will be to your cost that I unloose
That tongue-tied and begrudging voice of yours.

He sprinkles yellow water on the CORPSE *and afterwards begins to thrash it.*

You evil spirits! Will he not learn better?
Then wait! The drops of this enchanted water
Will make him satisfy my will entirely
While he defies and disobeys your own.
Lashed with this whip he will acquire new life,
Though slightly, from the pain that it inflicts.
Rebellious soul, return to your old inn
Where you so lately had your board and lodging!
Now you return. You show it. I can feel you
Entering, though with pain, into yourself.

As he says this the CORPSE *throws itself back into its grave though it remains visible.*

THE CORPSE. Marquino, cease your rigour, fierce and rough!
The torments I must suffer are enough,
In the dark realm down there, for me to bear
Without your adding to my dark despair.
For you are wrong in thinking that I yearn
Back to that dismal short life to return
Which I have lived down there, where I must haste
Since I am missed. But you cause me far worse pain
Since now I have to agonise again;
For death a second time with bitter strife
Must triumph o'er my spirit and my life.
My demon foe expects me with clenched hand,
And with the others of that murky band
Who serve your pleasure, waits with growing ire
For me to finish off what you require
And tell you of the lamentable end
On which the doomed Numantia can depend,
Destroyed by that which was her nearest friend—
The strength of her own hands. Neither the Roman
Will win the victory, nor o'er her foemen
Will strong Numantia ever vaunt the glory,
Friend being good to foe, and foe to friend.
But do not dream that peace will end the story:

These two conflicting fronts will never bend
Because without assistance from her foes
The sword of friends will deal the fatal blows
And be the murderer of this brave city!
Stay here, Marquino! Let me go, in pity!
The Fates forbid that longer I delay
And though you may not trust in what I say
All will be verified upon the day.

The CORPSE *disappears in the grave.*

MARQUINO. O dismal omens! Lamentable end!
If this must happen between friend and friend,
Within this very tomb I'll end my life.

He throws himself into the grave.

MARANDRO. See, Leonicio, if it is not true
That everything goes dead against my luck.
The road is blocked that leads to any good
(Marquino says) save to the tomb and death.

LEONICIO. These things are all delusions and chimeras,
Fantasies, witcheries, abracadabras,
Auguries, fortunetellers' whimsies, dreams,
And things of diabolical invention.
You have a gift for finding care and trouble.
The dead don't care for living folks' affairs.

MARANDRO. Marquino never would commit such folly
Were not our future doom seen in the present.
Let us announce this to the people. But
To bring such news, how can one stir a foot?

ACT III

Enter SCIPIO, JUGURTHA, CAIUS MARIUS.

SCIPIO. I'm thoroughly delighted with the way
 Good fortune has conformed to my desire,
 And to be taming this free, stubborn people
 By dint of prudence, without wasting strength.
 Seeing occasion for this plan, I chose it,
 Since I know that through rushing things in haste,
 Especially in the affairs of war,
 Much life is lost, and credit runs to waste.
 They thought it was an error to surround
 The enemy, and that our Roman strength
 Lost honour by not conquering the foe
 In the outmoded, antiquated way.
 I know all that was said, but yet I trust
 That all good, practical commanders reckon
 That victory the best which costs least blood.
 What victory can redound to greater glory,
 Judging it from the point of view of war,
 Than one that's won without a single sword
 Leaving its sheath, and yet can subjugate
 And conquer a strong enemy completely?
 But when a victory's acquired with loss
 Of friendly blood, it spoils the joy of it
 To win with blood what might be won without.

They sound a trumpet from Numantia's ramparts.

JUGURTHA. Hark, sir. A trumpet from Numantia sounds,
 And I am sure they've got something to tell you
 Because the wall prevents their exit here.
 There's Caravino on the battlements.
 He gives the sign of safety. Let's approach.

SCIPIO. Approach no further. We can hear him here.

CARAVINO *enters on the wall with a flag on a lance.*

CARAVINO. Ho! Romans! can you hear my voice from here?

SCIPIO. If only you don't shout so loud and fast
  Anyone can both hear and understand you.

CARAVINO. Then tell your general to stretch his legs
  Here to the trench because an embassy's
  Coming to him.

SCIPIO.   Out with it, quick! I'm Scipio.

CARAVINO. Well, hear the rest, most prudent general!
  Numantia says, Consider what long years
  Between us and the Romans have endured
  The evils of a long and tedious war,
  And that the pestilence of those same evils
  May not increase, Numantia wishes this—
  If you, too, wish the same—in one brief fight
  To end the war by means of single combat.
  One soldier volunteers out of our ranks
  To fight, in a closed space, with any stout
  Champion of yours, and end this stubborn strife.
  If he whom the harsh Fates condemn to die
  Be ours, we shall deliver up our country:
  If he be yours, then glory to the war!
  For the security of this arrangement
  We'll send you hostages if you require them.
  I know you will accept, since you command
  Soldiers, the least of whom in the open field
  Can make the best of ours break out in sweat,
  And so you can be certain of success.
  So now to expedite the execution
  Of this affair, tell me if you agree.

SCIPIO. You *are* a wit! What quips and jests are these?
  What mad hilarity would you excite?
  Employ the means of humble supplication
  If you still hope to save your scrannel necks
  From the sharp Roman blade and our strong arms!
  The wild beast, once it's shut within a cage
  Because of its ferocity and rage,
  And also because there, by patient wile
  And time, he can be tamed in proper style—
  Why, any fool who lets that creature out
  Not only puts his sanity in doubt

But life in danger! Beasts you are, I say,
And caged as beasts: to learn, the only way
That beasts can learn, their masters to obey.
Numantia will be mine to your vast woe,
Yet not a drop of Roman blood will flow!
Come, let the greatest fighter you can find
Cross this great trench, if so he has the mind;
And if you think there is a little shame
In my refusal, or that I'm to blame,
Why, all that will be whisked off by the wind
When this great victory restores my fame!

SCIPIO *and his companions retire while* CARAVINO *remains.*

CARAVINO. You'll not hear more? You craven! You'll go hide?
In a fair, equal fight you take no pride?
Your conduct ill accords with your great name.
Since all at once a coward you became,
Answering me. You Romans are all craven!
In your huge numbers you may find a haven
But man to man and hand to hand you'll not
Answer an honest challenge on the spot.
Disloyal swindlers, sodomites, pernicious,
Treacherous, lewd, perverse, foul, avaricious
Tyrants, reducing anyone to slavery,
Known rather for base cunning than for bravery—
What glory can you gain from killing us
By keeping us incarcerated thus?
In the formed squadron or the skirmish free,
Out on the open field for all to see,
Where neither ditch nor dyke impede the jolt
And shock of death's impetuous thunderbolt,
It would be well for that so-very-gallant
Army of yours to show its fighting talent
Against our weak, starved few, but it's your way
To fight by unfair means, craft, and delay.
The straight, fair fight, which valour most concerns,
Is ill adapted to your twists and turns.
Rabbits! who go disguised in lions' hide,
Let your brave deeds by you be magnified!
But yet I trust great Jupiter, one day,

Will bend you down beneath Numantia's sway,
Her laws and statutes humbly to obey.

CARAVINO goes out, then returns with THEOGENES, MAR-
ANDRO, *and others.*

THEOGENES. Our fate now hems us in such narrow limits,
Dear friends, that it would be most fortunate
To finish off our ills with death. You saw
The grievous omen of the sacrifice
And how the grave has swallowed up Marquino.
The challenge was worth nothing. What is left?
One way is to accept our final end.
Let us Numantines show the reckless courage
That burns within our breasts. Let's get to work,
Break through the hostile wall, and rush to die
Out in the open field, not here, like cowards,
As captives. Well I know that such an exploit
Can only change the manner of our death,
Which is a certainty in this case, too.

CARAVINO. With this idea I sympathise. I wish
To die breaching the wall and dealing havoc.
But there's one thing that makes me feel uncertain—
That if our wives get knowledge of this plan
It will prove quite impossible, for sure.
When we had all decided once before
Each one of us to trust in his swift horse
And make a dash for it, learning our drift
They were so vexed, they stole and hid our snaffles
So that we could not find a single one.
If then they could prevent us from a sortie
They'll do it just as easily, I say,
When once they show the tears they showed that day.

MARANDRO. Our plans are evident to all of them.
Each woman knows them. There's not one of them
Who's not complaining bitterly about it.
They say that both in good and evil fortune
They wish to follow us in life or death
Although we find their company a hindrance.

*Enter four women of Numantia, each with a child in her
arms, and* LIRA, *a maiden.*

See, here they come to beg you not to leave them
In such predicaments, and were you made
Of cold, hard steel, the sight of your young children,
Which they so sadly carry in their arms,
Would soften you. Do you not see the loving
Manner in which they bid them their farewell
And give their last embraces and caresses?

FIRST WOMAN. My dearest lords, in hundreds of misfortunes
We've suffered in Numantia up till now
(Death being among the least of those we suffer)
And in the happiness, now gone for good,
We always shared with you as wives and partners,
And you shared with us, too, as loving husbands.
Then why, on this most sinister occasion
With which the angered heavens threaten us,
Do you show us so little of that love?
We've learned, and it is obvious to us all,
You wish to rush into the Roman's hands
To ask a kinder death than that from Hunger,
Who hems us in and from whose clammy hands
Escape is now impossible to hope.
You wish to perish fighting and to leave us,
Shelterless, to dishonour, shame, and death.
First let our necks be severed by your swords
Before we are dishonoured by your foes.
It is my firmly-constituted will,
And I will do the utmost that is in me
To perish with my husband, if I can;
And so would any wife who wished to show
That fear of death can never hinder one
Who loves from loving well, in joy or grief,
In happiness or misery alike.

SECOND WOMAN. What are you thinking of, you men? Do you
Persist in this mad fantasy of leaving
Us women here and absenting yourselves?
Perhaps you want the virgins of Numantia
To fall a prey to the insulting Romans
And your free sons to serve as fettered slaves?
Would it not be far better with your own

Strong arms to strangle them? What! Would you feed
The vaunting Roman's lechery and greed,
To his injustice sacrifice the just,
And leave us as a trophy for his lust?
Must foreign hands destroy our houses? Must
Promised espousals be enjoyed by Romans?
In going forth you'll make a fatal error
Which will give rise to many thousand worse
Because you leave your flock, without its shepherd
And sheepdogs, to the wolf. If you go forth,
Take us along with you because our life
Is to die at your side. Then do not hasten
Your way to death. For Hunger weaves her curtain
Slowly but surely, and its fall is certain.

THIRD WOMAN. Children of these sad mothers—what is this?
What! are you tongue-tied that you do not plead
With tears that your dear fathers will not leave you?
Tell them that they begot you free, and that
You were born free, and that your mothers reared you
In freedom. Tell them, now our fate declines,
That they who gave you life must give you death!
O walls of this sad city, if you can,
Cry out these words, a thousand times repeat them:
"Numantines! free your temples, towers
And these belovèd homes of ours
Which we raised up in love and peace!
The wives and children of your city
Plead that you will be moved to pity,
Their souls from bondage to release.
Let pity move you! Be our friends
Since not in breaking through the wall
Is any remedy at all
For the disaster that impends!"

LIRA. Now the sad maidens as they grieve
Seek your protection, for they know
A cure that's certain to relieve
Their evil plight. What? Will you leave
So rich a plunder to the foe
And our virginities bestow

On those that ruthlessly destroy us?
Must the same hands that lay you low
Be those that strip us and enjoy us?
The Romans are as wolves ferocious,
Rapacious, bloody, and atrocious:
To leave us for them is a crime.
It's desperation and notorious
Folly, to find quick death, though glorious—
Making a sally at this time.
What city in the whole of Spain,
Were you to win, would entertain
Or dare to favour you? Not one.
My poor opinion is, if you
Insist on trying to break through,
You'll give your lives to Rome but none
To poor Numantia, only death—
Her own and yours. Your vital breath
Will animate them. They'll make fun
Of your small number. What can three
To eighty thousand soldiers be
Except a hapless prey? Although
You broke the walls to reach the foe,
You'd reap poor vengeance though good ends.
It's better far that we abide
By Fortune. Let our Fate decide
Whether it worsens or it mends,
And whether life or death betide!

THEOGENES. Dry your eyes, tender women! Know from me
Your anguish has afflicted us so sorely
That it has called forth our most fervent love.
Now grief takes hold of us, now piercing pity
To see how all our happiness has faded.
Never in life or death will we desert you,
Never in life or death will cease to serve you!
We thought to cross the ditch, not to escape,
But to get killed (since it was far more certain)
Because those who avenge themselves while dying
Enjoy a sort of life even in death.
But since our plans have been found out by you

It would be madness now to hazard it.
Belovèd children, and belovèd wives,
From this day forward, our devoted lives
Are yours more than they ever were before.
The one thing we must guard against is this—
The enemy, by our discomfiture,
Must not acquire a single grave of honour,
Profit, or glory. Rather must our foes
Be witnesses to blazon forth *our* glory.
And if you'll all agree to what I say
A hundred thousand years will seem a day
To our immortal fame. This is my plan.
Nothing in all Numantia must remain
That to the enemy could prove a gain.
Right in the central square, we'll make a fire
In which we'll burn all that those swine desire
Of trinkets, even from the poorest penny
Of the poor pauper who has hardly any,
To all that the rich merchant has of worth—
We'll melt it down and hide it in the earth!
This loss seems child's play when each priceless jewel
And heirloom, too, is sentenced to be fuel.
And now for a few hours we must allay
The hungry pangs that gnaw our guts away.
Take out our Roman prisoners and slaughter
The poor devils. Their carcasses we'll quarter
And share together for our final feast.
Sparing neither the grown-up nor the younger,
We'll make our banquet of the Roman beast—
Such is the grim necessity of hunger!

CARAVINO. Friends, how does this strike you? Do you agree?
    This project more than satisfies me. Come!
    Let's make this strange yet honourable act,
    As soon as possible, a living fact!

THEOGENES. Now I'll inform you of my further plans.
    When we have done what I have said, each one
    Must be a minister of fell destruction
    And kindle up the rich, red-blazing fire!

FIRST WOMAN. At once we shall begin with willing hands

To give our ornaments and jewelry
And like them we shall then give up our lives
As we have given up our vain desires.

LIRA. Then let us hurry! Come along, then, come!
And let us pile and burn in one fixed place
Aught that by way of trophy might enrich
The Roman's hands or feed his avarice.

All go out except MARANDRO *who, on the point of departure
takes* LIRA *by the hand. She stays with him. Then* LEONICIO
enters unseen by them and watches them.

MARANDRO. Do not go off at such a speed,
Lira, but let me taste and feed
Upon the only blessing that
Life can provide me ere I die,
And on your beauty feast my eye
For my ill-fortune has grown fat
Feeding upon my care and woe.
O lovely Lira, you that so
Divinely agonise my whole
Continuously thwarted dreams
Till anguish to be glory seems
Since you're the glory of my soul,
What are your thoughts?

LIRA.   Well, I was thinking
How my delight with yours is sinking
And my life, ere war be done,
But not by it cut off and slain,
Is setting like the setting sun
That bleeds to death on yonder plain.

MARANDRO. What's that you say, my soul's delight?

LIRA. That with such hunger I contend
I am near vanquished in the fight
And feel my life is at its end.
What sort of nuptials can you dream
With one whom, in this fierce extreme,
Such agonising pangs devour
That she must perish in an hour?
It was but yesterday my brother
Perished of it. Today my mother

Has died of this same gnawing hunger.
And if against its drawn-out length
And irremediable strength
I still survive, it's that I'm younger
And from my youth I draw some force.
But for some days I've ceased to strive
Against it, let it take its course,
And now I scarcely feel alive.

MARANDRO. O Lira, dry your eyes! Let mine
Like rivers, for these griefs of thine,
Flow forth instead! Though hunger-stricken,
You shall not die! Across the trench
Out of the Romans' hands I'll wrench
The bread for want of which you sicken,
And put the bread between your lips
For your sweet life with death at grips.
For I would die your life to quicken
And it is death to me to see
Your pain. I'll snatch bread from the Roman
And with some damage to the foeman
If my hands are as they used to be.

LIRA. You speak as lovers always speak, Marandro,
But it's unjust that I enjoy the taste
Of something bought of peril to your life.
What you could steal could not sustain me now
And would be likelier fatal than reviving.
Enjoy your youth and health. Your life is of
More value to the city than my own.
You can defend her from the foe's onslaught
But the weak powers of this poor girl here
Are useless. So, my dear love, do not think
Anything more about it. I want nothing
That's won at cost of sweat or blood by you.
Even if for a day you could prolong
My life, you could not end this fearsome hunger.

MARANDRO. In vain you try to shackle me, dear Lira,
From the straight course where both my will and fate
Invite me, nay, compel me. You will pray,
In the meantime, to the great gods on high,

That I may come back safely with the spoils
That will relieve your misery and my pity.

LIRA. Marandro, my sweet friend, oh, do not go!
I would go frantic should the foeman's sword
Be reddened with your blood. Marandro, dearest
Blessing of all my life, if to go out
Is perilous, far worse is the return.
I will placate your ardour: witness heaven!
I dread your peril more than I love life.
But if, belovèd friend, you still persist
Then give me your embrace as a fast pledge
That you will take me with you when you go.

MARANDRO. Lira, may heaven keep you company!
Go! here is Leonicio.

LIRA.   May you thrive,
And nothing happen to endanger you!
Exit LIRA.

LEONICIO. The offer you have made is terrible,
And proves too well, Marandro, as you said,
That in a lover's breast can dwell no coward—
Although from your rare valour and your virtue
One could expect this. But I fear that Fate
Will prove most grudging to our urgent need.
I overheard attentively the piteous
Plight of your Lira, undeserved in one
Of such rare virtue, and I heard you vow
To free her from her present misery
By hurling yourself on the Roman swords.
Well, my good friend, I'm coming with you too.
In such a just and urgent enterprise
It's fit that my small strength should aid your own.

MARANDRO. O friendship of my happy soul! O friendship
That undivided in despair and travail
Endures as in prosperity and pleasure!
Rejoice in your sweet life, my Leonicio!
Stay in the city here! I do not wish
To be the homicide of your green years.
I have to go alone. Alone I wish

To come back with the spoils that should reward
My own inviolable faith and love.

LEONICIO. Well, now you know, Marandro, that my wishes,
In good or in bad luck, still conform
To yours, and that not fear nor death itself
Can swerve them from you by a single hair.
Nothing is stronger than my will to serve you.
I *will* go with you and with you return
If heaven does not bid me to remain,
Killed in defence of you, upon the plain.

MARANDRO. Stay here, my friend, stay here in safety
Because, if in this risky enterprise
I chance to lose my life, you may console
My mother and my most belovèd bride.

LEONICIO. You are so very gracious, my dear friend,
To talk about your death in such a way—
So calmly and so restfully—and say
That I might serve for any consolation
To your sad mother or your grieving bride,
But in your death my own would be accomplished,
And of this doubtful fact I've now made sure.
You see it has to be, my friend Marandro,
So say no more to me about remaining.

MARANDRO. Since I cannot prevent your going with me,
Then, in the silence of this murky night,
We'll leap upon the foemen, lightly armed
And lightly harnessed, since it is to luck
We're trusting in our lofty enterprise
Rather than to the toughness of our armour.

LEONICIO. Come, I will never falter in your service!

Exeunt.

Enter TWO NUMANTINES.

FIRST NUMANTINE. Weep, my dear brother, let your soul flow
     out
Of both your eyes and turn to bitter tears!
Let death descend and take the piteous spoils
Of our most sad and miserable lives!

SECOND NUMANTINE. Our miseries can endure but little longer

Because death now is visibly approaching
To carry off in rapid flight the whole
People which treads upon Numantine soil.
I see the grim beginnings which presage
The swift, sad end of our belovèd country,
Without the hostile ministers of war
Taking the slightest part in it at all.
Ourselves it is to whom life has become
So much of an insufferable load,
Who have pronounced the irrevocable sentence,
Though it's a cruel one, of death. Already
Up in the central square they've made a huge
Blazing and hungry conflagration, which,
Fed with our riches, soars to the fourth sphere.
There with sad, fearful haste runs every one,
As with a sacred offering, to feast
The roaring flames with his own goods and chattels,
Sustaining them with households and estates.
There pearls, brought from the rosy Orient,
With gold wrought in a thousand precious vases,
Diamonds and rubies exquisitely cut,
And costly purple robes and rich brocades—
All have been hurled into the midst of this
Raging volcano, to the slightest scrap
Of anything which any Roman could
Stuff in his chest or occupy his hands with.

*Here people come in on one side loaded with linen and
clothing, and go out on the other side.*

Oh, turn your gaze on this sad spectacle
To see with what wild speed and keen good will
All of Numantia runs in crowds to nourish
The roaring mad inferno of the flames—
And not with green wood or with dried-up straw
Nor with such things as men consign to flames
But with the homes and properties and wealth
They can no longer live with or enjoy.

FIRST NUMANTINE. If in these things our only harm consisted,
With patience we could bear it. But alas!
If I am not deceived, they will decree

That we must all die by a cruel death.
Before the barbarous cruelty of Rome
Severs our necks, ourselves with our own hands
Must be our own fierce butchers, not the Romans!
The orders are that neither women, children,
Nor old folk shall be spared, since in the end
To die of hunger is a death more cruel.
But see! there is a woman coming out
For whose sake once I suffered pangs of love
As fierce as those she's suffering from hunger.

Enter a woman with a child in her arms leading another by the hand, and carrying a bundle of clothes to be burned.
Translator's note: *Spanish women still carry all burdens on their heads.*

MOTHER. O woeful life and bitter agony!

SON. Mother! will they give us some bread to eat
For all these clothes?

MOTHER.   What? Bread, my son?
No, neither bread nor anything to eat!

SON. Well, Mother, must I perish in this rage
Of hunger? If you give me just a crumb
I will not ask for more! Dear mother, do!

MOTHER. Son, how you make me suffer!

SON.   Don't you wish
To give me any?

MOTHER.   Yes, of course, I wish
To give you tons, but I don't know where to find it.

SON. Well, you can buy some, then. Or if not you,
Then I can buy it. But to save me trouble
If I can come across some bread I'll trade
All of these clothes for it—just for one piece!

MOTHER, *to the baby.* Poor creature, what is that you're
        sucking
Out of my breast? Can you not taste? It's blood,
Not milk. Come, bite my breasts in pieces
And eat them if it satisfies your hunger.
My thin, tired arms can carry you no more.
My little ones, delighters of my soul,

What more can I provide you than my blood?
O Famine! Terrible and ghastly Famine,
You've swallowed up my life. O useless war!
You came to kill me. I can do no more.

SON. O Mother mine, I'm dying! Come, let's hurry.
It seems that hunger grows the more we walk.

MOTHER. Belovèd son, we're near the square
Where we will throw into the fire
Our pain, our hunger, and despair
And burn our troubles up entire.

The woman staggers out with her children. The TWO
NUMANTINES *remain.*

SECOND NUMANTINE. That woman scarcely now can lift a foot—
Poor piteous, doomed, and desolated mother
On whom her little children still depend!

FIRST NUMANTINE. We all are moving to the same sad end
But now we'd better move along with speed
To find out what the Senate has agreed.

ACT IV

The call to arms is sounded hastily in the Roman camp. At
the sound SCIPIO *comes in storming with* JUGURTHA *and*
CAIUS MARIUS, *who are also agitated.*

SCIPIO. What is this, captains? Who sounds this alarm?
  Is it, by chance, some lunatics who've come
  To ask for burial here instead of there?
  I hope it's not some mutiny that causes
  This call to arms—because I am so sure
  The foe is finished that I dread much more
  From the curbed-in impatience of my friends.

  Enter QUINTUS FABIUS *with his sword drawn.*

QUINTUS FABIUS. Don't be alarmed, my prudent general!
  We know now why this call to arms was sounded:
  But it was at the cost of some of our
  Bravest and strongest soldiers. Two Numantines,
  Whose valour cannot be denied, jumped over
  The gaping ditch, having slid down the rampart,
  And they've put the whole camp in a furore!
  They rushed the outpost guards with such a fury
  That they gave way; then, through a thousand spears,
  They charged with such mad frenzy that these, too,
  Gave way; then charging to Fabricius' tents
  They cut their way, transfixing six more soldiers.
  Not when the red-hot lightning shoots from heaven
  Is it so swift to strike and to return,
  Or when a meteor streaks along the sky
  Is it so swift, as with their rapid pace
  They sliced your ranks and coloured all the place
  Crimson with Roman blood, which right and left
  They drew with peerless skill, they were so deft.
  Fabricius through his chest was pierced clean through.
  Eracius' brains are open to your view.
  Almido had his right arm cut in two,
  And there is little hope that he'll survive

For more than a few hours. Estacio's fleetness
Was little to his profit (nor his valour):
When he caught up with them, they struck him down.
Then rushing round the camp from tent to tent,
They found a few dry biscuits as they went,
And having found them, they turned swiftly back
But could not stem the rage of the attack.
One of them went scot-free, but then his mate
A thousand sword thrusts finished off—too late!
What reason lay behind this valiant deed?
It all was due to hunger and to need.

SCIPIO. If having been starved so, and circled in,
They show such huge excess of valour, what
Would they not do were they in their prime fettle
And free to come and go? O tameless hearts!
But in the end you shall be tamed at last,
For your fierce violence is not in the running
With calculation, industry, and cunning.

Exeunt omnes.

Enter MARANDRO *mortally wounded and bleeding badly, with a basket full of bread.*

MARANDRO. You have not come with me, ah, Leonicio!
How could I come while you remained behind?
The true friend that you stayed to me through all
Has stayed behind, and yet you never left me,
But I left you. And is it possible
That your hacked limbs bear witness to the price—
And what a price!—this luckless bread has cost?
And is it possible that by the wound
Which laid you dead I am not murdered too?
But cruel Fate denied my death with yours
To do me more and greater harm and prove
Your faithfulness was greater than my own.
You carry off the palm in the contention
As to which of us was the better friend.
Soon, to excuse me, I'll send you my soul,
Yes, soon enough because I'm due to die
At Lira's feet, giving to her this bitter
And costly bread, this bread won from the foe

But at the cost of the unlucky blood
Of two devoted friends.

Enter LIRA *with some clothes to put in the fire.*

LIRA.   What's this I see?

MARANDRO. A thing that very soon you'll see no more,
So rapidly do my misfortunes hasten
My end. Lira, you see I've kept my word
That while I was alive you should not die.
And yet more truly could I say that now
You'll not lack wherewithal to eat: but I,
The wherewithal to live.

LIRA.   What do you say,
Belov'd Marandro?

MARANDRO.   Lira, sate your hunger
While cursèd Fate is severing my thread.
But the salt blood I've lost today, sweet love,
Mingling with it, will make that bread taste bitter.
This is the bread, guarded by eighty thousand
Enemy soldiers, that has cost the lives,
Which each of them loved best, of two good comrades.
And that you know for certain what I'm saying,
Know that I'm dying, and that Leonicio
Died too, to get this bread. Receive my love
Forever and my pure and honest prayers
As a still better banquet—for your soul!
And since you've always been, in calm or tempest,
My lady and my love, receive this body
Now, as you've just received from me my soul!

He falls dead and LIRA *takes his head in her lap.*

LIRA. Marandro: my sweet friend! What's wrong with you?
How do you feel, that suddenly you've lost
Your usual stalwart bearing? Oh, my husband
Is dead—my luckless and unlucky husband!
Oh! The most piteous thing that ever happened!
What cruel Fate, belovèd, made you so
Valiant, so amorous, so excellent,
But so unlucky as a soldier too?
You made a sortie to prevent my death

And by it took away my life! This bread
Stained with the blood that he has shed for me
Is now no longer bread but deadly venom.
My lips shall never touch it, but to kiss
The dear-loved blood that spatters it.

A BOY, *Lira's youngest brother, enters, speaking faintly.*

BOY. Lira, dear sister, Mother's dead already
And, now my father's dying, I must too.
Hunger by now has finished him. My sister,
So you have bread? Oh, bread, you've come too late
Since not a crumb can pass! So tight has hunger
Throttled my throat, that if this bread were water
No drop could pass. You keep the bread, dear sister:
There's bread to spare, when life cannot be spared.

He also falls dead.

LIRA. What, are you dead, dear brother? He has lost
Both breath and life. Ill luck is good
When it comes unaccompanied. Why, Fortune,
Do you still join affliction to affliction
For me to suffer in a single moment,
Making me both a widow and an orphan?
Hardhearted Roman army! Your sharp swords
Keep me surrounded with my dead, a husband
And now a second brother. In this plight
Where can I turn my face, seeing these two
Were the most precious treasures of my soul?
Oh, my sweet husband and my dear young brother,
I shall requite your love, for very soon
I shall be seeing you in heaven or hell.
I'll have to imitate the way you both
Perished, for both by steel and hunger too
My life must end. I'd sooner give a knife
To my throat than this bread. For death is welcome
To those who live like me in anxious care.
What am I waiting for? I am a coward!
My arm, you flinch to strike? My most dear husband
And darling brother, wait for me: I'm coming!

Enter a woman fleeing. Behind her A NUMANTINE SOLDIER
with a dagger to kill her.

WOMAN. Eternal Father Jupiter, protect me
  In this dire strait!

SOLDIER.   However swift you flee
  My hard hand must destroy you!
  Exit the woman.

LIRA.   Turn on me
  The hard steel and your warlike arm! Let life
  Be spared to one who's pleased with hers! Take mine
  For my life is my bane!

SOLDIER.   Although the Senate
  Decreed no woman to remain alive,
  What arm or what impetuous heart would dare
  Bury his falchion in a breast so fair?
  I, lady, am not of such evil fame
  That I can be your homicide. Alas!
  Some other hand, some other sword must do it,
  Since I was born to worship and adore you.

LIRA. O valiant soldier, I can swear by heaven,
  This pity that you have expressed for me
  Is a most harsh misfortune in my eyes.
  I would consider you a friend if, with
  Resolute heart and spirit, you transpierced
  My own sad heart and took my bitter life.
  But since you wish to show me pity, show it,
  Kind author of my comfort, in this plight
  By helping me to give the funeral rites
  Of burial to my unlucky husband,
  Also to him, my brother, lying here,
  Free now from vital breath. My husband died
  To give me life, but hunger slew my brother.

SOLDIER. I'll do what you command me, that is easy,
  Provided that you tell me as we go
  The circumstances that have led to this.

LIRA. My friend, speech is no longer in my power.

SOLDIER. What! have you come to such a pass? You feel
  Truly like that? Well, you can bear your brother:
  He is a lighter burden than your husband
  Whom I shall carry since he weighs the most.

They take out the bodies: and now a woman personifying WAR *enters with a spear and a shield. She brings with her* PESTILENCE *and* HUNGER. PESTILENCE *is a woman who is supported on a crutch with her head swathed in bandages; she wears a yellow mask.* HUNGER, *wearing a robe of glazed buckram and a pale, discoloured mask, carries a figurine of a naked corpse.*

WAR. Hunger and Pestilence, you who administer
My dread commands, terrific, grand, and sinister,
Consumers both of life and health, who scorn
Prayers, pleadings, threats, commands, or tears forlorn,
Now that you know my plans there is no need
For me to praise again the willing speed
With which you have rejoiced me in your mission,
Obeying orders with such expedition.
The inexorable Fates, in their design,
Force me at last my favour to incline
To the sagacious Romans who must rise,
By victory exalted, to the skies.
At the same time these Spaniards must be felled
And slaughtered wholesale in the town they held.
But in the end will come a time when I
Shall change, and, casting down what's proud and high,
Raise what was once so small and weak before—
For I am the most powerful Queen of War,
By mothers so detested, though in vain,
Since those who wrongly hold me in disdain
Ignore the valour of my heart and hand.
I know that through the world in every land
The valour of the Spaniard will attain
Triumph at length beneath the happy reign
Of Philip, Charles the Fifth, and Ferdinand.

PESTILENCE. If Hunger, our dear friend here, had not done
Her duty in Numantia so quickly
Killing them all till not a single one
Will live it out, I, with a doom as sickly,
Could well have executed your designs
So that the soldiers in the Roman lines
Could have reaped easy and great gains which now

Even the partial Fates cannot allow.
But Hunger here has worked at such a rate,
In such a way, on the Numantine folk
That they rush headlong to anticipate
And take the wind out of the sails of Fate.
Now all their riches have gone up in smoke.
What Rome will gain is hardly worth a joke.
For us to go to work now, it's too late.
They on themselves have worked your dread design
So that you need not Hunger's help nor mine.
Fury and Rage (your followers) have taken
Such hold upon their hearts that they awaken
A ruthlessness that, were each friend a foeman,
Could not be worse. As if each were a Roman,
Numantine kills Numantine.

HUNGER.   There's the omen!
Turn to the city! See the high roofs burning!
Hear the sad sighs that, from a thousand yearning
And desolated breasts, groan forth their grief!
Hear the high screams of the most lovely ladies
Whose tender limbs are charring in that Hades
Of fire and blood. No friend can bring relief,
Father, nor lover! Death commands in chief.
As tender lambs and ewes, when by their shepherd
Deserted to the wolves or to the leopards,
Rush bleating here and there in mad career,
So children and their mothers, crazed with fear,
Seeing the drawn sword slash from street to street,
Go rushing round on panic-stricken feet,
Hoping in vain their destiny to cheat.
From his young, newly-wedded bride, the spouse
Cuts with a sword his lately-whispered vows.
Against his mother, whom he once adored,
Unheard-of thing! the son uplifts his sword.
Against the son, his father and his sire,
Whom these contrarious clemencies inspire,
Lifts his strong arm, and what he did beget
Is unbegotten—though with fierce regret
Yet with deep satisfaction. There's no square
Street, alley of that whole great city there

That is not full of corpses. Steel and fire
Rage everywhere, ferocious, fell, and dire,
And soon the highest turret of the town
To match the level earth will topple down,
The sumptuous temple and the richest home
Crumble to dust and ashes—tower and dome!
Come! You will see Theogenes at work
Honing the edges of his sword and dirk
To plunge them in the throat of his dear wife
And rob his tender children of their life,
And now that he has lost them and without
Them does not care to live, he casts about
To seek a death more strange and dread than all
That to a human being may befall.

WAR. Come, then! But let each one in her dire course
Exert the very utmost of her force!
From my commands you must not swerve or flinch
But carry out my orders to the inch!
Exeunt.

Enter THEOGENES *with his two small* SONS, *one* DAUGHTER,
and his WIFE.

THEOGENES. Though my paternal love cannot delay
The execution of my dread design,
Consider, my dear children, ere you die,
The honourable motives of my thought.
Terrible is the pain that must be borne
In dying violent deaths. My fate is worse
Since I am doomed to be your butcher first.
But you must not remain, belovèd children,
To live as slaves, nor by the Roman power
Be led in triumph as a trophy, since
To humble us exalts the Romans' pride.
The least rough path which heaven allows to us—
Nay, offers us and shows us, and instructs us
To take—is this into the arms of death.
Nor must you, dearest wife, remain to see
Your tender breast a prey to the rude hands
And lustful eyes of Rome. My sword must free you
From such an agony, and render vain

The lust and greed which goad them on to gain
The dust and ash which will be all we leave
Of our Numantia. My belovèd wife,
It was myself who first put the suggestion
That all of us should perish rather than
Be subject to the lawless power of Rome,
So I must not be backward to enact it,
Nor must my children be the last to die.

WIFE. Can we escape them by no other means?
Heaven knows I would rejoice, could such be found,
But since it seems impossible to me,
And either way my death is near and certain,
You take the trophy of our lives, my husband,
Rather than leave them to perfidious Rome.
Now, since I have to perish, let it be
Inside Diana's temple. Take us there,
And give us up to lightning, steel, and fire!

THEOGENES. Let it be done! Come, let us not delay!
My sorry fate is calling me away.

SON. Mother, why do you cry? Where are we going?
Wait for me, for I have no strength to walk.
It would be better if we had a meal,
For I am faint with weariness and hunger.

WIFE. Then come into my arms, dear son of mine.
Death is your meal, and it is time to dine.
Exeunt.

Enter two other boys, one of whom is SERVIUS, *and the other*
BARIATUS, *who later throws himself from the tower.*

BARIATUS. Servius, where is it that you wish to flee?

SERVIUS. I? Where you like.

BARIATUS.   Come on! How weak you are!
You sentence us to death by lagging here.
Do you not know two thousand swords are drawn
To kill us?

SERVIUS.   It's not possible to fly.
Where do you think of going? What's your plan?

BARIATUS. To hide myself away inside a tower
Belonging to my father.

SERVIUS.   You can go then,
  My friend. I am too weak and tired with hunger.
  I cannot follow you a single step.

BARIATUS. What? Won't you come along?

SERVIUS.   I would, but cannot.
  If you can't walk you'll have to perish here,
  Either by steel, from hunger, or from fright.

BARIATUS. I'm going. Life is going cheap, I fear,
  And fire or sword must end my short career.

    BARIATUS *goes to the tower.* SERVIUS *remains.* THEOGENES
    enters with a drawn sword and bloody hands. Seeing him,
    SERVIUS *runs off the stage.*

THEOGENES. Spilt blood of my own entrails, since you are
  That of my sons! O hand, impetuous hand,
  That for its honour struck against itself
  So cruelly! O Fortune to my bane
  Ever conspiring! O heavens so devoid
  Of pity and of justice! Grant to me,
  I here beseech you, in my dismal plight,
  An honourable though a speedy death!
  O brave Numantines, take me for a base
  Perfidious Roman, and on him avenge
  The injury and insult you have suffered,
  Dyeing your hands and dagger in my blood.
  In my mad sorrow and my desperate fury,
  It's such a sword I offer to you all—
  Since in a fight to feel the pang of death
  Hurts less than in cold blood. He who deprives
  The other of his life must then consign
  His body to the fire, a pious office!
  Come! What is keeping you? Come on! At once!
  Come, make a sacrifice of me, and turn
  The tender love you had for me as friends
  Into the rage and fury of the foe!

    Enter A NUMANTINE.

NUMANTINE. To whom, stalwart Theogenes, do you
  Address yourself? Say what new way to die
  Are you inventing? Why to such wild and jaggèd

Heights of disaster do you still provoke us,
Inciting us to frenzy?

THEOGENES.   Brave Numantine!
If fear daunt not the vigour of your arm,
Take up your sword, and kill yourself with me
As if you were my enemy! This way
To die I find more pleasing than all others
In such a pass as this.

NUMANTINE.   It satisfies
And suits me too. Let's go to the main square,
For there the great fire burns, and he who wins
Can put the victim on his funeral pyre.

THEOGENES. Well said. Let's hurry. It is getting late
To die the death I anxiously desire.
Honour and glory are in either fate,
Whether by steel it comes, or else by fire.
Exeunt.

Enter SCIPIO, JUGURTHA, QUINTUS FABIUS, CAIUS MARIUS,
ERMILIUS, LIMPIUS, *and other Roman soldiers.*

SCIPIO. If I am not mistaken in my thoughts
And if appearances have not deceived me,
The turmoil you have witnessed in Numantia,
The piteous sounds you've heard, the flames you've seen,
Beyond the slightest doubt proclaim to me
That the barbarian fury of the enemy
Has turned against his own fierce breast at last.
Nobody yet appears upon the walls,
The usual sentinels give out no challenge,
And everything is silent as the grave—
As if these wild Numantines suddenly
Had become tranquillised and lulled to rest.

CAIUS MARIUS. I'll soon resolve you of your doubts, my lord,
Since if you wish it, I will volunteer
To climb the wall, though it is dangerous,
Only to find out what our proud and fierce
Enemies have been doing in Numantia.

SCIPIO. Then, Marius, set a ladder to the wall
And do what you propose.

CAIUS MARIUS.   Go fetch a ladder
  At once. Bring, too, my shield and my white-plumed
  Helmet, for I will either lose my life
  Or else relieve the army of its doubts.

ERMILIUS. Here are your shield and helmet. Limpius
  Is coming with the ladder. Here it is.

CAIUS MARIUS. I recommend my soul to Jupiter
  For I will now perform the deed I promised.

JUGURTHA. Raise your shield higher, Marius! Crouch lower!
  Cover your head! Courage! Now you are there.
  What can you see?

CAIUS MARIUS.   You holy gods above!
  What do my eyes behold?

JUGURTHA.   What strikes such wonder?

CAIUS MARIUS. A lake of crimson blood! A thousand bodies,
  Transfixed upon a thousand points of steel,
  Lie stretched in all the streets. Numantia's dead.

SCIPIO. Are any of them living?

CAIUS MARIUS.   Not a soul—
  At least not so far as my sight can reach!

SCIPIO. Get down into the town, now, on your life
  And look about you. Follow him, my friend,
  Jugurtha. But let's all go with him too.

JUGURTHA. It does not suit your rank to go with us
  On such a risky enterprise. Be patient,
  My general, till Marius or I
  Bring back the answer as to what has happened
  In the proud city. Hold the ladder firm!
  Oh, what a terrible, horrific sight!
  What an unheard-of wonder-striking thing!
  Warm, steaming blood has flooded all the ground!
  Dead bodies populate the streets and squares!
  And now I'll go and see the whole of it.

  He jumps down into the city.

QUINTUS FABIUS. No doubt the fierce Numantines were incited
  To this barbarous fury when they saw
  That there was no escape for them, and so
  Much rather than surrender up their lives

To our victorious hands (abominated,
In the extreme, by their proud, tameless hearts)
They have preferred to give them up together
To their own swords.

SCIPIO.   If only one of them
Is left alive, then they will not deny me
A triumph back in Rome for having tamed
So proud a nation, so inveterate
And deadly an antagonist of ours,
Unbending in opinion, prompt, and daring
Through greatest perils and the direst trials!
Indeed no Roman soldier yet can boast
He ever saw Numantine turn his back.
Their valour and dexterity in arms
Force me, with perfect reason, to immure them
As if they were untamable, wild beasts,
And conquer them by assiduity
And wiles—it was impossible by force.
But look. I think here's Marius returning.

CAIUS MARIUS *returns to the top of the wall.*

CAIUS MARIUS. Illustrious and most prudent general,
In vain have we employed our strength, in vain
Has proved your defence! The victory
We felt so sure would crown your industry
And skill has now been turned to wind and smoke.
The lamentable end and tragic story
Of the unconquered city of Numantia
Deserves to live eternally in glory,
For they have cheated you of all your winnings
And wrenched your triumph out of your own hands.
Dying with such great-hearted constancy
That all our projects have been rendered vain,
The worn-out people of Numantia have
(Ending their misery by violence)
Put a sad ending to a long, long story.
Numantia is one mighty lake of blood
Strewn with ten thousand corpses whose own pride
And stubborn rigour was their homicide.
Of the unbearable and heavy chain

Of slavery they have escaped the strain
By their audacious and unflinching valour.
Up in the midst of their main square a fierce,
Tremendous blaze of fire is roaring, which
They've fed with their own bodies and possessions.
I was in time to see the furious
Theogenes, a valiant, proud Numantine
(Desiring to have done with life for good,
Cursing his brief and luckless lot on earth)
Hurl himself in the middle of the fire,
Saying these words: "Illustrious Fame, employ
Your tongue and use your eyes on this exploit
Which calls you to recount it! Romans, come!
Come, now, and revel in the promised plunder
Of this dead city, turned to dust and ashes,
With all its fruits and flowers turned to thorns!"
Thence, with my thoughts alert and nimble feet,
I wandered round, searching the most remote
And intricate recesses of the town,
But never one live person did I find
Whom I could fetch with me to bring you word
Of how this huge disaster has occurred.

SCIPIO. Could it have been, by chance, that in my breast
My savage arrogance, pregnant with their doom,
Had left no room for clemency at all?
And is my character, by chance, an alien
To that benignity which every victor
Should use to deal with a defeated foe?
Ill have they judged my heart there in Numantia
Since I was born to conquer and forgive!

QUINTUS FABIUS. Jugurtha now may satisfy you better
In what you want to know. Look, here he comes,
Full of foreboding.

JUGURTHA *appears on the wall.*

JUGURTHA.   Prudent general,
In vain do you employ your valour here.
Turn to some other place the diligence
And skill for which you are so justly famed.
All of them, all, are dead, except, I think,

For one, a boy, who still remains alive
To grace you with a triumph, as I see,
Here in this tower before me. He's well-dressed,
But wears a strange confusion in his looks.

SCIPIO. If this is only true, it will be worth
A triumph over the Numantine nation
In Rome. Why, it's the thing I prayed for most!
Let's go there. Coax him to come down. If only
He falls into my hands alive, that's all
That is important to me at this moment.

BARIATUS *speaks out of the tower.*

BARIATUS. Romans! What do you seek? Where are you going?
If here into Numantia you would enter
By force, you'll find it easy; there's no hindrance.
But I must tell you that I hold the keys,
Though feebly-guarded, of this city here
Over whom death has triumphed.

SCIPIO.   It's for them
That I am coming, and to show you that
Compassion is no stranger to my breast.

BARIATUS. You, cruel man, too late have come to offer
Your clemency, when there is no one left
On whom to use it. I myself intend
To carry out the sentence, too, by which
My own belovèd mother and my father
Met such a cruel and appalling death.

QUINTUS FABIUS. Tell me, boy, if, by chance, you've been struck
    blind
By some rash, headstrong madness, to despise
Your budding youth and hate your sweet, young life?

SCIPIO. Temper, my little man, your reckless courage!
Subject your valour to my glorious power,
Being yourself so little, since from now,
I give my faith and pledge my word on it
You shall be your own master and live free,
Endowed with all the jewels and the treasures
That I can give you or that you desire,
If you surrender to me with good will.

BARIATUS. The whole wild fury of all those who perished
   Within this town, now turned to dust and ash,
   Their rage at treaties and agreements broken
   And offers of submission laughed to scorn,
   All of their fiery anger and resentment
   Are here united in my breast alone!
   I have inherited Numantia's valour—
   If you think you can conquer me, you're mad!
   Belovèd country! O unlucky city!
   Never imagine it, nor fear, that I
   Would be nonplussed at what I owe to you
   Being by you engendered, or that I,
   For promises or fears, would flinch or falter!
   Now that I have no earth nor heaven nor destiny
   And the whole world to conquer me conspires,
   It is impossible that to your valour
   I should not pay the duty that I owe.
   If fear enticed me here to hide myself
   From imminent and terrifying death,
   Death now will take me forth with greater courage
   Since I desire to follow in your wake.
   For my vile fear that now has passed away
   The reparation will be strong and brave;
   For the late terror of my tender youth
   A death of bold resolve will pay in full.
   And I assure you, my brave citizens,
   That your resolve within me is not dead—
   That the perfidious Romans shall not triumph
   But over our mere ashes. Their designs
   Are all in vain, whether they strike me down
   Or tempt me with their doubtful promises
   To spare my life and ope wide gates to wealth.
   Hold back, you Romans! Do not waste your strength
   Or tire yourselves by swarming up the wall!
   Were you ten times more powerful, your power
   Could never hope to conquer me at all.
   Now let me show you my intention. That
   I loved my dear-belovèd country purely
   And perfectly, let this fall be the proof!

The BOY *throws himself off the wall. A trumpet sounds.*

SCIPIO. Oh, never in my life have I beheld
A deed so unforgettable as this!
Young child with ancient valour in your breast!
Not only has Numantia but all Spain
Acquired undying glory by an act
So spirited, of such heroic virtue!
You, with this fall, have raised your fame on high,
And levelled all my victories to the ground!
If proud Numantia were living yet
I would rejoice because you lived in her.
Alone you won this long and famous contest,
You only! Then, my child, be yours the victory
And yours the glory with which heaven prepares
To welcome you, who vanquished by your fall
Him who, exalted high, you've now brought low.

Enter FAME *clothed in white.*

FAME. Go forth, my voice, in accents sweet and low,
From race to race, and kindle as you go,
In every soul, a burning wish to keep
Deathless the memory of so brave a leap.
Raise up your downcast brows, Romans! and bear
Away this little body that could dare
Your might and wrest the triumph from your hands.
For I am Fame, proclaimer to the lands,
And I shall take great care (while highest heaven
Towers to the topmost sphere of all the seven
Pouring its strength and vigour on our earth)
To publish round the world Numantia's worth
And peerless valour with a truthful tongue,
From Bactria to Thule to be sung,
And reach from Pole to Pole! This peerless deed
Foretells the valour that the Spanish breed
Will in the coming centuries inherit
From ancestors and fathers of such merit.
Neither the scythe of Death nor course of Time
Shall make me cease to sing in deathless rhyme
The glory of Numantia's constant soul
And her strong arm. In her alone I find

All that can kindle the poetic mind
To fill long ages with sad lamentations,
Praising the bravest of unconquered nations.
And now, remembering her matchless glory,
We give a happy end to our sad story.

FUENTE OVEJUNA

Lope de Vega

English Version by Roy Campbell

In 1476 the peasants of Fuente Ovejuna, a village in Córdoba, rose against their feudal overlords, represented by Fernán Gómez de Guzmán. As Comendador, or Knight Commander, of the Order of Calatrava, Fernán Gómez derived his authority from the Master of that Order, the young Rodrigo Téllez Girón. The larger political background is sketched in Lope's opening scene where the Comendador champions the King of Portugal's claim to the Spanish throne. The rival claimant was Ferdinand of Aragón who had married Isabela of Castile: it is to these "Catholic Princes" that the peasants will later appeal, as to a Supreme Court.

Lope read of the events of 1476 in *A Chronicle of the Three Military Orders* by Rades y Andrada.

E.B.

DRAMATIS PERSONAE

QUEEN ISABEL (ISABELA) OF CASTILE

HER HUSBAND, KING FERNANDO (FERDINAND) OF ARAGÓN

RODRIGO TÉLLEZ GIRÓN, *Master of the Order of Calatrava*

FERNÁN (FERNANDO) GÓMEZ DE GUZMÁN, *Comendador of the Order of Calatrava*

ORTUÑO ⎱
⎰ *his servants*
FLORES

DON MANRIQUE, *Master of the Order of Santiago*

A JUDGE

TWO ALDERMEN OF CIUDAD REAL

AN ALDERMAN OF FUENTE OVEJUNA[1]

ESTEBAN ⎱
⎰ *mayors of Fuente Ovejuna*
ALONSO

LAURENCIA ⎫
JACINTA ⎬ *peasant women*
PASCUALA ⎭

JUAN ROJO ⎫
FRONDOSO ⎬ *peasants*
BARRILDO ⎭
MENGO

LEONELO, *a student of law*

CIMBRANOS, *a soldier*

MUSICIANS

ATTENDANTS

PEASANTS AND PEASANT WOMEN

SOLDIERS

---

[1] Fuente Ovejuna should be pronounced in five syllables, thus: Fwént–yov–e–hú–na. It is written as one word on the map today, but the two-word form is less formidable for non-Spanish readers and is not an innovation. *Fuente* means fountain or well; *ovejuna* means pertaining to sheep. [E.B.]

ACT I

The house of the Master of Calatrava in Almagro

Enter the COMENDADOR, FLORES, ORTUÑO.

COMENDADOR. The Master knows I'm here in town?

FLORES. He knows
Already.

ORTUÑO. He gets more serious, as he grows.

COMENDADOR. But does he know that it is I, Fernán
Gómez de Guzmán?

FLORES. He's not yet a man.
Do not be shocked.

COMENDADOR. My name he may ignore
But not my rank of Grand Comendador!

ORTUÑO. He has advisers who abet his pride
In setting common courtesy aside.

COMENDADOR. Then he will win but little love, for still
Courtesy is the key to men's good will.
Stupid discourtesy's the key to naught
But hate.

ORTUÑO. If a discourteous man but thought
How all must come to hate him in the end
Although to kiss his shoe they now contend—
He would prefer to die than be like this.

FLORES. How sickening and importunate it is
To suffer such discourtesy! In men
Of equal rank, it's foolishness, but when
Their rank's unequal, it becomes a curse,
And smacks of arrant tyranny or worse.
But you can well ignore a slight like this
From one too young even to've known the kiss
Of women.

COMENDADOR. But the sword he buckled on
The day the cross of Calatrava shone

First on his breast conferred the obligation
Of courtesy.

FLORES.   If in his estimation
You have been slandered, you will soon find out.

ORTUÑO. You still can go, if you are still in doubt.

COMENDADOR. It is a question I would fain decide.

Enter the MASTER OF CALATRAVA *with his train of* AT-
TENDANTS.

MASTER. Your pardon, on my life! Fernando Gómez!
I've only just been told you were in town.

COMENDADOR. With much good reason I had cause to frown
Thinking you slighted me, since mutual love
And noble birth should raise us both above
Such wrangling thoughts. You're Master of the Order.
I, Gómez, am your Grand Comendador
And very faithful servant ever more.

MASTER. I little guessed; I had no news of you.
Welcome! Embrace me!

COMENDADOR.   It is but my due
That you should honour me: I risked my life
On your behalf so often in the strife
Ere the Pope raised you to this lofty rank,
Waiving your youth.

MASTER.   It's you I have to thank,
That's true; and by the holy sign across
Our breasts, I shall repay your toil and loss
With my esteem, and as a father, too,
Shall honour you.

COMENDADOR.   I'm now content with you.

MASTER. What tidings of the war?

COMENDADOR.   Hear what I say
And learn how much you owe me.

MASTER.   Tell me, pray.

COMENDADOR. Grand Master of the cross of Calatrava,
Raised by the valour of a famous father
To that high station! He, eight years ago,
In favour of yourself renounced his Mastership.

This was confirmed and sworn by kings and captains
For greater surety. The most Holy Pontiff,
Pius the Second, sent some Bulls, and others
Were sent thereafter by Pope Paul,[1] appointing
That Juan Pacheco, Master of the Order
Of Santiago, should share equal rank
As your coadjutor. He died; and you,
Despite your tender years, were given sole
Dominion. You must realise your honour
Depends in such a case on serving truly
The cause of your great House. Hear how things stand:
Upon the death of Henry of Castile,[2]
Alfonso, King of Portugal, laid claim
To Henry's title—Joan, Alfonso's wife,
Is Henry's daughter. A like claim is made,
Though with less obvious right to your allegiance,
By Ferdinand of Aragón who cites
His marriage to Castilian Isabel.
Your House, great sir, supports Alfonso's claim.
Your cousin, as it happens, holds this Joan
Fast in his power . . . My advice is this:
To summon all the Knights of Calatrava
With those here of Almagro, and to capture
Ciudad Real, the city on the frontier
Dividing Andalusia from Castile.
Few forces will be needed. As their soldiers
They only have the natives of the place
And some few gentry who support the cause
Of Isabela and King Ferdinand.
It steads you now to make the whole world ring
And stun the misbelief of all beholders
Who deem your cross too broad for the slim shoulders
Of such a child as you are. Think of them—
Urueña's mighty counts from whom you stem
And how from forth their tombs, to urge your quarrel,
They show the garlands of unwithering laurel
They won in life! Think of Villena's lords

---

[1] Pius II (1458–64), Paul II (1467–71).
[2] Henry IV of Castile (1454–74), Alfonso V of Portugal (1438–81), Ferdinand of Aragón (1452–1516). [E.B.]

And other captains famous for their swords,
Too many for the wings of Fame to bear!
Remember them. Your pure, white blade make bare,
Which you must stain the colour of the sign
That spans with crimson cross your chest and mine—
Since Master of the red cross or its knight
No man can be while yet his sword is white!
Both cross and sword in scarlet must be dyed
One on your breast, the other at your side,
And you, the sovereign of your deathless line,
Must as the dome upon their temple shine!

MASTER. Fernando Gómez, rest assured, I'll fight
This quarrel for my lineage and my right,
And, when the city to my conquest falls,
Like forked, red lightning, scorch its battered walls.
So, though my uncle's dead, the world may know
That in my veins his deeds of valour flow,
And, when I draw my sword, its silver flare
Shall flush as crimson as the cross I wear!
But tell me how you're settled now, and where,
And have you any soldiers quartered there?

COMENDADOR. But few; yet trained by me. Inured to battle,
They'll fight like lions. But, as for the village,
Fuente Ovejuna's folk think more of tillage,
And care more for their humble crops and cattle
Than about martial glories. They know naught
Of war.

MASTER.   You live there?

COMENDADOR.   Yes, I've sought
A haven there in these rough times. But, mind,
Let not a single vassal stay behind!

MASTER. No fear of that! My horse I'll mount today,
Couching my lance, and eager for the fray!

Village square in Fuente Ovejuna

Enter PASCUALA *and* LAURENCIA.

LAURENCIA. Never may he return!

PASCUALA.　　　　　　　　　Why so?
　I thought, when you had heard the news
　Of his departure, you would show
　More sorrow.

LAURENCIA.　　　May heaven still refuse
　To let him come back here!

PASCUALA.　　　　　　　　　I've heard
　Oaths angrier far than those you utter,
　But when it came to test the word
　The hearts have proved as soft as butter.

LAURENCIA. D'you think you'll find a holm-oak drier
　Than I am?

PASCUALA.　　Get along with you!
　It is the driest cork takes fire.
　Yet when one's talking of desire,
　And when the gentry come to woo,
　What girl can say, and prove no liar,
　"I shall not go the same way too"?

LAURENCIA. By this bright sun, I swear it's true,
　Though the whole world would say I lie!
　Why should I love Fernando who
　Pursues me? Here's the reason why:
　D'you think he'd marry me?

PASCUALA.　　　　　　　　Why, no!

LAURENCIA. His infamy I then condemn.
　How many girls have suffered for
　The ruin that was made of them
　All by this same Comendador!

PASCUALA. I'll hold it as a marvel, though,
　If from his clutches you go free.

LAURENCIA. It's nonsense—all that you foresee!
  For ever since a month ago,
  In vain, he has been after me.
  Ortuño, that sly cur, and Flores,
  His pandar, showed me silks and pearls
  And costly headgear for my curls,
  And tried to frighten me with stories
  About his power to do me harm.
  Yet, though they filled me with alarm,
  They could not bait me with their hook.

PASCUALA. Where did they tempt you?

LAURENCIA.   Last weekend,
  While washing linen by the brook.

PASCUALA. I fear they'll trick you in the end.

LAURENCIA. What? Me?

PASCUALA.   Or, if not you, the priest.

LAURENCIA. Though toothsome, I am just too tough
  To serve His Reverence for a feast.
  But of this "love" I've had enough.
  I am more interested far
  In any slice of roasted bacon
  That from the embers I have taken
  And placed between the bread I've kneaded;
  Or from my mother's favourite jar
  To steal a cup of wine unheeded;
  Or watch at noon the simmering broth
  Where beef chunks in the humming froth
  Of greens are somersaulting round;
  Or, if I've come in tired from walking,
  To splice an *aubergine* well-browned
  With a ham-slice; or else be caulking
  The crannies of my appetite
  With a grape-bunch from my own vine
  (Which God preserve from hail or blight)
  Till we on salmagundi dine
  With oil and pepper seasoned fine;
  And then to bed—to my oration
  Of "Lead me not into temptation"—
  And sleep contented with my prayer.

These are the things for which I care
And prize a hundred times above
The foolish, foxy wiles of love
With which these villains weave their snare.
For if you wish to take their measure
Their only aim's to work us harm,
To make us go to bed with pleasure,
Then to awake in dire alarm.

PASCUALA. You're right, Laurencia, and when
They leave off loving us, the men
Deal with us as the thankless sparrows
Deal with the peasant in the winter:
For when the days begin to narrow
And the fields with frosts to splinter,
Then down, as fast as they are able,
They flit from chimney, cave, and gable
With melting voice to croon and coo
"Tweenie-tweenie-tweenie-twoo"
While with the crumbs swept from his table
The fool regales the faithless crew.
But when the cold has ceased to freeze them
And the fields their flowers reveal,
Past delights no longer please them,
Thanklessness is all they feel.
For all the largesse of his table
They miscall the friend they knew
For an unbelieving Jew
Flitting up to cave and gable
No longer chirping "tweeny-tweeny"
But cursing "Sheeny-sheeny-sheeny!"
Such are men with every maiden:
When they need us, then we are
The wealth with which their hearts are laden,
Their life, their soul, their guiding star,
But when their flames die down to embers,
They chirrup, bill, and coo no more:
All the names their faith remembers
Are the names of "bitch" and "whore"!

LAURENCIA. Trust no man that comes to woo!

PASCUALA. So say I, Laurencia, too!

Enter MENGO, BARRILDO, FRONDOSO.

FRONDOSO. Your arguments have got lopsided,
  Barrildo.

BARRILDO. Look! Here's one at hand
  By whose decision we may stand.

MENGO. But ere the point has been decided,
  You both must swear to pay the cost
  You've wagered if the verdict's mine.

BARRILDO. I swear we shall! But, if you've lost,
  What prize, in turn, have you provided?

MENGO. I'll bet you, then, my flute of box
  Worth a lot more than barns or flocks
  Were you to value it as I did.

BARRILDO. I'm satisfied.

MENGO.   Then let's proceed.

FRONDOSO. Ladies! Good day!

LAURENCIA.   "Ladies" indeed!

FRONDOSO. Yes, it's the fashion and the law
  Which euphemises every flaw.
  The fat man's "well-set-up"; the lean
  Is "slim" and "graceful in his mien";
  The fledgling scholar, still at college,
  Is called "a doctor" for his knowledge;
  The stone-blind has a "visual failing";
  The squint-eyed has a "roving glance";
  The cripple "does not like to dance";
  The big-mouthed churl who's always railing
  Is "fearless"; the potato-eyed
  Old blinkard is called "shrewd and sharp";
  The ignorant is magnified
  For "wisdom"; he who loves to carp
  And cavil, why, he's "persevering";
  The busybody's "most endearing";
  The gasbag's "deep" and "wise"; the shameless
  Is "daring"; and the coward's blameless,
  Though "falling short"; the domineering,
  Insulting ruffian is miscalled

"A martial figure"; he who's bald
For "grave authority's" extolled;
The grudging sulk is praised for "gravity";
There's "wit" in ignorant depravity;
The insolent is "brave and bold";
The madman goes for "free and easy,"
For "humourous" the tout who's broke;
"Companionable, bright, and breezy"
They call the brandy-gozzled soak;
The snuffler and the bulbous-snouted
Are only "suffering from a cold";
Arrogance for "reserve" is doubted,
And grumpiness for "shyness" goes;
The hunchback passes for "well-loaded" . . .
And so, lest I should be outmoded,
I call you "Ladies" I suppose.
But that's enough, for in this way
I could talk nonsense all the day.

LAURENCIA. Up in the cities, those in fashion
Use gentler words to be polite.
But, by my faith, the terms they ration
For human faults, appear more right
Than the rough terms that can be flung
At random by a spiteful tongue.

FRONDOSO. Well, could you let us have a sample?

LAURENCIA. I'll take the opposite example
To each of yours. The man who's serious
Is "grumpy." One who speaks the truth
They call "self-righteous" and "uncouth."
They call the grave man "sad"; "imperious"
And "tiresome"—one who reprehends;
"Importunate"—who counsels youth;
"Officious"—one who helps his friends;
"Cruel" they call the man who's just,
Impartially though he should try us;
"Listless and tame"—the humbly pious;
And one who's constant in his trust
They take for "simple, dull, and dense";
Courtesy is to "cringe and flatter";

Christian behaviour's "all pretence";
Merit that earns is no such matter,
But "merely luck"; misfortune's "shame"—
For which the sufferer is to blame;
A girl who's virtuous is "a fool";
A wife who does not break the rule
Is merely "dull" . . . But that should be
More than enough to bring me level
In answering your philosophy.

MENGO. By heavens, she is the very devil!
The priest who functioned at your christening
Laid on the salt, in handfuls too!

LAURENCIA. But what's your strife (if I've been listening
Correctly)?

FRONDOSO. Hark, Laurencia, do!

LAURENCIA. Well, what is it you want?

FRONDOSO. Laurencia,
Lend me your hearing.

LAURENCIA. Only lend?
To give it you for keeps, I'll venture,
From this day onwards.

FRONDOSO. I depend
On your discretion.

LAURENCIA. What's your bet?

FRONDOSO. I and Barrildo both have set
A wager against Mengo here.

LAURENCIA. What does he say?

BARRILDO. —Denies a fact
That's certain, absolute, and clear.

MENGO. To put it plainly, I've come here
To floor them with the truth exact.

LAURENCIA. What's that?

BARRILDO. That love does not exist
Is what *he* holds.

LAURENCIA. But who can doubt it?
Surely there's love.

BARRILDO.   Of course. Without it
How on this earth could life persist?

MENGO. Philosophy is all a mist
To me. I know nothing about it.
The written word is Greek to me.
But can you watch, and dare to scout it,
The strife between each element,
The endless war they represent?
And it's from them our bodies borrow
Their nourishment, their wrath and sorrow,
Their phlegm and blood—you must agree.

FRONDOSO. The worlds around us and above,
Mengo, are harmony entire.
Harmony is pure love, and love
Is harmony.

MENGO.   I state the worth
Of self-love, native to this earth:
That is the love which governs all things.
Affinities in great and small things
Must regulate all that we see:
I don't deny *that*. I agree
That everything is truly fond
Of what to it may correspond
In keeping its integrity:
My hand against a coming blow
Leaps up to guard my face, and so
My feet, by running off, forestall
A danger that might else befall
My body. My eyes, blinking tight,
Avoid whatever harms their sight.
Such love is natural.

PASCUALA.   Then why
Object? What is it you deny?

MENGO. That anyone in love can fall
(Except with his own self) at all.

PASCUALA. Your pardon, Mengo, but you're lying,
Since is it any good denying
That force is not material

By which men love their womenkind,
Or animals their mates?

MENGO.   It's blind,
Sheer *amour-propre*, self-satisfaction,
Not love. What's love, then? I'll enquire.

LAURENCIA. Why, love is a divine desire
Of beauty.

MENGO.   Why does love pursue
Beauty? Why? Surely, to acquire
It for one's own good self.

LAURENCIA.   That's true.

MENGO. To love one's own self, one must woo
The thing that self does most require.

LAURENCIA. That's so.

MENGO.   Well, there's no love
Except what for one's own delight
One hunts, to feed one's appetite,
For one's own self the prize to grapple,
To be of one's own eye the apple,
And the sole eye of one's potato!

BARRILDO. The preacher in his recent sermons
Mentioned a certain man called Plato
Who, speaking about love, determines
That we should selflessly admire
The soul and virtue of the one
We love—to set our hearts on fire.

PASCUALA. Right off the beaten track you've run
And bogged your axle in the mire
Where only doctors from the colleges
Find foothold.

LAURENCIA.   You are right: our knowledge is
Too shallow. Do not grind too hard
And fine, but thank the heavens above,
Mengo, that you're so lucky-starred
As to be ignorant of love.

MENGO. Are you in love?

LAURENCIA.   With my good name.

FRONDOSO. May God chastise you for the same
  With jealous pangs!

PASCUALA.   The wisest plan
  Is to consult the sacristan.
  He, or the priest, could answer best . . .
  Laurencia's never loved a man
  And I have scarcely stood the test.
  Our judgment would be all in vain.

FRONDOSO. A curse upon your cold disdain!

  Enter FLORES.

FLORES. God be with you, good people!

PASCUALA.   Look!
  The page of the Comendador.

LAURENCIA. Rather his carrion-kite and rook.
  What news abroad, friend?

FLORES.   From the war
  I've just returned, as you may see.

LAURENCIA. And what of Don Fernán? Is he
  Expected back?

FLORES.   The war at last
  Has ended. Though it cost some lives,
  Our cause victoriously thrives.

FRONDOSO. Well, señor, tell us how it passed.

FLORES. Why, yes. Although myself I say it,
  There's no man better could portray it,
  Since I was there from first to last,
  And with my own eyes saw it all.
  Against that city which we call
  The Royal City, our young Master
  Of Calatrava raised his troop,
  Two thousand infantry, to swoop,
  And carry slaughter and disaster
  Together with three hundred horse
  Of seculars and monks and friars—
  For even priests must join the force
  When our great Order so requires
  (Though that is chiefly with the Moors)
  To take up arms and fight in wars.

The youthful Master of our Order,
In doublet green with gilded border,
Slit at the sleeve-ends to unfold
The bracelets held with links of gold,
On a huge dapple horse was seen
With grey hairs shot with hairs of silver,
Whose underlip the Guadalquivir
Had bathed, and who had grazed its green.
Its tail with deerskin plaits behind,
Its mane, in front, was deftly twined
With many a ribbon, lace, and bow
Whose flattering whiteness, row by row,
Vied with the dots and dancing speckles
That starred his flanks with fiery freckles
And showered his stalwart croup with snow.
Our own Fernando Gómez rode
With him. The horse that he bestrode
Was of the honey-coloured hue
But mane and tail and fetlock, too,
Were jetty-black at each extreme;
The muzzle was as black to view,
Save that it turned as white as cream
From snorting, slavering, and drinking
The froth that from its snaffle clinking
And champing jaws, flaked sud by sud,
The foam of its aspiring blood,
And smoke to which its wrath was flame.
In glittering scales his chain-mail bound him;
Bright plates of armour spanned his frame
And clipped his shoulders. In wide swirls
His orange tunic-fringe around him
Sparkled with gold and orient pearls.
Over his helmet, wreathed in curls,
The cream-white ostrich-plumes were towering
As if 'twere orange-blossom flowering
Out of his orange-coloured lace—
Slung on a white and scarlet brace,
An ash-tree, lifted on his arm,
To threaten all the Moorish race
And fill Granada with alarm!

The city rose in the King's name
Since for the Crown they all proclaim
Their loyalty to the King's succession.
They made resistance worthy fame.
But in the end, their strength to tame,
The Master entered in procession,
And those who had denied his right
He had beheaded upon sight.
As for the common people there,
He had each snaffled with a bit,
And, having stripped their bodies bare,
He flogged them in the public square
Till they could neither stand nor sit.
He made himself so roundly feared,
So popular and so revered,
Who in so short a time could win,
Chastise, and rule, though adolescent!
They augured that the pale blue crescent
Of Islam in eclipse would spin
To ignominy, shame, and loss,
Before the sun of his red cross.
After he'd lightened, struck, and thundered,
Out of the city's wreck, he plundered
Such vast largesse and wealth for all
(But chiefly the Comendador)
It seemed he had flung wide the door
Of his own house and dining-hall
And bade them ransack all the store.
But now I hear the band approaching.
Rejoice! Forget your cares and quarrels!
To win all hearts, with none reproaching,
Is worth a forest full of laurels.

Enter the COMENDADOR *with* ORTUÑO, JUAN ROJO, *and the
mayor and deputy mayor,* ESTEBAN, *and* ALONSO.

MUSICIANS, *singing*.

>   You're welcome in our village,
>   Comendador, to stop!
>   Battlefields are his tillage
>   And lives of men his crop!

Long live the Guzmán faction
And the Girones line
Invincible in action
In peace the most benign.

Who stronger than the oak
Against the Moors did sally
And quelled the sturdy folk
Of Ciudad Reále.[3]

Fuente Ovejuna greets him
The village where his home is
Shout, everyone who meets him:
Long live Fernando Gómez!

COMENDADOR. Dear village, let me thank you from my heart,
For all these signs of love that you have shown.

ALONSO. Of what we feel we've only shown a part
Of all the love you merit as your own.

ESTEBAN. Fuente Ovejuna's mayors and corporation
(Whom you've so graced), along with this ovation,
Beg that you will accept, as from our hearts,
The humble gifts that pile these rustic carts.
You'll find as much good will and homely thanks
Borne in the cradle of their creaking planks
As in more wealthy gifts. Here, two glazed jars
Brim with preserves. Here, from the wooden bars
A flock of geese poke forth their heads to cackle
Your valiant fame. Ten fattened hogs, to crackle
Upon your fire, here offer up their loves,
And their smooth hides, as soft as scented gloves.
A hundred pairs of chanticleers and chickens
For whom full many a widow sighs and sickens
And many an orphaned fledgling joins the mourners
Round dunghills, village-greens, and farmyard corners.
We bring no coats of arms nor gold-trapped steeds
But all from rustic loyalty proceeds
Offered by loyal vassals—men who hold
That love's more lasting and more pure than gold.

[3] Mispronounce "Re/álly" as in original. [R.C.]

And (talking about purity) here's wine—
Twelve skins of it! which could defend a breach
In January, if it did but line
Your warriors' skins inside. It's common speech—
For furbishing clean steel, to make it shine
And cut like lightning, there is naught like wine.
Armour without, I say, but wine within,
Against all comers, they will always win!
I will not speak of cheeses and the rest:
Our house is yours, and you, most honoured guest,
Have won your own deserts from every heart.

COMENDADOR. Thanks, councillors, in peace may you depart.

ALONSO. Now rest, thrice welcome to our countryside!
If these poor rushes that we strew before you
Were pearls and rubies which we could provide,
Even then, they would be insufficient for you.

COMENDADOR. I well believe you. Thank you all. Good-bye.

ESTEBAN. Now, singers, raise your voices up on high.

MUSICIANS *sing*.

> You're welcome in our village,
> Comendador, to stop!
> Battlefields are your tillage,
> And slaughtered men your crop!

Exeunt.

Enter COMENDADOR, LAURENCIA, PASCUALA, ORTUÑO, FLORES.

COMENDADOR. Here! Wait, you two!

LAURENCIA.   What does Your Lordship wish?

COMENDADOR. You turned me down the other day. Yes! Me!
What does this mean?

LAURENCIA.   Pascuala, is he talking
To you?

PASCUALA. No! Leave me out of it! Not me!

COMENDADOR. It is to you I'm talking, cruel beauty,
And to this other wench. Are you not mine?

PASCUALA. Your servants, yes. But not for other use.

COMENDADOR. Go in, get in this doorway here. Come on!
There are a lot of men here. Don't be frightened.

LAURENCIA. I'll go in if the councillors go too
  (One of them is my father) not unless . . .

COMENDADOR. Flores . . .

FLORES.   My lord!

COMENDADOR. What do they mean not to obey my orders?

FLORES. In with you!

LAURENCIA.   Here, don't claw us!

FLORES.   Don't be foolish!
  Go in!

PASCUALA. No! If we do, you'll bolt us in.

FLORES. Go in! He only wants to let you see
  The trophies he's brought back.

COMENDADOR.   Once they're inside,
  Ortuño, bolt the door.
  Exit COMENDADOR.

LAURENCIA. Flores, please let us pass.

ORTUÑO.   What! Don't you know
  That you're included with the other presents?

PASCUALA. Out of my way, or I shall scream for help!

FLORES. That's taking things too far.

LAURENCIA.   Cannot your master
  Be satisfied with all the meat they've brought him?

ORTUÑO. Yours is the sort of meat he likes the best.

LAURENCIA. Well, may it choke his throat and burst his innards!
  The women leave.

FLORES. And now we're in a fix! Think what he'll say!

In the palace of the Catholic kings at Medina del Campo

Enter KING FERDINAND, QUEEN ISABEL, DON MANRIQUE,
Master of Santiago, and ATTENDANTS.

QUEEN. My lord, we must be wary in this matter.
  The King of Portugal has got his army
  Ready to march. So we must pounce at once
  And win outright, or else we'll court defeat.

KING. Aragón and Navarre are sending help
And I can soon reorganise Castile
To bring us swift success.

QUEEN.   Your Majesty,
Our victory is ensured by that, believe me.

DON MANRIQUE. Two aldermen from Ciudad Real
Beg leave of audience. Shall I bid them enter?

KING. Do not deny our presence. Let them in.

Enter TWO ALDERMEN *from Ciudad Real.*

FIRST ALDERMAN. Great Catholic King Ferdinand, whom
        heaven
Sent to Castile from Aragón to bless
And shelter us. From Ciudad Real
We've humbly come to sue for the protection
Of your unrivalled valour. In the past
We have been happy as your subjects; now
Our adverse fate has brought us down from that
High honour. For the famous Don Rodrigo
Téllez Girón (though young to be the Master
Of Calatrava) that fierce thunderbolt
Of reckless valour, both for his own glory
And to extend the frontiers of his rule,
Laid close siege to our city. Though we fought,
Opposing bravery to violent force,
Till the blood ran in streams, we lost the war.
So then he took possession of the town,
Which he could not have done, save for the help,
Tactics, and counsels of Fernando Gómez.
So he remains our ruler, we his vassals,
Against our will, unless some remedy
Is soon applied.

KING.   Where is Fernando Gómez?

FIRST ALDERMAN. He's in Fuente Ovejuna, I believe,
Since that's his fief. He has a house and land there,
And there, more freely than we dare to tell it,
He tyrannises over his poor vassals
Keeping them alien from content and peace.

KING. Have you a captain left among you?

SECOND ALDERMAN.   Sire,
  No one of noble blood escaped from death,
  Capture, or wounds.

QUEEN.   This case brooks no delay.
  We must strike quickly without losing strength
  Before our daring enemy can act.
  The King of Portugal, advancing through
  Estremadura, finds a sure, safe gateway
  And may cause far more harm if he's not checked.

KING. Now, Don Manrique, Master of Santiago,
  Go! Take two regiments! Repair these harms
  And grant no respite to the foe! The Count
  Of Cabra can go with you: Córdova
  Can claim in him a captain of world fame.
  This is the most that I can send you now.

DON MANRIQUE. Yes, I think this solution is the best.
  I'll stamp out his disorders, or I'll die.

QUEEN. Since it is you we send, victory's certain!

The countryside near Fuente Ovejuna

Enter LAURENCIA *and* FRONDOSO.

LAURENCIA. I had come back from the river
  Although my washing's hardly wrung
  Lest we should be on every tongue
  Because, Frondoso, you're so reckless
  In what you say, that old and young
  Are spreading rumours through the village
  That I on you and you on me
  Are casting looks for all to see.
  They know that of the farmer people
  You are most bold, and proud, and free
  And wear the finest clothes, and so,
  In all the village, there's no man

Or girl that does not claim to know
That you and I will soon be one
And that the village sacristan
Will leave off playing his bassoon
To see us from the vestry soon.
For my own part I wish them thrift,
Full barns in August, with the gift
Of brimming must in every jar.
Their tittle-tattle's very far
From getting on my nerves. A lot
Of sleep I'll lose on that account!
I do not care one tiny jot.

FRONDOSO. Lovely Laurencia, this disdain
Causes my soul such dreadful pain.
It breaks my heart to see and hear you
And makes me frightened to come near you.
If you but realise that I
For you alone would live and die
Your faithful husband—my reward
Is poor!

LAURENCIA. It's all I can afford.

FRONDOSO. But can you really feel no ruth
To see the pain you cause? Mere thinking
Of you prevents me eating, drinking
Or sleeping, in my prime of youth.
Can savagery so uncouth
And cruelty so fierce, be hid
Behind an angel's face? In truth
I fear I shall go raving mad.

LAURENCIA. Try magic spells, if you feel bad.

FRONDOSO. No! I am begging for my life!
My dear Laurencia, be my wife
And let us both, like turtledoves,
With beaks and hearts in amorous strife
Solemnly consummate our loves
When we come from the church together
To bill and coo through life forever.

LAURENCIA. You ask my uncle, old Juan Rojo!
Even if I'm not mad about you

And very well could do without you—
Yet I could care for you.

FRONDOSO.   Confound!
Here comes the Grand Comendador.

LAURENCIA. He's hunting roebuck, I'll be bound.
Hide in this bush.

FRONDOSO.   I'll hide, but where
Can I escape my jealous care?

Enter the COMENDADOR *with a crossbow.*

COMENDADOR. It's not so bad when hunting buck
To fall in with such damned good luck
In place of *buck* to find a *dear*—
A deer so timorous and shy
And so precisely now and here!

LAURENCIA. I am just resting while I dry
Some linen, and, with your good will,
I shall return now to the rill.

COMENDADOR. This ugly kind of frown and fret
Insults my rank which you forget,
And does great havoc to the grace
Both of the figure and the face
Which heaven gave you. Though chance gave
You, other times, a way to save
Your virtue, now good fortune yields
These hushed, conniving, lonely fields
And you alone cannot deny
Your Master's rights, nor hope to fly
From one who holds you in control
And owns your house, your body, and your soul—
One whom, moreover, you insult by this.
Pedro Redondo's wife granted me bliss,
Sebastiania, too—they never parried
The strong urge of my love, though newly married.
Martin del Pozo's wife, two days a bride,
Gave herself up, and laid her by my side.

LAURENCIA. My lord, those women long were at the game
Before their husbands or Your Lordship came!
Follow your roebuck, sir, by God be blessed!

But for that Christian cross upon your chest
I'd say you were the fiend—

COMENDADOR.   I will not stand it:
I'll fling my bow aside, and like a bandit
Will plunder you with my brute-strength alone,
For you are a mere chattel that I own!

LAURENCIA. What? Are you mad?

COMENDADOR.   Don't struggle!

FRONDOSO *steals out and takes the crossbow.*

FRONDOSO.   Now I've got
The crossbow. Heaven help us all! If not,
I'll have to shoulder it and shoot.

LAURENCIA.   Heaven be my aid!

COMENDADOR. Look, we are all alone. Don't be afraid!

FRONDOSO. Most generous Comendador, let go
Of this poor girl, or else with your own bow
I shall transfix your body without sparing.
Although I tremble at the cross you're wearing!

COMENDADOR. Villainous dog!

FRONDOSO.   No dog, sir!

LAURENCIA.   Have a care,
Frondoso, what you're doing.

FRONDOSO, *to* LAURENCIA.   Run away!

Exit LAURENCIA.

COMENDADOR. Oh, what a fool I was to leave my sword,
Thinking that it would frighten her.

FRONDOSO.   My lord,
I've but to press this trigger and you die.

COMENDADOR. She's gone, you lowborn villain. Leave that bow!
I tell you, put it down, quick!

FRONDOSO.   How can I
Leave it, when you will kill me if I do?
True love is deaf to reason or to rhyme
When he is on his throne for the first time:
So take good warning.

COMENDADOR.   Shoot me villain, do!

Rather than that upon a clod like you
One nobly born should turn his back and flee,
Shoot me, and see what it will lead you to!
Shoot, dog! I break the laws of chivalry
By speaking to you.

FRONDOSO.   I'll not shoot you. No.
But as I'm forced to save my life, I'll go,
Taking your crossbow.

Takes the bow off with him.

COMENDADOR.   How could I foresee
This danger? But by heaven I shall be
Revenged for this rebellion and attack.
God give me patience till I've paid it back!

ACT II

Village square in Fuente Ovejuna

Enter ESTEBAN *and the* FIRST ALDERMAN.

ESTEBAN. My view is this, good sir: let no more grain
    Be taken from the public granary.
    The year wears on. The harvest augurs badly.
    Let us store up reserves in case of need,
    Whatever voices murmur other views.

FIRST ALDERMAN. That's always been my own idea in ruling
    The village peacefully in its best interests.

ESTEBAN. We must present a plea to Fernán Gómez.
    We don't want these astrologers to make
    Long speeches about things they do not know
    Concerning secrets known to God alone.
    What right have they presumptuously to claim
    Deep theologic knowledge and to find
    The future corresponding with the past?
    The present is the time that counts; the wisest
    Of them is ignorant of all but that.
    You'd think they had the clouds on tap at home!
    You'd think the stars were at their beck and call!
    How can they know the goings-on in heaven
    Which fill us with such anxious hopes and fears?
    They think that they can regulate the seedtime
    And deal out laws to barley, wheat, peas, beans,
    Cucumbers, calabashes, pumpkins, and mustard!
    They are the pumpkin-heads! They prophesy
    A beast will die, and then they say it's happened
    Not here but somewhere else—in Transylvania!
    They say there'll be a shortage in our wine,
    But plenty of good beer in Germany.
    In Gascony the cherries will be frozen
    And there'll be lots of tigers in Hircania,
    But after all, whether we sow or not,

The year is always ended in December!

Enter LEONELO, *the student, and* BARRILDO.

LEONELO. We're not the first to get here for a gossip.

BARRILDO. What's Salamanca like?

LEONELO.   That's a long story.

BARRILDO. You'll be a learnèd doctor.

LEONELO.   Not so learnèd.

There's not much future in my faculty.

BARRILDO. Then some are cleverer than you?

LEONELO.   Of course.

BARRILDO. I'm sure that they must think you a fine scholar.

LEONELO. I've done my best to learn what mattered most.

BARRILDO. Now that the printing press has been invented
Everyone seems to pride himself on knowledge.

LEONELO. In spite of that I think they know far less:
There is a strange confusion in excess
Which always must defeat its own intention
And that is one result of that invention.
Not that I would deny the printing art
Finds genius out, and lifts it far apart
From the base throng, where it would lie neglected,
Raising it up by time to be respected.
We owe the press to Gutenberg, a clever
And worthy man from Mainz whose fame forever
Will fill the world. But some deserve the curse
Of the whole world for printing their own verse.
Some people, till their works were printed, had
Been much revered—but now we find them bad.
Others, in envy, signed an honoured name
To their own works, and brought it evil fame.

BARRILDO. Come, come, I can't think that.

LEONELO.   Oh yes, it's true!

Illiterates still grudge scholarship its due.

BARRILDO. But printing is important all the same.

LEONELO. Long centuries had passed before it came
And yet it has not given us a second
Augustine or Jerome who could be reckoned
As due to it.

BARRILDO. Don't let us get so heated,
Calm yourself down, and let us both be seated.

Enter JUAN ROJO *and another* PEASANT.

JUAN ROJO. Four farms are not sufficient for a dowry
If gifts be reckoned in the modern way:
Take heed, all you who have enquiring minds,
Opinion in this town has gone astray!

PEASANT. Don't lose your temper. The Comendador—
What news of him?

JUAN ROJO.   He has ill-used Laurencia.

PEASANT. No brute is so lascivious as he.
Would he were hanged upon that olive tree!

Enter the COMENDADOR, ORTUÑO, FLORES.

COMENDADOR. God save you all, good people.

ALDERMAN.   Oh! My lord!

COMENDADOR. Please remain seated everyone.

ESTEBAN.   Your Lordship
Be seated. We are quite contented standing.

COMENDADOR. I say you must sit down.

ESTEBAN.   All decent people
Delight in honouring rank. One can't pay honour
To any one, unless one has it.

COMENDADOR.   Come.
We'll have a talk. Sit down there, all of you.

ESTEBAN. You've seen the greyhound, sir.

COMENDADOR.   Yes, my good mayor,
My servants are enchanted with its speed.

ESTEBAN. It's a rare dog. I think it could keep up
With any gaolbird on the run from justice
Or any coward confessing on the rack.

COMENDADOR. I only wish that you could send it after
A certain bit of game that always beats me
By giving me the slip.

ESTEBAN.   Of course I'll send it.

COMENDADOR. I mean your daughter.

ESTEBAN.   What! My daughter!

COMENDADOR.   Yes!

ESTEBAN. What! Is she worthy to be wooed by you?

COMENDADOR. She's very difficult, my worthy mayor.

ESTEBAN. How do you mean?

COMENDADOR. She's causing me annoyance!
Why, there are women of high class, and married
To some I see around me in the square,
Who, at the first advance, gave themselves to me.

ESTEBAN. Well, they did wrong, my lord, and you yourself
Are doing wrong in talking thus so freely.

COMENDADOR. Oh, what an eloquent old country bumpkin!
Flores, you ought to give him Aristotle's
Treatise on *Politics*.

ESTEBAN. My lord, this village
Would fain live peacefully beneath your rule.
And surely they include some worthy people.

LEONELO. His shamelessness is surely without equal!

COMENDADOR. Alderman, have I said something to hurt you?

ALDERMAN. Yes. What you say is most unjust. Unsay it,
And do not try to rob us of our honour.

COMENDADOR. *Honour?* Do such as *you* pretend to *honour?*
You should be called the Calatrava Friars!

ALDERMAN. And some there are boast of the cross you gave
them
Whose blood, for all that, is not all it might be!

COMENDADOR. Do I pollute your blood then if I join
My blood with it?

ALDERMAN. Yes! When it's fouled with lust,
Your blood's unclean.

COMENDADOR. But surely you'll admit
I do your wives great honour when I woo them?

ESTEBAN. Your words dishonour you. We can't believe them:
And what you said at first—forget that too!

COMENDADOR. How dull and stupid is the country peasant!
It's only in the city life is pleasant,
Where husbands thank you to attend their wives
And men of wit can lead amusing lives.

ESTEBAN. That's false. You cannot fob us off with that.

God lives in cities, too, and there are people
Quicker to punish crime than you'll find here.

COMENDADOR. Clear out!

ESTEBAN.   Is that from you to me alone?

COMENDADOR. Clear out, the lot of you, let none remain!

ESTEBAN. We'll go, then.

COMENDADOR.   Not in that way, in one bunch!

FLORES. My lord, contain yourself, beware!

COMENDADOR.   They've banded
Together in my absence to defy me.

ORTUÑO. My lord, for God's sake, have some patience!

COMENDADOR.   Patience?
I marvel at the patience I have shown.
Go, separately, each to his own home!

LEONELO. Heavens, do you permit this?

ESTEBAN.   I'll go this way.

PEASANTS *go slowly and sullenly.*

COMENDADOR. What do you make of them?

ORTUÑO.   They do not know
How to dissimulate; and you refuse
To take the measure of their discontent.

COMENDADOR. What! Would they rank themselves, as equals,
     with me?

FLORES. It's not exactly ranking as your equals . . .

COMENDADOR. And that base boor that ran off with my cross-
     bow—
Must he remain unpunished?

FLORES.   Last night I thought
I'd caught him by Laurencia's door. I hit
Him hard. But it was someone else.

COMENDADOR.   Where is he?

FLORES. Frondoso? Oh, he's slinking round about.

COMENDADOR. What! Does he dare to show himself round
     here—
A man who wished to kill me?——

FLORES. Yes, like an unsuspecting bird, or else
A fish that glides towards the baited hook.

COMENDADOR. A man that makes Córdoba and Granada
Tremble on their foundations—to be dared
And daunted by a yokel! Really, Flores,
I think this world is coming to an end!

FLORES. The course of love was never smooth.

ORTUÑO.   He must
Be a good friend of yours to be still living.

COMENDADOR. Ortuño, I have used dissimulation.
Otherwise in two short hours, I'd have put
The whole town to the sword. You wait and see,
The moment that they give me the occasion,
How I shall be revenged. Have you no news
Of Pascuala?

FLORES.   She's getting married soon
She tells me.

COMENDADOR. And till then she asks for credit?

FLORES. As far as I can see, it won't be long
Till the whole debt is paid.

COMENDADOR. What of Olalla?

ORTUÑO.   Why, she showed some humour
In answering.

COMENDADOR.   She is a lively wench!
What did she say?

ORTUÑO.   Her bridegroom's getting jealous,
To see the many messages you send
And how you pay her visits with your servants.
But when he's off his guard, you'll still be welcome.

COMENDADOR. I swear upon my knighthood she's a fine one!
But as for that young whippersnapping husband
Let him beware!

ORTUÑO.   He's scared enough already.

COMENDADOR. What news of Inés?

FLORES.   Which one?

COMENDADOR.   Antón's wife.

FLORES. She's game at any time with all her charms,

I spoke to her outside her stableyard
By which she bids you enter when you like.

COMENDADOR. These easy women I like very well
And yet I pay them poorly. They don't know
The value of a decent reputation.

FLORES. You do not get the necessary setbacks
To contrast with their favours. Quick surrender
Undoes the interest and excitement of
Crowning a hope deferred. But there are women
(So the philosopher relates) who need
Men, just as abstract forms require a substance.
That men become mere habit with such women
Is not so strange.

COMENDADOR.　　　When a man's mad with love
He's pleased with quick surrender, but he values
The woman less, tires quickly, and forgets her.
For even the most grateful man esteems
At a low value that which cost him least.

Enter CIMBRANOS, *a soldier.*

CIMBRANOS. Where's the Comendador?

FLORES.　　　　　　　　　　You're in his presence.

CIMBRANOS. Valiant Fernando Gómez, change that green
Cap of a hunter for your shining morion
And change this tunic for your bright new arms.
The Master of the Knights of Santiago,
Joined with the Count of Cabra, has laid siege
In Ciudad Real to Don Rodrigo
Girón—and in the name of Isabela
Queen of Castile. And so we are in danger
Of losing that which cost us so much blood
As well you know. At early dawn were sighted,
From the high battlements, the crests and colours,
The lions and the castles of Castile
And the bright bars of Aragón. Although
The King of Portugal would aid Girón,
The best that he can hope for, at this pass,
Is to escape, alive, home to Almagro.
So mount your horse. The sight of you alone
Should send them limping back into Castile.

COMENDADOR. Stop! Say no more! Ortuño, in the square
  Get them to sound the trumpet. Say, how many
  Soldiers are quartered here?

ORTUÑO.   Fifty, I think.

COMENDADOR. Get them all mounted.

CIMBRANOS.   If you are not quick,
  Ciudad Real will be the King's and Queen's.

COMENDADOR. Oh, never fear that such a thing could happen!

Countryside round Fuente Ovejuna

Enter MENGO, PASCUALA, *and* LAURENCIA, *fleeing.*

PASCUALA. Don't go away from us!

MENGO.   Whom do you fear?

LAURENCIA. Mengo, let's all return to town together
  In case we meet with him.

MENGO.   The cruel devil—
  Where will he end?

LAURENCIA.   He never lets us rest
  Either in sun or shade.

MENGO.   Would heaven could send
  A thunderbolt to finish with this madman!

LAURENCIA. A foul bloodthirsty beast, I'd rather call him—
  The pestilence and arsenic of the place!

MENGO. They tell me that in this same very meadow
  Frondoso threatened him with his own arrow
  To rescue you, Laurencia, from his lust.

LAURENCIA. Before that day I hated all men, Mengo.
  But now I see them in another light.
  Frondoso was so valiant! Now, I fear
  That it will cost his life.

MENGO.   That man must leave
  The village.

LAURENCIA.   Though I've come to love him dearly

That is what I advised him, too. But he
Receives my loving counsels with disdain
And rage, though the Comendador has sworn
To have him hanged head downwards by the feet.

PASCUALA. May he be throttled!

MENGO.   Stoning would be better.
I wish I had the sling I used when herding—
To lodge one in the cracked shell of his noodle!
Galabalo, the Roman emperor,
Was not so wicked.

LAURENCIA.   Heliogabalus,
You mean, who was a foul inhuman beast.

MENGO. "Pelly, oh, gaballer"? I don't care how
You say it. History's not my strong point!
But his revolting memory is outstunk,
In this Fernando Gómez, by a mile!
Is any man in nature quite so evil?

PASCUALA. No: for he is a tiger in his harshness!

Enter JACINTA.

JACINTA. Help me, for God's sake, if you are my friends!

LAURENCIA. What's wrong, Jacinta dear?

PASCUALA.   We are yours.

JACINTA. The pimps of the Comendador, more strongly
Armed with their native infamy than with
Their weapons, are about to drag me with them
To Ciudad Real, whither they're bound.

LAURENCIA. If that is so, Jacinta, I must flee
Since if with you he takes such liberty
What would he do with me? May God protect you.
Exit.

PASCUALA. Jacinta dear, since I am not a man
I can be of no use.
Exit.

MENGO.   It seems that I'm
Forced now to be a man, bearing the gender
And name of one. Jacinta, come with me!

JACINTA. But have you arms?

MENGO.   The first in all the world.

JACINTA. Oh! if you only had.

MENGO.   Why, here are stones,
Jacinta. Yes, and plenty of them too!

Enter FLORES *and* ORTUÑO.

FLORES. You thought you could escape from us on foot!

JACINTA. Oh, Mengo, I am lost.

MENGO.   Why, gentlemen . . .
You surely don't molest poor countryfolk?

ORTUÑO. Can I believe my eyes? You have the cheek
To try to save this woman?

MENGO.   With my pleadings,
Yes, as a near relation, I would save her!

FLORES. Kill him at once.

MENGO.   I swear by this bright gun
If you get in such tantrums, I shall loosen
This hempen sling—to make it life for life.

Enter COMENDADOR *and* CIMBRANOS.

COMENDADOR. What's this? You two have caused me to dismount
For such a vile and trivial cause.

FLORES.   The vile
And common folk of this place are defying
Our arms—it's time you had them massacred—
In nothing do they seem disposed to please you.

MENGO. My lord, if pity lives within your breast to see
This unjust act, chastise these soldiers here
Who have misused your name to rob this woman
From her own husband and her honest parents
And give me leave to take her to her people.

COMENDADOR. I'll give them leave to punish you, vile dog!
Let go that sling!

MENGO.   My lord . . . !

COMENDADOR.   Flores! Ortuño!
Cimbranos! Tie his hands up with that thing!

MENGO. Is that how you protect a woman's honour?

COMENDADOR. What do Fuente Ovejuna and its peasants
   Say about me?

MENGO.   Sir, how have we offended
   You in the slightest thing?

FLORES.   Shall he be killed?

COMENDADOR. No, do not foul your swords upon such dirt,
   Since you must honour them in nobler work.

ORTUÑO. Your orders then?

COMENDADOR.   To flog him. Strip him naked,
   And tie him to that oak, then with the reins . . .

MENGO. Have pity, since you are a noble! Please!

COMENDADOR. And do not cease from flogging him until
   The buckles and the studs jump from the thongs
   And leave the leather naked . . .

MENGO.   Oh, you heavens!
   How long until such evil deeds are punished?

   FLORES, ORTUÑO, *and* CIMBRANOS *carry off* MENGO.

COMENDADOR. Why do you run away, you countrywoman,
   Am I not better than a sweaty peasant?

JACINTA. Is that the way that you restore the honour
   My name has lost by being chased out here
   By your paid bloodhounds?

COMENDADOR.   How can it have harmed you?

JACINTA. I have an honourable father, sir,
   Who though he's lower in his rank than you
   Is nobler in his dealings, yes, by far!

COMENDADOR. The troubles and the insolence I get
   From such as you will not appease my anger.
   Come on, this way!

JACINTA.   With whom?

COMENDADOR.   With me!

JACINTA. Take care!

COMENDADOR.   Of course I'll take good care. You're now
   A woman of the commissariat,
   The baggage train, and brothels for the army
   At large, but for myself, no more! Away!

JACINTA. I will not live to let them outrage me!

COMENDADOR. Gee up! You dirty slut! Get on the march!

JACINTA. Have pity on me, sir!

COMENDADOR.   Pity, be damned!

JACINTA. I solemnly appeal to the divine
Justice of God against your cruelty!

JACINTA *is dragged off.*

ESTEBAN'S *house*

Enter LAURENCIA *and* FRONDOSO.

LAURENCIA. How do you dare to come here, risking death?

FRONDOSO. Only to show how deeply I adore you.
I saw, from that far slope, the bloody squadron
Of the Comendador go marching out—
So trusting in your faith, I lost all fear.
May he have left us, never to return!

LAURENCIA. Don't curse him, for the ones men curse the most
Always appear to go on living longest.

FRONDOSO. If that's so, may he live a thousand years!
That ought to settle him, if wishing well
Can do him any harm. Laurencia, listen!
I want to know if my deep loyalty
Has found the harbour it deserves. All round
The people think we are already one.
And that we're not united yet they wonder.
Leave off your coyness. Tell me yes or no.

LAURENCIA. To you, and all the village, I'll say yes.

FRONDOSO. Then let me kiss your feet for this great mercy
It's like receiving a new life, I swear.

LAURENCIA. Enough of compliments. Talk to my father,
That's the important part. He's coming here
Now with my uncle. And I'm sure that I shall be
Your wife. Good luck.

FRONDOSO.   I trust it all to God!

Exit LAURENCIA. FRONDOSO *hides.*

Enter ESTEBAN *and the* ALDERMAN.

ESTEBAN. It finished up like this. In the town square
  There was almost a riot. His behaviour
  Passed all belief or toleration. All
  Are stunned by his excesses. Poor Jacinta
  Has had to pay the cost of his last madness.

ALDERMAN. All Spain will soon be for the Catholic Princes
  (As now they call Queen Isabela and
  King Ferdinand) and their just laws obey.
  The Master of the Knights of Santiago,
  Now as the captain general of their armies,
  Sweeps on his way to Ciudad Real
  Where still Rodrigo Girón holds the town.
  But I am sick to think of poor Jacinta;
  She was a well-bred girl, so good and honest.

ESTEBAN. The way they flogged poor Mengo too!

ALDERMAN.   His skin
  Was black with weals as ink or pitch or tar!

ESTEBAN. Don't speak about it. Why, it burns me up
  To see and suffer this most fiendish treatment
  And live beneath the stench of his bad name.
  I'd like to know what use is this damned bauble,
  A mayor's staff of office? It's a mockery!

ALDERMAN. These dastard crimes were done by his own men,
  Not yours. Why should you feel so sore at it?

ESTEBAN. And there's another thing. Redondo's wife—
  After he'd finished with her in the valley,
  He gave her to his flunkeys after him!

ALDERMAN. But someone's lurking here. Who can it be?

FRONDOSO. It's only I. I hope you do not mind.

ESTEBAN. Frondoso, to my house you're always welcome.
  You owe your father one life, but to me
  You owe another since I reared you up
  And loved you as a son.

FRONDOSO.   Trusting in that
  I'll ask a favour. Sir, you know full well
  Whose son I am.

ESTEBAN.   Has mad Fernando Gómez
  Done you some foul injustice?

FRONDOSO.   Yes. A great one.

ESTEBAN. The heart within me warned me that was so!

FRONDOSO. Well sir, taking advantage of your kindness,
  I came to beg the hand of your Laurencia,
  With whom I am in love. Forgive my haste
  If I have spoken it too soon, for others
  There are who would opine that I'm too daring.

ESTEBAN. Frondoso, from your words I draw new life
  Because great dread was growing in my soul.
  Thank heaven, my dear son, that for the honour
  Of me and mine, you venture this. I thank
  Your love, and bless the dear, fine zeal you show.
  First now, consult your father, since I'd like
  To know how it strikes him. As for myself
  I could not have been happier about it.

ALDERMAN. But you should know the girl's opinion first.

ESTEBAN. Don't worry about that. The bargain's made.
  I'll bet they had it settled long ago.
  As for the dowry, we can deal with that
  Now, on the spot. I've got a little hoard
  Which I'll be pleased to settle on you both.

FRONDOSO. I don't want any dowry, sir, at all:
  Don't let's get saddened about such affairs.

ALDERMAN. You should be glad he doesn't ask for her
  Stark naked.

ESTEBAN.   Well, we'll ask *her* what she thinks
  If you don't mind.

FRONDOSO.   Yes, that is just. You ask her.
  Opinions should be studied, not ignored.

ESTEBAN, *calling.* Daughter! Laurencia!

  LAURENCIA, *entering to them.*

LAURENCIA.   Yes, my lord and father?

ESTEBAN, *to the* ALDERMAN.

  See if I told you right! You see how quickly
  She answered me.

To LAURENCIA.

     Laurencia, my darling,
I've sent to know your mind about this question.
Come over here. D'you think that your friend, Gila,
Should be the wife of young Frondoso? He
Seems to be quite as upright a young man
As any in the village.

LAURENCIA.   Gila's marrying?

ESTEBAN. If any one deserves him, she's his equal.

LAURENCIA. I say so too.

ESTEBAN.   Yes, but I say she's ugly
And that Frondoso would be better mated
With you.

LAURENCIA. Why, Father, haven't you forgotten
In your old age this scurvy jesting habit?

ESTEBAN. Well, do you love him?

LAURENCIA.   Yes, I am his. He's mine
But there is this affair . . .

ESTEBAN.   Shall I agree?

LAURENCIA. You say the word for me.

ESTEBAN.   The keys are mine
And it is done.

  To the ALDERMAN.

    Let's go and find his father
Down in the village square.

ALDERMAN.   Yes, come, let's go.

ESTEBAN, *to* FRONDOSO. What shall I say to him about the
  dowry?
I can well spare for you a cool four thousand
Maravedis.

FRONDOSO. Why, sir, discuss it now?
It's wounding to my honour.

ESTEBAN.   Don't talk nonsense.
That is a thing you will get over quickly.
To lose a dowry, why, you'll miss a lot.

  Exeunt ESTEBAN *and* ALDERMAN.

LAURENCIA. Frondoso, are you glad?

FRONDOSO.   What! Am I glad?
  I think I shall go mad with all the joy
  And the good feeling in my heart. Laurencia,
  My heart seems darting laughter from my eyes
  To see you at long last in my possession.

The country near Ciudad Real

Enter the MASTER OF CALATRAVA, *the* COMENDADOR, FLORES,
and ORTUÑO.

COMENDADOR. Fly, Master, now there is no other way!

MASTER. It was the weakness of the rampart caused it
  And the great strength of the invading army.

COMENDADOR. It cost them blood and many thousand lives.

MASTER. But they can never boast it to their glory
  The flag of Calatrava graced their spoils
  With other captured standards.

COMENDADOR.   None the less,
  Girón, your proudest hopes are in the dust.

MASTER. It's not my fault if fortune blindly heaves me
  Aloft today, and then tomorrow leaves me.

VOICES *within.* Victory for the monarchs of Castile!

MASTER. The battlements are crowned with lights, the windows
  Of all the highest towers are hung with banners
  And with victorious flags.

COMENDADOR.   It cost them dear,
  Rather a funeral than a feast, I fear
  For them today.

MASTER.   I'll home to Calatrava,
  Fernando Gómez.

COMENDADOR.   I to Fuente Ovejuna
  While you continue following your cause
  Or yield yourself up to the Catholic King.

MASTER. I'll write to you what I intend to do.

COMENDADOR. Yes, time will teach you.

MASTER.   Though so young, yet time
With his deceitful rigour proves my master.

The country near Fuente Ovejuna

Enter, in a crowd, MUSICIANS, MENGO, FRONDOSO, LAUREN-
CIA, PASCUALA, BARRILDO, ESTEBAN, *and* JUAN ROJO.

MUSICIANS, *singing.*
                    Long live the bridegroom
                    Long live the bride.

MENGO. Your singing must be difficult.

BARRILDO. D'you think that music made by you
Would have a happier result?

FRONDOSO. Poor Mengo, you're so black and blue,
You know far more of blows and curses
Than notes and tremolos and verses.

MENGO. There is one in this place knows how
To stop your junketing I vow,
And that's the grim Comendador!

BARRILDO. That's enough, Mengo! Say no more!
That foul, barbarian, murderous stot
Has of our honour robbed the lot.

MENGO. He had me beaten by a hundred
Men in turn. Is it to be wondered,
When I had nothing but a sling,
That I submitted to this thing?
It was both heathen and herètic
To force so powerful an emetic
Upon a man of such good fame
Though modesty conceals his name . . .
How can you bear with it? For shame!

BARRILDO. Why, for a joke!

MENGO.   There is no laughter

In such a dose. It feels like flame,
And makes you wish to die thereafter.

FRONDOSO. I ask you if your rhyme's in season—
Too coarse either for rhyme or reason!

MENGO. Well, listen. "May the bride together
With her bridegroom make good weather,
Nor ever feel the need to quarrel,
Nor jealousy at things immoral,
And may they in this way behave
Till, tired of living, to the grave
They're trundled off in the same hearse!
Long live the pair!"

FRONDOSO.   May heaven curse
The poet who spawns such a verse.

BARRILDO. He made it quickly on the spot.

MENGO. Talking of poets, have you not
Seen doughnut-bakers at their toil
Chuck chunks of dough into the oil
To fill their cauldron on the boil?
Some come out cooked, some come out charred,
Some come out soft, some come out hard.
Well, that's how poets (I suppose)
Deal with the poems they compose.
Choosing one's matter, just like duff,
In different shapes one kneads the stuff
Then flings it in his paper pot
Hoping to make a lucky shot
And smother up with treacle thick
Such thoughts as might make people sick.
But when he touts the things for sale
On nobody can he prevail.
At last then (without praise or pelf)
He must digest them by himself.

BARRILDO. Hush! let the lovers speak, quit fooling, Mengo.

LAURENCIA. Give us your hands to kiss.

JUAN ROJO.   Yes, my dear niece,
After you and Frondoso kiss your father's.

ESTEBAN. Rojo, to her and her good man, may heaven
   Grant deepest blessings!

FRONDOSO.   You two, bless us both.

JUAN ROJO. Now all together sing, since they are one!

MUSICIANS *sing.*

>   Through Fuente Ovejuna's valleys
>   A long-haired girl goes light of foot
>   A knight of Calatrava sallies,
>   With his red cross, in her pursuit.
>   So she hides in bushes green
>   To conceal her wrath and shame,
>   Feigning that she has not seen
>   That running on her tracks he came.
>   *O why do you hide there*
>   *My lovely girl, alone?*
>   *For my desires can fare*
>   *Through walls and see through stone.*
>
>   The nobleman comes near her now
>   And, she confused and frightened, tries
>   Closer to pull each sheltering bough
>   To hide her beauty from his eyes.
>   But since, for one who is in love,
>   No obstacle was ever met
>   On seas beneath or peaks above,
>   He goes on singing to her yet:
>   *O why do you hide there,*
>   *My lovely girl, alone?*
>   *For my desires can fare*
>   *Through walls and see through stone.*

Enter the COMENDADOR, FLORES, ORTUÑO, CIMBRANOS.

COMENDADOR. On with the wedding! Don't let *me* disturb you.

JUAN ROJO. This is no game, my lord; we're glad to take
   Your orders. May we find a seat for you?
   What tidings of your warlike enterprise?
   I'll wager that you conquered.

FRONDOSO.   I am lost!
   May heaven save me!

LAURENCIA.   Fly from here, Frondoso!

COMENDADOR. Don't let him go. Arrest him. Tie him up.

JUAN ROJO. Obey, my lad.

FRONDOSO. You want them, then, to kill me?

COMENDADOR. I'm not the sort of man to kill a fellow
Who's guiltless. If I were, these soldiers here
Would have already riddled you clean through.
I order him to gaol where his own father
Will have to judge and sentence him, as mayor.

PASCUALA. Why, sir, he's getting married.

COMENDADOR. Getting married?
What's that to me? Are there no more young men?

PASCUALA. If he offended you, you should forgive him
Being who you are.

COMENDADOR. Pascuala, I don't count
For anything in this affair at all.
It was that he insulted the Grand Master,
Téllez Girón, whom God preserve; he raised
His arm against the Order; aimed a crossbow
At its most holy symbol; and must suffer
Due punishment to stand as an example
Because it touches on the Master's honour.
Some others might rebel against his rule
Elsewhere, and raise their standards in the field.
It would not do to pardon one who threatened
The Master's Grand Comendador with death
As you all know he did the other day.
What loyal subjects!

ESTEBAN. As his father-in-law
I'll plead for him. Surely it is not much
That a young man in love should lose control
With you since you were ravishing his bride!
Surely he might defend her! That's no crime!

COMENDADOR. Mayor! You are an interfering fool!

ESTEBAN. It's for your virtue's sake, my lord.

COMENDADOR. I never
Annoyed his bride—since she was not his bride then!

ESTEBAN. Yes, you molested her. Let this suffice you.

There are a pair of monarchs in Castile
Who are giving out new laws and making havoc
Of old abuses. They would do great wrong,
When resting from their victories, to permit
That lords and barons in the villages
Should be allowed to tyrannise and murder
Because they wear big crosses on their breasts!
Let great King Ferdinand put on the cross,
For such a symbol is for true-born princes!

COMENDADOR. Hey! Take away his staff of office from him!

ESTEBAN. Take it! You're welcome to the useless bauble.

COMENDADOR. And now I'm going to batter him with it
As I would any horse that gets too frisky!

Breaks the staff on ESTEBAN's *head.*

ESTEBAN. Being a vassal, I must suffer this.

PASCUALA. How dare you strike an aged man like that?

LAURENCIA. If you thrash him because he is my father—
What is it in me you would take revenge on?

COMENDADOR. Take her and guard her for me with ten soldiers!

Exeunt COMENDADOR *and his followers, dragging* LAURENCIA *and* FRONDOSO.

ESTEBAN. May justice come down from on high!
Exit.

PASCUALA.   The wedding
Has turned into a day of bitter mourning.
Exit.

BARRILDO. Will no man raise his voice?

MENGO.   I've had my flogging
Already, just for raising it a little.
I've got the seven cardinal colours striped
Upon my hide, and yet I never went
To Rome to fetch them.

JUAN ROJO.   All shall raise our voices!

MENGO. Well, sirs, it seems to me all should be silent.
My buttocks are like slices of raw salmon.

ACT III

Council chamber in Fuente Ovejuna

Enter ESTEBAN, ALONSO, BARRILDO.

ESTEBAN. Have they not come yet to the council?

BARRILDO.   No.

ESTEBAN. Unless they're quick, we run a mortal danger.

BARRILDO. Most of the people have been warned already.
Frondoso is in shackles in the tower.
Laurencia, my girl's in such a plight
That unless God comes quickly to our aid . . .
Enter JUAN ROJO *and the* ALDERMAN. MENGO *after them.*

JUAN ROJO. Why are you shouting, when our enterprise
Depends on secrecy, Esteban?

ESTEBAN. That I'm so silent should surprise you more
Considering my wrongs.

MENGO.   I've also come
To sit on this great council.

ESTEBAN.   An old man
Whose snow-white beard is watered by his eyes,
You honourable farmers, asks of you
What funeral oration should be made
For our lost country and its trampled honour?
Yet of what use to mourn our honours now,
Since which of you has not been vilely injured
By this barbarian? Answer! Is there one
Among you who does not feel that his honour
And life have not been utterly destroyed?
Are all of you not sick of mere lamenting?
Then, since you have lost all that is worth while,
What are you waiting for? What worse misfortune?

JUAN ROJO. We've suffered that already—the world's worst!
But since it now is manifest and public
The King and Queen have pacified Castile,

And now, from Córdoba, are on the way.
Let's send two councillors to beg their mercy
And ask them to deliver us from woe.

BARRILDO. While Ferdinand is humbling to the earth
So many stronger enemies far off,
The greater wars absorb his time and strength:
Some other swifter method should be found.

ALDERMAN. If you would hear my voice, my vote should be
That we desert this village, one and all.

JUAN ROJO. There is not time enough for such a move.

MENGO. If anyone should hear this noisy meeting
It would cost several lives amongst the council.

ALDERMAN. But now the mast of patience has been splintered
Our ship drives on beyond the scope of fear
To that of desperation. From her wedding
They take the daughter of an honoured mayor,
Breaking his staff upon his own white head.
What slave has ever suffered such injustice?

JUAN ROJO. What do you think the people should attempt?
Die, or else perish in the bold attempt
Since they are few and we are many.

BARRILDO.   How!
To arm ourselves against our rightful lord?

ESTEBAN. The King alone, after our God in heaven,
Is our true lord. All right of mastership
Is forfeited by inhumanity.
With God to help our zeal, why fear the cost?

MENGO. Look, sirs, be very cautious in such projects.
I came here on the part of simple peasants
Who suffer the worst injuries of all—
And I must also represent their fears.

JUAN ROJO. If what we've suffered far outweighs the loss
Of life that's scarce worth living—why hold back?
They burn our barns, our vineyards, and our farms.
Tyrants they are. To vengeance let us go!
Enter LAURENCIA, *dishevelled and torn.*

LAURENCIA. Let me inside! For well I have the right

To enter into council with the men
Since if I cannot vote, at least I can
Scream out aloud. Do any of you know me?

ESTEBAN. Great God in heaven! Can this be my daughter?

JUAN ROJO. Do you not know Laurencia?

LAURENCIA.   I have come
In such condition, that you well may wonder
Who this is here.

ESTEBAN.   My daughter!

LAURENCIA.   Do not call me
Your daughter!

ESTEBAN.   Why, my dear one, tell me why?

LAURENCIA. For many reasons and of these the weightiest
Is that you neither rescued me from traitors
Nor yet took vengeance on those bestial tyrants
Whom you let kidnap me! I was not yet
Frondoso's, so you can't fob off on him
The duty of avenging me. On you
The duty lies as well. Until the night
When marriage is fulfilled and consummated,
It is the father's duty, not the husband's.
When one has bought a gem, till it's delivered
The buyer does not pay. It is not he
Who has to guard it from the hands of robbers
Till it's been handed over. I was taken
Under your eyes to Fernán Gómez' house
While you looked on like coward shepherds, letting
The wolf escape uninjured with the sheep.
They set their daggers to my breasts! The vileness
And filth of what they said to me! The threats
They made to tear me limb from limb! The foul
And bestial tricks by which they tried to have me!
Do you not see my hair torn out? These cuts
And bruises and the bleeding flesh that shows
Through my torn rags? You call yourselves true men?
Are you my parents and relations, you
Whose entrails do not burst with grief to see me
Reduced to this despair? You're all tame sheep!

Fuente Ovejuna means the fount where sheep drink—
And now I see the reason! Cowards, give
Me weapons! You are stones and bronze and marble
And tigers—tigers? no! for tigers follow
The stealers of their cubs, and kill the hunters
Before they can escape back to their ships.
No, you are craven rabbits, mice, and hares!
You are not Spaniards but barbarian slaves!
Yes, you are hens to suffer that your women
By brutal force should be enjoyed by others.
Put spindles in your belts. Why wear those swords?
As God lives now, I shall make sure that women
Alone redeem our honour from these tyrants,
And make these traitors bleed! And as for you,
You chickenhearted nancy-boys and sissies,
Spinning-wheel gossips and effeminate cowards,
We will throw stones at you and have you dressed
In petticoats and crinolines and bonnets,
With rouge and powder on your pansy faces!
Now the Comendador's about to hang
Frondoso up alive, to starve and die,
Head downwards from the castle's battlements,
And so he'll soon be doing with you all!
But I am glad of it, you half-men, since
The town will thus be ridded of its women,
And thus become a town of Amazons
Like me, to be the wonder of the age.

ESTEBAN. I am not one who suffers such vile titles.
I shall rebel, though it should be alone
And all the world against me.

JUAN ROJO.   So will I!
Though frightened by the greatness of our foe.

ALDERMAN. Let us all die, rather than cringe!

BARRILDO.   Unfurl
A cloth upon a pole to be our banner!
Death and destruction to this breed of monsters!

JUAN ROJO. What order shall we march in?

MENGO.   Without order!
Let's kill him straight! One cry will join the people

Since they are all agreed upon his death!

ESTEBAN. Then arm yourselves! Grab swords and pikes and
    cudgels,
Crossbows and slings and anything you can!

MENGO. Long live the Catholic Kings, our rightful masters!

ALL. Long live the Kings!

MENGO.   Death to the bloody tyrants!

ALL. Death to the traitor-tyrants one and all!

    Exeunt all the men.

LAURENCIA. March on! And may the heavens hear your cry!

    Shouting very loudly.

All women of the village, join the ranks!
The time has come now to retrieve our honour!

    Enter PASCUALA, JACINTA, *and other women to* LAURENCIA.

PASCUALA. What's this? What are you shouting for so loudly?

LAURENCIA. Can't you see how they've all gone off to kill
Fernando Gómez—dotards, boys, and men,
All furiously rushing to the fray?
And we, the women, must we yield the honour
Of such a noble action to the men,
Since we have suffered far more harm than them?

JACINTA. Well, what do you propose to do?

LAURENCIA.   Line up!
In order! For we'll show the world today
A deed which centuries will hear with awe
When we are dead and gone. Jacinta, here,
Your greater wrongs earn you the higher rank
So you will be the corporal of the band.

JACINTA. Your own wrongs are not less than mine.

LAURENCIA.   Pascuala,
You will be the ensign.

PASCUALA.   Give me the flag
To hoist upon a lance, and you will see
Whether I merited the rank or not.

LAURENCIA. There is no time. Strike while the iron's hot!
Let kerchiefs, shawls, and bonnets be our standards!

PASCUALA. Now we'll elect our captain.

LAURENCIA.   There's no need.

PASCUALA. Why?

LAURENCIA.   Because, when I go into action—watch me!
You will not need the Cid or Rodomont![4]

The hall in the Comendador's castle

Enter FRONDOSO *with his hands tied,* FLORES, ORTUÑO,
CIMBRANOS, *and the* COMENDADOR.

COMENDADOR. Whatever rope's left over from his hands
Will do to hang him from and hurt the worse.

FRONDOSO. Oh, what an evil name your birth retrieves!

COMENDADOR. Now hang him from that nearest battlement.

FRONDOSO. My lord, I never did intend the deed
When shouldering the crossbow.

A great noise is heard.

FLORES.   What's the uproar?

COMENDADOR. What does it mean?

FLORES.   Like thunder from the highest
It breaks in on our judgment.

More noise.

ORTUÑO.   All the doors
Are being crashed and splintered into dust!

A tremendous noise.

COMENDADOR. What? Breaking in the doors of my own house?
And the headquarters of the Order?

FLORES.   Yes!
The whole town has arrived in force together.

JUAN ROJO, *within.* Kill, destroy, burn, crush, and smash them
all!

4 Heroes of rival peoples (Spanish and Saracen) and of rival
literatures (Spanish and Italian). The latter gave a word to the
English language: rodomontade. [E.B.]

ORTUÑO. These mob revolts are nasty to controll!

COMENDADOR. You mean they've risen against me?

FLORES.   Not only risen.
Your gates are sprawling headlong to their fury
And they are here on top of you!

COMENDADOR, *pointing to* FRONDOSO. Untie him.
And humour this poor bumpkin of a mayor,
Frondoso, if you can.

FRONDOSO.   I'll go: it's only
Through love they have committed this offence.
He goes out. The voice of MENGO *is heard from within.*

MENGO, *within.* Long live King Ferdinand and Isabel!
Death to the traitors here!

FLORES.   Don't be found here,
My lord, for God's sake!

COMENDADOR.   Let them try to force it!
This central hall is very strongly walled
And guarded. Soon enough they will slink home.

FLORES. When a whole people which has been outraged
Makes up its mind, it never goes back home
Without its freight of vengeance and red blood.

COMENDADOR. In this great door, as if at a portcullis,
We can defend ourselves against them all.

FRONDOSO, *within.* Long live Fuente Ovejuna!

COMENDADOR, *derisively.*   What a captain!
Set on them, and you'll see their fury fade!

FLORES. By your own fury, sir, I'm more dismayed!

Enter ESTEBAN, FRONDOSO, JUAN ROJO, MENGO, BARRILDO,
and other PEASANTS, *all armed.*

ESTEBAN. Now we confront the tyrant and his flunkeys!
Fuente Ovejuna, let those tyrants die!

COMENDADOR. Wait, my good people.

ALL.   Insults cannot wait!

COMENDADOR. Tell me your injuries, and I'll repair them,
I swear upon my knighthood and my faith.

ALL. Fuente Ovejuna! Long live the Catholic Kings!
And death to all bad Christians and to traitors!

COMENDADOR. Will you not listen to me? I'm your master!

ALL. The Catholic King and Queen are now our masters!

COMENDADOR. Here, wait a minute!

ALL.   Die, Fernando Gómez!
Long live Fuente Ovejuna!

Exeunt fighting, the COMENDADOR *driven back by the insurgents.*

Enter the women, armed.

LAURENCIA. Halt at this door. You are no longer women
But desperate legionnaires.

PASCUALA.   Those poor old pansies
We once called men, it seems, are men once more
And letting out his blood!

JACINTA.   Throw down his body
And we'll impale the carcass on our spears.

ESTEBAN, *within.* Die, foul Comendador!

COMENDADOR, *within.*   I'm dying
And may the Lord have mercy on my soul
And pity for my monstrous sins.

BARRILDO, *within.*   Here's Flores!

MENGO, *within.* Have at him! He's the very man that sliced me
Across my back two thousand fiery lashes.

FRONDOSO, *within.* I would not be avenged were I to spare him.

LAURENCIA. We'll enter now.

PASCUALA.   Wait! Let us guard the door!

BARRILDO, *within.*
What! soften us with tears? You scurvy cowards
Who were the lords and masters of us all?

LAURENCIA. I can't wait, Pascuala, I must enter.
My sword is sick of loafing in its sheath.
Exit.

BARRILDO, *within.* Ortuño too! Ortuño!

FRONDOSO, *within.*   Slash his face!

Suddenly enter FLORES *from within,* MENGO *pursuing him.*

FLORES. Have mercy, Mengo, it was not my fault:
  I was obeying orders.

MENGO.   If you don't
  Deserve it 'cause you are a filthy pimp
  You more than merit it for flogging me!

PASCUALA. You give him to us women, Mengo, now.
  Stop flogging him. Just hand him over. Lovely!

MENGO. I've given him enough to pay my stripes.

PASCUALA. I shall avenge you more.

MENGO.   Well, fire ahead!

JACINTA. Die, dirty rat!

FLORES.   What, to be killed by women?

JACINTA. Weren't women in your line?

PASCUALA.   What tears are those?

JACINTA. Die, traitor, and the pandar to his vices!

LAURENCIA, *within.* Die, you dirty devil!

FLORES.   Have pity on me, ladies!

  Enter ORTUÑO *fleeing,* LAURENCIA *after him.*

ORTUÑO. Look, but I am not him you mean!

LAURENCIA.   I know
  The creature that you are.
  To the women.

                            Go in, you women,
  Kill! Finish off these villains once for all!

PASCUALA. I shall die killing.

ALL THE WOMEN.   Live the Catholic Kings!
  Long live Fuente Ovejuna! Tyrants, die!

King's palace in Toro

  Enter KING FERDINAND, QUEEN ISABEL, *and* DON MANRIQUE,
  Master of Santiago.

DON MANRIQUE. Having foreseen and calculated well
  We carried out our plans with few obstructions.

There wasn't much resistance. If there had been
It would have fizzled out. Cabra is busy
And well-prepared against a chance attack.

KING. He has done well. The way to help him best
Is to reorganise our force and send
Covering troops. The King of Portugal
Can be checkmated thus. The Count of Cabra
Is in the key position where he is.
That's to the good. He's one who knows his work.

Enter FLORES, *wounded.*

FLORES. Great Catholic King Ferdinand, to whom
God grants, as worthiest of His knights, to wear
The diadem of Castile, I come to tell you
Of the worst cruelty the sun has seen,
From rise to set, among the whole world's peoples!

KING. Come, come, contain yourself.

FLORES.   My sovereign lord,
My wounds prevent me from more lengthy detail,
Since I am near my death and bleeding fast.
I've come from Fuente Ovejuna where
The village people slew their rightful lord
Fernando Gómez who lies mangled by
Disloyal vassals for a trivial cause.
The countryfolk proclaimed him as a "tyrant"
And worked themselves to frenzy with this cry.
They burst his doors in though he made the promise,
Upon his knightly faith, of reparation
To all whom he had injured. Deaf to prayers,
With ruthless fury, they all fell on him
And, with a thousand cruel wounds, destroyed
A breast that bore the cross of Calatrava.
Then, from the topmost windows, down they hurled him
To fall upon the serried pikes and swords
The women held upright to catch his body.
They clawed out all his beard and half his hair
And hacked his face about with fearful gashes
As his poor corpse was carried to the channel.
Their brutal fury raged to such a height,
His very ears were bargained for, as trophies,

And fetched high prices. After this was done
They chipped away with pikes the coat-of-arms
Over his gateway, saying they were hateful,
And that they would supplant them with your own.
They sacked his palace, and they shared the plunder
As though he'd been a foe in open war.
I saw all this from where I hid, for fate
Would not permit my miserable life
To end just then but thus I lay till night
Permitted my escape to tell of it.
Great lord, since you are just, punish the villains
With a just sentence for their barbarous crimes.
Fernando's blood cries out to you for vengeance
And rigorous justice.

KING.   You may rest assured
They'll not remain unpunished. This sad thing
Amazes me. A judge must go forthwith
To verify this case and make examples
Of those who're guilty. Let him take a captain
For his protection. Such barefaced rebellion
As this requires exemplary chastisement.
Attend that soldier's wounds.

Town square in Fuente Ovejuna

*The village people and their women come in with the head
of* FERNANDO GÓMEZ *on a lance.*

MUSICIANS, *singing.*

> Long life to Ferdinand our King
> And to Queen Isabel
> But death to all the tyrants
> That on this earth may dwell!

BARRILDO. Now it's Frondoso's turn, to say
His piece of verse.

FRONDOSO.   I have no art.
Although my lines may limp astray

Forgive them, coming from my heart:
Long live the lovely Isabel
And Ferdinand of Aragón,
In one and other's arms to dwell,
Each with each, and both as one!
Then may the great Archangel Michael
Raise them in glory to the sky!
Long live the Kings for many a cycle
But let all tyrants quickly die!

LAURENCIA. Your turn, Barrildo!

BARRILDO.   I don't mind.
I've thought mine out with studious care.

PASCUALA. Say it with care, too; then you'll find
It will sound even yet more rare!

BARRILDO. Long live the famous Kings, since they
              Have been so many times victorious,
              And may they come to reign, some day,
              As our own masters, great and glorious!
              In triumph, over dwarfs and giants,
              We wish them power to rise on high
              But to all tyrants shout defiance!
              Forever may they burst and die!

MUSICIANS, *singing*.

              Long life to Ferdinand our King
              And to Queen Isabel
              But death to all the tyrants
              That on this earth may dwell!

LAURENCIA. Now, Mengo, you recite.

FRONDOSO.   Yes, you!

MENGO. I am no "true-blue" as to verse.

PASCUALA. Rather you mean, and it's quite true,
You're black and blue on your *reverse!*

MENGO. Well, here goes, without more verbosity:
That fellow, on a Sunday morning
Had my back thrashed with such ferocity
It put my hide in hues of mourning
But now I feel no animosity.

Long live the Kings of Christianosity
And perish thus all Tyrannosity!

MUSICIANS, *singing*.

>   Long life to Ferdinand our King
>   And to Queen Isabel
>   But death to all the tyrants
>   That on this earth may dwell!

ESTEBAN. Take out that head.

MENGO.   How horribly it grins!

Enter JUAN ROJO *carrying the Royal Arms on a shield.*

ALDERMAN. The new Arms have arrived.

ESTEBAN.   Let's look at them!

JUAN ROJO. Where shall we place them?

ALDERMAN.   Here, on the Town Hall.

ESTEBAN. A splendid shield!

BARRILDO.   What happiness it means!

FRONDOSO. With this new sun, our day begins to break.

ESTEBAN. Long live Castile, León, and Aragón!
Die, tyranny, forever! But now heed me,
Fuente Ovejuna! Hear an old man's words,
Whose counsel never harmed a soul among you.
The King will wish to clarify this case
And, since the town lies in his journey's route,
You should agree on what you'll have to say
When they examine you, as well they may.

FRONDOSO. What's your advice?

ESTEBAN.   If they ask who is guilty,
Die saying "Fuente Ovejuna" only.
Not one word more.

FRONDOSO.   Nothing could be more straight!
Fuente Ovejuna did it.

ESTEBAN.   Will you all
Answer thus?

ALL.   Yes.

ESTEBAN.   Now let me just pretend
I'm the examiner, and we'll rehearse

The better, thus, what we must say and do.
Say Mengo, here, is being put to torture.

MENGO. Can you find no one thinner to stretch out?

ESTEBAN. Come, don't be foolish, Mengo! Were you thinking
This was in earnest?

MENGO.   Well, say on, then! Do!

ESTEBAN. Who was it murdered the Comendador?

MENGO. Fuente Ovejuna did it.

ESTEBAN.   Now, you dog!
Do you want to be racked in half?

MENGO.   My lord!
Although I die . . .

ESTEBAN.   Confess, you knave!

MENGO.   I do.

ESTEBAN. Well, who was it?

MENGO.   It was Fuente Ovejuna.

ESTEBAN. Give him an extra turn!

MENGO.   Why, that is nothing!

ESTEBAN. A fig, then, for the worst the judge can do!

Another ALDERMAN *enters.*

SECOND ALDERMAN. What's going on here?

FRONDOSO.   Why, what is the matter,
Cuadrado?

SECOND ALDERMAN. The examining judge has come.

ESTEBAN. Then scatter round the town.

SECOND ALDERMAN.   He is attended,
Too, by a captain and his troops.

ESTEBAN.   Although
The devil came himself, we'll not be daunted.
You know now the one word we all must answer.

SECOND ALDERMAN. They are arresting everyone on sight.

ESTEBAN. Don't fear. Who murdered the Comendador,
Eh, Mengo?

MENGO.   Who? Why, Fuente Ovejuna!

Palace of the Master of Calatrava in Almagro

Enter the MASTER *and a soldier.*

MASTER. That such a thing could happen! What a fate!
I almost feel like putting you to death
For bringing such black news.

SOLDIER.   I only brought it
As messenger, not to arouse your anger.

MASTER. To think an angry mob could dare so much!
I'll take five hundred men to raze the village
That not one person's name shall be remembered!

SOLDIER. Contain your rage, my lord. They have declared
Their loyalty to the King. Your one last hope
Is not to anger him more than you've done.

MASTER. How can they give their village to the King
Since they are of my Order?

SOLDIER.   That will be
A legal matter to discuss with him.

MASTER. No legal powers affect the papal tenure,
Yet I must recognise the King and Queen
And pay them homage; so I'll curb my rage
Till I have come to some accommodation.
For though they hold me heavily to blame,
My youth will plead for me. I go with shame—
Compelled to go that I may save my honour,
For one must not be careless in that cause.

The square in Fuente Ovejuna

Enter LAURENCIA, *alone.*

LAURENCIA. Loving, to know the loved one is in danger
Doubles the pangs of love; foreseeing harms

Adds fears to fears and multiplies alarms.
The firm untroubled mind, to tears a stranger,
Melts at the touch of fear. The steadfast faith,
If fear comes near it, flickers like a wraith,
Imagining the dear one snatched away.
I love my husband. Yet when he is near,
Fearing his harm, I am a prey to fear;
And when he's absent, I am in worse dismay.

Enter FRONDOSO.

FRONDOSO. Laurencia!

LAURENCIA.   My beloved husband, how
Dare you be seen round here?

FRONDOSO.   Is this the way
You welcome my most loving care?

LAURENCIA.   My dearest,
Seek safety. You're in deadly peril here!

FRONDOSO. May heaven forbid that you're not glad to see me!

LAURENCIA. Do you not fear the cruelty of the judge?
And how he's treated others? Save your life
And do not court worse danger!

FRONDOSO.   Save a life
So ill-received? Should I desert my friends
And lose the sight of you in this great danger?
Do not tell *me* to fly. It is unthinkable
That I should make an alien of my blood
On such a terrible occasion.

Cries within.

                          Listen
I can hear cries—of someone being tortured,
If my ears tell me truly. Listen hard.

The voice of the JUDGE *can now be heard from within with
the replies of the* PEASANTS.

JUDGE, *within.* Now, good old man, speak nothing but the
    truth!

FRONDOSO. It's an old man they're putting on the rack.

LAURENCIA. How dastardly!

ESTEBAN, *within.*   Can they leave off?

JUDGE, *within*.   Relax him.
Now speak! Who was it killed Fernando Gómez?

ESTEBAN, *within*. Fuente Ovejuna did it.

LAURENCIA.   Oh, my father!
Your name be praised forever to the skies!

FRONDOSO. Oh, grand example!

JUDGE, *within*.   Now let's rack that boy there.
You, puppy! Yes, I know you've got the answer!
Who was it? Are you silent? Give more turns,
You bungling torturer!

BOY, *within*.   Fuente Ovejuna!

JUDGE, *within*. I'd have you hanged, you riffraff, were I able.
Now on the King's life, tell me who it was!
Who murdered the Comendador?

FRONDOSO.   That they
Could torture a child thus, and he resist them!

LAURENCIA. Oh, valiant people!

FRONDOSO.   Very brave and strong!

JUDGE, *within*. Let's have that woman on the rack at once.
To torturer.
And get that lever working there, come on!

LAURENCIA. He's blind with rage!

JUDGE, *within*.   I'll kill the lot of you
Upon this rack here, on my word, you wretches!
Who murdered him?

PASCUALA, *within*.   My lord, Fuente Ovejuna!

JUDGE, *within, to torturer*. Tighter!

FRONDOSO.   In vain!

LAURENCIA.   Pascuala lasted out.

FRONDOSO. When children last, how can you be surprised?

JUDGE, *within, to torturer*.
Give her some more. It seems that you enchant them.

PASCUALA, *within*. Oh, pitying heaven!

JUDGE, *within, to torturer*. You swine, can you be deaf?
Stretch her, I said!

PASCUALA, *within*.   Fuente Ovejuna did it!

JUDGE, *within, to torturer.*
  Now let's have that half-naked bag of guts,
  That fattest one of all, him, over there!

LAURENCIA. Mengo, no doubt!

FRONDOSO.   He will break down, I fear.

MENGO, *within.* Ay! Ay!

JUDGE, *within.* Now turn the lever of the screw!

MENGO, *within.* Ay!

JUDGE, *within, to torturer.*
  Turn! More! Are you in need of help?

MENGO, *within.*   Ay! Ay!

JUDGE, *within.* Who murdered the Comendador, base villain?

MENGO, *within.* Ay! Ay! I'll tell Your Lordship.

JUDGE, *within, to torturer.*   Now relax it.

FRONDOSO. He will confess!

  A pause—no answer from MENGO.

JUDGE, *within, to torturer.* Put your shoulder this time
  Against the lever!

MENGO, *within.*   Wait! I've had enough.
  I'll tell you all, if you'll but let me free.

JUDGE, *within.* Who was it?

MENGO, *within.*   Why, my lord, to tell the truth . . .
  Little old Fuente Ovejunita did it!

JUDGE, *within.* Was ever such a stubborn villainy?
  They seem to make a jest of agony,
  And he from whom I hoped the most results
  Was far more strongly stubborn than the rest.
  Leave them. I am exhausted. Let them go!

FRONDOSO. Oh, Mengo, may God bless your honest soul!
  With fear enough for two I trembled here
  But fear for you had quite effaced that fear!

  Enter MENGO, BARRILDO, *and the* ALDERMAN.

BARRILDO. Mengo has conquered!

ALDERMAN.   As you see!

BARRILDO. Mengo's the victor!

FRONDOSO.   I agree!

MENGO. Ay! Ay! Ay! Ay!

BARRILDO. Come drink and eat!
Here, take this bowl, this stuff's a treat!

MENGO. Ay! Ay!

FRONDOSO. Pour him another jug!

BARRILDO. The way it gurgles down his mug!

FRONDOSO. It does him good. He soaks it neat.

LAURENCIA. Now give him something more to eat.

MENGO. Ay! Ay!

BARRILDO. This other is with me!

LAURENCIA. Just look how solemnly he's drinking.

FRONDOSO. One who defies the rack, I'm thinking,
Needs a good drink!

ALDERMAN. The next, with me?

MENGO. Ay! Ay! Yes! Yes!

FRONDOSO. Drink! You deserve it!

LAURENCIA. He soaks as fast as one can serve it.

FRONDOSO. Arrange his clothes: he's getting frozen.

BARRILDO. Some more to drink?

MENGO. Yes, three rounds more!

FRONDOSO. He needs more wine.

BARRILDO. There's lots in store.
Come drink, man, drink! for you're our chosen!
To be so brave a rack-defier
Must give a thirst like raging fire.
What's wrong?

MENGO. It has a tang of rosin,
And also I've a cold in store.

FRONDOSO. Why, here's some sweet wine, if you'd sooner.
But: who killed the Comendador?

MENGO. Why! little old Fuente Ovejunita!

Exeunt all but FRONDOSO *and* LAURENCIA.

FRONDOSO. It's right that they should do him greatest honour
But who killed the Comendador, my darling?

LAURENCIA. Fuente Ovejuna killed him, dearest love.

FRONDOSO. Who really killed him? Between you and me?

LAURENCIA. Fuente Ovejuna! Do not terrify me!

FRONDOSO. And how did *I* kill *you*, then? Tell me that.

LAURENCIA. You made me die of loving you so much!

Palace of the King at Tordesillas

Enter KING FERDINAND *and* QUEEN ISABEL.

QUEEN. I did not know I'd meet with the good fortune
To find you here, my lord.

KING.   The sight of you
Brings me new glory. I was on the way
To Portugal, and had to come past here.

QUEEN. Your Majesty did well indeed to come
Since it was convenient.

KING.   What of Castile?

QUEEN. All peaceful, quiet, and smooth.

KING.   Since it was you
Who did the smoothing, I don't marvel at it.

Enter DON MANRIQUE, *Master of Santiago.*

DON MANRIQUE. Seeking an audience with Your Majesties
The Master of the Calatrava Order
Has just arrived.

QUEEN.   I've always longed to see him.

DON MANRIQUE. I swear it by my faith, Your Majesty,
Though very young, he is a valiant soldier.

Exit.

Enter the MASTER OF CALATRAVA.

MASTER. Rodrigo Téllez Girón is my name,
Grand Master of the cross of Calatrava,
Who never stints your praises. I have come
To sue your royal pardons. Ill-advised
By those around me, I broke all just bounds,
In rash excess to brave your royal wills.

It was Fernando's counsel that deceived me,
And then my own self-interest. I was wrong.
So humbly now I beg forgiveness of you,
Which, if my supplication can deserve,
Amidst the foremost of your ranks I'll serve
And, in your next crusade against Granada,
No man shall draw his sword with fiercer verve,
For I shall plant my crimson crosses farther
Than any, on the topmost battlements!
Five hundred men I'll bring to join your tents
And I shall sign and seal a solemn oath—
Never to discontent you—to you both!

KING. Rise up then, Master, from the ground, for since
You've come to me, you shall be well received.

MASTER. You are the comforter of the afflicted.

QUEEN. You're quite as good at talking as at fighting.

MASTER. You are the lovely Esther of our age;
And you its godlike Xerxes, Majesty.

Re-enter DON MANRIQUE.

DON MANRIQUE. My lord, the judge examiner is here,
The one who went to Fuente Ovejuna.

KING, *to the* QUEEN.
Now you must judge these riotous aggressors.

MASTER, *thinking erroneously the* KING *addressed him.*
Had I not learned the lesson of your mercy,
I would have served them all a bloody lesson
In how to kill Comendadors.

KING, *to the* MASTER.   Not you.
The days when you gave judgments are no more.

MASTER *falls back rebuked.*

QUEEN, *to the* KING. Would but to God this military might
Were subject to your orders or put down.

Enter the JUDGE.

JUDGE. I went to Fuente Ovejuna, sire,
As I was bid. With all my diligence
And special care, your orders were obeyed.
But as to finding out who did the crime,

No scrap of writing can I bring in proof
Because, with one accord and single valour,
When to the question racked, they all reply:
"Fuente Ovejuna did it" and no more.
Three hundred of them, tortured on the rack
With terrible severity, replied
No other answer. Little boys of ten
Were stretched yet it was useless. Quite as vain
Were flatteries and promises and tricks.
It is so hard to verify the truth
That you must either hang the whole mad village
Or pardon every man-jack of them all.
All of them now are coming here before you
To certify the truth of all I say.

KING. Let them come in, then.

Enter the TWO MAYORS, FRONDOSO, *all the* WOMEN *and the rest of the villagers.*

LAURENCIA.   Are these two the Kings?

FRONDOSO. And very powerful ones!

LAURENCIA.   How beautiful
They are, by my faith! Saint Anthony bless them!

QUEEN. Are these the fierce aggressors we were told of?

ESTEBAN. Fuente Ovejuna greets you here, my lady,
Wishing to serve you. The dire cruelty
And most unsufferable tyranny
Of the Comendador caused all these troubles.
A thousand vile insults were showered upon us.
Our farms were robbed, our daughters forced and raped,
Because he was a man who had no pity.

FRONDOSO. So much was this the case that this young farm girl,
By heaven granted for my wife, with whom
I am by far the happiest man on earth,
Even at our wedding feast, on the first night,
Was forced into his house for his own pleasure
And if she hadn't fought with desperation . . .
There is no need to tell you any more.

MENGO. Is it not time I also had a word
If you will give me leave. You'll be astounded

At how they treated me for once defending
A girl of ours. Seeing his pimp and pandar
About to do her violence, I protested—
When that perverted Nero ordered them
To thrash my back into red salmon slices!
My bum still trembles to remember it
And I have had to spend more cash on balm
Than on my farm.

ESTEBAN.   All that we wish, my lord,
Is to become your own, whom we acknowledge
As our most natural sovereign. And your arms
Are hoisted on our village hall. Before you
We sue for mercy and yield up ourselves
As pledges of our innocence. Have mercy!

KING. Since what has happened is not verified
In writing (and it was a dreadful crime
Worthy of direst punishment), you're pardoned.
As to the town I'll keep it in my name
Until, or if, we find a rightful heir.

FRONDOSO. The King spoke grandly as one would expect
From one who such great wonders could effect.
Good night, discreet spectators, all be friends!
And with this line FUENTE OVEJUNA ends.

ناشه

THE TRICKSTER OF SEVILLE AND HIS GUEST OF STONE

Tirso de Molina

English Version by Roy Campbell

DRAMATIS PERSONAE

DON DIEGO TENORIO

DON JUAN TENORIO, *his son*

CATALINÓN, *Don Juan's lackey*

THE KING OF NAPLES

DUKE OCTAVIO

DON PEDRO TENORIO, *Don Juan's uncle and Spanish
   Ambassador in Naples*

THE MARQUIS OF LA MOTA

DON GONZALO DE ULLOA, *father of Doña Ana*

THE KING OF CASTILE [Alfonso XI, 1312–50]

DOÑA ANA

DUCHESS ISABEL

THISBE ⎫
ANFRISO ⎪
CORIDÓN ⎬ *fisherfolk*
BELISA ⎭

BATRICIO ⎫
GASENO ⎪
AMINTA ⎬ *farmfolk*
BELISA ⎭

RIPIO ⎫ *servants*
FABIO ⎭

Servants, guards, musicians, etc.

*The scene is laid in Naples, Tarragona, Seville, and Dos
   Hermanas.*
The time is the 14th Century but not consistently so.

ACT I

A room in the palace of the KING OF NAPLES

Enter DON JUAN, *with muffled face, and* ISABEL.

ISABEL. Here, Duke Octavio, here's a safe way through.

DON JUAN. Once more, dear Duchess, let me swear my troth!

ISABEL. Then may I glory in each promise, oath,
Flattery, gift, and wish—when they come true!

DON JUAN. You shall, my love.

ISABEL.   Wait while I fetch a light.

DON JUAN. Why?

ISABEL.   To convince my soul of this delight.

DON JUAN. I'll crush the lamp in pieces if you do!

ISABEL. Heavens above, what man are you? For shame!

DON JUAN. Who, I? I am a man without a name.

ISABEL. You're not the duke?

DON JUAN.   No.

ISABEL.   Help! the palace guard!

DON JUAN. Come, Duchess, give your hand. Don't shout so
hard!

ISABEL. Let go, you beast! I'll make the palace ring.
Help, soldiers, guards, and servants of the king!

Enter the KING OF NAPLES *with a lighted candle in a candle-stick.*

KING OF NAPLES. Who's there?

ISABEL, *aside.*   The king, alas!

DON JUAN.   Why, can't you see—
A man here with a woman? Her and me.

KING OF NAPLES, *aside.* Prudence in this would seem the better
plan.

He runs back so as not to recognize ISABEL.
Aloud.

Call out the palace guard! Arrest this man!

ISABEL, *covering her face*. Oh, my lost honour!

Enter DON PEDRO TENORIO, *ambassador of Spain, and guards.*

DON PEDRO.   From the king's rooms, cries
And shouting? Sire, from what did this arise?

KING OF NAPLES. Don Pedro, you take charge of this arrest.
Be shrewd and yet be prudent in your quest.
Seize and identify this muffled pair
In secret. Harm may come of this affair.
But if it proves as it appears to me,
The scandal will be less, the less I see.
Exit.

DON PEDRO. Seize him at once!

DON JUAN.   Come, which of you will dare?
I'm due to lose my life and much I care!
But I shall sell it dear and some will pay!

DON PEDRO. Kill him at once!

DON JUAN.   Now, don't be led astray.
I'm resolute to die. For not in vain
Am I a noble cavalier of Spain
And of her embassy. That being known,
Each one of you must fight with me alone:
Such is the law.

DON PEDRO.   Go, all of you, in there;
And take the woman. Leave him to my care.

The guards take ISABEL *into the next room.*

DON PEDRO. And now that we two are alone at length
Let's test this vaunted valour and this strength.

DON JUAN. Although, dear uncle, I've enough of both,
To use them on yourself I'm something loth.

DON PEDRO. Say who you are!

DON JUAN, *unmasking himself*. I shall. Your nephew, sir.

DON PEDRO, *aside*. My heart! I fear some treason is astir.

Aloud, to DON JUAN.

What's this you've done, base enemy? How is it
That in this guise you come to such a visit?

Tell me at once, since I must kill you here.
Quick! Out with it at once! And be sincere!

DON JUAN. My uncle and my lord, I'm still a lad,
As you were once. Such youthful loves you had.
Then don't blame me that I too feel for beauty.
But since you bid me tell it as a duty:
In this disguise I cheated Isabel
(Who took me for another man) and, well,
Enjoyed her——

DON PEDRO.   How could you so?
If you can lower your voice, sir, let me know.

DON JUAN, *in a lower voice.*
Pretending I was Duke Octavio.

DON PEDRO. What? Say no more! Enough!
   Aside.   If the king learns
The truth, I'm lost. Oh, by what twists and turns
Can I escape so dangerous a maze?
   Aloud.

Say, villain, was it not enough to raise,
With treachery and violence, such shame,
And with another great and noble dame
Back home in Spain but you repeat the crime,
With one that is of princely rank this time,
In the king's palace? May God punish you!
Your father from Castile had shipped you through
Safely to Naples' hospitable strand,
Who might have hoped for better at your hand
Than in return have such shame heaped upon her—
The greatest of her ladies to dishonour!
But here we're wasting time with this delay.
Think what to do and how to get away.

DON JUAN. Pardon for this offence I can't implore.
It would be insincere and, what is more,
Unmanly. My blood's yours—for you to take.
Come, let it out, and let me pay my stake!
Here at your feet, my uncle and my lord,
I offer you my lifeblood and my sword.

DON PEDRO. Curse you! Get up and fight! Prove you're a man!

This meek humility has spoilt my plan.
To slaughter in cold blood I never would.
Would you dare jump that balcony? You could?

DON JUAN. Your favour gives me wings. I surely can.

DON PEDRO. Then down you go! Seek hiding in Milan
Or Sicily!

DON JUAN.   Why, soon enough!

DON PEDRO.   You swear?

DON JUAN. Oh, surely!

DON PEDRO.   You'll be hearing from me there
The consequences of this sad affair.

DON JUAN. A pleasant one for me, you must consent.
Though I may be to blame, I'm well content.

DON PEDRO. You're led astray by youth. Quick, jump the railing!

DON JUAN. And now for Spain how happily I'm sailing!
Exit.

Enter KING OF NAPLES.

DON PEDRO. I tried to execute your orders, sire,
As well as your strict justice would require.
The man . . .

KING OF NAPLES. Is dead?

DON PEDRO.   No, he escaped the sword
And the fierce thrusts of it.

KING OF NAPLES.   How?

DON PEDRO.   Thus, my lord.
You'd hardly told your orders, when, without
More said, he gripped his sword and wheeled about,
Winding his cape around his arm, and so,
Ready to deal the soldiers blow for blow
And seeing death too near for hope of pardon,
Leaped desperately down into the garden
Over this balcony. Followed by all
They found him agonizing from his fall,
Contorted like a dying snake. But, when
They shouted "Kill him!" turning on the men
With such heroic swiftness he upstarted
As left me in confusion; and departed.

Isabel, whom I name to your surprise,
Says it was Duke Octavio in disguise
Who by this treachery enjoyed her.

KING OF NAPLES.   What?

DON PEDRO. I say what she confessed upon the spot.

KING OF NAPLES. Poor Honour! If by you our value stands
Why are you always placed in women's hands
Who are all fickleness and lightness?
Calls.   Here!
Enter a servant, and, after, ISABEL *with guards.*
Bring me the woman now! Let her appear!

DON PEDRO. The guards are bringing her already, sire.

ISABEL, *aside.* How shall I dare to face the king?

KING OF NAPLES.   Retire,
And see the doors are guarded.
Servant and guards retire.
                   Woman, say,
What force of fate, what angry planet, pray,
Makes you defile my palace and my board
With your lascivious beauty?

ISABEL.   Oh, my lord——

KING OF NAPLES. Be silent! For your tongue can never cleanse
Or gild the glaring fact of your offence.
Was it the Duke Octavio?

ISABEL.   My lord——

KING OF NAPLES. Can nothing cope with Love—guards within call,
Locks, bolts, and bars, and battlemented wall—
That he, a babe, can penetrate all these?
Don Pedro, on this very instant, seize
That woman! Place her prisoner in some tower!
Arrest the duke as well. Once in my power
I'll have him make amends for this disgrace.

ISABEL. My lord, but once upon me turn your face!

KING OF NAPLES. For your offences when my back was turned,
By the same back you now are justly spurned.

DON PEDRO. Come, Duchess.

ISABEL, *aside.*   Though I know I am to blame
    Beyond excuse, it will decrease the shame
    If Duke Octavio's forced to save my name.

Exeunt.

Enter OCTAVIO *and his servant* RIPIO.

RIPIO. You're bright and early, sir!

OCTAVIO.   No sleep or rest
    With love so fiercely burning in my breast!
    For since Love is a child, he is not eased
    With softest sheets, nor yet with ermine pleased.
    He lies down sleepless, long before the day,
    Already longing to be up and play;
    And like a child he plays and keeps on playing.
    The thoughts of Isabela keep me straying,
    Ripio, in the doldrums of despair,
    For, since she lives within my soul, my body
    Goes suffering with a load of anxious care
    To keep her honour safe whether I'm present
    Or absent.

RIPIO.   Sir, I find your love unpleasant.

OCTAVIO. What's that, you dolt?

RIPIO.   I find it very wrong
    To love as you do. Would you like to learn
    The reason why I do?

OCTAVIO.   Yes: come along!

RIPIO. You're certain that she loves you in return?

OCTAVIO. Of course, you idiot!

RIPIO.   *You* love *her?*

OCTAVIO.   I burn!

RIPIO. Why, what an idiot would I be
    To lose my reason for the dame,
    If I loved her and she loved me.
    Now, did she not return your flame,
    Then you might well keep such a coil
    Adore and flatter her and spoil
    And wait till she rewards your toil;
    But when you mutually adore

And neither in your faith miscarry,
What difficulty is there more,
What is preventing that you marry?

OCTAVIO. Such weddings are for lackeys, slaves,
  And laundry wenches.

RIPIO.   Well, what's wrong
  With a fine laundry girl who laves
  And sings and washes all day long?
  She who defends and then offends
  And spreads her linen out to see
  And is obliging to her friends
  Is good enough for such as me.
  There are no kinder people living
  Than those who give for giving's sake.
  If Isabel is not for *giving*
  Then see if she knows how to *take*.

  Enter a servant. After him, DON PEDRO.

SERVANT. The ambassador of Spain has even now
  Dismounted here. He wears a stormy brow,
  Insisting, with a fierce and angry zest,
  To speak to you. I fear it means arrest.

OCTAVIO. Arrest? For what? Go, show his lordship in.

DON PEDRO, *entering.*
  His conscience must be clear who so can win
  So late a sleep.

OCTAVIO.   But when such men as you,
  Your Excellency, come, as now you do,
  To honour and to favour such as me,
  It's wrong to sleep at all. My life should be
  An endless vigil. But what could befall
  To bring you at such hours on such a call?

DON PEDRO. The king sent me.

OCTAVIO.   Well if the king's kind thought
  Bend to me thus, I reck my life as naught
  To serve my liege, and would not count the cost
  If in the cause of honour it were lost.
  Tell me, my lord, what planet of good cheer,

What stroke of goodly fortune, brought you here
To say I am remembered by the king?

DON PEDRO. For you, Your Grace, a most unhappy thing!
I am the king's ambassador. I've brought
An embassy from him.

OCTAVIO.   Yes, so I thought.
That doesn't worry me. Say on. What is it?

DON PEDRO. It is for your arrest I make this visit,
Sent from the king: do not resist the laws.

OCTAVIO. For my arrest he sent you? For what cause?
Tell me my crime!

DON PEDRO.   You ought to know far more
Than I do, for I'm not entirely sure.
Though I may be mistaken, here's my thought,
If not my own belief, why you are sought.
Just when the giant Negroes fold their tents
Of darkness like funereal cerements,
And furtively before the dusky glow
Run jostling one another as they go,
I with His Majesty, while talking late
Of certain treaties and affairs of state
(Arch-enemies of sunlight are the great)
Heard then a woman's scream ("Help! Help!") resound
Through all the halls and corridors around,
And, as we all rushed forth to these alarms,
Found Isabel there, clasped with all her charms
By some most powerful man in lustful arms.
Whoever it could be aspired so high,
Giant, or monster of ambition, I
Was ordered to arrest him. Held at bay
I vainly strove to wrest his arms away
And well I could believe it was the Fiend
Taking a human form, for, ably screened
In dust and smoke, the balcony he lept
Down to the roots of the vast elms that swept
The palace roof. The duchess I assisted,
Who, in the presence of us all, attested
It was yourself who, husband-like, had known her.

OCTAVIO. What's that you say?

DON PEDRO.   Why, man, the whole world over
It is notorious to the public gaze
That Isabel, yes, in a thousand ways
Has . . .

OCTAVIO.   Say no more! Have mercy! Do not tell
So vile a treachery of Isabel.

Aside.

But say this were but caution on her part.

Aloud.

Go on. Say more! Speak out! But if the dart
Is poisoned that you're shooting at my heart,
Impervious to the scandal may I prove—
Unlike those gossips whom their own ears move,
Conceiving there, to give birth through their lips.
Could it be true my lady could eclipse
The memory of me, to deal me doom?
Yes: those who dream too brightly wake in gloom.
Yet in my heart I have no doubt: it seems
These happenings are naught but evil dreams
That, so to give more impulse to my sighs,
Entered my understanding in disguise.
Sir Marquis, could it be that Isabel
Deceived me? that my heart in ambush fell
And so my love was cheated? That can't be . . .
Why, the whole thing's impossible . . . that she . . .
Oh, woman! What a dreadful law is cloaked
In that word honour! Whom have I provoked
To this foul trick? Am I not honour-bound?
A man in Isabela's arms was found
Within the palace . . . Have I lost my mind?

DON PEDRO. Just as it's true that birds live in the wind,
Fish in the wave in keeping with their kind,
That all things have five elements to share,
That blessèd souls in glory know no care,
That staunchness is in friends, in foes is treason,
In night is gloom, in day is light—so reason
And truth are in the very words I say.

OCTAVIO. Marquis! My own belief will scarce obey,

And there's no thing that could astound me more!
That she, whom I as constant did adore,
Should prove no more than woman! More to know
I do not want, since it disgusts me so.

DON PEDRO. Well, since you seem so prudent. Take your pick
Of the best means . . .

OCTAVIO.   I would escape: and quick!
That's my best remedy.

DON PEDRO.   Then go with speed——

OCTAVIO. Spain then will be my harbour in my need.

DON PEDRO. —And slip out by this door while you are able.

OCTAVIO. O bending reed! O weathercock unstable!
Upon yourself alone you've turned the table
Inducing me to flee my native land
And seek my fortunes on a foreign strand!
Farewell, my country!

Aside.

                    Madness, death, and hell,
Another in the arms of Isabel!

Seashore near Tarragona

Enter THISBE, *with a fishing rod.*

THISBE. Of all whose feet the fleeting waters
Kiss (as the breezes kiss the rose
And jasmine), of the fishers' daughters
And longshore maidens, of all those
I am the only one exempt
From Love, the only one who rules
In sole, tyrannical contempt
The prisons which he stocks with fools.
Here where the slumbrous suns tread, light
And lazy, on the blue waves' trance,
And wake the sapphires with delight
To scare the shadows as they glance;

Here by white sands, so finely spun
They seem like seeded pearls to shine,
Or else like atoms of the sun
Gilded in heaven; by this brine,
Listening to the birds, I quarter,
And hear their amorous, plaintive moans
And the sweet battles which the water
Is waging with the rocks and stones.
With supple rod that bends and swishes
And seems to stoop with its own weight
I snare the little, silly fishes
That lash the sea and scarce can wait.
Or else with casting-net, deep down,
I catch as many as may live
Within the many-steepled town
Of conch-shells. I could not be gladder
Than with this freedom I enjoy,
I, whom the poison-darting adder
Of Love did never yet annoy.
And when a thousand lovelorn hearts
Pour forth their bitter plaints forlorn
I am the envy of these parts
Whose tragedies I laugh to scorn.
A thousand times, then, am I blest,
Love, since you never were my lot
But left me tranquil in my nest
And scatheless in my humble cot.
It's just an obelisk of thatch
That crowns my dwelling with its cone,
Though no cicadas it may catch,
Attracting turtledoves alone.
My virtue is preserved in straw
Like ripening fruit, or glass, that's packed
In hay (as by the selfsame law)
In order to arrive intact.
As for the fisherfolk around
Whom Tarragona's lights defend
From pirates in the Silver Sound
I am the one they most commend.
But I their soft approaches mock:

I am as granite to the wave,
To their implorings I'm a rock.
Anfriso to whom Heaven gave,
In soul and body, wondrous gifts,
Measured in speech, in action brave
Resourceful in the direst shifts,
Modest, long suffering of disdain,
Generous, valiant, tough as leather,
Has hung around my hut in vain
Haunting my caves in every weather,
Night after night, in wind or rain,
Till with his health and youth together
He gave the dawn its blush again.
Then also, with the fresh green boughs
Which he had hacked from elm-trees down,
He loves to deck my straw-built house
Which wears his flattery like a crown,
And then beneath the midnight stars
Each evening he would come to woo me
With tambourines and soft guitars.
But all of that meant nothing to me
Because in tyrannous dominion
I live, the empress of desire,
And love to clip love's rosy pinion
And of his hell to light the pyre.
The other girls for him go sighing,
Him, whom I murder with disdain.
For such is love—still to be dying
For those who hate and cause you pain.
In such contentment I employ
Without a care, each youthful year,
And any folly that I hear
Serves but to make me loth and coy
And like the wind to disappear.
My only pleasure, care, and wish
Is forth to cast my trace and hook
To every breeze, and give the fish
My baited line. But as I look
Two men have dived from yonder boat
Before the waves can suck it down.

It strikes the reef and keeps afloat
But now its poop begins to drown,
It sinks, releasing to the gale
Its topsail which finds there its home,
A kite upon the winds to sail,
One with the spindrift and the foam,
A lunatic locked in a cage—

A VOICE OUTSIDE. Help, I am drowning! Save my life!

THISBE. A man, caught in the ocean's rage,
And bravely with the seas at strife,
Upon his back his comrade saves
As once Aeneas bore Anchises,
And, strongly cleaving through the waves,
Subdues them as he falls and rises.
But on the beach there's no one standing
To lend a hand, or pull them clear.
Anfriso! Here are wrecked men landing!
Tirseo, Alfredo! Can't you hear?
But now miraculously come
Through the white surf, they step ashore
Quite out of breath the man who swum,
But still alive the one he bore.

Enter CATALINÓN *carrying* DON JUAN.

CATALINÓN. Oh, for the gift of Cana's wine!
The sea with too much salt is flavoured.
By all who swim to save their lives
Freely it may be quaffed and savoured
But deep down there is doom and slaughter
Where Davy Jones lives soused in brine.
Strange, that where God put so much water
He should forget to mix the wine!
Master! It seems he's frozen quite.
Master! What if he should be drowned?
It was the sea that caused the trouble:
What if with me the fault be found?
Bad luck to him who planted pine
As masts upon the sea to grow
And who its limits would define
With measures made of wood! Ah, no!

Cursèd be Jason and his Argo,
And Theseus, cursèd may he be,
Forever, under God's embargo!
Catalinón, unhappy me!
What can I do?

THISBE.   Why in such trouble,
Good man? Why is your life so rough?

CATALINÓN. Ah, fishermaid, my ills are double
And my good luck is not enough.
I see, to free me from his service,
My master's lifeless, is he not?

THISBE. Oh no, indeed, he's breathing yet.
Those fishermen in yonder cot—
Go call them here.

CATALINÓN.   Would they agree?

THISBE. At once! This noble—who is he?

CATALINÓN. Son of the king's high chamberlain
Expecting very soon to be
Raised to a count within a week
In Seville by His Majesty.
That's if the king and I agree.

THISBE. What is his name?

CATALINÓN.   Don Juan Tenorio.

THISBE. Then call my people.

CATALINÓN.   Yes, I'll go.

Exit CATALINÓN. THISBE *has* DON JUAN's *head on her lap.*

THISBE. Noble young man, so handsome, gay,
And exquisite, wake up, I say!

DON JUAN. Where can I be?

THISBE.   Safe from all harms
Encircled by a woman's arms.

DON JUAN. I live, who perished in the sea,
Only and utterly in thee,
And now I lose all doubt to find
Heaven about me is entwined
After the hell that was the ocean.
A frightful whirlwind wrecked my fleet

And swept me with its fierce commotion
To find a harbour at your feet.

THISBE. A lot of breath you have to waste
For one who nearly lost it all
If after such a storm you haste
To raise a tempest and a squall.
Cruel must be the ocean's thunder
The waves most vicious in their hate
If they can pull your limbs asunder
And make you talk at such a rate!
Beyond all doubt you must have taken
Salt water in above your ration,
More than you'd need to salt your bacon;
You talk in such a saucy fashion—
Quite eloquent enough, I'd say,
Lying as dead upon the beach
With all your senses well in reach
And shamming lifeless as you lay.
You seem the wooden horse of Greece
Washed at my feet for vengeance dire
Seemingly full of cold seawater
But pregnant with deceitful fire.
And if, all wet, you can ignite,
What won't you burn when you are dry?
You promise heat and fire and light,
Please God it will not prove a lie!

DON JUAN. Ah, would to God, dear country maid,
I had been swallowed by the main
So in my senses to remain
And not to lunacy betrayed
For love of you! The sea could harm me
Drowned between silver waves and blue
That roll forever out of view,
But with fierce fire it could not char me!
You share the quality that flashes
In the great sun like whom you show,
Though seeming cold and white as snow
Yet you can burn a man to ashes.

THISBE. The frostier seems your desire

All the more flame you seem to hold
That from my own kindles its fire.
Please God, it was not lies you told!

Enter CATALINÓN, ANFRISO, CORIDÓN, *and other fisherfolk.*

CATALINÓN. They have all come.

THISBE.   Your master's living.

DON JUAN. But only by your presence giving
The breath I yielded.

CORIDÓN, *to* THISBE.   What's your will?

THISBE. Anfriso, Coridón, and friends . . .

CORIDÓN. We seek to gratify you still
By every means to all your ends,
And so your orders, Thisbe, tell,
Out of those lips of fresh carnation,
To us who in your adoration
Would see that all for you goes well,
And ask no more than thus to be,
To dig the earth, to plough the sea,
To trample air or wind or fire
To satisfy your least desire.

THISBE, *aside.* How stupid used to seem to me
Their vows, and how they used to jar
But now in very truth I see
How far from flattery they are!

To the fishermen.

My friends, as I was fishing here
Upon this rock, I saw a barque
Sink in the waves. Two men swam clear.
I called for help but none would hark:
It seemed that none of you could hear.
But one of them lay lifeless here—
Brought on the back of this brave fellow—
A nobleman, who, on the yellow
Sands, lay as though upon his bier,
Very near swamped by wave and tide,
And so I sent his man to guide
And call you to revive him here.

ANFRISO. Well now, we've all arrived. You say

Your orders, though it's not the way
I usually expect from you.

THISBE. Now to my hut we'll gently take him
Where, with the gratitude that's due,
His clothing we'll repair, and make him
His rocktorn garments clean and new.
This bread of kindness that we break him
Will please my dear old father too.

CATALINÓN, *aside.* Her beauty is superb indeed.

DON JUAN. Come, listen here!

CATALINÓN.   I am all heed.

DON JUAN. If here they ask you who I am
You do not know—nor care a damn.

CATALINÓN. D'you try to tell me what to do?
Even here have I to learn from you?

DON JUAN. Why, for her love I'm almost dying.
I'll have her now, then scamper flying—

CATALINÓN. But what d'you mean?

DON JUAN.   Be dumb and follow me!

CORIDÓN. Anfriso, in an hour the fête will be.

ANFRISO. Come on, it's an occasion for good wine,
Sliced melons, and slashed bunches from the vine!

DON JUAN. I'm dying, Thisbe.

THISBE.   Yet you talk and talk!

DON JUAN. You see, yourself, I scarce can move or walk.

THISBE. You speak too much!

DON JUAN.   But you perceive my trend.

THISBE. Please God it be not lies from end to end!

The Alcazar at Seville

Enter KING OF CASTILE *with* DON GONZALO DE ULLOA *and attendants.*

KING OF CASTILE. How did your embassy succeed, my lord
Commander?

DON GONZALO.   There I found your cousin king,
Don Juan,[1] preparing, arming, and reviewing
Some thirty vessels of his fleet in Lisbon.

KING OF CASTILE. Bound whither?

DON GONZALO.   They said Goa, but I guess
It is some closer quarry, like Tangiers
Or Ceuta, which they may besiege this summer.

KING OF CASTILE. May God on high reward and help the zeal
With which he arms His glory! You and he—
Upon what general points did you agree?

DON GONZALO. My lord, he asks for Serpa, Olivenza,
Mora, and Toro. In return for these
He'll give you Villaverde, Mértola,
Herrera, and the districts round about
Which lie between Castile and Portugal.

KING OF CASTILE. At once confirm the contract, Don Gonzalo,
But what about your journey? You return
Both tired and out of pocket, I presume?

DON GONZALO. To serve you, sire, no hardship is too much.

KING OF CASTILE. What's Lisbon like? A good place?

DON GONZALO.   In all Spain
It is the largest city.[2] If you'd like it
I'll paint a picture of it in the air.

KING OF CASTILE. I'd like to hear it. Someone fetch a chair.

DON GONZALO. Why, Lisbon is the world's eighth wonder!
Cleaving the heart of her asunder
To travel half the breadth of Spain,
The sumptuous Tagus swirls its train
And through the ranges rolls its thunder
To enter deep into the main
Along the sacred wharves of Lisbon
Of which it laves the southern side.

[1] John I, who became King of Portugal in 1385. He was not in fact a contemporary of this King of Castile (Alfonso XI). [E.B.]

[2] Portugal was united to Spain from 1580 to 1640. The proper nouns that occur in the ensuing paean to Lisbon are commented on in the scholarly editions of which a convenient one for American readers is to be found in *Cuatro Comedias*, ed. Hill and Harlan, W. W. Norton & Co., New York, 1941. [E.B.]

But just before its name it loses
And its own course, into the tide,
It makes a port in the sierras
Where ships of all the navies ride
That can be numbered in this world
Where like the pikes of massed battalions
The masts of caravels and galleons,
Dhows, galleys, schooners, barques, and sloops
Of Indians, Norsemen, or Italians,
In such innumerable troops
Are mustered upon either hand,
They seem to form a pine-wood city
Which Neptune rules for miles inland!
Up on the side where sets the sun,
Guarding the port on either hand
Of where the Tagus makes its entry,
With many a grimly-snouted gun—
One called Cascaes and one Saint John,
Two fearsome fortresses keep sentry
The navies of the world to stun—
The mightiest strongholds on this Earth!
Just half a league along this firth
Is Belén, convent of Jerome—
The saint whose guardian was a lion
And for his emblem chose a stone—
Where Catholic and Christian princes
Are keeping their eternal home.
After this most astounding fabric,
Beyond Alcántara, you sally
A league, to reach Jabregas' convent
Which fills the centre of a valley
That is encircled by three slopes.
Here, with his paintbrush, would Apelles
Have to renounce his proudest hopes
For, seen from afar, there seem to be
Clusters of pearls hung from the sky,
Within whose vast immensity
Ten Romes would seem to multiply
In labyrinths of convents, churches
With streets and pathways winding by

To many a vast estate and mansion,
Extending to the sea and sky,
And on, in infinite expansion,
Through empires, sowing deathless seeds
Wherever thought of man can fly,
In buildings, arts and letters, deeds
Of glory, feats of arms, and high
Impartial rectitude of law.
But reaching nearest to the sky
And towering over all I saw,
Outrivalling the pen and sword,
The summit of her christian pity,
And, most of all to be adored,
The peak of this imperial city
Is in her vast Misericord!
The thing most worthy of amaze
That in this glorious pile I found
Was that, from its high top, the gaze
For seven leagues could sweep its rays
On sixty villages all round,
And each of them the sea, through bays,
Could reach, and at its door was found.
One of these ports is Olivelas
A convent where myself I counted
Eight hundred cells: the blessed nuns
To full twelve hundred souls amounted.
Lisbon just hereabouts contains
Full fifteen hundred parks and halls—
The sort that here in Andalusia
The populace "sortijo" calls,
And each with poplar groves and gardens,
Surrounded, too, with stately walls.
Right in the center of the city
Rucío lies, a noble square,
Well-paved, with statues, lawns, and fountains.
A century ago, just there,
The sea was lapping cold and green
But thirty thousand houses now,
From sea to city, intervene.
Where fishing yawls were wont to plough

A mighty township stands between.
The sea has lost its bearings here
And gone to rage in other parts
For here they call it New Street where
The treasure of the East imparts
Grandeur and wealth in such a wise
That there's one merchant counts his treasure
(So the king told me) not in coins
But in the old two-bushel measure
We use for fodder for our mules.
Terrero, so they call the place
Wherefrom the royal household rules,
Collects a countless shoal of boats
Constantly grounded in its port
From France and England. The royal court
Whose hands the passing Tagus kisses
Derives its name from its foundation
By him who conquered Troy—Ulysses.
And worthy such a derivation
Ulissibona was its name
As spoken by the Roman nation:
Lisbon's a shortening of the same.
The city arms are represented
By a great sphere on which displayed
Are the red wounds that Don Alonso
Got in the terrible Crusade.
In the great arsenal you spy
All kinds of vessels, among which
Those of the Conquest tower so high
That, looked at from the ground below,
Their mastheads seem to touch the sky.
It struck me as most excellent
That citizens, while they're at table,
Can buy great loads of living fish,
And most from their own doors are able
To catch as many as they wish,
And from the nets where salmon flounder
It's scarce a stone's throw to the dish.
Each afternoon a thousand laden
Vessels are docked, each by its shed,

With diverse merchandise and common
Sustenance—oil, and wine, and bread,
Timber, and fruits of all variety,
With ice that's carried on the head
And cried by women through the street.
(They fetch it, from the peaked Estrella's
Remote sierra, for the heat.)
I could go on like this forever
The city's marvels to repeat
But it would be to count the stars,
Number the sands, and grains of wheat . . .
Of citizens two hundred thousand
It boasts, and, what is more, a king
Who kisses both your hands and wishes
You all success in everything!

KING OF CASTILE. I couldn't have enjoyed so much
Seeing the town in all its grandeur
As thus by your creative touch
To have it brought before my eyes.
By the way, have you children?

DON GONZALO.   Sire,
I have one daughter. She is such a beauty
That Nature in her features may admire
And marvel at herself.

KING OF CASTILE.   Then let me give her
In marriage, from my hand endowered.

DON GONZALO.   My lord,
Your will is mine. But who is it you've chosen?

KING OF CASTILE. Although he is not here, he's a Sevillian.
Don Juan Tenorio is the young man's name.

DON GONZALO. I'll go and tell the news to Doña Ana,
My daughter.

KING OF CASTILE. Go at once, Gonzalo. Yes,
And let me have the answer very soon.

Seashore near Tarragona

Enter DON JUAN *and* CATALINÓN.

DON JUAN. Now go and get those horses ready
Since they are stabled close at hand.

CATALINÓN. Although I'm only just your servant
Catalinón, please understand,
Of decencies I am observant.
People don't say before my nose
Nor even yet behind my back:
"Catalinón is one of those . . ."
Bad names don't fit me. That's a fact.

DON JUAN. While these gay fishermen are spending
The hours in revel, fix the horses!
Galloping hoofs, when danger's pending,
Have always been my best recourses.

CATALINÓN. But surely, sir, you won't abuse her,
Who saved your life?

DON JUAN.   As a seducer
You've always known me. Why, then, ask me
And with my own true nature task me?
Not only that: her hut I'll fire
To daze their minds while we retire.

CATALINÓN. Too well I know you are the scourge
Of womankind.

DON JUAN.   I'm on the verge
Of dying for her: she's so good.

CATALINÓN. How generously you repay
Your entertainment!

DON JUAN.   Understood!
Aeneas paid in the same way
The Queen of Carthage, you poor dolt!

CATALINÓN. The way you tempt the thunderbolt!
Those who cheat women with base sham

In the long run their crime will damn
After they're dead. You'll find out when!

DON JUAN. Well on the credit side I am
If you extend my debt till then
You'll wait till death to punish me.

CATALINÓN. Follow your bent. I'd sooner be
Catalinón than you in what
Pertains to cheating women. See!
The poor unhappy soul draws near.

DON JUAN. Saddle those horses, do you hear?
And get them ready, now, for dodging.

CATALINÓN. Poor trustful creature, oh, how dear
We've paid you for our board and lodging!

Exit CATALINÓN.

Enter THISBE.

THISBE. When I am not with you I seem without
Myself.

DON JUAN. Such a pretence I beg to doubt.

THISBE. Why so?

DON JUAN.   If you loved me, you'd ease my soul.

THISBE. I'm yours.

DON JUAN.   If you were truly mine heart-whole,
How could you kill me thus and make me wait?

THISBE. It is love's punishment at last I've found
In you, and that's what makes me hesitate.

DON JUAN. If, my beloved, I live solely in you
And ever so to serve you will continue
And give my life for you, why do you tarry
Since I shall be your husband? Yes, we'll marry!

THISBE. Our birth is too unequal.

DON JUAN.   Love is king
And under him he matches everything:
Silk with sackcloth, lace with corduroy.

THISBE. I almost could believe you in my joy . . .
If men were not such cheats.

DON JUAN.   With your least wish
You trawl me in your tresses like a fish.

THISBE. And I bow down beneath the hand and word
  Of husband.

DON JUAN.   Here I swear, O peerless eyes!
  Where he who looks within them swoons and dies,
  To be your husband.

THISBE.   Darling, save your breath
  But, oh, remember God exists—and death.

DON JUAN, *aside*. Yes, on the credit side I seem to be
  If it's till death you'll keep on trusting me!
  Aloud.
  While God gives life, I'll be a slave to you,
  And here's my hand and word to prove it's true.

THISBE. Now to repay you I shall not be coy.

DON JUAN. I cannot rest within myself for joy.

THISBE. Come, in my cabin love has built his nest
  And there forever we shall be at rest.
  Come in between these reeds, my love, and hide.

DON JUAN. But how on earth am I to get inside?

THISBE. I'll show you.

DON JUAN.   With your glory, dearest bride,
  You've lit my soul.

THISBE.   May that compel you, love,
  To keep your word. If not, may God above
  Chastise you.

DON JUAN, *aside*. Well in credit I must be
  If not till death my reckoning: lucky me!
  Exeunt.
  Enter CORIDÓN, ANFRISO, BELISA, *and musicians.*

CORIDÓN. Call Thisbe and the other folk
  So that the guest alone may see
  Our retinue.

BELISA.   This is her cot.

ANFRISO. No better piece of ground could be
  For dancing than this very spot.
  Then call her out to join our glee.

CORIDÓN. Now, steady on, for can't you see
  She's occupied with other guests?

There's going to be some jealousy—
Enough to fill a thousand breasts.

ANFRISO. Thisbe is envied far and wide.

BELISA. Let's sing a little to betide
Her coming, since we want to dance.

ANFRISO, *aside*. How can one's cares find peace and quiet
When jealousy within runs riot
And on our revel glares askance?

ALL, *singing*.

> The girl went out to fish, she thought,
> Casting her net among the shoals
> But there instead of fish she caught
> A thousand lovesick souls.

THISBE. Fire, oh, fire! I'm burning, burning!
My cabin burns, my flames and sighs.
Oh, sound the tocsin, friends, I'm turning
The water on from my own eyes!
My poor hut seems another Troy
Since love, eternally at war,
For want of cities to destroy
Must fire the cabins of the poor.
Fire, oh, fire, and water, water!
Have pity, love, don't scorch my spirits!
Oh, wicked cabin, scene of slaughter,
Where honour, vanquished in the fight,
Bled crimson! Vilest robber's den
And shelter of the wrongs I mourn!
O traitor guest, most curst of men,
To leave a girl, betrayed, forlorn!
You were a cloud drawn from the sea
To swamp and deluge me with tears!
Fire, oh, fire! and water, water!
Diminish, love, the flame that sears
My soul! I was the one that ever
Made fun of men and cheated them,
Then came a cavalier to sever
The thread, and by base stratagem
Destroy and kill my honour dead
By swearing marriage as his bait,

Enjoy me and profane my bed
And, heartless, leave me to my fate.
Oh, follow, follow him, and bring
Him back to me. But no, do not!
I'll take it even to the king
And ask him to avenge my lot.
Fire, oh, fire! and water, water!
Have mercy, love, and grant me quarter.

Exit THISBE.

CORIDÓN. Follow that fiendish cavalier!

ANFRISO. In silence I must bear my lot
But I'll avenge me, never fear,
Against this thankless, misbegot,
Impostor of a cavalier.
Come, let us catch him in the rear
Because he flees in desperate plight
And who knows whether, far or near,
He may contrive more harm?

CORIDÓN.   It's right
That pride should finish, thus, in mire
And such proud confidence should bite
The dust at last.

THISBE.   Oh, fire! Oh, fire!

ANFRISO. She's thrown herself into the sea.

CORIDÓN. Thisbe! Don't do it! Stop! Retire!

THISBE. Fire! Oh, fire! and water, water!
O spare me, love, your furnace dire!
Have pity on a poor man's daughter!

ACT II

The Alcazar at Seville

Enter KING OF CASTILE *and* DON DIEGO TENORIO.

KING OF CASTILE. What's that you say?

DON DIEGO.   My lord, I know it's true.
This letter's just arrived here from my brother,
Your own ambassador. They caught him with
A noble beauty in the king's own quarters.

KING OF CASTILE. What sort of lady?

DON DIEGO.   The Duchess Isabel.

KING OF CASTILE. But what temerity! Where is he now?

DON DIEGO. From you my liege I can't disguise the truth:
He's just arrived in Seville with one servant.

KING OF CASTILE. You know, Tenorio, I esteem you highly.
I'll get particulars from the King of Naples
And then we'll match the boy with Isabel
Relieving Duke Octavio of his woes,
Who suffers innocently. But, on this instant,
Exile Don Juan from the town.

DON DIEGO.   My lord,
Where to?

KING OF CASTILE. He must leave Seville for Lebrija
Tonight, at once; and let him thank your merit
His sentence is so light. Meanwhile determine
What can be told Don Gonzalo de Ulloa.
For now the thought of marriage with his daughter
Is quite beyond the question.

DON DIEGO.   Well, my liege,
I hope that your commands will be to honour
The lady in some other way as worthy
The child of such a father.

KING OF CASTILE.   Here's a plan
That will absolve me from Gonzalo's anger:

I'll make him major-domo of the palace.

Enter a servant; afterwards, OCTAVIO.

SERVANT. A noble, sire, has just come from abroad.
He says he is the Duke Octavio.

KING OF CASTILE. The Duke Octavio?

SERVANT.   Yes, my lord.

KING OF CASTILE.   Let him enter.

OCTAVIO. A miserable pilgrim and an exile
Offers himself, great monarch, at your feet,
Forgetting all the hardships of his journey
In your great presence.

KING OF CASTILE.   Duke Octavio!

OCTAVIO. I have come fleeing from the fierce pursuit
Of a demented woman, the result
Of the unconscious fault of some philanderer—
For which I have to seek your royal feet.

KING OF CASTILE. Already, Duke, I know your innocence.
I've written to the king my vassal, also
Restoring your estate, and any damage
You might have suffered owing to your absence.
I'll marry you in Seville (if you like
And she agrees) to one beside whose beauty
Isabel's would seem ugly, even were she
An angel. Don Gonzalo of Ulloa,
The grand commander of Calatrava
Whom pagan Moors praise highly in their terror
(For always cowards are flatterers and praisers)
Has a young daughter whose outstanding virtue's
A dowry in itself (I count it second
To beauty)—and a living marvel too!
She is the sun, the star of all Castile
And it is she I wish to be your wife.

OCTAVIO. The very undertaking of this voyage
Was worth while, sire, for this one thing alone
That I should know and do what gives you pleasure.

KING OF CASTILE, *to* DON DIEGO.
See that the duke is entertained and lodged
Down to his least requirement.

OCTAVIO.   O my lord,
The man who trusts in you wins every prize.
You're first of the Alfonsos, though eleventh!

Exeunt KING OF CASTILE *and* DON DIEGO.

Enter RIPIO.

RIPIO. What's happened?

OCTAVIO.   All my toil's rewarded well.
I told the king my wrongs. He honoured me.
Caesar was with the Caesar: as you see
I came, I saw, I conquered, and as well
He's going to marry me from his own palace
And make the King of Naples understand
And so repeal the law by which I'm banned.

RIPIO. With real good reason do they call this king
The benefactor of Castile. And so
He's offered you a wife?

OCTAVIO.   Yes, a friend, a wife
And one from Seville. Seville breeds strong men
And bold ones and breeds strapping women too.
A dashing style within a veiling mantle
Which covers a pure sun of dazzling beauty
—Where do you see such things except in Seville?
I am so happy, it was worth my troubles.

Enter DON JUAN *and* CATALINÓN.

CATALINÓN, *aside to his master*.
Wait, sir, there is the injured duke,
Isabel's Sagittarius—
Rather, I'd say, her Capricorn.[3]

DON JUAN. Pretend.

CATALINÓN.   You flatter those you sell.

DON JUAN. I went from Naples in such haste
Upon the summons of the king

---

[3] In this elaborate allusion, Isabel stands to Octavio as Heracles
to Sagittarius, who is also the ninth sign of the zodiac and as such
is followed by Capricorn. Catalinón drags the latter in because of
the connotation of horns—cuckoldom. For a fuller account of such
points, the reader is again referred to the Hill and Harlan edition. [E.B.]

I had no time to say good-bye,
Octavio.

OCTAVIO.   For such a thing
I hold you blameless.

Aside.

          So we two
Today have met in Seville.

DON JUAN.   Who
Would think I would see you in Seville
Where I would serve you if I may
At your commands in every way?
You leave good things behind, for Naples
Is good, but only Seville's worth
Exchanging for so fine a city
Of all the cities on this earth.

OCTAVIO. If you had told me that in Naples
Before I ever came this way
I would have laughed the thought to scorn
But now I credit what you say.
In fact you would have said much more:
Why such understatement, pray?
But who's that coming over there?

DON JUAN. The Marquis of la Mota! Now
I'll have to be discourteous . . .

OCTAVIO. If ever you should need my sword
I'm at your service, my good lord.

CATALINÓN, *aside.*
And if he wants another dame,
Too, to dishonour in your name
I suppose you're at his service just the same.

OCTAVIO. I'm very pleased with meeting you.

Exeunt OCTAVIO *and* RIPIO.

Enter the MARQUIS OF LA MOTA *with servant.*

MARQUIS. All day I've been upon your track
But couldn't find you anywhere.
How strange you should be safely back
And your old friend be in despair
Of finding you!

DON JUAN. For heaven's sake,
That seems a lot of fuss to make.
What news in Seville?

MARQUIS. The whole court
Has changed.

DON JUAN. What women? Any sport?

MARQUIS. Of course.

DON JUAN. Inés?

MARQUIS. She has retired
To Vejel.

DON JUAN. Oh, she's time-expired!
And Constance?

MARQUIS. She's in sorry plight—
Moulting—both hair and eyebrows too!
A Portuguese said she was *old*
And she thought he meant *pretty*.

DON JUAN. True!
Our word for "lovely to behold"
Is like the Portuguese for "old."
And Theodora?

MARQUIS. Why, this summer
She cured herself of the French ill
That seemed about to overcome her,
Sweating it out in streams, until
She is grown so tender and polite
She pulled a tooth for me and quite
Surrounded me with heaps of flowers.

DON JUAN. And what of Julia Candlelight?
Does she still sell herself for trout?

MARQUIS. For stale salt cod, I have no doubt.

DON JUAN. How's Catarranas, the old slum?

MARQUIS. Why, crawling with the same old scum!

DON JUAN. Are those two sisters still on view?

MARQUIS. Yes, and that monkey of Tolú
The Celestina, their old dame,
Who read them scriptures on the game.

DON JUAN. Oh, her! Beelzebub's old sow!
  How is the elder of them now?

MARQUIS. She's spotless, and reformed at last,
  And has a saint for whom to fast.[4]

DON JUAN. A single lover, and no share?

MARQUIS. She's firm and faithful as she's fair.

DON JUAN. The other?

MARQUIS.   Leads a livelier dance
  And never yet would miss her chance.

DON JUAN. What jokes or scandals have you played?
  What harlots have you left unpaid?

MARQUIS. De Esquival and I both made
  A cruel fraud last night. Tonight
  We've got a better hoax in sight.

DON JUAN. I'll come with you. Tell me: what's brewing
  I' the way of courting, suing, wooing?
  For I already, sir, have got
  My nest eggs hatching out a plot.

MARQUIS. Speak not of territory where
  My heart is buried deep in care!

DON JUAN. How so?

MARQUIS.   I love one that is not
  Attainable.

DON JUAN.   The girl, does she
  Reject you?

MARQUIS.   No, she favours me
  And loves me.

DON JUAN.   Who is it?

MARQUIS.   My cousin,
  Ana, who has arrived here newly.

DON JUAN. Where has she been?

MARQUIS.   In Lisbon with
  The embassy.

DON JUAN.   Good-looking?

MARQUIS.   Truly

---

[4] Metaphor for being a kept woman true to one lover. [R.C.]

She's Nature's masterpiece. In her
Nature has strained her powers.

DON JUAN.   Such beauty?
By God, I'd like to see her!

MARQUIS.   Yes,
You'll see in her the greatest beauty
The king has seen in all his state.

DON JUAN. Get married then, since it's your fate.

MARQUIS. The king's betrothed her to some other.

DON JUAN. But she accepts it that you love her?

MARQUIS. Yes, and she writes me daily too.

CATALINÓN, *aside.* Keep your mouth shut or you'll be sorry:
Spain's greatest trickster marks his quarry.

DON JUAN. Who, then, more satisfied than you?

MARQUIS. I've come to see what resolution
Is taken on the lady's fate.

DON JUAN. Yes, go and see, and here I'll wait
For your return.

MARQUIS.   I'll come back soon.

CATALINÓN, *to the servant.*
Mister Round or Mister Square,
Good-bye.

SERVANT.   Good-bye.

Exeunt MARQUIS *and servant.*

DON JUAN, *to* CATALINÓN. Now we're alone.
Shadow the marquis, keep his track,
He went into the palace there.
See where he goes and then come back.

Exit CATALINÓN.

A servant woman at a barred window speaks to DON JUAN.

WOMAN. Who am I speaking to?

DON JUAN.   Who called me?

WOMAN.   Now, sir,
Seeing you are a good friend of the marquis,
Prudent and courteous, take this note, and give it

Into the marquis' hands, for it contains
The happiness and honour of a lady.

DON JUAN. As I'm a gentleman and his good friend
I swear to give it to him.

WOMAN.   Stranger, thanks.
Good-bye.

The servant woman disappears.

DON JUAN.   The voice has gone and I'm alone.
Does it not seem like magic, what has passed
This minute? That this letter should arrive
As if the wind were carrier to my thoughts
And luck my letter-box? Why, this must be
A letter to the marquis from the lady
His speeches so endeared to me. In Seville
I'm called the Trickster; and my greatest pleasure
Is to trick women, leaving them dishonoured.
As soon as I have left this little square
I'll open this and read it. Idle caution!
It makes me want to laugh outright. The paper's
Open already. And it's plain it's hers,
For there's her signature, and here it says:
"My unkind father secretly has forced me
To marry. I cannot resist. I doubt
If I can go on living, since it's death
That he has given me. If you respect
My will and my dear love of you, then show it
This once. For, just to see how I adore you,
Come to my door this evening at eleven
And you will find me waiting, and it open,
So to enjoy the very crown of love.
Wear for a signal (that the maids may know it
And let you in) a cape of crimson colour.
My love, I trust in you; farewell; your own
Unhappy love." Why, it's as good as done!
Oh, I could roar with laughter! I'll enjoy her
By the same trick that limed the other one,
Isabel, back in Naples.

Enter CATALINÓN.

CATALINÓN.   Here's the marquis
Returning now.

DON JUAN.   Tonight the two of us
Have lots to do.

CATALINÓN.   You've some new swindle!

DON JUAN. This one's a wonder!

CATALINÓN.   Well, I disapprove.
You claim that we'll escape being caught out
But those who live by cheating must be cheated
In the long run.

DON JUAN.   You've turned a bloody preacher,
Have you, you cheeky boor?

CATALINÓN.   Right makes men brave!

DON JUAN. Yes, and fear makes men cowards, just like you.
You earn by serving. If you'd always earn,
Act always on the spot. He who does most
Wins most.

CATALINÓN.   And those who say and do the most
Collide with things the most and come to grief.

DON JUAN. But now I'm warning you! So, for the last
Time, listen, for I shan't warn you again!

CATALINÓN. Well, yes, from now, whatever you command
I'll do as if you were flanked on either side
By a tiger and an elephant, Don Juan!

DON JUAN. Hark! here's the marquis.

CATALINÓN.   Must he be the victim?

Enter MARQUIS OF LA MOTA.

DON JUAN. Out of this casement, Marquis, someone gave me
A very courteous message for yourself.
I could not see who gave it but the voice
Was of a woman, and she said at twelve
You are to go in secret to the door,
Which at that hour will be open to you,
And you must wear a cape of crimson colour
So that the maids will know you.

MARQUIS.   What?

DON JUAN.   This message

Was passed me at the window here without
My seeing who it was who whispered it.

MARQUIS. This message has restored my life, dear friend:
May God reward you for it without end!

DON JUAN. I haven't got your cousin here inside
So why should your embraces be applied
To one so worthless?

MARQUIS.   You delight me so
That I am quite outside myself, I know.
O sun, go down!

DON JUAN.   It slopes towards its setting.

MARQUIS. Come, friends. Come, night. My reason I'm for-
        getting.
I'm mad with joy.

DON JUAN.   One sees that quite all right.
You'll reach the peak at twelve o'clock tonight.

MARQUIS. Crown of my very soul! My heart's delight
Who are to crown my loving faith tonight!

CATALINÓN, *aside*. Dear Christ! I would not even bet a dozen
Bad halfpennies on that belovèd cousin.

Exit the MARQUIS *and enter* DON DIEGO.

DON DIEGO. Don Juan!

CATALINÓN.   Your father calls you.

DON JUAN.   At your orders.

DON DIEGO. I'd like to see you far better behaved,
Good-natured, with a better reputation.
Can it be possible you wish to kill me
With your behaviour?

DON JUAN.   Why in such a state?

DON DIEGO. For your behaviour and your madness now
The king has bade me ban you from the city,
For he is justly angered by a crime
Which, though you hid it from me, *he* has heard of
In Seville here—a crime so grave and evil
I scarcely dare to name it. Make a cuckold
Of your best friend and in the royal palace!
May God reward you as your sins deserve:

For though it now appear that God above
Puts up with you, consenting to your crimes,
The punishment is certain—and how fearful
For those who've taken His great name in vain!
His justice is tremendous after death.

DON JUAN. What, after death? How long you give me credit!
A long, long time, before I need repentance!

DON DIEGO. It will seem short when you receive your sentence.

DON JUAN. And now what would His Highness with myself?
Will it be for a long, long time as well?

DON DIEGO. Until you have repaired the august insult
Done to the Duke Octavio, and appeased
The scandals you have caused with Isabel,
You have to live in exile in Lebrija.
The king requires you go there instantly.
The sentence is too slight for such a crime.

CATALINÓN, *aside*. And if he also knew about the case
Of that poor fishergirl the good old man
Would be far angrier.

DON DIEGO.   Since no punishment,
Nor anything I say or do, affects you,
Your chastisement I here confide to God.
Exit.

CATALINÓN. The dear old man was overcome.

DON JUAN. Tears are well suited to old age.
Well now, the night is coming down.
We'll seek the marquis. Come, my page.

CATALINÓN. And now you will enjoy his bride.

DON JUAN. Which promises to be great sport.

CATALINÓN. Pray God that we come out of it
Alive!

DON JUAN. Now, now!

CATALINÓN.   I think the best
Way to describe you, sir, would be
As a locust to whom girls are grass,
And so by public proclamation
Whenever you're about to arrive

Towns should be warned: "Here comes the plague
Of women in a single man
Who is their cheater and betrayer,
The greatest trickster in all Spain."

DON JUAN. You've given me a charming name.

It is night time.

Enter the MARQUIS *with musicians who move up and down the stage.*

MUSICIANS, *singing.*

> To him who waits a promised pleasure
> Delay is like despair to measure.

MARQUIS. May never break of day destroy
The night in which I take my joy.

DON JUAN. What's this?

CATALINÓN.   Why, music.

MARQUIS, *aside.*   It appears
The poet speaks to me.
Aloud.

                              Who's there?

DON JUAN. Friend!

MARQUIS.   It's Don Juan?

DON JUAN.   The marquis, you?

MARQUIS. Who other would it be?

DON JUAN.   I knew
You by the coloured cape you wear.

MARQUIS, *to the musicians.*
Sing, since Don Juan's come here to.

MUSICIANS, *singing.*

> To him who waits a promised pleasure
> Delay is like despair to measure.

DON JUAN. Whose house is that you gaze at so?

MARQUIS. Why, Don Gonzalo's.

DON JUAN.   Where shall we go?

MARQUIS. To Lisbon.[5]

[5] "Evidently refers to a street or district of Seville inhabited by Portuguese courtesans" [Hill and Harlan, *op. cit.*].

DON JUAN.   How,
  Being in Seville?

MARQUIS.   Don't you know?
  And do you wonder that the worst
  Of Portugal live on the first
  And best of Spain, right here and now?

DON JUAN. Where do they live?

MARQUIS.   Why, in the street
  Called "Of the Serpent." There one sees
  Adam, become a Portuguese,
  Wooing a thousand Eves to eat
  And take a bite out of their pockets.
  And, sure, it's quite a hole they make
  With all those big doubloons and ducats.

DON JUAN. You run along there while you can.
  I have to play a scurvy joke.

MARQUIS. I'm being shadowed by a man
  Some pimp or bravo . . .

DON JUAN.   Leave him to me.[6]
  I shan't let him escape, you'll see.

MARQUIS. Around your arm, then, wrap this cloak
  The better so to deal your stroke.

DON JUAN. A good idea; then come and show
  The house to which I have to go.

MARQUIS. Now, while you carry out the plan,
  Alter your voice and talk as though
  You were indeed some other man.
  D'you see that "jealousy"?

DON JUAN.   I do.

MARQUIS. Then go to it and whisper there:
  "Beatrice." Then pass right through.

DON JUAN. What sort of woman?

MARQUIS.   Soft and pink.

CATALINÓN. Some water-cooling jar, I think.

MARQUIS. I'll wait for you at Gradas Stair.

[6] Here Don Juan takes on Mota's enterprise, which proved more
dangerous than the latter had bargained for. [R.C.]

DON JUAN. Till then, dear Marquis! I'll be there.

CATALINÓN. Now whither bound?

DON JUAN.   Shut up, you bear!
  I go to where my jest is played.

CATALINÓN. Nothing escapes you unbetrayed.

DON JUAN. I adore cheating.

CATALINÓN.   Now to the bull!
  Pass me your cape.

DON JUAN.   Not so, the fool
  Beast has passed his cape to me.

MUSICIANS. The trick appeals to such as we.

MARQUIS. That is succeeding by mistake.

MUSICIANS. And the whole world doth errors make.

MUSICIANS, *singing*.

> When one awaits a promised pleasure
> Delay is like despair to measure.

Room in the House of DON GONZALO

DOÑA ANA *within, with* DON JUAN *and* CATALINÓN

DOÑA ANA, *within*. False friend, you're not the marquis! You
  have tricked me!

DON JUAN. I tell you who I am.

DOÑA ANA, *within*.   False foe, you lie!

Enter DON GONZALO *with drawn sword*.

DON GONZALO. I hear my daughter Doña Ana's voice.

DOÑA ANA, *within*. Will nobody kill this false traitor here,
  The murderer of my honour?

DON GONZALO. Can such effrontery exist? She said:
  "My honour murdered." Then alas for me!
  Her giddy tongue is like a bell to clamour
  Our sad disgrace to all.

DOÑA ANA, *within*.   Kill him!

DON JUAN and CATALINÓN enter with drawn swords.

DON JUAN.   Who's this?

DON GONZALO. The closed and fallen barbican is here
Of the strong fortress of my honour, which,
Base traitor, you have falsely undermined,
Though there my life was warden.

DON JUAN.   Let me pass!

DON GONZALO. Pass? You shall pass the point of this bare sword.

DON JUAN. You'll die for this.

DON GONZALO.   That is no matter.

DON JUAN.   Look,
I'll have to kill you.

DON GONZALO.   Die yourself, base traitor.

DON JUAN, *thrusting with sword.*
This is the way I die.

CATALINÓN, *aside.*   If I get free
Then no more feasts and scurvy tricks for me!

DON GONZALO. He's given me my death.

DON JUAN.   You took your life
By being rash.

DON GONZALO.   What use was it to me?

DON JUAN. Come, let us run.

Exeunt DON JUAN and CATALINÓN.

DON GONZALO.   My frozen blood you've swelled
With fury. I am dead. I can expect
No better thing. My fury will pursue you.
You are a traitor, and a traitor is
A traitor, being first of all a coward.

He dies. Servants enter and carry off the corpse.

Enter MARQUIS OF LA MOTA and musicians.

MARQUIS. Now midnight will be striking soon:
Don Juan's[7] surely very late.
How hard a thing it is—to wait.

Re-enter DON JUAN and CATALINÓN.

_____

[7] R.C. evidently used the traditional, anglicized pronunciation
of Don Juan—Byron rhymed it with "true one." [E.B.]

DON JUAN. Is that the marquis?

MARQUIS.   You're Don Juan?

DON JUAN. I am. Here, take your cape.

MARQUIS.   Your pranks . . .

DON JUAN. Have had a most funereal end
  In death.

CATALINÓN. Oh, flee from the dead man!

MARQUIS. Tell me, whom did you trick, my friend?

CATALINÓN, *aside*. You are the latest victim, thanks
  To him.

DON JUAN. This prank has cost most dear.

MARQUIS. Don Juan, the whole debt I'll clear . . .
  Because the girl will be complaining
  Of me . . .

DON JUAN.   The stroke of twelve draws near.

MARQUIS. May never break of day destroy
  The night in which I take my joy!

DON JUAN. Farewell then, Marquis!

CATALINÓN.   What a treat
  Awaits the wretch!

DON JUAN.   Let's run!

CATALINÓN.   My feet
  Than wings of eagles feel more fleet.

  Exeunt except the MARQUIS OF LA MOTA *and servants.*

MARQUIS. Now you can all go home. I'll go
  Alone.

SERVANTS. God made the night for sleeping.

  Exeunt servants.

VOICES *within.* Was ever such a sight of woe?
  Alas! How pitiless a blow!

MARQUIS. God shield me! I hear cries and weeping
  Resounding from the castle square.
  At such an hour what could it be?
  Ice freezes all my chest. I see
  What seems another Troy aflare,
  For torches now come wildly gleaming

With giant flames like comets streaming
And reeking from their pitchy hair,
A mighty horde of tarry hanks.
Fire seems to emulate the stars
Dividing into troops and ranks.
I'll go and find out . . .

Enter DON DIEGO TENORIO *and guards with torches.*

DON DIEGO.   Who goes there?

MARQUIS. One who would know of this affair,
And why there's such a hue and cry.

DON DIEGO, *to the guards.*
Bind him!

MARQUIS, *drawing his sword.*
                    What? Me? I'd sooner die!

DON DIEGO. Give me your sword. The greatest valour
Is speech without recourse to steel.

MARQUIS. And is it thus that you would deal
With me, the Marquis of la Mota?

DON DIEGO. Your sword! Whatever you may feel,
The king has ordered your arrest!

MARQUIS. Ye gods!

Enter the KING OF CASTILE *and his attendants.*

KING OF CASTILE.   Through Spain from east to west
See that he can't escape. As well
In Italy (for who can tell
If he should get there?) start the quest.

DON DIEGO. He is here.

MARQUIS.   Then, sire, I'm apprehended,
Truly, by your own orders. Why?

KING OF CASTILE. Take him, and have his head suspended
Upon a rampart near the sky.
—Don't linger in my presence, sir.

MARQUIS, *aside.* The ecstasies of am'rous passion
Always so light as they occur
Grow heavy after in this fashion.
"There's many a slip," once said the sage.
But why the king's revengeful rage?

Aloud.

I can't make out what crime I've done.

DON DIEGO. You know as well as anyone.

MARQUIS. Me?

DON DIEGO.   Come!

MARQUIS.   What strange confusion!

KING OF CASTILE.   Try him
And cut his head off before day.
For the commander, don't deny him
Solemnity and grave display
Such as men grant to royal or sacred
Persons. The funeral must be grand.
Statue and tomb of bronze and stone
With Gothic letters see them planned
Proclaiming vengeance is at hand.
And where has Doña Ana gone?

DON DIEGO. To sanctuary swift she ran
In the convent of Our Heavenly Queen.

KING OF CASTILE. This loss is grave, for such a man
Has Calatrava seldom seen.

Countryside near Dos Hermanas

Enter a betrothed couple, BATRICIO *and* AMINTA. *Also*
GASENO, BELISA, *and shepherd musicians.*

MUSICIANS, *singing.*

Brightly April's sun shines over
The orange flowers and scented clover
But though she serve him as a star
Aminta shines out lovelier far.

BATRICIO. Upon this carpet made of flowers,
When the red earth seems turned to snow,
The sun exhausts his dazzling powers
And freshens to his dawning glow.
Come, let us sit, for such a place
Invites us with its charm and grace.

AMINTA, *to the singers.*

A thousand, thousand favors show
To my betrothed, Batricio.

MUSICIANS, *singing.*

> Brightly April's sun shines over
> The orange flowers and scented clover
> But though she serve him as a star
> Aminta shines out lovelier far.

GASENO, *to the singers.*

As well has sung each lad and lass
As sings the choir at Holy Mass!

BATRICIO. Aminta, when the sun sees thee
It is o'erwhelmed with jealousy!

AMINTA. Batricio, when I hear thee,
I hear the voice of flattery!
But take my thanks, good lad, for soon
I'll be content to be the moon
If thou'lt give light to everyone
And be the all-commanding sun.
I'll wax and wane contentedly
Taking my light, dear sun, from thee!
May the dawn ever sing to us
Its subtle salutation, thus:

MUSICIANS, *singing.*

> Brightly April's sun shines over
> The orange flowers and scented clover
> But though she serve him as a star
> Aminta shines out lovelier far.

Enter CATALINÓN *in travelling clothes.*

CATALINÓN. Good people all, for your espousal
More guests have come to the carousal.

GASENO. Let everybody be invited.
I hope that all will be delighted.
Who's coming?

CATALINÓN.   Don Juan Tenorio.

GASENO. The old one?

CATALINÓN.   No, I mean the young.

GASENO. He must be something of a rake.

BATRICIO, *aside*. This omen very hard I take.
  For being a cavalier and young,
  It brings on envy, takes off lustre.
  Aloud.

Who gave him notice of our muster?

CATALINÓN. He heard of it along the road.

BATRICIO, *aside*. That to the devil must be owed.
  But why anticipate the load?
  Aloud.

Then come to my sweet wedding night
All those who wish to dance and dine
  Aside.

Except that one of them's a knight:
I take this as an evil sign.

GASENO. Let the Colossus be invited
  From Rhodes, the Pope and Prester John
  With Don Alfonso the Eleventh,
  His court, and all who follow on!
  Loaves of bread are piled in mountains
  For this wedding! Wine stands ready
  To overflow in springs, in fountains,
  In Taguses and Guadalquivirs!
  Babels and Babylons of ham,
  Thrushes and quails in timid flocks
  Are here your bulging sides to cram—
  And tender doves and basted cocks!
  To Dos Hermanas, welcome here!
  Bring in the noble cavalier
  To honour these white hairs of mine!

BELISA. Son of the chancellor!

BATRICIO.   A sign
  Of evil is this guest of mine
  For they must place him by my bride.
  To eat and drink I am not zealous
  Since heaven dooms me to be jealous,
  To love, to suffer, and abide.
  Enter DON JUAN.

DON JUAN. I heard by chance there was a marriage-feast
  When I was passing by this village here
  And so I've come to revel in it too
  Being so lucky as to pass just then.

GASENO. Your Lordship comes to honour and ennoble it.

BATRICIO, *aside*. And I, who am the host and master, say,
  Within me, that you come in evil hour.

GASENO. Won't you make room there for the cavalier!

DON JUAN. With your permission, I will take this place.
  Sits next to the bride.

BATRICIO. If you sit down before me, sir, you'll seem
  The bridegroom.

DON JUAN.   If I were, I could choose worse!

GASENO. He *is* the bridegroom.

DON JUAN.   Oh, I beg your pardon
  For my mistake.

CATALINÓN, *aside*. Oh, poor unhappy bridegroom!

DON JUAN, *aside to* CATALINÓN.
  He seems annoyed.

CATALINÓN.   I'm quite aware of that
  But if he has to serve you for a bull
  What does it matter if he seems annoyed?
  I would not give one horn-toss for his wife
  Nor for his honour. Poor unhappy man
  To fall into the hands of Lucifer!

DON JUAN. Can it be possible I am so lucky?
  I'm almost feeling jealous of your husband.

AMINTA. You seem to flatter me.

BATRICIO, *aside*.   Well is it said:
  "A great one at a wedding brings bad luck."

GASENO. Come, let us eat and drink a while
  So that your Lordship, while we dine,
  May rest himself!

  DON JUAN takes AMINTA's hand.

DON JUAN.   Why hide your hand?

AMINTA. It's mine.

GASENO.   Let's go.

BELISA.   Strike up the song again!

DON JUAN. What do you make of it?

CATALINÓN.   I fear a vile
Death at the hands of those same sturdy peasants.

DON JUAN. What lovely eyes and spotless hands—
They're burning me with flaming torches!

CATALINÓN. It's *you* will brand *her* with your mark
Then put her out to winter-grazing.
Three little lambs, and this makes four.[8]

DON JUAN. How all of them are staring at me!

BATRICIO. It is an evil-boding thing
A noble at my wedding.

GASENO.   Sing![9]

BATRICIO. God! I feel as if I'm dying.

CATALINÓN, *aside.*
They sing now, who will soon be crying.

[8] Isabel, Thisbe, Doña Ana, and now Aminta. As Act II closes, we have met all of the Don's women as far as this play is concerned; the threads are drawn together in the third and last act. [E.B.]

[9] Gaseno's trying to keep up appearances. [R.C.]

ACT III

GASENO's *house in Dos Hermanas*

Enter BATRICIO, *pensive.*

BATRICIO. Jealousy, timepiece of our cares, who strikes
Fierce torments and alarms at every hour,
Torments, with which you kill, although you give
Disjointed blows, cease from tormenting me,
Since it's absurd that, if love gives me life,
You should give death. What do you wish of me,
Sir Cavalier, that you torment me so?
Well did I say, seeing him at my wedding:
"An evil omen." Was it not well done
That he should sit beside my bride, not letting
Me even put my hand in my own plate?
Because each time I tried to do so, he
Would brush it off exclaiming: "What ill breeding!"
And when I turned to others and complained
They answered: "You have nothing to complain of!
Don't take this thing so hard! And don't get scared!
At court it's quite the custom. Just keep quiet!"
The custom! And they laughed! Fine custom this!
A worse one (in my eyes) than that of Sodom!
Another man at table with the bride
While the bridegroom goes hungry! And this other
Kept saying to me: "Don't you eat that, ha?"
The scoundrel then would snatch it from my plate
Saying that I was wrong not to enjoy it.
I am ashamed. This wedding was a jest
And not a marriage. None will suffer me,
Nor let me pass among them. Now he's supped
With both of us, I suppose he has to come
To bed with us, and, when I take my wife,
To chide me: "What ill breeding! What ill breeding!"
He's coming now. I can't resist. I'll hide.
But that can't be, since he has seen me now.

Enter DON JUAN.

DON JUAN. Batricio.

BATRICIO.   Yes, my lord.

DON JUAN.   It's just to tell you—

BATRICIO, *aside.* What can it be but more ill luck for me?

DON JUAN. It's just to tell you that I lost my soul
Some days ago to our Aminta and
Enjoyed . . .

BATRICIO.   Her honour?

DON JUAN.   Yes.

BATRICIO, *aside.*   A certain proof
Is all that I've just seen. Did she not love him
He never would have ventured to her house.
Aloud, to DON JUAN.
She's only proved a woman, after all.

DON JUAN. Aminta, in the end, grew jealous, desperate
In fact, thinking herself forgotten by me,
And being married to another man,
And so she wrote this letter sending for me
And in return I promised to enjoy
That which our souls had promised long ago.
Well, that's how things stand. Give your life a chance.
For ruthlessly I'll kill whoever stops us.

BATRICIO. Why, if you leave it to my choice, I'll further
Your wishes. For when rumour breathes abroad,
Honour and woman suffer worst of all,
And women in the general opinion
Will always lose more than they gain. For women
Are tested, just as bells are, by their sound,
And it is known how reputation suffers
When in the common speech a woman's name
Rings with the sound of a cracked bell. Since you
Subdue me, I no longer want the bliss
That love commanded me to take. A woman
Half good, half bad is like a piece of gold
Seen in the twilight. For a thousand years
Enjoy her, sir! I'd sooner die un-hoodwinked
Than live the dupe of others.

Exit.

DON JUAN.   Through his honour
I conquered him, and always, with these peasants
They hold their honour in both hands, and look
To their own honour first. For honour
Was forced, by so much falsity and fraud,
To leave the city for the countryside.
But now, before I work the final damage,
I shall pretend to remedy it too.
I'll go and talk to her old father and get him
To authorise the deed against his will.
O stars of morning, give me luck in this
Deception since you keep the payment, due
In death, for such a long, long time ahead!
Exit.

Enter AMINTA *and* BELISA.[10]

BELISA. See, where your bridegroom comes, Aminta. Come,
Enter and strip.

AMINTA.   Of this unhappy wedding,
I don't know what to think. For my Batricio
All day was bathed in melancholy tears.
All's jealousy and wild confusion. What
A terrible misfortune!

BELISA.   But what young knight
Was that . . . ?[11]

AMINTA.   Leave me, for I am all confusion
Since Shamelessness was made a knight of Spain.
Evil befall the knight that lost me my
Good husband!

BELISA.   Quiet! for I think he's coming.
Let no one tread the floor of so robust
A bridegroom.

AMINTA.   Now farewell, my dear Belisa.

[10] Belisa in the dark mistakes Don Juan for the bridegroom coming. [R.C.]
[11] There are two interpretations of this. I take it that Belisa, who was a snob and formerly proclaimed Don Juan's rank, pretends to be ignorant when he becomes unpopular. [R.C.]

BELISA. You will appease his anger in your arms.

Exit.

AMINTA. May it please Heaven my sighs might seem endearments

And these poor tears appear to him caresses!

Exeunt.

Enter DON JUAN, CATALINÓN, GASENO.

DON JUAN. Good-bye, Gaseno.

GASENO.   Let me keep you company

So that I may congratulate my daughter.

DON JUAN. Oh, there'll be time enough for that tomorrow.

GASENO. Yes, you are right. I offer my own soul

Together with the girl.

DON JUAN.   Rather, my bride.

Exit GASENO.

DON JUAN. Catalinón, go saddle up.

CATALINÓN.   For when?

DON JUAN. For dawn, and when the sun, half-dead with laughter,

Rises to see the hoax.

CATALINÓN.   For in Lebrija

There is another bridal that awaits us.

For God's sake, hasten with the one in hand.

DON JUAN. But this will be the greatest hoax of all.

CATALINÓN. I only hope we come out safely from it.

DON JUAN. Seeing my father is chief justice and

The king's most private friend, what can you fear?

CATALINÓN. God is accustomed to take vengeance on

Those who use privacy just to deprive,

And often, when there's gambling on, spectators

Are apt to lose as badly as the gamblers.

I've long been a spectator of your gambles,

And for this office I would dread to be

Struck by the thunderbolt to dust and cinders

When it gets you.

DON JUAN.   Go saddle up those horses!

Tomorrow night I have to sleep in Seville.

CATALINÓN. In Seville?

DON JUAN.   Yes.

CATALINÓN.   What are you saying? Look
At what you've done, master, and look how short
Even the longest life is until death!
And there's a hell behind the gates of death.

DON JUAN. If you concede me such a long, long time
You'll be deceived . . .

CATALINÓN.   Listen, my lord!

DON JUAN.   Get out!
Get out! You bore me with your farfetched fears!

CATALINÓN. How we admire the fearless Scythian
The brave Galician, Persian, Lybian!
But, I confess, for all of me,
They all can keep their bravery.
Exit.

DON JUAN. Night spreads across the world. Silence is black.
The Pleiades now tread the highest pole
'Mid starry clusters. Now I set my trap.
Love guides me to my joy—none can resist him.
I've got to reach her bed. Aminta!

AMINTA.   Who
Calls for Aminta? Is it Batricio?
He is at her door. She comes out, as from bed.

DON JUAN. I'm not Batricio. No.

AMINTA.   Then, who?

DON JUAN.   Look slowly,
And you'll see who I am.

AMINTA.   Why, sir, I'm lost,
With you outside my bedroom at these hours!

DON JUAN. Such are the hours that I am wont to keep.

AMINTA. Return, or I shall shout. Please don't exceed
The courtesy you owe to my Batricio.
You'll find, in Dos Hermanas, there are Romans—
Emilias and Lucreces who avenge!

DON JUAN. Just hear two words and hide the blushing scarlet
Of your fair cheeks deep down within your heart!

AMINTA. Go, go! My husband's coming.

DON JUAN.   I'm your husband.
  So what have you to marvel at?

AMINTA.   Since when?

DON JUAN. From now on, and forever, I am he!

AMINTA. But who arranged the marriage?

DON JUAN.   My delight.

AMINTA. And who was it that married us?

DON JUAN.   Your eyes.

AMINTA. By what authority?

DON JUAN.   Why, that of sight!

AMINTA. But does Batricio know?

DON JUAN.   Yes! He forgets you.

AMINTA. Has he forgotten me?

DON JUAN.   Yes. I adore you.

AMINTA. How?

DON JUAN. Thus with all my heart I swoon before you.

AMINTA. Get out!

DON JUAN.   How can I when you see I'm dying
  With love for you alone?

AMINTA.   What shameless lying!

DON JUAN. Aminta, listen and you'll know the truth,
  Since women are the friends of truth. I am
  A noble knight, the heir of the Tenorios,
  The conquerors of Seville. And my father,
  Next to the king, is honoured and esteemed
  Beyond all men in court. Upon his lips
  Hang life or death according to his word.
  Travelling on my road, by merest chance,
  I came and saw you. Love ordains these things
  And guides them, so that even He, Himself,
  Forgets that they were anything but chance.
  I saw you, I adored you, I was kindled
  So that I am determined now to wed you.
  Even though the king forbid it, and my father
  In anger and with threats tries to prevent it,
  I have to be your husband. What's your answer!

AMINTA. I don't know what to say. Your so-called "truths"
Are covered with deceitful rhetoric—
Because if I am married to Batricio
(As is well known) the fact is not annulled
Even if he deserts me.

DON JUAN.   Non-consummation,
Either by malice or deceit, is reason
For an annulment.

AMINTA.   In Batricio all
Was simple truth.

DON JUAN.   Tush! Come, give me your hand,
And let's confirm our vows.

AMINTA.   You're not deceiving?

DON JUAN. I'd be the one deceived.

AMINTA.   Then swear before me
To carry out your promised word.

DON JUAN.   I swear
By this white hand, a winter of pure snow.

AMINTA. Swear then, to God. Pray that he curse your soul
If you should fail!

DON JUAN.   If in my word and faith
I fail, I pray to God that by foul treason
I be murdered by a man!
   Aside.

                    I mean a dead one,
For living man, may God forbid!

AMINTA.   This promise
Has made me your own wife.

DON JUAN.   My very soul
I offer you between my outstretched arms.

AMINTA. My life and soul are yours.

DON JUAN.   Ah, my Aminta,
Tomorrow you will walk in silver buskins
Studded with tacks of gold from heel to toe.
Your alabaster throat will be imprisoned
In necklaces of diamonds and rubies,

And your white fingers, in their flashing rings,
Will seem transparent pearls.

AMINTA.   From now to yours
My will bows down, and I am yours alone.

DON JUAN, *aside*. Little you know the Trickster of Seville!

Near Tarragona

Enter ISABEL *and* FABIO *in travelling costume with an oxcart.*

ISABEL. He robbed me of my master—
By treason—of the man whom I adored!
O pitiless disaster
To truth! O night abhorred!
Black mask of day, who aided the deceit,
Antipode of the sun, and spouse of sleep!

FABIO. What serves it, Isabel,
Always upon your sorrows so to dwell?
—If love is naught but cunning,
Always through fields of scorn and anger running,
If he who laughs today
Tomorrow has to weep his woes away?
The sea is swelled with anger
And from this mighty tempest and its clangour,
Out of the foamy welter,
Duchess, the galleys now have sun for shelter
Beneath the towers that crown
This rocky strand.

ISABEL.   Where are we?

FABIO.   At the town
Of Tarragona. Hence,
By land, we'll reach the city of Valence
In very little time,
The palace of the sun, a most sublime
And stately city. There
For several days you may divert your care
And then to Seville sailing

You'll see the world's eighth wonder. What of failing
To win Octavio's hand?
Don Juan is more famous in the land!
Then why so sad? They say
He's made a count already. Anyway,
The king himself is giving
Your hand to him. Of all the nobles living
The nearest to the king,
His father is the first in everything.

ISABEL. My sadness is not due
To marrying Don Juan, since it's true
He is most nobly born
And the world knows it. What makes me forlorn
Is honour which, though wife,
I must lament the years of all my life.

FABIO. A fishermaid appears
Sighing most tenderly and bathed in tears.
Surely she's come to you
Some favour or some sympathy to woo.
So while I fetch your train
You two may all the sweetlier complain
Together.

Exit FABIO *and enter* THISBE.

THISBE.   Sea of Spain,
Rough sea with waves of fire and fleeting foam!
Burned Troy of my poor home!
O fire, conceived and hatched deep in the main,
Which waves brought forth,[12] to turn
Again to running water, though it burn
With flames in these salt tears.
Cursed be the wood that on the wave careers
To work the woe that was Medea's!
Cursèd be those that had the mad ideas
Of twisting hemp or lint
To crucify the canvas on a splint
And be the engines of deceiving—
Serpents of rope their deep enchantments weaving!

[12] Don Juan was the fire who came to her out of the water and
then produced more water in the form of her tears. [E.B.]

ISABEL. Why, lovely fishermaid,
  Do you make complaint so sadly of the sea?

THISBE. Why, madam, I have made
  A thousand such, and happy must you be
  To laugh at such a thing.

ISABEL. I also have such sad complaints to sing.
  Where are you from?

THISBE.   Behind
  There, where sore-wounded by the wind
  You see those huts, the gales
  Over them so victoriously rampage
  That through their shattered pales
  Each bird can find a nesting place, their rage
  Forces so many a rift!
  Of these great bulls, are you the prize they left,
  O beautiful Europa, in this cart?

ISABEL. Though much against my heart,
  They're taking me to Seville to be wed.

THISBE. If my sad lot has bred
  Some pity in you, and if you as well
  Some woes of the injurious sea can tell,
  Then take me with you, and I'll be your slave.
  I have an audience with the king to crave
  For reparation of an evil hoax
  Played by a noble on us humble folks.
  Lifeless and stranded by the angry wave
  Was Don Juan de Tenorio, whom to save
  I sheltered until he was out of danger,
  When this ungrateful and relentless stranger
  Proved to my foot a viper in the grass.
  With promises of marriage he confused me
  And for his own mere pleasure then abused me.
  Woe to the woman who believes man's oath!
  He ran away and left me to my woe.
  Say have I right to vengeance then, or no?

ISABEL. O cursed woman, hold your tongue,
  By which even to death I have been stung!
  After reflecting.

But, if it's grief that's actuating you,
It's not your fault. Proceed! But is it true?

THISBE. How happy, were it false!

ISABEL. Woe to the woman who believes man's oath!
Who's coming with you?

THISBE.   One old fisherman,
My father, and the witness of my wrongs.

ISABEL. No vengeance can suffice so great an evil.
Come in my company, and welcome both!

THISBE. Woe to the woman who believes man's oath.

The cloister or nave of a church in Seville. In one of the side chapels is the tomb of the commander Don Gonzalo with a statue of the dead man.[13]

Enter DON JUAN *and* CATALINÓN.

CATALINÓN. I tell you things are looking bad.

DON JUAN.   How so?

CATALINÓN. First, that Octavio has got to know
That hoax in Italy. The marquis, too,
Knows that the message which he got from you
And which you said his cousin gave was faked.
Then Isabela's on the way: she's staked
A marriage claim, and also it is spoken . . .

DON JUAN. Here, hold your tongue!

Hitting him.

CATALINÓN.   Look, master, you have broken
A molar in my mouth.

DON JUAN.   Then hold your jaw.
Who told you all this nonsense?

CATALINÓN.   Nonsense?

DON JUAN.   Yes.

---

[13] Fugitives from justice cannot be arrested in a church in Seville. That is why Don Juan goes to one. [R.C.]

CATALINÓN. It's gospel truth!

DON JUAN.　　　　　　I don't care if it is.
And what if Duke Octavio tries to kill me—
Have I not hands as well? Where is our lodging?

CATALINÓN. Down in the darkest, hidden street.

DON JUAN.　　　　　　　　　　That's good.

CATALINÓN. Here in this church, it's holy ground.

DON JUAN.　　　　　　　　　　Just so.
D'you think they'll kill me here in broad daylight?
And have you seen the groom from Dos Hermanas?

CATALINÓN. I saw him, too, looking both grim and sad.

DON JUAN. For two whole weeks Aminta has not known
How she's been tricked.

CATALINÓN.　　　　So thoroughly she's hoaxed
She goes about calling herself the countess!

DON JUAN. God, what a funny hoax!

CATALINÓN.　　　　　　Funny enough;
And one for which that girl must weep forever.
They both look at the sepulchre.

DON JUAN. Whose sepulchre is this?

CATALINÓN.　　　　　　Here Don Gonzalo
Lies buried.

DON JUAN.　　What? the same one I killed?
They've done him very nobly for a tomb.

CATALINÓN. This tomb was ordered by the king. What says
That writing there?

DON JUAN, *reads.*　　HERE, TRUSTING IN THE LORD
FOR VENGEANCE ON A TRAITOR, THE MOST LOYAL
OF ALL TRUE KNIGHTS LIES BURIED. What a joke!
So you think you'll avenge yourself on me?
Pulling the statue's beard.

So now you sprout a beard of solid stone,
Good gaffer?

CATALINÓN.　　There are beards that can't be plucked.
You watch yourself with beards that are too strong.

DON JUAN, *addressing the statue.*

Tonight I will await you at my inn
For supper. There we can arrange a duel
Although it will be difficult to fight;
A granite rapier must be stiff to handle.

CATALINÓN. Come, sir, it's getting dark. We'd better go!

DON JUAN, *to the statue.*

How long this vengeance seems to be in coming
Especially if you are going to wreak it!
You mustn't be so motionless and sleepy!
And if you're willing still to wait till death,
Why, what a lot of chances you are wasting
That for so long a time you give me credit!

A room in an inn

Two servants of DON JUAN *are laying the table.*

FIRST SERVANT. We must prepare the room because Don Juan
Dines here tonight.

SECOND SERVANT.   The tables are prepared.
If he's so late there's nothing one can do
But let the drinks warm and the food grow cold.
But who could order order from Don Juan,
The ace of all disorder?

Enter DON JUAN *and* CATALINÓN.

DON JUAN.   You've locked the doors?

CATALINÓN. I've locked the doors exactly as you ordered.

DON JUAN. Then bring my supper, quick.

FIRST SERVANT.   It's here already.

DON JUAN. Catalinón, sit down.

CATALINÓN.   I sup more slowly.

DON JUAN. Sit down, I tell you.

CATALINÓN.   Well, if you insist.

FIRST SERVANT, *aside.* He must be on a journey, now, as well,
To sup with his own lackey.

DON JUAN.   Come, sit down.

A loud knock is heard on the door.

CATALINÓN. Say, that's some knock!

DON JUAN.   It must be someone calling.
See who it is.

FIRST SERVANT. I fly, sir, to obey you.

CATALINÓN. What if the police have come?

DON JUAN.   What if they have?
No need for fear!

FIRST SERVANT *enters, fleeing in terror.*

                    What's this? You're all atremble.

CATALINÓN. He has seen something evil. One can tell it.

DON JUAN. Don't make me lose my temper. Speak, man, speak!
What have you seen? Some devil's terrified you?
Go, you, and see whatever's at the door.
Go on! Go, quick!

CATALINÓN.   Who, I?

DON JUAN.   Yes, you, at once.
Yes, you, get your feet moving. Aren't you going?

CATALINÓN. Who's got the keys?

SECOND SERVANT.   Only the bolt is slid.

DON JUAN. What's wrong with you then? Move! Why don't
    you go?

CATALINÓN. What if the raped and ravished have arrived
To have their final vengeance?

He goes out to see.

CATALINÓN *rushes back in panic, trips, falls over, and
gets up.*

DON JUAN.   What's all this?

CATALINÓN. God help me! You can kill me if you like.

DON JUAN. Who's killing you? What is it? What have you seen?

CATALINÓN. Master . . . there . . . I saw . . . well, when I
    got there . . .

Aside.

But what has seized me? What has snatched my mind?
Aloud.

I got there to the door . . . then after, I was blind . . .

But there I saw . . . I swear to God . . . I saw it . . .
I spoke and said: "Who are you?" And he answered.
I opened, went ahead, and bumped into—

DON JUAN. Well, who? Bumped into who?

CATALINÓN.   Oh, don't ask me!

DON JUAN. How wine confuses people! Here! That candle!
I'll go and see myself who it can be.

DON JUAN *takes the candle and goes towards the door.* DON
GONZALO *walks in to meet him in the form of the statue
that was on the sepulchre.* DON JUAN *staggers backwards
in a state of perturbation, holding his sword by the hilt
In the other hand he carries a candle.* DON GONZALO
advances towards him with slow, short steps, and DON
JUAN *retreats before him till they reach the middle of the
stage.*

DON JUAN. Who's this?

DON GONZALO.   It's I.

DON JUAN.   But who on earth are you?

DON GONZALO. The person you invited here to dine.

DON JUAN. Why, there's enough for both of us, and more
If you've brought any friends along with you.
The table's set already. Sit down here.

CATALINÓN. May God be with me now in my sore need
With Saint Panuncio and Saint Antón.
What? Do the dead eat too?
Aside.

                                He nods in answer.

DON JUAN. Catalinón, sit down with us.

CATALINÓN.   Excuse me:
I take it that he's dined.

DON JUAN.   You've lost your head.
Are you afraid of a dead man? What then?
If he were living, how much more you'd fear him!
What an illiterate and rustic fear!

CATALINÓN. Dine with your guest, sir. I have supped already

DON JUAN. You wish to make me angry?

CATALINÓN.   Sir, I stink

And that's the reason I would not offend you.
I smell too bad.

ᴏɴ JUAN.   Sit down! I'm waiting for you.

ᴀTALINÓN, *aside*. I'm dead with fear. My bum has mis-
    behaved.

The two servants are trembling with fear.

ᴏɴ JUAN. You others there! What about you? You're trem-
    bling?

ᴀTALINÓN. I never liked to eat with foreigners
Who come from other countries. Me, my lord—
You'd have me feasting with a guest of stone?

ᴏɴ JUAN. What stupid fear! If he is stone, what matter?

ᴀTALINÓN. It knocks me all to pieces all the same!

ᴏɴ JUAN. Speak to him courteously.

ᴀTALINÓN.   Sir, are you well?
That "other life," is it a pleasant country?
What is it like—all plains? Or steep sierras?
Do they give prizes there for poetry?

ʀsᴛ SERVANT. To every question he has nodded: Yes.

ᴀTALINÓN. And are there lots of taverns there? Why, surely,
If Noah lives around there, there must be!

ᴏɴ JUAN. Fetch wine.

ᴀTALINÓN.   Señor Dead Man, say, in your country,
Do the drinks there have ice in?

DON GONZALO *nods*.

                Ah! with ice!
What a good country!

ᴏɴ JUAN.   If you want a song
I'll make them sing.

DON GONZALO *nods*.

                Then sing!

ᴀTALINÓN.   The Señor Dead Man
Has real good taste.

ʀsᴛ SERVANT.   He's nobly bred, and so
He is a friend of pleasure, naturally.

They sing within.

> If you expect it of us men
> That our deserts shall find adjusting
> But not till after death, why then,
> A long, long time you are for trusting!

CATALINÓN. Either he finds the heat is overpowering
Or else he is a man who eats but little.
I cannot keep from trembling at my dinner.
It seems that they don't drink much over there
And so I'll drink, for both of us

Drinks.

a pledge
Of stone. I feel less terrified already.

They go on singing within.

> If that's the date you ladies give
> To enjoy all for whom I'm lusting
> You grant a long long time to live
> And burnish up my joys from rusting.

> If you expect it of us men
> That our deserts shall find adjusting
> But not till after death, why then
> A long, long time you are for trusting!

CATALINÓN. Of which of all the ladies you have cheated
Do they make mention?

DON JUAN.   I laugh at them all,
My friend, on this occasion. Why, in Naples
With Isabel . . .

CATALINÓN.   She's not so badly cheated
Since you will have to marry her, quite rightly.
But that poor girl who saved you from the sea,
You treated in a pretty sorry fashion.
You cheated Doña Ana.

DON JUAN.   Hold your jaw!
For here is someone who has suffered for her
And waits for his revenge.

CATALINÓN.   He is a man
Of mighty valour, being made of stone,
And you of flesh. It's not a pleasant problem.

DON GONZALO *makes a sign for the table to be cleared, and for* DON JUAN *and himself to be left alone together.*

DON JUAN. Here, clear this table, since he's making signs
The rest should go and leave us both together.

CATALINÓN. It's bad! For God's sake, master, don't remain!
For here's a dead man that with one sole fist-cuff
Could floor a giant.

DON JUAN.   All of you, get out!
Were I Catalinón, then I might flinch.
But go; for he approaches.

The servants go out, and DON JUAN *and* DON GONZALO *remain alone together.* DON GONZALO *signs to* DON JUAN *to close the door.*

DON JUAN.   The door's shut
And I am at your service. What's your will,
Shade, vision, or phantasma? If your soul
Is travailing in pain, if you await
Some satisfaction or relief, then tell me,
And I will give my word to do whatever
You should command me. Are you in the grace
Of God? Or was it that I killed you recklessly
In a state of mortal sin? Speak! I am anxious.

DON GONZALO, *speaking slowly, as if from another world.*
And as a gentleman you'll keep your word?

DON JUAN. I keep my word with men, being a knight.

DON GONZALO. Then give your hand on it. Don't be afraid!

DON JUAN. What! *Me* afraid? Were you both hell and death,
I'd dare to give my hand.
He gives his hand.

DON GONZALO. Now lower both your hand and voice. To-
morrow
At ten, *I'll* be awaiting *you* for supper.
You'll come?

DON JUAN.   Why, I expected something far
More dangerous than what you ask of me.
Tomorrow I shall be your guest. But where?

DON GONZALO. In my side-chapel, by my tomb.

DON JUAN.   Alone?

DON GONZALO. No, you can bring your servant. And you'll honour
  Your word, as I have done the same to you?

DON JUAN. Of course. I am Tenorio born and bred.

DON GONZALO. And I a born Ulloa.

DON JUAN.   I'll be there,
  And without fail.

DON GONZALO.   I trust your word. Good-bye.

He goes towards the door.

DON JUAN. Wait, let me get a torch to light your way!

DON GONZALO. My soul requires no light. I am in grace.

He retires very, very slowly, looking at DON JUAN, *until he
disappears, leaving* DON JUAN *in a state of panic.*

DON JUAN. God save me, all my body's bathed in sweat!
  My very heart seems frozen here inside.
  For when he took me by the hand and squeezed it
  It seemed I was in hell. Such was the heat.
  And yet his breath and voice were like the blizzard
  Of an infernal frost. But all these things,
  Begot by fear on the imagination,
  Are quite unreal. To fear the dead is baseness.
  If I am not afraid of noble bodies
  With all their powers, alive with wits and reason,
  To fear dead bodies is a stupid thing.
  Tomorrow I will go there to the chapel
  Where it invited me, that all of Seville
  May make a living legend of my valour.

The Alcazar at Seville

Enter the KING OF CASTILE, DON DIEGO TENORIO, *and their
suite.*

KING OF CASTILE. So Isabela has arrived at last.

DON DIEGO. Against her will.

KING OF CASTILE.   She does not like this marriage?

DON DIEGO. She feels the worst at losing her good name.

KING OF CASTILE. It is some other cause that thus torments her.
  Where is she?

DON JUAN.   She has taken up her lodging
  With the Barefooted Nuns.

KING OF CASTILE.   Then fetch her here
  And at her leisure she may serve the queen.

DON DIEGO. And if her marriage must be with Don Juan,
  Then, please, command it, that he may appear.

KING OF CASTILE. Yes, let him come here, full-dressed as a
      bridegroom!
  I'll have this marriage famed throughout the land.
  For from today Don Juan is the Count
  Of Lebrija: to rule it and possess it.
  If Isabel has lost a duke, her equal,
  At least she's won a most outstanding count.

DON DIEGO. For this great kindness I could kiss your feet.

KING OF CASTILE. You have deserved my favours worthily.
  I still am far behindhand in requiting
  Your services. It seems, too, that today
  The Lady Ana should be wedded also.

DON DIEGO. What! with Octavio?

KING OF CASTILE.   Should it not be
  That Duke Octavio must save the shame
  Of this great scandal? Doña Ana and the queen
  Have begged the marquis' life, and now the father
  Is dead, she wants a husband of her choice.
  So now she loses one and wins the other.
  Go to Triana's fort, and tell the marquis
  That for his injured cousin's sake he's pardoned.

DON DIEGO. Now I have seen what most I have desired!

KING OF CASTILE. This evening, then, the weddings will take
      place.

DON DIEGO. All's well that ends well. It should be easy to
  Convince the marquis he was greatly loved
  By his fair cousin.

KING OF CASTILE.   Also, warn Octavio:

The duke is always luckless with his women.
For him they're all appearances and rumours.
They say he's furious against Don Juan.

DON DIEGO. I shouldn't be surprised, since he found out
The truth about that dirty trick he played
Which has done so much damage on all sides.
Here comes the duke.

KING OF CASTILE.   Don't leave my side at all,
For in this crime you, too, are implicated.

Enter OCTAVIO.

OCTAVIO. Give me your feet, unconquered Majesty!

KING OF CASTILE. Rise, Duke. Put on your hat. What is your
    trouble?

OCTAVIO. I come to ask a right that should be granted.

KING OF CASTILE. Duke, if it's just, I swear to grant it. Name it.

OCTAVIO. Already, sire, you know by letters from
Your own ambassador, and the whole world
Knows by the tongue of rumour, how Don Juan,
With Spanish arrogance in Naples lately
In my own name defiled the sacred virtue
Of a great lady.

KING OF CASTILE.   Don't go any further!
I know of your misfortune. What's your plea?

OCTAVIO. To fight it out with him in open country
For he's a traitor.

DON DIEGO.   No, his blood's too noble!

KING OF CASTILE. Don Diego!

DON DIEGO.   Sire!

OCTAVIO.   Why, who are you who speak
Before the king in such a fashion?

DON DIEGO.   I
Am one who holds his peace when the king bids it.
Otherwise I would answer with this sword.

OCTAVIO. You're far too old!

DON DIEGO.   I once was young in Italy.
My sword was known from Naples to Milan.

OCTAVIO. Your blood is frozen. "I was once" is nothing
　　To: "I am now."

DON DIEGO.　　　　　　I am both "was" and "am."

KING OF CASTILE. Come, come, restrain yourselves! Enough!
　　Be silent, Don Diego. For my person
　　You have shown disrespect. As for you, Duke,
　　After the marriages are celebrated
　　We'll speak of this affair at greater leisure.
　　Don Juan's my creation and my henchman,
　　And of this trunk a branch. So keep your distance!

OCTAVIO. Your Majesty, I'll do as you command.

KING OF CASTILE. Come, Don Diego.

DON DIEGO, aside.　　　　　　Oh, my son, my son,
　　How badly you repay the love I bear you!

KING OF CASTILE. Duke!

OCTAVIO.　　　　Sire!

KING OF CASTILE.　　　　Tomorrow we shall have you
　　married.

OCTAVIO. So be it, if it is Your Highness' wish.

　　Exeunt KING, DON DIEGO, and their suite.
　　Enter GASENO and AMINTA.

GASENO. This gentleman may tell us where to find
　　Don Juan Tenorio. Is he round about?

OCTAVIO. You really mean Don Juan Tenorio?

AMINTA. Yes, that's the one I mean, and no mistake.

OCTAVIO. Oh yes. He's here. What do you want with him?

AMINTA. Why, that young man's my bridegroom. Yes, he is.

OCTAVIO. What's that?

AMINTA.　　　　You, being of the palace, haven't
　　Yet heard of it? That's strange.

OCTAVIO.　　　　　　He didn't tell me.

GASENO. Can that be possible?

OCTAVIO.　　　　　Well, so it seems.

GASENO. Lady Aminta is most honourable,
　　And now they're marrying. She is by lineage
　　One of the ancient Christians, pure Spanish,

And is the heir to our own cattle-farm
Which we rule just like counts or marquises.
Don Juan took her from Batricio
And was betrothed to her.

OCTAVIO, *aside.*   This is another
Of his foul tricks, and for my own revenge
They're giving it away.

To GASENO.

What is your wish?

GASENO. I want to see the marriage celebrated
Because the time is passing. Otherwise
I'll take it to the king.

OCTAVIO.   And very justly too.

GASENO. All I require is reason and just law.

OCTAVIO, *aside.* It just fits in, in keeping with my thoughts.
Aloud.

Today there is a wedding in the palace.

AMINTA. Why then, it must be mine!

OCTAVIO.   To make quite sure,
I have a little plan. You come with me,
Lady, where you'll be dressed in courtly fashion
Then into the king's quarters go with me.

AMINTA. Give me your hand and lead me to Don Juan.

OCTAVIO. This is a wise precaution.

GASENO.   Reason prompts it.

OCTAVIO, *aside.* So these good people give me my revenge
Against that traitor villain, base Don Juan,
And his foul injuries to Isabel.

*A street in full view of the church wherein the commander
is buried*

Enter DON JUAN *and* CATALINÓN.

CATALINÓN. How did the king receive you?

DON JUAN.   Lovingly.
As if he were my father.

CATALINÓN.   Did you see
The Duchess Isabel?

DON JUAN.   Yes. Her also.

CATALINÓN. How did she seem?

DON JUAN.   An angel.

CATALINÓN.   She received you
Courteously?

DON JUAN.   Her face seemed bathed in milk
And blushing with her blood like a white rose
With all its dews lit by the red aurora.

CATALINÓN. And so the wedding is this evening, sir?

DON JUAN. Yes, without fail.

CATALINÓN.   If it had been before
Perhaps you'd not have harmed so many women.
But now you take a wife with heavy charges
And grave responsibilities.

DON JUAN.   Are you being
Impertinent and stupid once again?

CATALINÓN. You might at least have waited till tomorrow.
Today's unlucky!

DON JUAN.   What day is it?

CATALINÓN.   Tuesday.
"Never travel or get married on a
Tuesday."

DON JUAN.   Oh, to hell with all that nonsense
Which only fools and madmen take to heart!
That day alone's unlucky, cursed, and foul
When I run out of money. Other days,
All other days, are revelry and laughter.

CATALINÓN. Come, let us go, for you must dress in style.
They're waiting for you now and it grows late.

DON JUAN. We have another business first at hand.
So they'll just have to wait.

CATALINÓN.   What other business?

DON JUAN. To sup with the Dead Man.

CATALINÓN. What need for that?

DON JUAN. Well, don't you know I gave my word upon it?

CATALINÓN. And if you broke it, sir, what could it matter?
  A jasper figure can't expect so much
  From a live man as to insist on vows.

DON JUAN. The Dead Man, then, could say I was a coward.

CATALINÓN. But anyway you see the church is shut.

DON JUAN. Knock, then.

CATALINÓN. What does it matter if I knock?
  There's nobody to open it inside
  And all the sacristans are sleeping.

DON JUAN. Knock!
  Here at this postern.

CATALINÓN. It is open.

DON JUAN. Enter.

CATALINÓN. Let friars enter with their stoles and hyssops!

DON JUAN. Then follow me and hold your tongue. Be silent.

CATALINÓN. Silent?

DON JUAN. Yes.

CATALINÓN. I am silent. Oh, my God,
  Please bring me out alive from such a feast!
  They go out on one side and will come in on the other.

Interior of the church

Enter DON JUAN *and* CATALINÓN.

CATALINÓN. It's very dark for such a great big church.
  Oh, sir, protect me, someone grabbed my cloak!

  DON GONZALO *comes in as before in the form of a statue.*

DON JUAN. Who's that?

DON GONZALO. It is I.

CATALINÓN. I am dead with fright!

DON GONZALO. I am the Dead Man: do not be afraid.

I did not think that you would keep your word
Since you delight in breaking it so often—

DON JUAN. I suppose that you imagine me a coward!

DON GONZALO. Why, yes! Because, that night, you fled from me
When you killed me.

DON JUAN.   I fled from recognition.
But here I stand before you. What's your will?

DON GONZALO. Why, only to invite you here to supper.

CATALINÓN. Pray let us be excused. Here all the victuals
They serve are cold—cold supper and cold lunches.

DON JUAN. We'll sup then.

DON GONZALO.   Well, to do so, you must lift
The lid, here, off this tomb.

DON JUAN.   Why, if you wish it
I'll lift these pillars too!

DON GONZALO.   You're very willing.

DON JUAN, *lifting by one end the lid of the tomb which
folds back easily, leaving discovered a black table already
laid and set.*

DON JUAN. Yes, I have strength and courage in my body.

CATALINÓN. This table must have come from Guinea's coast
It is so black. Are there none here to wash it?

DON GONZALO. Be seated.

DON JUAN.   Where?

CATALINÓN.   See two black servants come
With stools

Enter two figures in black with stools.

            So here, too, people go in mourning
With flannel made in Flanders?

DON JUAN.   You! Sit down!

CATALINÓN. What, me, sir? I've already fed this evening.

DON JUAN. Don't answer back!

CATALINÓN.   All right, I will not answer.
Aside.

O God, in safety get me out of this!

Aloud.

What dish is this?

DON GONZALO.   Tarantulas and vipers.

CATALINÓN. Really? How nice!

DON GONZALO.   That is our diet here.

But you're not eating.

DON JUAN.   I shall eat it

Were all the snakes in hell upon one plate.

DON GONZALO. I'd like to have them sing to you a little.

CATALINÓN. What sort of wine do they have here?

DON GONZALO.   There, taste it.

CATALINÓN. Vinegar, frost, and ice. That's what this wine is!

DON GONZALO. Well, that's the sort of wine that we press here.

They sing within.

> Let all those know who judge God's ways
> And treat his punishments with scorn
> There is no debt but that he pays,
> No date but it is bound to dawn.

CATALINÓN. How terrible! I've heard this tune before
And now it is addressed to me.

DON JUAN, *aside.*   My breast

Is frozen, and the ice tears me apart.

They sing.

> While in the world one's flesh is lusting
> It is most wrong for men to say:
> "A long long time in me you're trusting"
> For very shortly dawns the day.

CATALINÓN. What is this: fricassee?

DON GONZALO.   Of fingernails.

CATALINÓN. Then they must be the fingernails of tailors
They are so sharp and claw-like and rapacious.

DON JUAN. Now I have eaten, let them clear the table.

DON GONZALO. Give me your hand. Don't be afraid! Your hand.

DON JUAN. Afraid, you say. *Me* frightened? Here's my hand.

He gives it.

I'm roasting, burning! Do not burn me so
With your fierce fire!

DON GONZALO.   That's nothing to the fire
Which you have sought yourself! The wondrous ways
Of God, Don Juan, are not fathomable.
And so He wishes now for you to pay
Your forfeits straight into the hands of death.
This is God's justice. What you've done, you pay for.

DON JUAN. I'm roasting. Do not grip my hand so hard!
I'll kill you with this dagger. But the blows
Strike only empty air. Look. With your daughter
I did no harm. She saw the hoax in time.

DON GONZALO. That does not matter. It was your intention.

DON JUAN. Then let me send for a confessor quickly,
So to absolve my soul before I die.

DON GONZALO. Impossible. You've thought of it too late.

DON JUAN. Oh, I am burning! Oh, I am roasting, burning!
I'm dying!

He falls dead.

CATALINÓN.   There is no escape. I, too,
Must die for having been your companion.

DON GONZALO. Such is God's justice. What is done is paid for.

The tomb sinks with a rumbling thunder, taking DON JUAN
and DON GONZALO *with it.* CATALINÓN *creeps out of the
wreckage.*

CATALINÓN. So help me God! What's this? The chapel's burning
With wondrous light. And I'm left with the corpse
To watch with it and guard it. To his father
I'll creep away now and proclaim the news.
Saint George and Holy Lamb of God protect me
That I may come in safety to the street!

The Alcazar

Enter the KING OF CASTILE, DON DIEGO, *courtiers, and attendants.*

DON DIEGO. The marquis wants to kiss your royal feet.

KING OF CASTILE. Then let him enter. Call the Count Don Juan
As well, that he be kept no longer waiting.

Enter BATRICIO *and* GASENO.

BATRICIO. Where are such foul monstrosities permitted
That your own servants should affront, unpunished,
The humble people?

KING OF CASTILE.   What is that you say?

BATRICIO. Don Juan Tenorio, treacherous, detestable,
Stole my young wife the evening of our marriage,
And here I have the witnesses.

Enter THISBE *and* ISABEL.

THISBE. Sire, if Your Highness will not do me justice
On Don Juan Tenorio, both to God and men
I will complain through all my days to come!
When dying he was swept ashore, I gave him
Both life and hospitality. With lust
And promises of marriage he repaid
This kindness. He abused me and then left me.

KING OF CASTILE. What do you say?

ISABEL.   She's telling you the truth.

Enter AMINTA *and the* DUKE OCTAVIO.

AMINTA. Where is my spouse?

KING OF CASTILE.   Who is he?

AMINTA.   What, you don't
Know, even yet? Don Juan Tenorio,
With whom I've come this evening to be wedded,
Because he owes it to my name and honour
And, being noble, will not break his word.

Enter the MARQUIS OF LA MOTA.

MARQUIS. It's time to drag some truths into the light,
My lord. Know then that of the selfsame crime
For which you sentenced me, Don Juan is guilty
(A cruel fraud to put on a best friend)
And I've the witnesses to prove it here.

KING OF CASTILE. Could any shamelessness compare to this?

DON DIEGO. Sire, to reward my services to you,
Let him be made to expiate his crime
So that the heavens themselves don't shoot their lightning
At me, for having bred so foul a son.

KING OF CASTILE. So it is thus my favourites behave!

Enter CATALINÓN.

CATALINÓN. My lords, all listen to the greatest wonder
That ever happened in this world, and kill me
If, listening, you don't believe it's true.
Don Juan, making fun of the commander,
Having divested him of life and honour,
And all the gems and ornaments of life,
Pulling the beard upon his granite statue,
Insulted him by asking him to dine.
Oh, that he'd never done so! Then the statue
Went to his house, inviting him in turn,
And then (to make it short, and not to tire you)
When they had finished supper, took his hand
And squeezed it till he squeezed his life out, saying:
"God ordered me to kill you thus, and punish
Your monstrous crimes. For what you've done, you pay."

KING OF CASTILE. What are you saying?

CATALINÓN.   It's the gospel truth.
Don Juan pleaded, first, that he had not
Seduced the Lady Ana: she discovered
The fraud in time.

MARQUIS.   For this delightful news
A thousand gifts I wish to give you.

KING OF CASTILE. Just punishment from Heaven has been dealt.
Now let them all be married, since the cause
Of all their harm is dead.

OCTAVIO.   Since Isabela's
A widow now, I wish to marry her.

MARQUIS. And I to wed my cousin.

BATRICIO.   And us others
With our own girls. For now THE GUEST OF STONE
Is ended.

KING OF CASTILE. Take the tomb to San Francisco,
The great church in Madrid, and there install it
And so preserve this memory through all time.

LOVE AFTER DEATH

Calderón de la Barca

English Version by Roy Campbell

From the time that Spain had been liberated from the Moorish yoke by Ferdinand and Isabella, the descendants of the Arabs had continued to live upon the same soil . . . until the 1st of January, 1567, when the edict of Philip II which had for its object the extirpation of all Moorish customs was published at Granada . . . The principal Moors . . . sent addresses and petitions to . . . the king; but all in vain. Every day they saw themselves exposed to every species of . . . annoyance; until at length they resolved to have recourse to arms . . . and in the month of December, 1568, the insurrection burst out in the Alpujarra . . . Towards the end of 1570 . . . the insurrection was finally put down.

DENIS FLORENCE MACCARTHY

DRAMATIS PERSONAE

DON ALVARO TUZANÍ
DON JOHN MALEC, *an old nobleman* } *"New Christians" of ancient Moorish descent*
DON FERNANDO DE VÁLOR

ALCUZCUZ, *a Spanish Moor, drunken and fat, who speaks in a pidgin patois*

CADÍ, *an old Moor*

DON JOHN OF MENDOZA

PRINCE DON JOHN OF AUSTRIA

DON LOPE DE FIGUEROA

DON ALONZO DE ZUÑIGA, *supreme magistrate or Grand Corregidor*

GARCÉS, *a soldier*

DOÑA ISABEL TUZANÍ, *sister to Don Alvaro*

DOÑA CLARA MALEC, *daughter to Don John Malec*

BEATRICE
INÉS } *servant maids*

A MANSERVANT

Moorish men and women, Christian soldiers, Moorish soldiers

The scene is laid in Granada and in the Alpujarra (a mountain range parallel to the Sierra Nevada and south of it).

ACT I

A room in the house of CADÍ *in Granada*

*Moors, in short jackets and trousers. Moorish women in white
doublets, with musical instruments.* CADÍ *and* ALCUZCUZ[1]

CADÍ. Are all the doors locked?

ALCUZCUZ.   All ze doors
  Is shutly tighted. Yes! All right!

CADÍ. Let none else enter here but Moors
  Who give the countersign. Our rite
  Must now proceed. Because today
  Is Friday, we must keep it holy
  According to our people's way,
  Without the Christian people knowing—
  Under whose rule we live today
  As captives, in a state of woe—
  Lest they insult us or betray
  Our ceremonies.

ALL.   As you say!

ALCUZCUZ. If we must sing, and dance also,
  Alcuzcuz all to pieces go.

ONE MOOR *sings.*

       Though grieving at its captive state
       Through Allah's deep designs of fate
       The Afric Empire now bewail
       Its lost dominion brief and frail!

ALL *sing.*

       May Allah's law prevail!

SECOND MOOR *sings.*

       Long live the memory great and glorious

---

[1] This latter is a clown. He is called Alcuzcuz after his national dish, *Kouss-Kouss,* as we call an Italian a Macaroni or a Frenchman a Froggie, after certain dishes they eat and some of us don't. I have used a more or less phonetic spelling for Alcuzcuz' first few speeches, afterwards leaving his pronunciation more and more to the imagination of the reader. [R.C.]

Of deeds that made our cause victorious
In our old liberty when Spain
Was captive in her own domain!

ALL *sing*.

May Allah's law remain!

ALCUZCUZ *sings*.

Hooray vor zat great vamous tuzzle
Ven Muza he voz put ze muzzle
On Christian dog and twist his tail
And make ze Spaniolites to wail!

ALL *sing*.

May Allah's law prevail!

Loud knocking within.

CADÍ. What's that?

A MOOR.   They're bursting in the doors!

CADÍ. No doubt they've come to raid us Moors
At our close meetings, since it's true
The edicts of the king pursue
Our rites: and having seen the entry
Of crowds in here, some spy or sentry
Has warned the law of what we do.

More knocking—then it ceases.

ALCUZCUZ. Him give it up now.

MALEC, *within*.   To such knocks,
Can you delay? Undo the locks!

ALCUZCUZ. Upon our zouls you virst must call,
Or locks—zey vill not vork at all!

A MOOR. What shall we do then?

CADÍ.   Hide away
The instruments that serve our rites,
And swear you visit me today
As friends do whom their host invites.

A MOOR. A good plan.

CADÍ.   Now dissimulate.
Alcuzcuz! Run! Why stand and wait?

ALCUZCUZ. Me frighten, if me open gate,
Policeman cudgel me mein belly,

Which wood of cudgel do not sate
Half so agreeably and welly
As Kuz-kuz do, when on a plate.

ALCUZCUZ *opens. Enter* DON JOHN MALEC.

MALEC. Don't be afraid.

CADÍ.   Why, John Malec!
Whose blood, illustrious, without fleck,
Proclaims you twenty-fourth in name
Of proud Granada's line—though first
From Africa your parents came.

MALEC. With right good reason I have burst
Upon you here. Enough to say
That outrages the most accursed
Have dragged me hither in this way.

CADÍ, *aside to other Moors.*
No doubt he's come here to upbraid us.

ALCUZCUZ. *Upb*-raid is very goot, I tink!
Upb-raid is nicer zan just *raid* us
And round us up into ze clink.

CADÍ. My lord Malec, what is your will?

MALEC. Control yourselves, my friends, be still!
When to the council where we frame
The country's laws today I came
The secretary read aloud
A letter in King Philip's name
That to your injury was vowed,
Yes, to your detriment and shame
In every detail and instruction.
How aptly Fortune has been held
The twin of Time for each, propelled
Upon one wheel with wings unfurled,
Either for welfare or destruction
On his relentless course is hurled
Unswervingly without a pause,
And with his speed revolves the world.
The old restrictions, bans, and laws
He read the first, and then the new
Written with a more drastic view:

That no one of the Moorish nation
(Today the merest ash and embers
Of that once radiant conflagration
Whose glory all the world remembers,
Which burned up Spain)—none of our nation
May celebrate the feasts or rites
Or festivals of Islamites.
We may not dress in silks, attend
The baths, or even (here is the end)
Speak our own language, by this token
That, even in private, friend to friend,
Only Castilian may be spoken.
   I, as behoved the oldest man
To speak the first, mildly began
Protesting that, though it was just
That Arab speech and customs must,
In the long run, give place to Spanish,
Yet such a harsh and furious thrust
Some few surviving traits to banish
Which of their own accord would vanish
I thought excessive and unjust,
And begged them to restrain their zeal
Lest violence prove resort to steel,
When ancient custom's spurned as dust.
John of Mendoza next arose
A relative of the great Counts
Of Mondéjar: "I must suppose
Don John has got his own accounts
To square, by pleading in this fashion,
And that his words are swayed by passion,
Since he, by lineage and descent,
Stems from the neighbour continent,
And Nature forced him to protect
(Using so merciful a style)
His own dear people, class, and sect
The Moors—despicable and vile!"
"Don John," I then replied, "when Spain,
A prisoner in her own locked doors,
A captive in her own domain,
Was in subjection to the Moors

The Christian stock that mingled there
(Whom now we call Mozarabs) care
But little, do not take it hard,
Nor as an infamy regard
Having been subjects as they were,
Since often it makes men more great
Unflinchingly to suffer fate
Than lord it over chance and fortune.
And as for being slaves and vile,
When men are brought low by misfortune,
Those that were knights of Moorish style
Owed nothing to the Christians when
They were baptised as Christian men
With the same sacraments and water—
Especially when the arms they quarter
Stem from a line of kings, like mine."
"Yes, but mere kings of Moorish line,"
He sneered. And thus I answered him:
"Does dynasty become more dim
For being Moorish, when Válores,
Cegris and Venegas, too,
Granadas, with all their glories
Are Christians—and as good as you!"
    Words led to words amongst the lords
And as we'd come in without swords,
All in mere argument engaging,
A wordy battle soon was raging . . .
Oh, surely it's an evil chance,
When, lacking swords to glint and glance,
The deadlier tongues begin to rip!
For we can cure most wounds of steel
But wounds from words will never heal.
Perhaps some word that I let slip
Outraged his pride—at this I shiver!—
To wrest my staff out of my grip
And raising it on high . . . deliver . . .
Enough! For harder to declare
Some insults can be than to bear!
    This insult which on your behalf
I earned and suffered in this way

Has struck you all with the same staff.
I have no son who can repay
The insult done to my white hair.
Only one daughter, my sole heir,
Consoles me, to increase my care.

O valiant Moors, you who descend
From the great Africans of yore,
All that the Christian race intend
Is to enslave you more and more!

The Alpujarra range of peaks,
Whose nape the sun at noonday seeks,
A billowy waste of woods and rocks
Dotted with villages like flocks,
Whose towns ride on the silver waves
Of granite, over gulf-like caves,
Cresting the heights of yawning valleys
And take their names from ships and galleys,
Suggested by their shape and view,
Storm-tossed by crags into the blue—
Galera, Berja, Gavia—meaning
Galley and Brig and Topsail too—
That region's ours, its people leaning,
All, to our cause. We've but to store
The heights with food and ammunition,
And man it for the whole position
To be impregnable in war.
Elect a leader from the Royal
Abenhuméyas (from a score
You have your choice) and turn to loyal
Free señors, who were slaves before!
I'll go around, persuading all.
It would be infamous disgrace
Such wrongs as mine in vain should call
Demanding vengeance from our race.

CADÍ. In this great enterprise to share . . .

A MOOR. And for the action which you dare . . .

CADÍ. I'll give my life and wealth up whole . . .

A MOOR. I offer up my life and soul . . .

ALL. And all of us will swear the same!

MOORISH LADY. And I will offer, in the name
  Of every true Moriscan dame
  That in Granada here may dwell,
  My jewels and my silks as well.
  Exit MALEC *with some of them.*

ALCUZCUZ. Myself, Alcuzcuz, only gotting
  Von little shop, vot's next to notting,
  In Vevarambla, nicely smelling,
  Vere almostly all tings I selling—
  Oil, vin'gar, garlic, onions, figs,
  Pimentos, little vons and bigs,
  Broom made of palm-leaf, long dog-leashes,
  Paper, in big or small-one pieshes,
  Tobacco, sealingwax, and tape,
  Needles, pins, threads, and quills to shape
  For writing-pens and valking-sticks
  And seeing Moors are in a fix
  I offer (like the desert camel he
  Do same) up on my back to carry
  Any Alcuzcuz, with his family,
  Chattels, and goods—Tom, Dick, or Harry—
  Vether of base or dukely station—
  For ze var-effort of my nation . . .

A MOOR. You're mad, you idiot, cut it short!

ALCUZCUZ. I'm madness in no kind of sort.

A MOOR. You're drunk then.

ALCUZCUZ.   No! (hic) Much far from it!
  I knowing well our boss Mahomet
  Write in ze Alcohol,[2] his book,
  That when Alcoran can be took—
  You must not—through ze mouth nor look
  Upon it even with your eyes
  I got von system very vise:
  To proof zat I'm devoutly reared
  I drink it only through my beard.

[2] I could not translate the joke where Alcuzcuz calls the Alcoran (the Moorish Bible) the Alacran (or scorpion), so I made him confuse the Alcoran with Alcohol. [R.C.]

A room in the house of DON JOHN MALEC

Enter DOÑA CLARA *and* BEATRICE.

CLARA. Let me weep, Beatrice. My woe
  And fury both together owe
  My eyes a debt. I cannot kill
  The foe that hurts my honour. Still,
  I may lament the dire disgrace
  That I inherit from my race
  And, since I cannot kill, can die.
    How base of Nature and how cruel
  To trick us out for ear and eye
  With wit and beauty, each a jewel,
  And honour, too, with them to vie,
  A blazing diamond, brighter yet—
  But ah! how insecurely set!
  What greater woe is there to feel
  For women, than that we can steal
  A husband's honour, or with shame
  Besmirch even a father's name—
  Yet not restore or wash the same.
  Had I been only born a son,
  Granada and the world should see
  If with a wrong, so base a one
  As to my father he has done,
  Mendoza would have bearded me.
  I'd have him know this furthermore:
  It is not as a woman, nor
  For weakness, that I scorn the churl,
  Since he who fights the old and hoar
  Might well fight duels with a girl.
    But all these hopes are empty speech
  And folly! Would to God on high
  That only these two hands could reach
  My vengeance! Then I'd gladly die.

But worse than all it is for me
That in one day my loss should be
Both of a father and a spouse,
For since this shame fell on our house
Don Alvaro will none of me.

Enter DON ALVARO TUZANÍ.

ALVARO. As a bad augury I heard
You, lovely Clara, speak my name
(While still my love remained unstirred)
As if it had not stayed the same.
If your voice echoed, word for word,
Your heart, I take it to proclaim
That I have hurt you, since you wrest
My name so fiercely from your breast.

CLARA. I can't deny my heart with woes
Is thronged—and you the chief of those.
Alvaro, since the powers above
Now tear me from you past recall
You are my worst despair of all.
So strong and lasting is my love
I cannot yield to be your wife
Since you must never mate for life
With one whose name is in disgrace.

ALVARO. Clara, I need not here retrace
How much I honour and adore
You and your love. I must implore
Your pardon that I came before,
Not after, I'd avenged your father.
Forgive me this delay, the rather
As it is chiefly on your score.
    Although it is against the laws
Of duels, that they be discussed
With women—when you hear the cause,
Clara, you'll pardon me, I trust.
I could console you with the fact
That between gentlemen and lords
There's no dishonour in an act
That's undertaken without swords.
A blow struck in a court of law

Or royal court (as in this case)
Is not in code and does not draw
The least dishonour or disgrace.
The reason that I've called on you
Before I pierce Mendoza through
Is that true vengeances require
Two things: that short of death entire
No wounds suffice and that a brother
Or son should right the wrong: no other
Can arrogate true satisfaction
If not a relative by right.
That is the reason for my action
In coming here before I fight—
To ask your father for your hand,
That when in arms we take our stand,
True satisfaction may be won
Not by a stranger but a son!
For this I came, and if, before,
To ask your hand I have been slack,
The reason for my hanging back
Was that you had been born so poor.
Now all the dowry I implore
Is your deep wrong and injury.
Grant it: that all the world may see
Wrongs are the dowry of the poor!

CLARA. I do not hope, Don Alvaro,
By tears to put more proofs before you
Of the clear truth that I adore you,
And of the faith with which I glow.
I need not say that, twice offended,
Two times today my life has ended
And that I am (though not your wife)
Devoted to your love heart-whole,
Who of my soul have been the life
And of my life have been the soul.
But you must learn this, furthermore,
In spite of what it takes to say:
I would have been your slave before
But cannot be your wife today,
Since if, reluctant yesterday,

You did not ask me for your wife
Then I would never, for my life,
That now of us the world should say:
"He had to overlook so much
Before he'd wed the such-and-such."
I thought myself beyond degree
Honoured, and rich (it seemed to me)
Before I'd yet deserved to capture
Your hand (how vain a heart can be!)
And only doubted in my rapture
In that the bliss pertained to me.
But now, today, I set you free:
To punishment I turn my favour
And into bitterness my savour,
Señor, "that all the world may see"
That honourless I had to bide
Before you'd claim me for your bride!

ALVARO. It's to avenge you that I try!

CLARA. And I, in fear for you, refuse.

ALVARO. This proof of love can you deny?

CLARA. Or this esteem for you?

ALVARO.   No use!
You cannot pass off that excuse.

CLARA. I still can kill myself, and will . . .

ALVARO. And I can ask your father still . . .

CLARA. You're wrong.

ALVARO.   You think this loyalty?

CLARA.   Pride
And honour.

ALVARO.   Is it kind?

CLARA.   It's faith.
Because I swear to heaven above
No other man shall have my love,
And that my honour take no scathe
Is all I would ensure by death.

ALVARO. All this is lunacy. What matter
If . . .

BEATRICE. . . . Madam, I can hear the master,
With others, judging from the clatter,
Already coming up the stair.

CLARA. Go! Quickly! Hide, in that room there!

ALVARO. What a misfortune!

CLARA.   A disaster!

Exeunt ALVARO *and* BEATRICE.

Enter DON ALONZO ZUÑIGA, DON FERNANDO DE VÁLOR, *and*
DON JOHN MALEC.

MALEC. Clara—

CLARA.   My lord—

MALEC, *apart.*

                              (Alas, what pain
It is to meet with her again!)
Aloud.

Go, Clara, to that room and wait.

CLARA, *apart to* MALEC. What is it?

MALEC, *apart to* CLARA. Listen while they prate.[3]

Exit DOÑA CLARA *to the room where* DON ALVARO *is hidden, and they both listen behind the half-open door.*

ZUÑIGA. Mendoza is a prisoner, pending
The settlement of all this row,
Detained in the Alhambra now,
Until we reach some peaceful ending
And the whole quarrel is composed.
Don John Malec, you are requested
To keep indoors, while all is tested,
Your word is all that is imposed.

MALEC. I give my word to keep enclosed.

VÁLOR. It will not be for long, because
The Lord Corregidor's so kind.

[3] It is well to realize here that both Malec and Clara, as will be
seen later, are fooling Zuñiga and Válor. Neither has renounced
the idea of vengeance. Malec, in discussing the marriage at all, is
simply marking time and trailing red herrings till the revolt gets
going. Clara in marrying Mendoza only wants to get near enough
to him to shove a knife in him—now that she has turned down
Tuzaní for slighting her poverty. [R.C.]

(The laws of honour and state-laws
To one another must be blind.)
Yet kindly he permitted me
To act between you two and see
If some solution I could find.

ZUÑIGA. One would think bearded men were youths!
For Don Fernando (through two plain truths)
Could cut this whole sad business short.
There has been, can be, no offence
By laws of honour or of sense
In brawls that are begun in court.
To law or royalty import
No private rancour or pretence.
The whole thing could be settled here.

VÁLOR. I think I have a good idea . . .

ALVARO, *apart to* CLARA. Did you hear that and were you weighing
The gist?

CLARA, *apart to* ALVARO. I did.

VÁLOR.   . . . As I was saying
Don John of Mendoza is a knight
Of valour, beauty, and delight,
Unmarried, and of lordly line.
And you, John Malec, can combine
The royal blood of twenty reigns
Both in your breeding and your veins
And, for a better coat of arms,
Rose-of-the-winds of all the charms,
You have a daughter, known for brains,
Beauty and wit and sterling mettle.
If anybody wants to settle
This business, then it's clear (why wait?)
That Doña Clara be the mate
Of John Mendoza . . .

ALVARO, *apart*.   Oh, my fate!

VÁLOR. So strange a quarrel cannot fight
Against itself without a right.
The thing is to confound it quite.
Bridegroom, offender, and offended

Would then be one, the matter ended.
Since once he is the plaintiff's son
And the insulter, both in one,
And the avenger, too, you see—
Either three times (were he so dense)
At his own guts he'd have to fence
Against himself—or else agree,
Rather than split up into three
(And all antagonists by code)—
To settle down, and let things be:
When such complexities are truckled
To such an infinite degree,
Everyone might be his own cuckold
Or countermand his pedigree.

ALVARO, *aside.* I'll answer them, or I'll explode!

CLARA, *aside.* No, for God's sake, don't ruin me.

ZUÑIGA. Why, that would settle the affair!

MALEC. Only one hindrance, I declare,
(Without more need of splitting hair)
Is whether she would take upon her
What she might think . . .

CLARA, *aside.*   An answered prayer
Thus to avenge our joint dishonour . . .

MALEC. . . . What she might think incumbent on her
In taking to herself a mate
Whom she has so much grounds to hate.

Enter DOÑA CLARA.

CLARA. Yes, I could love him, all the more
That you, sir, wished me to be married.
Life without honour is so arid
Of happiness. Though if I bore
The title of your son, my ire
Would challenge him to mortal war,
Either to kill him or expire,
Being your daughter I am willing
To save your honour and defend it.
Aside.
And since it can't be done by killing

Alone, by killing and by dying
Together, I can safely mend it.

ZUÑIGA, *to* VÁLOR.

I could not solve it for my trying:
Only your brain could have unravelled
A problem that had got me gravelled.

VÁLOR. I have no doubt but this will end it.
Write the arrangement down in ink
And right away I'll take or send it.

ZUÑIGA. We'll take it, both of us.

MALEC, *aside*.   I think
This is the best means to delay
Till the rebellion's under way.

VÁLOR. All will end happy as you'll see,
Which comes of leaving things to me.

Exeunt MALEC, VÁLOR, ZUÑIGA.

CLARA. They've gone into a room to write
Their new arrangement. Alvaro,
It's time that you come out and go.

ALVARO. Yes, go I will, with great delight,
No more to see a heart so light
In such a noble breast. That I
Committed no rash act of spite,
When with your words you made me die,
Was neither from respect nor fright
But from relief so base a whore . . .

CLARA. Heavens preserve me!

ALVARO.   . . . out of hand,
With vile intent and coldly planned,
While one man hid behind her door
Could give herself to one man more.
It almost makes me feel unmanned,
That such a thing of crumbling sand
I could believe in and adore.

CLARA. I beg you, Alvaro, no more!
The day will come to prove you wrong
And Clara resolute and strong
To perish and to satisfy . . .

ALVARO. What satisfaction could there be
  In such a lunatic transaction?

CLARA. You'll see there can be satisfaction.

ALVARO. Did I not hear you just agree
  To be Mendoza's wife?

CLARA.   Just so.
  The motive you have yet to know.

ALVARO. What motive, save the death of me?
  If you've a motive, then impart it,
  Any excuse you care to name
  Since he has caused your father's shame
  And left me dead and brokenhearted.

CLARA. Alvaro, time will undeceive you
  One day quite soon when my firm faith
  With clear, unbandaged eyes will leave you
  To see my honour without scathe:
  And that, in spite of all, this seeming
  Inconstancy was purest faith.

ALVARO. What sly deceit! Can I be dreaming
  Or did I hear you pledge your hand?

CLARA. You did.

ALVARO.   And you're to be his wife?

CLARA. No! No! You do not understand.

ALVARO. What's your intent?

CLARA.   To take his life
  As soon as he is near my hand
  And it is nearer to my knife.
  Now are you satisfied?

ALVARO.   No! No!
  If he should die within your arms,
  He dies amidst the fairest charms
  That ever mortal man did know.
  It shall not be, for long before
  He has the luck to die in them
  I have bethought a stratagem
  To stretch him in his own red gore.

CLARA. Is this your love?

ALVARO.   It is my honour.

CLARA. And is it kindness?

ALVARO.   No. I'm jealous:
Of such a death I would be zealous
And to be killed in such a style.

CLARA. They've finished writing there inside.

ALVARO. Well, I must run then. To abide
So long was scarcely worth the while.

A room in the Alhambra

Enter DON JOHN OF MENDOZA *and* GARCÉS.

MENDOZA. Rage never can exist with right and reason.

GARCÉS. Do not excuse yourself. You did quite rightly
To strike him—not as an old man but new,
I mean as a "New Christian" which he is.
And then he thinks to claim immunity
And beard a true Gonzalez de Mendoza.

MENDOZA. Oh, there are thousands trusting to their rank
Who think that they can swagger and be proud.

GARCÉS. For such folk old Don Iñigo the constable
Wore two swords—one, as usual, at his belt;
The other served him as a walking-stick.
And when they asked him why, he answered them:
"This at my belt is for the sort of people
Who, like myself, wear sword-hilts at their belt.
This other one, here, serves me as a cudgel
For little cheeky insolents who don't."

MENDOZA. He set a good example to grandees
Carrying those two swords, in those two manners,
And now we're talking about swords, just give me
Your own, for though I am a prisoner here,
I never like to be without a sword
Whatever happens.

GARCÉS.   I am glad I came
  To visit you and be with you today
  If you have enemies.

MENDOZA.   Oh, by the way,
  Garcés, how did you fare, there, at Lepanto?

GARCÉS. Like other men who had the luck to be there
  Soldiering under the heroic hand
  Of him who is the offspring of the grand
  And god-like eagle whose vast wings unfurled
  Bracketed dawn and sunrise round the world!

MENDOZA. Don John of Austria, how did he return?

GARCÉS. Content and happy with the expedition.

MENDOZA. It must have been tremendous.

GARCÉS.   Just you listen.
  With the alliance . . .

MENDOZA.   Wait, here comes a woman,
  Masked.

GARCÉS.   How unfortunate! I had a hand
  I thought would sweep the bloody table clean
  And now my ace is trumped by this damned queen!

  Enter DOÑA ISABEL TUZANÍ, *masked.*

ISABEL. Señor Don John Gonzalez de Mendoza
  May one who comes to visit you in prison
  Inquire if it agrees with you?

MENDOZA.   Of course!
  Garcés, get out!

GARCÉS.   Look out, sir, that there's not some . . .

MENDOZA. Your fears are vain. I know the voice. Get out.

GARCÉS. You know the voice. I'll go, then.

MENDOZA.   Get along, then!

  Exit GARCÉS.

MENDOZA. I question what I see and hear
  For contradictory replies:
  The mystery is hard to clear
  As to which sense is telling lies
  Because if I believe my eyes
  You are not she whom you appear

And if I credit either ear
You are yourself in shape and size.
Put by, put by the subtle cloud:
Shine forth from the obscure disguise
That lies upon you like a shroud
That both my eyes and ears may say
That it has dawned two times today.

ISABEL. To put you out of further doubt
I'll have to show my person clear
Though haunted, too, by jealous fear—
Who other would have sought you out
Or in disguise have stolen here
But . . .

MENDOZA. Isabel! my dearest lady!
You here, to seek me in this way!
And in a dress so drab and shady!
And from your home so far away!
How can one dream from day to day
Impossible delights are vain
When in this way you make them plain?

ISABEL. On hearing that you had been taken
That instant, by the news so shaken
My love could brook no more delay
And while my brother was away
In this disguise I ran, I flew,
With just one handmaid and no more
Who's keeping watch there by the door.
You see how much I care for you.

MENDOZA. Now all misfortunes such as mine
May preen themselves and prink and shine
When with a kindness so divine—

Enter INÉS *with a cloak, frightened.*

INÉS.   My lady!

ISABEL. Inés, what's wrong?

INÉS.   Don Alvaro, your brother,
Is coming here.

ISABEL.   I wonder if he'd know me
In this disguise.

MENDOZA.   Now, what a thing to happen!

ISABEL. If he has followed me, I'm dead already.

MENDOZA. If you're with me you need not be afraid.
Go into that next room and shut the door.
If he should try to find you it will be
Over my own dead body.

ISABEL.   I'm in danger,
Terrible danger. May the heavens protect me!
Both women hide in the next room.
Enter DON ALVARO.

ALVARO. Don John of Mendoza, I must speak with you
Alone.

MENDOZA. And so you find me, all alone.

ISABEL, *aside from the door.* How pale he looks!

ALVARO.   Then I will
shut the door.

MENDOZA. Shut it, then.
Aside.

God! that was a good one, that was!

ALVARO. And now it's shut, please listen carefully
To what I say. I heard a conversation,
By chance, from which I learned you will be sent for . . .

MENDOZA. That's true enough.

ALVARO.   . . . Be sent for from this prison . . .

MENDOZA. That's no lie.

ALVARO. . . . . By some who by this action will insult me
Even to my very soul.

ISABEL, *apart.*   What more can he
Divulge?

MENDOZA, *apart.* He beats about the bush. Confound him!

ALVARO. So I came on ahead to save my honour
Before the rest come here to try to patch
Indecent and humiliating friendships
Between yourself and them.

MENDOZA.   You keep me puzzled.

ALVARO. Then let me make it clear.

ISABEL, *apart*.   I breathe again.
He was not on my track, then, after all.

ALVARO. The Grand Corregidor, Alonso Zuñiga,
With Don Fernando de Válor and Don John
Malec, his relative, are coming here
To make their peace with you, and it's my duty
To hinder and prevent them. With my reasons,
Though I have many, I'll not trouble you.
But chiefly I came here on the caprice
Of curiosity to find out whether
You were as valiant with the young and active
As you have proved yourself with weak old age.

MENDOZA. I'm very grateful to have heard your reason.
I thought it was a very different thing
And one of far more import to your honour
And far more interesting to myself.
Why, this is just a fleabite! I would never
Refuse a friend who only wants to fight.
So now before they come for these "indecent
Friendships" they want to patch and you to hinder . . .
Delighted to oblige you! Pull your sword out!

ALVARO. That's what I came for and to stop your breath
Sooner than you expect.

MENDOZA.   Here is the place then.
There's nobody around.

ISABEL, *within*.   My miseries
Increase from bad to worse: who would not blush
To see her brother fighting with her lover?
They fight. Clash of swords.

MENDOZA, *aside*. What bravery the lad shows!

ALVARO, *aside*.   God, what skill!

ISABEL, *aside*. What can I do? I wish the victory
To both of them, yet either way my loss
Would be as great and heavy as the cross.
Tripping over a chair, DON ALVARO *falls back.*

ALVARO. Confound it! Tripping on that stool, I've fallen!

ISABEL *comes out and shrieks*. Mendoza, hold your hand!
Aside.

What am I doing?
Love for my brother made me lose my head!
Returns again.

ALVARO. You see how wrong you were in telling me
Nobody was around.

MENDOZA.   Do not complain!
I would have spared your life in any case.
It makes it more like fighting two of you
Together and it gives me twice the fun.
I know the rules of cavaliers besides:
Seeing your fall was purely accidental
I would have let you rise.

ALVARO.   I owe two things
To that fair lady that she saved my life
Before you spared it: by that act she saved me
From any obligation to yourself
And also left me as I was, determined
To have your life at any cost.

MENDOZA.   Lay on, then!
What holds you back?

ISABEL, *aside.*   Would I could scream for help!
Knocking on the door within.

ALVARO. They're knocking at the door.

MENDOZA.   What shall we do then?

ALVARO. When one of us is dead, the live one then
Opens the door.

MENDOZA.   Well said!

ISABEL, *entering.*   Before that happens
I'll open it myself and let them enter.

ALVARO. Don't open it!

MENDOZA.   Don't open it!

She opens it.

Enter DON FERNANDO DE VÁLOR *and* DON ALONZO DE ZUÑIGA.

ISABEL.   My lords,
These men you see here wish to kill each other.

ZUÑIGA. Shame on you! for to see you muffled thus

And these two men contending in your presence
Proves clearly that you are the cause of this!

ISABEL, *aside*.

Poor me! The way I thought I might escape
Led to my own destruction.

ALVARO.   So as not
Unduly to imperil this fair lady
To whom I owe my life, I'll tell the truth.
It's not for love but as a relative
Of Don John Malec that I'm fighting here.
And that, I hope, should satisfy you all.

MENDOZA. That's true. This lady's only here by chance,
Visiting me.

ZUÑIGA.   Well, since that quarrel now
Has been sealed up in friendship, all this ceases.
Everything has been settled without blood
And bloodless victories win greater glory.

Enter INÉS.

ZUÑIGA. Go, ladies, and good-bye.

ISABEL, *aside*.   What a relief!

Exeunt INÉS *and* ISABEL.

VÁLOR. Señor Don John Mendoza your relations
And mine have settled this affair indoors
(As in Castile we use the phrase) as follows.
By marriage, as a relative, the breach
Is to be soldered once for all: you give
Your hand in marriage to the lovely daughter
Of John Malec, the phoenix of Granada,
And as a part of . . .

MENDOZA.   Hold your tongue! No more!
For, Señor Don Fernando Válor, hear me.
There are too many obstacles to this.
If Lady Clara is a blessed phoenix,
Let it be in Arabia, among Arabs.
We highlanders, the nobles of Castile,
Don't feel the need of phoenixes at all!
And men like me have no need of relations
To solder up such weird and doubtful honours!

It's indecent to mix Mendoza blood with
The blood of the Malecs. They do not ring
Together in the selfsame sort of key—
"Mendoza" with "Malec" cannot agree!

VÁLOR. Don John Malec's a man . . .

MENDOZA. And one like you!

VÁLOR. Yes, for his ancestors were a whole line
Of kings on either side, and so were mine.

MENDOZA. Yes, but my own, although they were not kings,
Were higher than the kings of Moors: they were
Castilian highlanders and mountaineers.

ALVARO. What Don Fernando says, I will uphold
Out in the open with my sword.

ZUÑIGA. Then here
My magistracy ceases, for before
They ever made me Grand Corregidor
I was a Zuñiga of high Castile,
And hereby laying down my staff of office
Beside Don John Mendoza, with blue steel
I will support him . . .

Enter a SERVANT.

SERVANT. There are people coming.

ZUÑIGA. Dissimulate then. I'll resume my office.
Don John, you must remain a prisoner here.

MENDOZA. In all things I obey you.

ZUÑIGA. You two, go.

MENDOZA. If either of you wish for satisfaction . . .

ZUÑIGA. You'll find us both wherever you may choose . . .

MENDOZA. With swords, good sirs . . .

ZUÑIGA. . . . And capes and nothing else.[4]

DON ALONZO DE ZUÑIGA *goes out and* DON JOHN MENDOZA *accompanies him.*

VÁLOR. To think my honour could put up with that!

ALVARO. To think my valour could consent to this!

---

[4] I think this means that they will not be wearing clandestine
mail or armour under their coats. [R.C.]

VÁLOR. That I became a Christian, thus to be
  Insulted.

ALVARO.   And since I became one too
  That it should be forgotten who I am.

VÁLOR. It's cowardice that I'm not yet revenged.

ALVARO. It's infamy that I have drawn no blood.

VÁLOR. Oh, heaven for the chance!

ALVARO.   For just one chance!

VÁLOR. If heaven should allow . . .

ALVARO.   If fate permits . . .

VÁLOR. I shall do such a thing that very soon . . .

ALVARO. Spain will repent a hundred thousand times . . .

VÁLOR. The valour . . .

ALVARO.   . . . The incendiary force
  Of the strong, arrogant, and fearless arm . . .

VÁLOR. . . . Of the proud Válors!

ALVARO.   . . . Of the Tuzanís![5]

VÁLOR. You heard me?

ALVARO.   Yes.

VÁLOR.   When tongues for once have spoken
  Then hands must speak and something must be broken.

ALVARO. Who says they are not ready to begin?

[5] This is a typical Calderonian construction. The exclamations
are supposed to help each other along. They have a double syntax,
making sense; and each single exclamation, also making sense, in-
terweaves through the double one. [R.C.]

ACT II

The Alpujarra in the neighbourhood of Galera

Drums and trumpets sounding.[6] *Enter* SOLDIERS, DON JOHN
OF MENDOZA *and* PRINCE DON JOHN OF AUSTRIA.

DON JOHN OF AUSTRIA. Insulting, bold, rebellious mountain
    range
Whose wild uncultured ruggedness, whose strange
Outlandish height, whose awful weight, whose horrid
Monstrous build and overwhelming forehead
Fatigue the ground, expand the air and earth,
And make the sky conceive a monstrous birth!
Primeval lair of bandits, thieves, and vandals,
Whose breast, a thundercloud of plots and scandals,
Gives forth seditious lightnings, word for word,
That striking here, in Africa are heard!
Today, this day will be the very last
That you will boast of your perfidious past
Because I bring with me, yoked to one tether,
My justice and your punishment together—
And both of them ashamed that they should be
Yoked to so mean an end. Not victory
I come for, since such victory were venal
Whose foes were rebels and its purpose penal.
But say what could have caused this fierce revolt.

MENDOZA. Listen, young eagle of the thunderbolt.
This range is called the Alpujarra. This,
Making a rampart of each precipice,
The Moors have made their stronghold, seeing Spain
Affords no shelter to their dusky strain.
Among these mountaintops they would restore

---

[6] As three battalions of the Legion or Tercio of the Duke of
Alba are being used, they should be playing "El Novio de la
Muerte" ("The Sweetheart of Death"), which is the marching
song of that ancient regiment, today the smartest in Europe. [R.C.]

A second Africa in Spain once more:
Here if the slopes are difficult to make
The peaks are nigh impregnable to take.
The range is fourteen leagues around, but fifty
If of the cliffs and canyons you are thrifty:
Because between the summits of the peaks
Are meadows, hanging gardens, rushy creeks
And fields of flowers and every kind of tillage.
On every col a hamlet or a village
You'll find, in such a wise that when the west
Goes red at sundown, flying crimson flags,
You'd think each village made of hollow crags,
For so the houses seem round every crest,
Though round the mountain-skirts they build no nest.
These towns their arsenal are, their wall,
Galera, Gavia, Berja most of all.
Full thirty thousand able Moors and tall,
Without the women or the children, can
Within this range be mustered to a man.
There are rich pastures in between the rocks
For browsing goats and grazing herds and flocks.
There is enough to safeguard their subsistence
Even in the fruits they grow. For their existence,
Added to meat, a thousand plants suffice,
Wild or domestic, terraces of rice
In irrigation, barley, wheat, and millet.
Even the crags bow to their horn and fill it;
A tribute of green herbs they draw from stone.
So learn'd in irrigation they have grown
That to each dint or scraping of a hoe
The rocks give birth and into gardens grow.
As for the cause of the rebellion, I
Having a part in it, should not reply
And hope you will forgive my silence, since
A partisan may speak but not convince.
Perhaps it would be better to admit
I was the cause, by me the flames were lit,
But the encroaching laws, the somewhat cruel
Restrictions, long before had laid the fuel.

But then if anybody is to blame
Better myself—to me, it's all the same!
It might have been our quarrel, or it may
Be that from Válor, just the other day,
The chief guard at the door of the Guild Hall
Took off a hidden dagger. Then with all
These new restrictions harassed and oppressed
As they have been, which daily, without rest,
The Court keeps sending out, the wretched nation
Was driven to rebel in desperation.
And so, before we others were aware,
They gradually armed those mountains there,
Found out and fortified the best positions,
And stored them up with rations and munitions.
This treason has been going on three years,
Unnoticed until now as it appears.
It's a strange thing that thirty thousand men
Could operate so secretly, and when
The women and the children knew it too,
Yet not a hint of it could trickle through—
Specially when you think how great a danger
A secret runs: when all the world's a stranger
To it, except some three, it worms its way,
Funnels and squirms into the light of day,
Then fills the world with thunder, blood or spray.
The first report of thunder from the bolt
Of lightning which they forged in this revolt
Up there among those craggy fells and clefts
Found echo then in sacrileges, thefts
From churches, blasphemies, assassinations,
Attacks, and treasonable machinations,
Until it seemed Granada was the stage
And theatre for tragedy and rage.
When necessary justice intervened
Stubborn resistance met it, although screened.
The staff of justice turned into a blade
And into force civility was made.
Mere disobedience was not long before
It burst out into open civil war.
They murdered first the Grand Corregidor,

Alonzo Zuñiga. With loud alarms
The drums of the militia called to arms.
But that was not enough, for chancy Fortune
Still sides with innovation, to importune
Set laws and wonted order. We'd the worst
Of it then, and were beaten at the first.
What huge misfortunes piled themselves on high
Like hydras which we lopped to multiply.
Disasters swelled the woe upon our side
While their successes puffed their windy pride,
And harm and havoc spread to both alike.
With help from Africa, they hope to strike
Our force in two, with one half to engage
The landing on the coast, while the rest wage
This war against the gorges and the crags.
It all depends the way their fortune wags.
If they have more successes at this stage
The whole of Spain will stream with Moorish flags
Because the Moors of Castile and Valencia
And of Estremadura, too, are set,
Upon our next defeat or misadventure,
To rise up as one man and beat us yet.
That you may learn that they are (quite apart
From being firm and daring) deep in art
And cunning in their politics, give ear,
And I'll describe their government round here.
The first thing that they did was to elect
The leader, nay, a monarch of their sect,
And though there were two claimants—Tuzaní
And Válor—in the end, they now agree
That Válor, marrying (at Malec's suggestion)
The sister of his rival, without question
Should reign supreme.
Aside.

                        My memory diverts me
Now from my theme, and pierces me, and hurts me,
Thinking of Tuzaní who might have been
Made king by them, though little that would mean,
Had I not of his sister made my queen!

Aloud.

And now, my lord, when Válor once was crowned,
The first act that he passed and published round
Was that neither his subjects nor their dames
Should call each other by their Christian names
Nor practice Christian rites. This first idea
He signed with the old name Abenhuméya
That the old Moorish kings were wont to use
In Córdoba, which kings with his infuse
Their blood, with his, directly by descent.
No speech but Arabic will he consent
To hear. No other clothes can they affect,
Nor creed, save those of Islam and the sect.
These edicts issued, next he organised
His forces, and his strategy devised.
Galera here, the "Galley," to Malec
He gave, to admiral the craggy deck—
This town that we have come on first, whose sheer
Fortifications stand without a peer
Since Nature was the learned engineer
That trenched and walled these labyrinths of rock,
Impregnable to almost any shock,
Nor to be won but by great loss of gore.
Malec commands it, as I said before,
Father to Clara, otherwise renowned
As the Maleca. Gavia the High,
By which the summit of the range is crowned
As by a topsail spread against the sky,
Was given in command to Tuzaní
Betrothed to Clara, the Maleca. He
Spends half his time at Berja lower down
Which is the heart that animates that giant
Of granite, yonder, with its craggy frown.
Those are their dispositions. Once defiant,
The towering Alpujarra beetles there
As if its crags and boulders all prepare
To avalanche in thunder to their base
And at your royal feet would sue for grace.

DON JOHN OF AUSTRIA. Don John, your warnings and your in-
     formation

Are worthy a Mendoza and yourself
Noise of drums.

For loyalheartedness. What drums are those?

MENDOZA. They're beating up the forces to the muster
For the march-past.

DON JOHN OF AUSTRIA. What troops are those in front?

MENDOZA. That's the battalion of Granada, sir,
Drawn from the lands the Genil feeds and waters.

DON JOHN OF AUSTRIA. And who commands them?

MENDOZA.   Lord Tendilla, sir,
Perpetual constable of the Alhambra
And all the lands pertaining thereunto.

DON JOHN OF AUSTRIA. His name, in Africa, makes the Moors
tremble.

Drums.

What is this next battalion?

MENDOZA.   That of Murcia.

DON JOHN OF AUSTRIA. In charge of whom?

MENDOZA.   The Marquis of
los Vélez.

DON JOHN OF AUSTRIA. His fame and actions crown him as a
hero.

More drums.

MENDOZA. These troops, my lord, come from Baeza, led
By such a soldier that fame owes him statues,
Sancho de Avila.

DON JOHN OF AUSTRIA. Although his name
Is dear to military fame and honour,
I think he can claim one distinction higher
Than all the rest because the Duke of Alba
Taught him, as his once-favourite disciple,
Never to yield but conquer all the time.

More drums.[7]

MENDOZA. Now here's the Tercio of the Legionaries—

[7] Here should be played, if possible, the Novio de la Muerte
because the Tercio or Legion is about to appear. [R.C.]

All veterans from Flanders. They have come,
Changing the pearls and crystal of the Meuse
For those of the Genil.

DON JOHN OF AUSTRIA.   Who leads this Tercio?

MENDOZA. A monster of nobility and valour,
Don Lope de Figueroa!

DON JOHN OF AUSTRIA.   I've heard wonders
Of his determination and resolve
And also of his lack of common patience.

MENDOZA. Oh, that's because he's got the gout and roars
And rages with impatience when it keeps him
From active service on the field of battle.

DON JOHN OF AUSTRIA. I'd like to meet him.

Enter DON LOPE DE FIGUEROA.

DON LOPE.   By the Lord Almighty
The only reason I can tolerate
These feet of mine is that they led me here
To meet Your Royal Highness.

DON JOHN OF AUSTRIA.   How did you
Arrive?

DON LOPE. As well as anybody could arrive
Who's marched from Flanders almost without rest
To Andalusia here to serve Your Highness.
You would not come to Flanders, so at last
Flanders has come to you!

DON JOHN OF AUSTRIA.   Someday I hope
To go there. But what sort of troops are these
You've brought?

DON LOPE.   So fine and tough a set of men
That were the Alpujarra hell itself
And were Mahomet in command of it,
They'd rush through every breach—except for some
Who cannot climb the cliffs for gouty feet.

A SOLDIER, *within.* Halt!

GARCÉS, *within.* Get out of my way and let me through!

Enter GARCÉS, *carrying* ALCUZCUZ *on his back.*

DON JOHN OF AUSTRIA. What's this?

GARCÉS. I was on picket in those foothills
  When hearing something rustle in the bushes
  I found this dainty greyhound stalking me
  Behind them. Without doubt he is a spy.
  I tied his hands up with my musket-sling
  And as he started yelping the alarm
  I took him on my back and brought him here.

DON LOPE. Good man, by God! And are there such down here?

GARCÉS. You think there are no men outside of Flanders,
  My lord.

ALCUZCUZ. Very bad business, poor Alcuzcuz!
  The apple of my windpipe smelling hemp!

DON JOHN OF AUSTRIA, *to* GARCÉS.
  I know you very well. You cannot fool me
  Twice over with your wondrous deeds of valour.

GARCÉS. How little it costs princes to reward one
  When but to honour merit is a prize.

DON JOHN OF AUSTRIA. You, there! Come here!

ALCUZCUZ. You spikking
    to myself?

DON JOHN OF AUSTRIA. Yes.

ALCUZCUZ. Though as a favour I might com-
    ing nearer,
  I feel nice stopping here.

DON JOHN OF AUSTRIA. Who and what are you?

ALCUZCUZ, *aside*. Alcuzcuz must be careful what he say.
  Aloud.
  I am Alcuzcuz. I one Moorish wallah.
  Other-one Moors, they fetch me here by force
  Because I be one Christian and I know
  The Creed, Hail Mary, the Fourteen Commandments,
  And everything. The Moors, she want to kill me
  Because I tell them I one Christian wallah
  And so I run away to fall in hands
  Of anyone who like to take me on.
  You spare my life, I tell you what the Moors
  Saying and doing in the mountains there.

I guide you to the passage in the mountains
Where you can enter in and no resistance.

DON JOHN OF AUSTRIA. Although I think he's lying, yet perhaps
It could be true.

MENDOZA.   Why doubt it? There are many
Among them who are Christians. I myself
Know one, a lady, whom they brought by force,
Against her will, as he may well have been.

DON JOHN OF AUSTRIA. Well, since we neither doubt him nor
    believe him
Retain him, Garcés, as your prisoner.

GARCÉS. I shall, my lord. I'll keep my eye on him.

DON JOHN OF AUSTRIA. Until we know if we were right or
    wrong.
And now, Don Lope, we'll inspect the camp
And settle where we'll start with the attack.

MENDOZA. Your Highness must decide with greatest care.
Although this undertaking seems of little
Importance to a warrior of your fame,
Some undertakings that yield little glory
Give grave dishonour when we fail in them.
So we must be both wary and attentive
Not so much to succeed in our attempt
As not to fail in it.

    Exeunt DON JOHN OF AUSTRIA, DON JOHN OF MENDOZA, DON
    LOPE DE FIGUEROA *and soldiers.*

GARCÉS. You! What's your name?

ALCUZCUZ.   In Christian—Dish of Rice—
Which in the Moorish tongue is Alcuzcuz.
But call me Rice since now I am converted
From Moor to Christian.

GARCÉS.   Listen, Alcuzcuz,
You are my slave. Speak truthfully!

ALCUZCUZ.   Thank you!

GARCÉS. You said to Prince Don John of Austria—

ALCUZCUZ. Was he that wallah?

GARCÉS.   Yes. You said you knew
An easy passage to the High Sierras.

ALCUZCUZ. Yes, master.

GARCÉS.   Now although it is a fact
  He's come to conquer you with all these generals,
  The Marquis of los Vélez, John Mendoza,
  The Marquis of Mondéjar, and Don Lope
  De Figueroa, the secret of the passage
  Must not be told to anyone but me.
  You've got to take me there and show me, now,
  Because I want to scout and reconnoitre.

ALCUZCUZ, *aside*. I'll have to lead him round and round the
      whole
  Range of the Alpujarra since the offer
  I made that Christian was a pack of lies.
  Aloud.
  You follow me.

GARCÉS.   Hang on a moment! Wait!
  I left my rations in the guardroom there
  Before I went on picket. I'll just stuff them
  Into my knapsack here to save the time
  And eat them as we walk along.

ALCUZCUZ.   All right.

GARCÉS. Come on then.

ALCUZCUZ.   Saint Mahomet, since you be
  My prophet, spirit me away to Mecca;
  For poor Alcuzcuz he swing about between deep sea and
      devil and get driven from caterpillar to post without
      stopping.

A garden in Berja

Enter MOORS *and* MUSICIANS, *followed by* DON FERNANDO DE
VÁLOR *and his wife*, DOÑA ISABEL TUZANÍ.

VÁLOR. Within the pleasant skirts of this crowned peak,
  Whose coronet's a city, Spring convenes
  Her court. In the republic of the flowers
  The rose, like you, has been elected queen.

Sit down, my love, and let the others sing
To see if melancholy yields to music.

ISABEL. Valiant Abenhuméya, whose great courage
Not only does the oak of Alpujarra
Crown with its leaves but also the green laurel
Ungrateful to the sun, it's not disdain
For the good fortune of your love that makes me
So melancholy but the dispensation
Of Fate. For Fate has that strange character
That it can never bring a happiness
To us but that it mates it with grief.
My grief is born without a cause.
Aside.

                         I would
To God that that were true!
Aloud.

                         It's the result
Of this strange character of Fate. How can I
Forego a shrewd presentiment of evil
When I am raised so high in happiness
That I am giddy and foresense a fall?

VÁLOR. Then, if to make you sad would make you happier,
I much regret that I cannot console you.
Oh, let your melancholy grow forever
Since with it grows your empire over me
And with it grows my love. Musicians, sing!
Music and sadness always are well met.
There is a pact of peace between them both.
SONG.

        My joys, you do not need to say
        Whom you belong to, since I know
        You must be mine, so brief your stay,
        So suddenly you go!

Enter MALEC, *who comes to talk to* DON FERNANDO DE VÁLOR *on his bended knee. On opposite sides* DON ALVARO *and* DOÑA CLARA *enter in Moorish costumes and remain at the entrance. Also* BEATRICE, *the maid.*

ALVARO, *aside.*

> My pleasures do not need to say
> Whom they belong to, since I know

CLARA.

> They must be mine, so brief their stay,
> So suddenly they go!

The instruments go on humming softly while the play continues.

CLARA, *aside.* How sad I am I overheard that song!

ALVARO, *aside.* What strange confusion strikes me in that voice!

CLARA, *aside.* Just when my father's treating of my marriage!

ALVARO, *aside.* Just when love was anticipating joy!

CLARA, *aside.* Oh, listen to the music, my scared hopes!

ALVARO, *aside.* Listen, my fancies! Listen to that song!

Music, and they both join in the last two lines.

ALVARO *and* CLARA, *aside.*

> They must be mine, so brief their stay,
> So suddenly they go!

MALEC. My lord, since in the thunderclouds of battle
Love also finds a place, I wish to tell you
I have a plan to get my daughter married.

VÁLOR. Who is so fortunate?

MALEC.   Why, Tuzaní
Your brother-in-law.

VÁLOR.   Why, nothing could be better,
Since each of them would die without the other.
Where are they both?

Both CLARA *and* ALVARO *approach him.*

CLARA.   What happiness to kneel
Here at your feet.

ALVARO.   What happiness that you
Give to us both your hand.

CLARA.   Rather my arms,
Thus, to embrace you both. In our most learned
And holy Alcoran, the law requires
No other ritual than that Tuzaní
Should make his settlement with the Maleca
In terms of wealth and jewels; and it's done.

ALVARO. All is too mean that I possess:
  Than you all splendour blazes less.
  To give you gems, I know, is stupid
  As giving diamonds to the sun.
  But here's a brooch made like a Cupid
  Of diamonds which flash to stun,
  With a whole quiverful of rays;
  He stoops before you here and lays
  His diamonds at your feet. This one
  'S a string of pearls such as Aurora,
  For nobody but only you,
  Would weep, mistaking you for Flora,
  If you would gather up their dew.
  And here's a lazuline, spread eagle,
  The colour of my hope, all blue,
  The only bird that at the regal
  White sun can stare and keep its view,
  Even as now it stares at you.
  And here's a ruby which the sun
  Lit up but has no more to do
  With me, since my good fortune's done
  With memories for good. Remember,
  Yourself, that in each blood-red ember
  Of ruby, and each ray-white jewel,
  Is nothing that I would recall;
  And if your memories find renewal,
  Let these not be the phoenix-fuel
  From which they are revived at all.

CLARA. Your gifts, my lord, are like your words, all flame.
  All my life long I'll wear them in your name.

ISABEL. I wish you happiness in your immortal
  Alliance.
  Aside.

        Which for me bodes little good.

MALEC. Now join your hands in token of your souls.

ALVARO. I am all yours.

CLARA.   Come let our arms confirm
  This deathless bond.

CLARA *and* ALVARO.   I'm happy now.

As they join hands, drums and marches are heard.

ALL.　　　　　　　　　　　　　　　What's that?

MALEC. Those are not Moorish drums that roll their thunder
　　Against our eyrie in the crags. They're Spanish!

ALVARO. What an unfortunate confusion this is!

VÁLOR. Suspend the marriage till we find what new
　　Prodigy this portends . . .

ALVARO.　　　　　　　　　　Why, don't you see
　　The prodigy was that I should be happy:
　　What greater prodigy than that could be?
　　The sun no sooner looked on my good luck
　　Than Spanish arms and thunders then eclipsed it
　　Out of alarm that such a thing should be!

More drums.

Enter ALCUZCUZ *with knapsacks on his shoulders.*

ALCUZCUZ. Give thanks to Allah and Mahomet that
　　I got to you at last.

ALVARO.　　　　　　　　Where have you been,
　　Alcuzcuz?

ALCUZCUZ.　Well, now, everybody's here!

VÁLOR. What happened to you?

ALCUZCUZ.　　　　　　　　　　I was at my post
　　Where I was posted when another fellow,
　　Posting himself behind me, bore me off
　　As if I was a post—to one Don John,
　　Who has arrived with all his men down there.
　　There, feigning that I was a Christian dog,
　　I told them I believed in God, not Allah.
　　They spare my life but give me for a servant
　　To the same Christian soldier that made off
　　With me, and scarcely do I told this fellow
　　I know a path into the Alpujarra
　　When he insist that I must show it him.
　　He did not want his comrades to observe him
　　And, giving me this knapsack with his food,
　　Told me to lead him on into the forest.
　　As soon as I was sure we were alone,
　　And he could not catch up, I gave the slip

To him. Just then a Moorish trumpet sounded
And scared him back to camp. I come with warning
That I just left Don John of Ostrich, with
The Marquises of Figura-aroma
And Lucifer and Sancho Deviller
Quite near here. And they come to fight with you,
All of them, sure, here in the Alpujarra!

VÁLOR. Now hold your tongue, or you will make me angry.

ISABEL. Now, from this lofty summit, where the sun
At dawn is scared to crease his scarlet banner
And at nightfall to quench his lonely watchfire,
Vaguely, in doubtful forms and blurred mirage,
One can distinguish the invading squadrons
Who trample on our boundaries.

CLARA.   Granada
Has sent a mighty host.

VÁLOR.   Whole worlds of men
Would be too few to conquer me! Were he
Who would subject this wondrous labyrinth
Not son of the Fifth Charles but the fifth planet,
And were the whole horizon to be covered
With martial standards, tents, and troops of war,
These crags would serve then for a funeral pyre,
These rocks would be the cairn upon their grave.
Now that the stern decision is approaching,
They find us well prepared against surprise,
Ready to meet them in full force. Malec
Must go now to Galera, Tuzaní
To Gavia. I'll remain in Berja here,
Trusting to Allah that he will provide
For all of us, and shelter and protect us
Since all of us are fighting on his side.
Go then to Gavia first. When we're victorious
Will be the time to celebrate your love.

Exeunt DON FERNANDO DE VÁLOR, MALEC, ISABEL, *other
Moors and musicians.*

CLARA, *to herself.*
          My pleasures do not need to say
          Whom they belong to, since I know

ALVARO, *to himself.*

> They must be mine, so brief their stay,
> So suddenly they go!

CLARA, *to herself.*

> Roses of happiness that shut
> And withered ere they could be born

ALVARO, *to himself.*

> That perished ere they could be cut
> And left me here to mourn!

CLARA, *to herself.*

> Since now you prove so frail and tender
> And cast your petals at one sigh—

ALVARO, *to himself.*

> Since joy has proved so mean a lender—

CLARA, *to herself.*

> The joys we win we must surrender,
> No sooner conquered, than to die—

ALVARO, *to himself.*

> My joys, you do not need to say
> Whom you belong to, since I know.

CLARA, *to herself.*

> Delights of those who've lost their way,
> As we have, you are sons of woe!
> Before you bloom, you fade away!
> If it was by mistake you found me
> For someone else, it is not kind
> Thus mockingly to hover round me.
> Then leave me to myself: go find,
> Lord of my joys, Don Alvaro,
> Whom you belong to, since I know.

ALVARO, *to himself.*

> Our joys seem marvels in our sight
> For scarcely can we deem them true
> But they will prove it by their flight:
> They're marvels in their fleetness too.
> I was half mad with joy, and now
> With melancholy. Vain delight,
> You sought me by mistake, I vow,

> For someone else whose heart is light.
> My sorrows need not tell me, no,
> Whom they belong to, since I know.

CLARA, *to herself*.

> Although, false pleasures, you entice
> Pretending you can be enjoyed

ALVARO, *to himself*.

> And though you might pretend it twice,
> You, once for all, were proven void.

CLARA, *to herself*.

> Twice prosperous you seemed today

BOTH, *to themselves*.

> You showed it in your haste to flee.
> You showed it in your long delay
> To come to us when you were free.

CLARA, *to herself*.

> And by the briefness of your stay

BOTH, *to themselves*.

> I know that you belong to me.

ALVARO. I have been talking to myself, Maleca,
Since for my grief I could not talk to you.
When my love crowned itself with the victorious
Palm of your own, then I was silent too,
Suspended in the pure calm of my heart
Since it is foolish that the noisy tongue
Should take upon it to express one's soul.

CLARA. Speech is a voluntary act, since men
Can well be silent of their own free will,
But hearing is involuntary passive
And cannot be turned on and off like speech.
Yet such is my despair and my distraction,
I cannot even hear for what I'm feeling.
If suffering can stop you speaking, think
How one must suffer—that one ceases hearing!

ALVARO. The king has ordered me to Gavia, you
Are for Galera. Love, with Honour wrestling,
Yields to that tyrant. Go, then, to Galera.
And may the pitying heavens grant the siege,

The storming, and the battle that awaits us
May fall on Gavia, leaving you in peace.

CLARA. And so I cannot see you till the war
Is finished?

ALVARO. Yes, you'll see me every night.
It's but two leagues from Gavia to Galera
And if Love cannot fly them with his wings
Then he was fledged in vain.

CLARA. Far greater distances,
I know, are measured by his wings. Each night
I'll wait you at this postern in the wall.

ALVARO. Sure of your love, I'll come here to the wall
Each night. Give me your arms now as a pledge.
Drums are heard.

CLARA. More drums are sounding.

ALVARO. What a curse it is!

CLARA. Oh, what a load to bear!

ALVARO. What pain!

CLARA. What grief!

ALVARO. And this is love, is it?

CLARA. It's more like death!

ALVARO. Well, can one die more deeply than to love?
The two lovers go out.

BEATRICE (*now Zara under the new laws against Christian
names*). Alcuzcuz, since we're left alone together,
Come here.

ALCUZCUZ. Zara, you speaking to zese rations?
Or is it me, Alcuzcuz, vat you vant?

BEATRICE. Why is it that you always think of gorging
When all is grief and moonlight? Listen to me!

ALCUZCUZ. Vas you addressing vith such loving kindness
To me, or to this knapsack full of rations?

BEATRICE. It is to you I speak, although my love
Is partly for the knapsack; it's so like you,
So full of food, I want to look inside.

ALCUZCUZ. I thought I knew your tricks. Then to the knapsack,
And not to me, address your tenderness.

BEATRICE *goes on pulling out of the knapsack the various things she mentions.*

BEATRICE, *horrified.*

Here's bacon! . . . Food of dogs! Mahomet
Forbids to us the flesh of swine!
More venom's here to make one vomit,
Accursèd alcohol and wine!
I'll see or touch no more of it!
Be warned Alcuzcuz, it's accurst!
There's enough poison in this kit
To blow you up and make you burst.

Exit BEATRICE.

ALCUZCUZ. All poison vas it? No mistake?
All venom vas it? And no doubt?
This woman Zara vas von snake—
She know vat poisons is about
And recognise them ven she see them
And though she voz so glutton, too,
She vould not eat them!—Vell, that heathen
Christian, I see now vat 'e do:
He put ze grub into ze sack
So that Alcuzcuz steal one snack . . .
Alcuzcuz poisoned . . . fall down dead . . .
And die of stomach-ache instead
Of eating ham and drinking sack.
Oh vot a villainous damn plot
To kill Alcuzcuz! He not catch me!
I laugh and spit upon the lot!
Mahomet from my death he snatch me!

Drums.

But nearer now ze trumpet come
And nearer, nearer sound ze drum,
Squeaking so fierce, and rumbling hollow
Along ze mountain. I must follow
Tuzaní. Is anybody knowing
Somevone vants poison, cheap and nice?
Good poison! . . . going . . . going . . . going . . .
Good poison, very cheap ze price!

Mountains round Galera

Enter DON JOHN OF AUSTRIA, DON LOPE DE FIGUEROA, DON
JOHN OF MENDOZA, *and soldiers.*

MENDOZA. You get a better view of all the landmarks
When just before the sun goes down it hangs
As now, less bright. That town on my right hand
Which from the concrete of a mighty rock
Was hung, thus falling through the centuries,
Is Gavia the Lofty. That town there
Upon its left whose towers compete with its
Own pinnacles and boulders is called Berja.
That other, there, they call Galera, maybe
Because its keeled foundation's like a galley's
Or that it rides an ocean of scrolled rocks,
Curling like waves, and heaves a foam of flowers
Spuming around it, like a shawl of spray.
It looks as though, subjected to the winds,
It turned and veered with them above the world.

DON JOHN. One of these two divisions must besiege . . .

DON LOPE. Well, let us see which one of them's best suited,
And has the best hands for the task, for feet
Don't count in sieges!

DON JOHN.   Fetch me that Morisco
Who gave himself up: we'll investigate
If there was any truth in what he said.
Where is Garcés, to whom I gave him prisoner?

MENDOZA. I haven't seen him since.

GARCÉS, *within.*   Alas! heaven help me!
Enter GARCÉS *wounded and falling down.*

DON JOHN. Look! What is this!

GARCÉS.   I've got here still alive,
Though only just alive.

MENDOZA.   My lord, it's Garcés!

DON JOHN. What happened to you?

GARCÉS.   Is Your Highness ready
To swap with me the dropping of a charge
For some priority intelligence?

DON JOHN. Go on! Speak!

GARCÉS.   That Morisco that you gave me
Said that he came here to deliver you
The Alpujarra by a secret path.
Your Highness, ridden by the one desire
To find this path, I disobeyed my orders.
(The love of glory is not base desire
For profit.) So I took the Moor to show me.
I followed him among those labyrinths
Where even the sun is bound to lose his way
Although he passes through them every day.
No sooner were we by those crags surrounded
Than he gave tongue, and all the rocks resounded
With Moorish horns responding to his yelp.
Like dogs they rushed their fellow-cur to help.
To fight them all was useless, so before
They came in numbers, soaked with my own gore,
Amid the thickest undergrowth my shoulders
I heaved, and rushed downhill until the boulders,
Under the ramparts of Galera, drawn
Asunder in a melancholy yawn,
As if to utter some tremendous groan
For being crushed beneath such weight of stone
As that which straddled it,[8] gaped wide its jaws
Which it can never close, seeing the cause
Is that it still must groan beneath that strain
Forever to bewail its fate in vain.
I crawled inside this tunnel, perhaps
They did not see me enter through its chaps,
Or else they thought me lost within its gloom
Or that they thought that there I'd found a tomb,
Sore bleeding as I was. No more they loitered.
And there, alone, the siege I reconnoitred.
I found that strong Galera had been mined

---

[8] *I.e.*, the yawn. [E.B.]

By Time, the greatest ally we could find,
For in the world no dapper engineer
Or miner to his strategy comes near.
This tunnel, then, approaching from the south,
If you with powder-barrels fill the mouth,
Without the need of a besieging train,
You'll shower the ramparts over half of Spain
And save whole months of slow starvation, sallies,
Battering-rams, and skirmishing in valleys.
Thousands of lives that swarm in that high city
I give you for my own. Have then no pity
On children, let the old men not escape,
And let the women be for spoil and rape—
It is this last I'm recommending chiefly.

DON JOHN. Staunch this man's wound! Away with him!

They take out GARCÉS.

                                     Now, briefly,
Don Lope, I accept as a good omen,
Fair as the right-hand eagle to the Roman,
That there's a town here which is called The Galley.
After Lepanto, all my fancies rally
Round that one word. So now the legion marches
Straight to Galera.

ONE SOLDIER.   Give the password!

ANOTHER SOLDIER.   Say it!

SOLDIERS. Galera!

DON JOHN.   Grant me for triumphal arches,
Heaven, these peaks! As for this campaign, may it
Prove, though on land, as fortunate to me—
Siege as the sea-fight, mountains as the sea!

Ramparts of Galera

Enter DON ALVARO *and* ALCUZCUZ.

ALVARO. I leave my life and honour in your hands,
Alcuzcuz, since if it is known I come

From Gavia on these errands, in an instant
I lose my life and honour at one blow.
Stay with my mare while I go in the garden.
Soon I'll return for I dare not be slow.
We must be back in Gavia ere they know
That we were absent from our post.

ALCUZCUZ. I'm always at your orders to oblige you,
Though vith such haste ve has to come and go,
I never get a chance to get my knapsack
Out of my room, ve has to hustle so.

ALVARO. If I find that you leave this post one instant
I'll kill you without mercy. Now you know!

DOÑA CLARA *comes out of a postern.*

CLARA. Is that you?

ALVARO.   Who but I could be so faithful?

CLARA. Enter at once in case they recognise you.
If I detain you here.

Exeunt ALVARO *and* CLARA.

ALCUZCUZ. By Allah, but I'm feeling sleepy!
With slumberness I'm getting limp.
There is no job that's half so creepy
As that of pander, bawd, or pimp!
In any other sort of job,
You're either on your job or off it—
Whoa, pony, whoa!—But, swap my bob!
A pander works for others' profit.
He takes the lover to his lady
And then gets paid in kicks and blows.
I better seek a job less shady—
A shoemaker, perhaps (who knows?)
They make themselves new shoes. A draper
In a new suit may cut a caper.
A cook would set me cock-a-hoop
At every turn to taste the soup.
Or it might be as good to take
A bakery, and eat some cake.
No job so mean but is far grander
Than this sad job to be a pander
Which neither gets you clothed nor fed

But only gets you stabbed instead—
Whoa, mare!—For god's sake, someone, catch her!
For my poor legs will never match her!

He runs out after the mare and is heard saying within:

Whoa! Mare, please stop to run away
And do the thing I ask from you:
I'll do the same for you one day
If for Alcuzcuz you will do.
I cannot catch him, that's the truth.
There is no luck for Alcuzcuz,
Yet I've done well enough forsooth.

He enters with the knapsack which he has fetched from his room.

Because when he comes back, my master
Will kill me, when he's finished kissing.
To Gavia he cannot get faster
Than they find out that he was missing.
"Where is my mare?" "I have not got."
"What did you do with her?" "She trot."
"And now I kill you on the spot!"[9]
Zip! He will take me from my life
And die me sudden vith his knife.
But yet Alcuzcuz, my dear son,
Zere is more deaths to choose than one.
Let's die by poison, vithout strife,
Seeing it is von hopeless case
And up to life I cannot face.

Pulls the leather bottle from knapsack and drinks.

Better like this, than all in slices
Bathed in my blood, like sauce or gravy.
How am I? Better, thanks! How nice is
This venom! makes me feel all wavy

Drinks.

With waves of warmth! it glows inside!
I see I did not take enough.

Drinks.

[9] Here Alcuzcuz is imagining his conversation with his master when the latter returns. [R.C.]

It must be weak. I have not died.
Once more I have to take ze stuff.
Drinks.

So I may die little by little
But now I think it acts. My eyes
Grow dim, my brain turns, dries my spittle,
And now my tongue is twice the size.
Come on, let's have two other tries.
Drinks more.

With poison I vill have to fill me
Before he gets a chance to kill me.
Vere is my mouth to pour it in?
I cannot find it! Round it spin!
Drums.

SOLDIER, *within.* Hey! Sentries of Galera! The alert!
They light beacons in the watchtowers.

ALCUZCUZ. When thus the lightning starts to flash around
Who doubts that thunder is about to sound?

Enter DON ALVARO *and* DOÑA CLARA, *startled.*

CLARA. The sentries, see, are lighting up the towers.

ALVARO. The Christians in the silence of the night
Have stolen to Galera through the shadows
Without a doubt.

CLARA.　　　　　　Go quickly! The whole castle
Is in a tumult.

ALVARO.　　　　　What a glorious action
To leave my lady here besieged and run!

CLARA. How miserable . . .

ALVARO.　　　　　　　Thus to turn my back?

CLARA. Go, for your honour lies on Gavia there.
Perhaps this is a providential warning
For you to get on duty.

ALVARO.　　　　　　Oh, my heart!
With love and honour tearing me apart,
What wild confusion whirls me!

CLARA.　　　　　　　　Answer first
Your honour: love's a thing that can be nursed.

ALVARO. I'll answer both at once.

CLARA. How?

ALVARO. I will carry
You with me. Love and Honour we will marry
Both to a single risk. Jump up behind
Here on my mare whose speed insults the wind.

CLARA. I'm yours. And with my husband I will share
Whatever comes.

ALVARO. Alcuzcuz, bring the mare!

ALCUZCUZ. Who's calling?

ALVARO. I am: bring the mare!

ALCUZCUZ. Yes (hic!),
I'm waiting for her too. She'll come back quick
For that is what she promised when she fled.

ALVARO. Where is she then?

ALCUZCUZ. Run off. But then she said
"Not long" and she's a mare who keeps her head.

ALVARO. By heavens, then, I'll kill you!

ALCUZCUZ. Not so quick
For I'm so badly poisoned and so sick
That I could knock you flying with my breath,
Just one whiff of my breath.

ALVARO. Dog! To your death
I'll send you now!

CLARA. Stop! Stop! Alas, don't do it!
She restrains him and is wounded in the hand.

ALVARO. What's this?

CLARA. It is my blood. Your dagger drew it,
When I restrained your hand.

ALVARO. Is any life
Worth such dear blood?

CLARA. On my own, as your wife,
I beg you not to kill him.

ALVARO. Over me
No other prayer so absolute could be.
Does it bleed much?

CLARA.   No.

ALVARO.   Bandage it with this.
Hands her a handkerchief.

CLARA. Since I cannot accompany my bliss,
  Go swiftly now: and if they fail to make
  The town tonight, tomorrow we will take
  The selfsame route, for always from this side
  The city it has been quite safe to ride.

ALVARO. Agreed!

CLARA.   Then Allah keep you!

ALVARO.   To what end,
  Since I abhor this life?

ALCUZCUZ.   Then you can mend
  Your griefs by loving it. Here in this bottle
  There is some poison left to close your throttle.
  They ignore him.

CLARA. Then go, my love!

ALVARO.   How sadly I depart!

CLARA. And I with what affliction in my heart!

ALVARO. To know that my opposing star . . .

CLARA. And that my fate, severer far . . .

ALVARO. . . . My true love from my heart has cut

CLARA. . . . The gates on my desire has shut

ALVARO. . . . And only shines to work me spite.

CLARA. . . . Since now the Christian arms have come
  With trumpet hoarse and rolling drum
  To rob me of my heart's delight.

ALCUZCUZ. Is this to sleeping or to dying?
  It's much the same, when all is said,
  So much the same I am not trying
  To know if I'm asleep or dead.

ACT III

Near Galera

Enter ALVARO *without seeing* ALCUZCUZ *lying asleep on the ground.*

ALVARO. Cold pallid night, to you I here entrust,
Most worthily, my hope and enterprise;
To you my love confides its happiness,
My soul its longed-for trophy and its prize.
For to your gloom (in spite of all these spangles
Above) Maleca will give nobler light
When, like a retiary, she entangles
Me in the snares and springes of her charms
Once she is stolen plunder in my arms.
Upon the wings of anxious care I've flown
To just a quarter of a league within
Reach of Galera. In this part here, Nature
Constructed, without art, thick leafy mazes,
Which, neither too distinct, nor too confused,
Afford a handy stabling for my horse.
And since there's nobody about to see me
I'll tether him to this strong olive, trusting
Tonight to leather thongs with far more reason
Than yesterday I trusted in a man.
Trips on the prostrate body of ALCUZCUZ.
What the . . . !

             But every accident forebodes
And seems an omen to my amorous breast.
Last night Maleca's blood, and now this body!
If it's an accident, then all the more
My valour should resent it, since the moment
I start approaching to Galera's walls
Upon a wretched carcase I must fall.
Each thing today I've touched or seen or heard
Of horror and dismay has brought me word.

Alas, poor miserable wretch, to whom
This homeless, rough sierra serves for tomb!
But no, since having lost the vital spark,
No longer now, beset with shades of gloom,
You fight with fears and terrors in the dark.

ALCUZCUZ *wakes.*

ALCUZCUZ. Who walks on me?

ALVARO.   What's this I see and hear?
Who's there? Who are you?

ALCUZCUZ.   I'm Alcuzcuz, here.
You told me I must waiting for the mare
And here I am, nobody having seen me.
If you, tonight, got to go back to Gavia,
Why you turn up so late? But always
Lovers are velly lackadaisical.

ALVARO. What are you doing here?

ALCUZCUZ.   What voz I doing?
You ask me! When I wait for you so long
Ever since you were going in the postern
To visit with Maleca!

ALVARO.   What a state
To be in! What a sot! So since last night
You've lain here? God! Who ever saw the like?

ALCUZCUZ. I may have slept (but was not drunk)
And had a little forty-wink
Because I swallowed poison-drink,
Because I die of a blue-funk,
Because the mare, she do a bunk,
Because you kill me too, I think.
But since the mare she not come back,
And poison do not make me crack,
And Allah makes me feeling bedder,
Come on! Let's go along together.

ALVARO. What idiocy! You were dead drunk last night!

ALCUZCUZ. If there are poisons that can make
One drunk, then, yes, I will allow
That I voz drunk, but by mistake.
My tongue tastes like a rusty plough,

My mouth of iron, and my lips
Of plaster splintered into chips!

ALVARO. Get out of here that not a second time
You spoil my chance of happiness sublime!
I do not want to fail of my delight
Through your good offices again tonight!

ALCUZCUZ. It was not Zara's fault, for why,
To stop me drinking it she try.
"This stuff voz poison, yes," she said,
"Alcuzcuz drink, Alcuzcuz dead."

A noise within.

ALVARO. Hide in these branches! I hear people coming.
Wait till they pass!

Exeunt.

Enter GARCÉS with soldiers.

GARCÉS.   Here, this cave is the mouth
Of the big mine, this gap beneath the wall.
Come silently, since nobody has seen us.
The fuse by now is lighted. Any moment
You can expect the mountain-side to burst
And fill the sky with thunderclouds of dust.
As soon as it goes up, not one of you
Must wait a second, but rush up and seize
The new positions which this mighty landslide
Will yield us on the crests of its moraines,
And, fighting, you must keep those same positions
Until the reinforcements can arrive
Who're hiding in these woods behind us there.

Exeunt.

Enter again ALVARO and ALCUZCUZ.

ALVARO. Did you hear anything?

ALCUZCUZ.   Nothing I heard.

ALVARO. It must have been some sort of night-patrol
Making its rounds. For this I must be careful.
Have they gone?

ALCUZCUZ.   Do you look, yet you cannot see?

ALVARO. I must approach the rampart now.

Firing of a cannon.

                              What's that?

ALCUZCUZ. Nothing voz speaking vith a clearer voice
    To tell you vot he is than von big piece
    Of ordnance. He voz saying: "I'm von cannon."
    Votever language he voz speaking in
    He mean the same.

Explosion of the mine, prolonged rumbling.

MOORS, *within.*   Help, Allah! Heaven save us!

ALCUZCUZ. Save me, Mahomet! Allah vill see to you!

ALVARO. It seems that jerked from their eternal axles
    The huge wheel of the adamantine earth
    And of the crystal heavens were unhinged.

DON LOPE, *shouting within.*
    The mine has worked! Everyone to the breaches!

Drums. Yells of attackers; screams of victims.

ALVARO. Monstrosity! What Etna or Vesuvius?
    What horrible Avernus in eruption?
    What huge volcano, got with child of mountains,
    Heaves up their molten lava to the sky?

ALCUZCUZ. What monasteriosity! What salubrious
    Vernal eruction and absurd volcation
    Make too much smoke and noise all round the place?

ALVARO. Who ever saw destruction vaster?
    While flames and flashing blades of steel
    Vie with each other which the faster
    Shall overwhelm and prove the master
    The burning city walls reveal
    Their dire abortions of disaster
    With livid horrors, more than real,
    And gape their entrails, carved with fire,
    Till that which was but brick and plaster
    With conscious pain begins to twire
    And twinge. The fire, if blood could take it,
    That had not had the time to die,
    (Yet only fiercer seems to make it)
    Would now be quenched, the flames would die.
    The town, if rushing smoke could take it,

Would be rebuilded there on high.
Each street, a writhing viper, streams
With blood and burning pitch. All adders
The houses are, of coiling flames,
Of spiral smoke, gyrating screams
That go on winding up the ladders
Of their own ruin till it seems
They re-establish there on high
A capital of ghastly dreams
And ghoulish nightmares in the sky!
Then what a nobleman were I
And what a lover, did I not
(With Death himself to cast my lot)
Rush climbing up these ramparts high
Until in my embraces furled
I hold the rare Maleca nigh
For whom Galera and the world
May burn to cinders! What care I?

Exit ALVARO.

ALCUZCUZ. I not von nobleman, nor I
Is not von lover, if I let
Zara go blazing to the sky.
Vat vould you like vith me to bet?
I'm not one, no, you're right! The whole wide earth
Is full of them—yet only one I be!
What is Galera and the whole world worth
If only I can get away scot-free?
There's only one Alcuzcuz, and that's me.

The ruins of Galera

Enter DON JOHN OF MENDOZA, DON LOPE DE FIGUEROA,
GARCÉS, *and soldiers.*

DON LOPE. Deliver up the town to fire and sword!
Let not a single soul remain alive!

GARCÉS. I'll go and fire the town.

FIRST SOLDIER.   I'll start the plunder.

Enter MALEC[10] *and Moors.*

MALEC. I will suffice alone, before this rampart
To serve for its defense.

They fight a battle.

MENDOZA.   That is Malec,
Señor, the chief commander of the town.

DON LOPE. Surrender!

MALEC.   What's the meaning of that word,
Surrender?

CLARA, *within.* Help me, Father! Help! Oh, Father!

MALEC, *aside.* That is Maleca calling me to help her.
I am torn in two halves!

CLARA, *within.*   Oh, help me, Father!
Help! I am being killed. A Christian's killing me!

MALEC. Now let them come and kill me! I'll not struggle.
So let my life be ended with your own!

DON LOPE. Die there, you dog, and take my compliments
Down to Mahomet with you as you go!

*The Moors retire, forced back by the Christians. After
the battle has been concluded off stage, re-enter soldiers.*

FIRST SOLDIER. I've never seen such plunder in my life!
Nothing but rubies, diamonds, and emeralds!

SECOND SOLDIER. Look, I am rich for life! All in one hour!

GARCÉS. My sword has spared no single life today
Either for being beautiful or feeble.
What I would give to catch that dirty Moor,
Alcuzcuz, and to slit his gizzard too!

DON LOPE. Now that Galera's all in flames, call back
The looters lest we have to rescue them!

MENDOZA. Pass on the order to retire!

---

[10] Malec's first name under the new Moorish rule is no longer
John (a Christian name) but Ladín. Both Mendoza and Clara call
him by that name in these scenes. But I make Mendoza call him
Malec as before and I make Clara call him Father instead of Ladín,
since the use of a new name only adds confusion. Isabel's Moorish
name, Lidora, is used once below. [R.C.]

FIRST SOLDIER. Pass on
  The order to retire!

SECOND SOLDIER. Pass it along!

  Exeunt.

  Enter DON ALVARO.

ALVARO. Through seas of blood and forests of red fire
  Stumbling on slaughtered bodies in the mire,
  At last to Malec's house I have arrived,
  A heap of ash, where nothing has survived
  The flames of sword-blades and the scythes of flame
  That reaped it bare.

CLARA *and voice within.* Alas! Alas!

ALVARO. There came
  Upon the breeze a piteous tender cry
  Soft as a dove's, sad as a parting sigh.
  And, there again! repeating the same tones,
  A gentle voice that on the night wind moans!
  But like a streak of lightning through my bones
  It volts the marrow, makes my heart beat faster.
  Who ever gazed upon such huge disaster?
  There by the last few flames to cease from feeding,
  I see a woman's form, who, with her bleeding,
  Quenches them, one by one. It is Maleca!
  O God on high! this one last prayer fulfill me,
  Either restore her to this life or kill me!

  He goes out and carries in DOÑA CLARA, *with hair dishevelled and loose, covered and blinded with her own blood,
  partly clothed, semi-conscious; she does not recognise him
  or his voice till just before she dies.*

CLARA. You, who have neither firmness nor remorse,
  Spaniard, but coldly steer a middle course:
  No pity, to have wounded me so sorely,
  No firmness, having wounded not to kill me.
  Finish me once for all! Strike with more force!
  What fouler cruelty can you contrive
  Than leave me thus unwomaned yet alive?

ALVARO. Oh, heartbreaking divinity (for such
  There are, and men from you may learn as much

Who study human fortune), I who hold you
Here in my arms with deepest love behold you
And sooner would divide my life in twain
Than do the slightest thing to cause you pain.

CLARA. Your kindness, though I cannot see your face,
Says also that you're of our Moorish race,
And if you are so kind, do then for me
Another kindness, and to Tuzaní,
My husband, who in Gavia leads the war,
Give him these last embraces, I implore,
From his most loving wife, for I am she.
Say that a Spanish soldier, less of honour
Than covetous of jewels, set upon her
And bathed her in her blood with his rude knife.
Tell him that in Galera here his wife
Lies dead.

ALVARO.   Belovèd, that embrace you gave me
I do not need to carry. For to save me
The errand, I came here for the supreme
She recognizes his voice.
Felicity and rapture of my dream.

CLARA. Only that voice, belovèd one, could give
New breath to these few moments I've to live.
It soothes, and robs my death of all alarms.
Oh, let me, let me, fold you in these arms!
She dies.

ALVARO. How ignorant a churl was he who said
Love melts two lives in one. If that were true
I would be dying now; and living, you.
For you this instant having struck me dead
By dying would be living in my stead.
You heavens that look down upon my pain,
You mountains that behold my wrongs in vain,
You winds that hear my sorrow and you fires
Who witness this the wreck of my desires,
How could you have permitted that the best
Light of this world, the star of all the west,
Should be put out? The fairest flower grow pale?
The sweetest breath be missing from the gale?

You scientists of love, can you discover
To me, what is expected of a lover
Who on the night his love was to be crowned,
After long days of waiting, came and found
His own belovèd drowning in her blood
A snow-white lily trampled in the mud,
The purest gold so mercilessly tested
By cruel fire! And can it be suggested
How one should act who finds his lady dead?
Who finds a tomb where he had sought a bed?
No goddess, but a corpse! Do not respond
Or counsel me since I am now beyond
All reasoning or sense! My sole belief,
Creed, faith, hope, or religion is my grief.
You mighty range, above my head up-towered,
Who saw the doughty deed of this foul coward,
Who saw the basest victory ever won,
And vilest triumph underneath the sun,
Would that your peaks or vales had never seen
The most unhappy beauty, though my queen,
That ever in your boundaries has been!
But what use are complaints in this affair?
To weep and wail is but to beat the air!

Enter VÁLOR, DOÑA ISABEL, *and Moors.*

VÁLOR. Galera called for help with tongues of fire
And yet we came too late. The foe retire.

ISABEL. So late we came that every street and square
Reflects the stars in each slow-dying flare
From pyramids of ashes and despair.

ALVARO. Don't wonder, don't astound yourselves that you
Were late, for I was somewhat tardy too!

VÁLOR. What strange presaging voice is this I hear?

ISABEL. What boding accent strikes upon my ear?

VÁLOR. What's this?

ALVARO.   It is the most unearthly grief,
A sorrow that surpasses all belief,
Beyond alleviation or relief,
To have seen die (how lamentably! how

Piteously!) the partner of one's vow,
The person that one loves! It is the summit
Of icy, piercing grief. It is the plummet
That deepest sounds the gulf of black despair.
Maleca, my dear wife and only care,
Is that dead person (can I overcome it?)
Who's lying (oh, what horrible despair!)
So pallid and so bloodstained. (Do I dare
To say it?) That's Maleca lying there!
Some coward hand had pierced this noble breast
Between the flames . . . and . . . you can see the rest!
Does it not horrify your hearts that fire
Could quench such fire? And do you not admire
That base pig-iron could carve a diamond too,
And mud cast shadows on a peak of snow?
You all are witnesses to the most savage
And sacrilegious outrage, the worst ravage,
The blasphemy most fiendish and obscene,
The ghastliest horror that has ever been
The lot of two true lovers. And I call
You now as witnesses (yes! one and all!)
To the most noble vengeance Time can claim
To keep inscribed upon the rolls of fame.
And here I swear to the belovèd name
Of this cut flower, this rose of all the roses,
That bloomed so briefly and forever closes,
A wonder in its life and in its death—
To her I swear with my most fervent breath,
In loving homage to her soul above,
To venge her death and vindicate our love.
And since Galera (not in vain they found her
So apt a name) has come at last to founder
In crimson tides of blood and waves of fire,
And in the whirlpool of its end, entire,
Sinks, tilting headlong, like a shattered galley,
From top to base of this predestined valley,
And since now to their camp the Spaniards are
Retiring, and their drums sound faint and far,
I shall go down to render them my thanks
And find the murderer within their ranks

By joining some battalion in the legion,
So that the fire that desolates this region
May see it, and the rolling world may know,
And all the winds may trumpet it that blow,
That Fate may help, that heaven may allow it
To happen, as exactly as I vow it,
That men, beasts, birds, fish, sun, stars, moon, air, fire,
Earth, water, and all nature may admire,
Take cognizance of, publish, and resound
That in a Moorish breast can still be found
A Moorish heart that's loyal, firm, and sound,
And, in that heart, a love that outlives death—
That he may never brag with vaunting breath
Our souls were farther parted by his knife
Or by the grave divided than in life.

Exit.

VÁLOR. Wait, do not go!

ISABEL.   As well to try to halt
A thunderbolt shot headlong from the vault
Above our heads.

VÁLOR.   Bear off the sad remains
Of this unhappy beauty. In your veins
Let not the blood run cold, nor valour cloy,
To see the ruins of this second Troy
Fall down as if in homage to the ground
Or fly in dust and cinders all around.
Moors of the Mountain Range, do not despair!
Abenhuméya has you in his care
And to avenge your wrongs on Christian Spain
Will not have girded on his sword in vain.

Exit.

ISABEL, *aside.* Oh, would to God each mountain-peak and
    spire,
These Atlases of self-consuming fire
And giants of the wind that rakes their crest,
Might totter and grow weak and so give rest
To all these woes with which we faint and tire.

A camp near Berja

Enter DON JOHN OF AUSTRIA, DON LOPE DE FIGUEROA, DON
JOHN MENDOZA *and soldiers.*

DON JOHN OF AUSTRIA. Now that Galera has surrendered
　　Its heap of ruins breathing fire,
　　To be (a phoenix many-splendoured)
　　Its own red furnace and its pyre,
　　And, in the uproar, to appear
　　A fragment of the burning sphere,
　　Where in a labyrinth of smoke
　　There rushed a minotaur of flame
　　Whom rage and hunger has provoked
　　To roar and thunder round the same
　　Till weariness had worn him tame,
　　We have not long to wait before
　　Aurora curdles into pearls
　　The tears she weeps along the shore
　　And on the oceans foamy swirls,[11]
　　And then we'll march on Berja. Rest
　　Will never soothe my tameless heart,
　　Or make me falter in my quest,
　　Or from my purpose swerve apart,
　　Until Abenhuméya, dead
　　Or living, stretches at my feet!

DON LOPE. If it's your order that we spread
　　The selfsame havoc and defeat
　　As at Galera, then so be it;
　　The die is cast. But if you care
　　From the king's point of view to see it,
　　The whole perspective changes there:
　　It never was the king's intent

[11] The Alpujarra overlooks the sea, of which both the Sierra
Nevada and it command a vast expanse to the South and East as
they rise from 8000 to 13,000 feet. They would therefore see the
dawn over the Mediterranean. [R.C.]

To extirpate his subjects so.
The lesson was severe he meant
To have delivered at one blow.
To set a stern example thus
And temper punishment with ruth,
I think, is what's required of us.

MENDOZA. My lord, Don Lope speaks the truth.
You showed them that your heart can harden
The day when you destroyed the city.
Let them glimpse, too, the face of pardon,
And be as noted for your pity
As for your wrath. Then soothe your rigour.
Temper the fierceness of your will
And lion heart. That heart is bigger
One needs to pardon with, than kill.

DON JOHN OF AUSTRIA. My brother sent me, it is true,
To pacify this fierce revolt.
I've never learned with words to sue,
And only in the thunderbolt
My wrath can find an arm to wield.
My only pulpit is my stirrup,
My law court is the open field,
It's not with syllabubs and syrup
I grease the axle of my car
Or whet my good sword that impales
The Crescent and the Morning Star.[12]
But since my royal charge entails
Both valiant force and pleasing arts,
Into two halves I'll cleave asunder:
With mercy's weapons piercing hearts,
With pardon's (not with cannon's) thunder
Appealing to their sense and reason.
My just severity I'll season.
Mendoza!

MENDOZA.   Yes, my lord?

DON JOHN OF AUSTRIA.   Away,
To Berja (where old Válor lives)
As my ambassador, and say

[12] The Turkish flag. [R.C.]

The king a public pardon gives
To all who'll take it and obey.
But he has two prerogatives:
Which are to pardon or to slay,
And public punishment today
Is one of two alternatives
Which they themselves can best decide.
A general pardon I'll provide
To those consenting to return
Among us, there to work, and earn
And as true citizens abide
In their professions, trades, or task
And live and prosper with their fellows.
Their safety's granted, if they ask,
But Berja must surrender whole.
If not, with the same pair of bellows
Of which Galera whiffed a sample,
I'll make of Berja one red blaze
Both as a warning and example
To further dalliance and delays!

MENDOZA. My lord, at once it shall be done.

Exit.

DON LOPE. No town was ever sacked or won
That gave such profit to the looter.
Why, every trooper is a magnate
And every sapper or sharpshooter
Is now set up in life forever.

DON JOHN OF AUSTRIA. Did so much treasure hoard and stagnate
In such a town?

DON LOPE. The soldiers never
Have been so happy.

DON JOHN OF AUSTRIA. I should claim
My own true portion and my measure
Of booty from the looted treasure
To send a trophy, in my name,
To her who is my queen and sister.
I'll have to bargain for a jewel.

DON LOPE. I've thought of that. Like solar fuel,
   Behold this necklace glint and glisten—
   This river of gigantic pearls
   That spills a cataract of fire
   Wherein the spectrum plays and swirls.
   I guessed, foresensing your desire,
   The sort of thing you would require,
   And here's the answer to your thought—
   Which from a soldier I have bought—
   The finest trophy of them all
   With pearls the size of musket-ball.

DON JOHN OF AUSTRIA. In not refusing it, I'll not refuse,
   Don Lope, any favour you would choose
   Or any service that would help your lot
   And comes within my own prerogative.
   For it's my turn to teach you to receive
   Since you so nobly taught me how to give.

DON LOPE. I ask a costly price: it's by your leave
   That it and I may serve you while we live.

Enter DON ALVARO *and* ALCUZCUZ *as Spaniards.*

ALVARO, *without seeing* DON JOHN.
   Alouzcuz, you're the one that I require,
   You only, for my comrade and my squire
   Upon this enterprize.

ALCUZCUZ.   You trust to me!
   Though vot you're up to here, I no can see.
   But hush! there's "Highness" so they call his name.

ALVARO. Don John of Austria?

ALCUZCUZ.   The very same!
   I must survey him carefully. His fame
   Warrants it.

DON JOHN OF AUSTRIA. See how uniform they are
   In size, and every one of them a star!

ALVARO, *apart.* My scrutiny was warranted. That same
   Rope of white pearls (alas!) that he holds there
   I know them well (alas, my soul!). They were
   The ones I gave Maleca.

DON JOHN OF AUSTRIA.   Come, let's go.
That soldier in amazement's staring so.

DON LOPE. Why, everyone who sees you, you amaze.

Exeunt DON JOHN OF AUSTRIA, DON LOPE DE FIGUEROA, *and soldiers.*

ALVARO. I am struck dumb: my mind is in a daze.

ALCUZCUZ. Now that we are alone, sir, what the reason
For coming down the range so out of season?

ALVARO. You'll know it soon enough.

ALCUZCUZ.   Yes, now I know
Enough and soon to wish I never go
With you.

ALVARO.   Well, what of that?

ALCUZCUZ.   You do not know
That I was captive here short time ago?
And that one Christian soldier was my boss
Who, if he catch me here, my life is loss?

ALVARO. How can he know you in this new disguise
Which, as we pass, will never draw their eyes,
Since we seem Christians now and soldiers too,
Resembling Moors in naught we say or do.

ALCUZCUZ. All right, my master, it's all right for you.
You spik ze language. You can pass for Spaniard.
I open mouth, they tie me with a lanyard
Both hand together. Then me captive twice
And have to call myself by name of Rice.
For you, all right. For Alcuzcuz, not nice.
How can Alcuzcuz 'scape from jail and flogging?

ALVARO. By speaking low, to none but me; by dogging
My footsteps; and behaving as a servant
Should do, of whom nobody is observant.

ALCUZCUZ. But if somebody ask me who I am?

ALVARO. Behave as if you do not care a damn!
Don't answer!

ALCUZCUZ.   Me not answer ven I'm spoken?

ALVARO. No, if you don't want trouble, or a broken
Pate for your pains.

ALCUZCUZ.   Only the great Mahomet
  When I got itch to speak could keep me from it.
  I always voz a conversocialist.

ALVARO. Many would call me mad that I persist
  (Of my opposing star the idolatrist)
  Among these thirty thousand men to seek
  A single man (without more track or spoor
  Than the wind leaves on rock) on whom to wreak
  My wrath, and yet one prodigy the more
  Among so many would not much surprise me.
  That it's impossible my wits advise me,
  Ever to be avenged. Then be it so:
  It's after the impossible I go.
  Since if I fail in it, I fail in all,
  Then on the thirty-thousandth chance I'll call.
  Although those pearls infallibly were plain
  They do not show by whom my love was slain,
  For it is clear no noble hand would spill
  A woman's blood, nor high-born valour kill
  For lucre, since nobility admires
  The power of beauty and its sacred fires.
  Therefore the present owner did not do it.
  The trail was false; and now, to lead me straighter,
  I must seek lower down, if I'd come to it,
  Among the ranks, to find that bestial traitor.

ALCUZCUZ. Is that what you were coming for down here?

ALVARO. Yes. Looking for a needle in the hay.

ALCUZCUZ. No good, no good; it's time to disappear.
  You got no chance to find him if you stay,
  Among so many.

ALVARO.   But I've sworn to do it.

ALCUZCUZ. And here's the proverb vot I tag unto it:
  "It's easy at the court to find my son
  Because he wears dark clothes like everyone."

ALVARO. It is not your concern.

ALCUZCUZ.   Hush! Someone come!
  I speak by signs, pretending I be dumb.

ALVARO. Yes.

ALCUZCUZ.   Allah, put your hand upon my tongue!
Enter soldiers.

FIRST SOLDIER. Our winnings are shared out and all is fair
Since everyone who gambles does his share
Of trickery even when he plays for two.

SECOND SOLDIER. That isn't fair. I do not see the sequel.
Our shares in both our winnings should be equal,
If equal in our losses.

FIRST SOLDIER.   Look, my friends, I don't
Like quarreling for selfish ends. My wont
Is quite the opposite. This man objects
But I refuse to answer.

SECOND SOLDIER.   Yes, but let's
Get someone neutral to decide. You there,
Hey, soldier!

ALCUZCUZ, *aside.* It's to me I'm being spoke!
Allah! Some patience!

SECOND SOLDIER.   Don't you answer folk
Who speak to you?

ALCUZCUZ.   Ah-ha!

THIRD SOLDIER.   Why, he's dumb, poor bloke.

ALCUZCUZ, *aside.* If you but knew . . .

ALVARO, *aside.*   I'll have to interfere
Or I'll be ruined by this jackass here.
Aloud.

Gentlemen, let me crave your pardon for
My servant here who cannot understand you
Because he's deaf and dumb.

ALCUZCUZ, *aside.*   I am not dumb.
But this time I know nothing. Not got answer.
Alcuzcuz never playing cards or poker.
Nothing I know of ace and trump and joker.

SECOND SOLDIER. You, sir, would settle what we want to know
Far better than your servant.

ALVARO.   I'll be pleased
If I can satisfy you.

FIRST SOLDIER. I won for both of us, since we were partners,
    Amongst the cash, this Cupid made of diamonds—

ALVARO, *aside.* Heavens above!

FIRST SOLDIER.   —This Cupid you see here.

ALVARO, *aside.* Alas, Maleca, all your wedding jewels
    Are nothing but the plunder of your grave.
    The tracks are more confused that, from a prince
    Down to a trooper, show on drifting sand!
    So much does plunder jump from hand to hand.

FIRST SOLDIER. Well, then, you see, while we shared out the
        winnings,
    Since I had won, I gave him this here Cupid
    Which well can be converted into cash:
    And took the ready cash all for myself.
    If I'm the winner for the pair, then, surely,
    I have the choice before my partner has.

ALVARO. I can compose this difference if you like
    And pay you the true value of this jewel
    So that you can make share and share alike
    But on this one condition: that's to know
    If it is regal booty, and if so
    Which soldier got it first.

SECOND SOLDIER.   It's quite all right!
    All that we gamble for, by day or night,
    Was looted from Galera's bloody sack.
    There's nobody alive can claim it back!

ALVARO, *aside.* Heavens, do you consent to what I hear?

ALCUZCUZ, *aside.* I'm burst with talkativity, not fear!
    I want to speaking!

FIRST SOLDIER.   Yes, I'll find the man.
    This fellow here showed me by different signs
    These gems was taken from a lovely bint
    Whom one of us proceeded then to kill.
    He shouldn't be so hard to find.

ALVARO, *aside.*   Ah me!

SECOND SOLDIER. I'll find him and he'll tell you it, firsthand.
    Just follow me. He'll give it to you straight

Out of the horse's mouth. I know him well.
You'll hear it all from him.

ALVARO, *aside.*   I will not listen
To one word more than to make sure that he's
The murderer. Then I will stab him through.
Aloud.
Lead on then, gentlemen, and I will follow.

Outside the guardroom in the same camp near Berja

SOLDIERS, *within.* Here! here! hang on a moment!

OTHER SOLDIERS, *within.*   Get outside!

Sound of fighting within, swords clashing.

ONE SOLDIER, *within.* Were all the world to help you, I would
    kill you.

ANOTHER SOLDIER, *within.* He's with our enemy.

ANOTHER SOLDIER, *within.*   Then let him die!

GARCÉS, *within.* I have to fight alone against the lot?
    What does it matter then? Have at you all!
    They come in fighting, GARCÉS *against the other soldiers.*
    DON ALVARO, *who has been waiting outside the guardroom*
    is trying to hold them back. ALCUZCUZ *is a long way behind.*

ALVARO. So many soldiers setting on to one!
    No, that is cowardly and base! Hold back!
    Or you will ask for what you get from me.

ALCUZCUZ. Very nice for Alcuzcuz, not allowed
    To pray for mercy, argue, or explain,
    When all the other dashing out the brain!

A SOLDIER. I've had it. Yes, he's killed me!
    Thud as he falls within.
    Enter DON LOPE DE FIGUEROA *and other soldiers.*

DON LOPE.   What's all this?

A SOLDIER. He's dead. We're for it, if we're found! Let's run!
    All those who were fighting flee.

GARCÉS, *to* ALVARO. I owe you, soldier, that you saved my life,
And will repay it.

He goes off.

DON LOPE.   Wait there, don't run off!

ALVARO. I'm here. I don't run off.

DON LOPE.   Disarm the two.

ALVARO, *aside.* O heavens!

Aloud.

                  Look here, my lord, I only
Drew forth this sword so as to stop them fighting.
The quarrel was not mine.

DON LOPE.   I only know
That, just outside the guardroom, here I found
A soldier dead, and you with a drawn sword.

ALVARO, *aside.* I've no defence. To think that I came here
To kill a man; yet, saving one man's life,
To lose my own.

DON LOPE.   And you, behind there, you
Who speak by signs, you do not yield your sword.
It seems that I have seen your face before
When you were very talkative. Arrest them
While I go on and round up all the rest.

ALCUZCUZ, *aside.* Two things I do not like, they don't agree—
To quarrel and be silent—not with me!
No, if I add them up right, there are three!
Yes, one, two, three: I don't like not to saying
Nothing, nor fighting, nor in jail to staying!

They are taken off under arrest.

Enter DON JOHN OF AUSTRIA.

DON JOHN OF AUSTRIA. What's all this noise, Don Lope?

DON LOPE.   Soldiers fighting
About the loot. One man has just been killed.

DON JOHN OF AUSTRIA. I will not stand for such indiscipline:
This sort of thing can lead to death by hundreds.
Although you're all for clemency, I know,
Justice must be respected, too.

Enter MENDOZA.

MENDOZA.   Your Highness,
  Give me your feet to kiss.
DON JOHN OF AUSTRIA.   What news, Mendoza?
MENDOZA. I blew the trumpet sounding truce
  To Berja on its towering crag
  And straightaway (as is the use)
  They answered with a snow-white flag.
  I was admitted under guard
  And to the canopy bestarred
  Of old Abenhuméya came
  Where he was sitting with his dame
  As beautiful as the Aurora
  (Once Isabel but now Lidora,
  Since she too had to change her name).
  Upon a cushion on the floor
  I sat as your ambassador
  With every honour to be had—
  Aside.

Remembered passion made me sad
And reawakened to adore.

Aloud.

I gave your ultimatum to them
  And told them of the offered pardon,
  And into ecstasies it threw them
  And there were fetes in every garden.
  Only Abenhuméya stern,
  The son of arrogance and pride,
  Their gratitude would not return
  But struck the sabre at his side,
  And this is what the tyrant cried:
  "I am the King Abenhuméya
  Of Alpujarra. At my feet
  The whole of Spain (that's my idea)
  Will soon be levelled like a street.
  So tell Don John, if life he prizes
  He better had retire and take
  Any base Moor who compromises
  And yields to him for mercy's sake.
  Let him of such his army make

And lead them out yourself I say,
To fight for Philip, in your wake
This moment when you march away.
The numbers' being on your side
Will bring my victory more pride."
Then Válor, having said his say,
Bade me return; but what I found
Was that the Alpujarra range
Was split in factions all around.
Opinions underwent a change.
For while some still as war cries sounded:
"Africa! Africa!" the main
Part of the echoes that rebounded
From cliff to crag were all for Spain.

DON JOHN OF AUSTRIA. The tyrant cannot hold much longer:
Those that are strongest first to cry
Rebellion are much louder, stronger,
And shriller, when their chances die,
To bathe their very leaders in
Their blood, their gravest deeds decry,
And help the other side to win.
And since the state of Alpujarra's
Like what you say, we'll take the chance
And now, without more stay, as far as
Berja, the whole post will advance
Before these suicides expire
Like scorpions when they're singed with fire.
I will not give them half a chance
To subjugate each other thus.
Whichever way the dice would dance,
The victory must be with us!

In the guardroom

ALCUZCUZ *and* DON ALVARO *with their hands tied behind them*

ALCUZCUZ. During the time we have to spend
Alone in here, as friend to friend,
Now while there's nobody to hear,
Lord Tuzaní, would you be willing
To tell me for what stupid end
We're here—for dying or for killing?

ALVARO. To die, it seems now, not to slay.

ALCUZCUZ. Damned be all peacemakers, I say,
Who'd butt into a private row!

ALVARO. As I was blameless, anyhow,
With no self-interest either way,
I foolishly made no resistance.
Had I been warned of this today,
A hundred would have kept their distance,
Till I'd a chance to slip away.

ALCUZCUZ. Well, I would join up with the hundred
Against you!

ALVARO.   What was worst to hear
Was how that beast who killed and plundered
Seems like a hero to appear.
That from a woman whom he killed
The craven brute his pockets filled
Made them all grin from ear to ear!

ALCUZCUZ. That's not the worst of it, by far!
The worst of it is that we are
Ordered to kneel down and confess
As though the creed that we profess
Were theirs. But when Sir Reverence comes
I'm going to go on playing dumb.

ALVARO. Well seeing, now, that all is lost
I'll sell my life at a high cost.

ALCUZCUZ. Why, what can you expect to do
Except to curse and rant and swagger?

ALVARO. Under my shirt, well hidden too,
I still have got my Moorish dagger.
Alcuzcuz, can't you come and chew
This lanyard here that binds my wrists,
With those big teeth of yours?

ALCUZCUZ.   No! Please!
It is not dignified to chew
A lanyard with its snaky twists
So near another person's bum.

ALVARO. Do what I say, Alcuzcuz, come!
Bite, gnaw, and gnash this lanyard through.

ALCUZCUZ. Well, maybe, seeing it's for you.

ALVARO. I'll do you the same favour too.

ALCUZCUZ. I've bitten through, and now you're free;
Then come and do the same for me.

ALVARO. I can't just yet. There's someone coming.

ALCUZCUZ. So poor Alcuzcuz still must be
Tied up behind and go on dumbing.

Enter one of the guards with GARCÉS *in shackles.*

GUARD. Here, with his man who's dumb and deaf,
Both of them handcuffed with a cord,
Is the young man who pulled his sword
And saved you from a dirty death.

GARCÉS. Although I'm sorry to be caught
Chased by so many at one time
I'm happy to be here in time
To save you, stranger (you who sought
To save me) and, my life for yours,
To swear you blameless of the crime.
Guard, when you go off duty, race
To John Mendoza, crave his ear,
Tell him I am a prisoner here
And with a mortal charge to face.
Then, when he once knows who it is,

My services will plead *my* life,
And my sworn evidence save *his*.
Indicates ALVARO.

GUARD. Yes, certainly, I'll run there, hard,
The moment that I come off guard.

ALVARO, *aside to* ALCUZCUZ.
You see in what a fresh and breezy
Familiar way they come and go.
To cut my way out will be easy:
Just wait and see.

ALCUZCUZ, *aside to* ALVARO. I will . . . Oh! Oh!

ALVARO, *aside.* What's up with you?

ALCUZCUZ, *aside to* ALVARO.   It's him. He's come!

ALVARO, *aside to* ALCUZCUZ. Explain!

ALCUZCUZ, *aside to* ALVARO.   No! Now I'm *really* dumb
With terror.

ALVARO.   Speak.

ALCUZCUZ.   I'm dead with fright.

ALVARO. What is it?

ALCUZCUZ.   That's the big, strong bully
Whose slave I was, from whom I snitched
The poison that I drank so fully
Out of the bag that was bewitched
With evil spells of pork and bacon.
In case he sees me, just in case,
I'll lie and snore upon my face.
May Allah never let me waken!
He lies down and hides his face as if to sleep.

GARCÉS. Since without knowing you and not
Once having done you a good turn,
You saved my life when things were hot,
Comrade, it gives me grave concern
To find you in so warm a spot.
If prison could give consolation
The greatest there could be, for me,
Would be that on investigation
My evidence could set you free.

ALVARO. God bless you for the thought.

ALCUZCUZ, *aside*.   So *he's*
  A prisoner too, and he's the fellow
  That caused the fight! Now he'll not seize
  So quick a chance to fight and bellow
  And make Alcuzcuz knock his knees!

GARCÉS. Don't be downhearted or despair!
  I'll take the blame and give the life
  I owe you to be fair and square
  Since it was I who caused the strife
  And you just happened to be there.

ALVARO. I would expect you to behave
  Exactly so, for you are brave.
  This plight of mine's not worth a sigh
  But that a mission I'd in hand,
  Sworn to achieve and deeply planned,
  Must be abandoned if I die.

SOLDIER. You needn't think that both of you
  Will hang, and here's the reason why:
  When the accomplices are two
  And but one wound to hang them by,
  Only one is condemned to die,
  And he who gets it in that case
  Is he who has the ugliest face.

ALCUZCUZ, *aside*. For saying that, I hope you burst!

SOLDIER. And so it is, between you three—
  Old Deaf-and-Dumb will catch it first!

ALCUZCUZ, *aside*. That's plainer than my face can be!
  The ugliest in the world is me!

GARCÉS. Another favour I would sue
  To swell my gratitude to you.

ALCUZCUZ, *aside*. The law is that the ugliest only . . .

ALVARO. What?

GARCÉS.   Tell me what you are, and who,
  To whom I owe my life.

ALVARO.   A lonely
  Soldier of fortune who relies
  Upon his sword for bread, I came . . .

ALCUZCUZ, *aside.* The law is that the ugliest dies!

ALVARO. To find a man.

ALCUZCUZ, *aside.* The law is that the ugliest dies!

GARCÉS.　　　　　　What is his name?

ALVARO. I do not know.

GARCÉS.　　　　　　In what division
And what battalion did he go?

ALVARO. I cannot tell you with precision.

GARCÉS. What is he like?

ALVARO.　　　　　　I do not know.

GARCÉS. You neither know his number, name,
Or what he looks like? What a go!

ALVARO. Yet strange! I feel I've found the same
Man that I wanted, though I know
Neither his number nor his name.

GARCÉS. In strange enigmas you go straying
But do not be downhearted since,
Once he has heard of this, the prince,
Who owes me (as I don't mind saying)
A most outstanding obligation,
For but for me and what I found,
Galera would remain unshaken,
Which by my stratagem was taken
And scattered to the winds around—
The prince will let me out intact.
We'll take advantage of the fact,
The pair of us, for from this day
Each by the other must be backed:
Blood-brothership in thought and act
Must bind us on our earthly way.

ALVARO. So you were one of those that stormed Galera?

GARCÉS. I would to God that it had not been so.

ALVARO. In such a feat of valour, not to share a
Distinguished part? Why? I would like to know.

GARCÉS. Because, since I was first of all to reach
That fated city, rushing through the breach,
I do not know what influence or doom

Shadows me with the shadow of the tomb.
For, since that dreadful day, nothing but ill
Has dogged my footsteps, and pursues me still.

ALVARO. Out of what cause was born this dread you feel?

GARCÉS. I killed a Moorish lady with cold steel
And heaven is offended with me still
And will be, whatsoever way I pull.
That girl was far too beautiful to kill.

ALVARO. So beautiful was she?

GARCÉS.   So beautiful!

ALVARO, *aside.* Oh, my lost heaven!
    Aloud.

                           Get it off your chest:
How did it happen?

GARCÉS.   One day, while on picket,
Amongst dark boughs, which, though noon reached its
    crest,
Prolonged the night before, in that dark thicket,
I took an Arab prisoner. In fine
(So not to tire you with this tale of mine)
He cheated me and led me all astray,
Having pretended he would show the way
To take the town. When he had got me there
He yelled in Arab. Horns began to blare.
Arabs began to swarm. One wounded me.
Being outnumbered, I was forced to flee.
I hid within a cave. This monstrous hollow
Was to become the womb in days to follow
(Through my discovery and inspiration)
The womb which then conceived the fatal shock
And sank, with its tremendous detonation,
That galley with the keel of solid rock,
That once was called Galera. It was I
Who told Don John that there was such a gap,
And while the engineers worked on the sly,
I, Garcés, mounted guard upon the sap.
I led the storming party and was first
Climbing the glacis, through the flames to burst,

A human salamander breathing fire
Which now became my element entire
Until I reached a house that seemed a fort
So many of their soldiers made resort
To it . . . But I grow tedious and you tire
Of listening.

ALVARO.   Not at all. I was comparing
My lot with yours. Mine also needs an airing.

GARCÉS. Filled with a rage which nothing then could check,
I reached that house, the palace of Malec
(But whether fort or palace, now a wreck)
About the same moment when Don Lope came
(Now, there's a soldier of immortal fame!)
And killed their old commander, when with sword
And fire the true allegiance was restored.
Profiting by the cheers, I sought for gain
(Though profit sorts with honour not at all)
And running fast through every room and hall
And corridor of all that vast domain
At last I came into a little room
The refuge of a Moorish girl than whom
My eyes had never seen a rarer sight.
No painter yet could match the grace and glow
But it's no time for picture painting. No!
Half in bewilderment and half in fright
As if the curtain that she went behind
Were flanked with ravelins and were the kind
We speak of in the language of our trade
As the curtain of a rampart—the poor maid
Retired and hid—— But look, you're deathly pale
And tears are in your eyes.

ALVARO.   It's that your tale
Reminds me of my own misfortune!

GARCÉS.   Oh!
Don't be downhearted! Do not sorrow so
For your lost chances! Why, man, don't you know
Watched kettles never boil? Plans come unstuck!
The one who never seeks it finds the luck!
The lucky moment comes when least expected!

ALVARO. That's true! On with the tale that I deflected!

GARCÉS. I followed her into her room and found her
With such a galaxy of gems around her,
Like starlight shimmering on a sea of glory,
She seemed more to expect some wondrous lover
Rather than death—a death so grim and gory
As she was on the way, then, to discover.
No sooner had I seized her hand, to shove her
To bed, than to these words she gave her breath:
"Christian, if you by compassing my death
Follow ambition more than glory, take
These gems and let me be, for pity's sake.
The blood of woman stains true swords, you know,
More than it ornaments them. Let me go.
Leave my bed pure and leave the faith untorn
Of this poor breast whose mystery's still unknown
Even to him to whom it has been sworn."
I came to clasp her . . .

ALVARO.   Wait? hold on a bit!
Don't get so near!
He pulls himself up.

                    Oh, my sore-troubled wit,
Tracking my own thoughts and my despairs
Made me cry out, at random, unawares.
Bear with me, soldier, and get on with it!

GARCÉS. She cried out loudly to defend her name
And life. But then, as other people came
Into the house, I saw my prize was lost
And seeing that my love for her was crossed
Irreparably, to such fierce extremes
Does passion swing that, whether it was thwarted
Fury to see my cravings thus aborted
Or by some other prompting (Ugh! it seems
Infamy even to repeat in speech!),
I made some movement with my hand to reach
And grab a necklace. I forget the rest
But found my blade was hilted in her breast,
A breast of snow tipped with a Cupid's kiss.

ALVARO. Was this the way you dealt the blow? Like this?

Stabs him.

GARCÉS. God help me! What d'you mean?

ALCUZCUZ.   That's done the trick.
Die, traitor, die.

GARCÉS.   What! Did you mean to kill me?

ALVARO. Yes, for that murdered beauty was my wife.
That trampled rose is still my soul and life,
And thus on you in vengeance I fulfill me.
You were the man that I was looking for.

GARCÉS. You took me weaponless by treason. Shame!

ALVARO. All things are fair in vengeance as in war.
Don Alvaro Tuzaní is my name.
I was her husband, as I am forever.

ALCUZCUZ. Yes, and my name's Alcuzcuz, Christian dog,
Who bore your knapsack full of poisoned hog.

GARCÉS. Why did you save my life if but to sever
It now? Call in the guard! Call in the guard!

He dies.

MEN, *within.* Hullo! What's this? Somebody's yelling hard.
It sounds like Garcés, whom I came to see.

Enter DON JOHN OF MENDOZA *and soldiers.*

ALVARO. Let go that sword. I'll wrest it from your hand.

Takes soldier's sword.

Señor Don John Mendoza, Tuzaní
My name is, called the Lightning and the Brand
Of the Alpujarra. I came here on my duty—
Which was the vengeance of a sovereign beauty.
For no one loves who will not venge his love.
'Twas in another prison that we strove
With equal arms and standing face to face.
Now if you came to seek me in this place
Surely you're man enough to come alone
Being who you are, but if by hazard, then,
My duty and my purpose being known
And true respect to noble sorrow shown,
Make way for me, and call off all your men.

MENDOZA. I could, without the slightest shame at all,

Turn you my back and leave you to the rest,
Since this is the king's army after all
In which you are an uninvited guest.
For that alone you'd have to be suppressed,
And I'm quite pleased to be the first to act
By killing you, though by the others backed,
Since you're outside the rules.

ALVARO.   You close my way?
Why then, I'll hack one through you, come what may.
They fight.

SOLDIER. He's killed me.
Soldier runs out and falls dead.

ALVARO.   Now you see I've earned my name
Tuzaní the Avenger of my Dame.
The other soldiers run out.

MENDOZA. I'll be the first to kill you after all.

ALCUZCUZ. Must he who is the ugliest die the first?

DON JOHN OF AUSTRIA *enters with* DON LOPE *and more
soldiers.*

DON JOHN OF AUSTRIA. What's this? What's this unseemly sort
    of brawl?

MENDOZA. It is a Moor, for vengeance all athirst,
Who came down from the range to take the life
Of Garcés here, saying he killed his wife.

DON LOPE. He killed your wife?

ALVARO.   Yes.

DON LOPE.   Then you've bravely done!
Rather than punishment, praise should be won
For such a deed. Your Highness, you would do
The very same, or you would not be you,
Don John of Austria!

MENDOZA.   But it's Tuzaní
A rebel leader! Surely he must be
Arrested?

DON JOHN OF AUSTRIA. Give your sword up.

ALVARO.   Pardon me,
Your Highness, that I have to turn my back

Upon your orders and your royalty.
Let those who dare now follow in my track!
Exit.

DON JOHN OF AUSTRIA. Follow him, everyone! Resume the
    attack!

Before the walls of Berja

Enter DOÑA ISABEL *with Moorish soldiers on the wall.*

ISABEL. Show this white banner to the Christian folk!
    Enter DON ALVARO.

ALVARO. Through all their halberds and their pikes I broke
    And now at the great mountain's foot I stand.

A SPANISH SOLDIER, *within.*
    Men, take your muskets! Shoot him out of hand!

ALVARO. Till you surround me quite you'll not get *me!*

A MOOR. Help him get back!

ISABEL.   Stop! Lord Tuzaní?

ALVARO. Those men are armed, Lidora: death is near.

ISABEL. Patience, my lord, one moment. Have no fear.
    She and the Moorish soldiers leave the wall.

DON JOHN, *within.*
    Go! Search from trunk to trunk, from bough to bough!
    Track him down, all of you! Capture him now!
    Enter from one side DON JOHN OF AUSTRIA *and his soldiers.*
    Enter from the other side DOÑA ISABEL *and the Moors with*
    DON ALVARO.

ISABEL. Don John of Austria, child of the eagle,
    That beauteous eagle on full pride of sail
    Who face to face could look upon the regal
    White sun at noon and as an equal hail
    Its majesty. The Alpujarra range
    Once in revolt, now quiet as you see,
    A woman lays before your feet, to change

Back to her own religion, and be free.
I'm Doña Isabela Tuzaní,
Who lived here, though constrained and not by choice.
Catholic in my soul, Moor in my voice,
I was Abenhuméya's wife by force—
Whose death, the outcome of his reckless course,
Has spattered both his crown and arms with gore.
For when the Moors were weary of the war,
On hearing they were like to be forgiven,
And on the point of giving in therefore,
To such excess of fury was he driven
And cursed them for their cowardice so sore
That suddenly the captain of the guard
Seized him and said: "Surrender to the king!"
"Lay hands on me?" he cried. His way was barred,
And as he fumbled with his hilt to bring
His rapier out, a halberd sent his head
Rolling along the floor, and he fell dead,
And with him fell the hopes of all he led.
Though for so long his deeds suspended
The world, the danger now is ended.
With horror now Spain seems to reel
Rather than from the clash of steel,
And if your thoughts no longer harden
And if it may deserve a pardon,
Before your feet here to lay down
Valiant Abenhuméya's crown,
A royal pardon then I crave
From one so generous and brave,
For Tuzaní, my own dear brother,
That he receive like any other
The same forgiveness that is yours,
Offered to all the race of Moors.
Another blessing too I crave
For one who'd rather be your slave
Than that which I too long have been,
Though so reluctantly: a queen.

DON JOHN OF AUSTRIA. Your prayers are easy to be granted.
Rise, Isabel! And, Tuzaní,
Long live your valour, to be chanted

In deathless verses by the swans
Of Helicon, inscribed in bronze,
And bruited over land and sea.

ALVARO. I kneel in thanks!

ALCUZCUZ. Alcuzcuz, he
Is pardoned?

DON JOHN OF AUSTRIA. Yes.

ALCUZCUZ. I thank my liege.

ALVARO. Thus, without further waste of breath,
Here ends the play LOVE AFTER DEATH
And the famous Alpujarra siege.

LIFE IS A DREAM

Calderón de la Barca

English Version by Roy Campbell

DRAMATIS PERSONAE

BASIL, *King of Poland*
SEGISMUND, *Prince*
ASTOLFO, *Duke of Muscovy*
CLOTALDO, *old man*
CLARION, *a comical servant*
ROSAURA, *a lady*
STELLA, *a princess*
Soldiers, guards, musicians, servants, retinues, women

The scene is laid in the court of Poland, a nearby fortress, and the open country.

ACT I

On one side a craggy mountain: on the other a rude tower whose base serves as a prison for SEGISMUND. *The door facing the spectators is open. The action begins at nightfall.*

ROSAURA, *dressed as a man, appears on the rocks climbing down to the plain: behind her comes* CLARION.

ROSAURA. You headlong hippogriff who match the gale
  In rushing to and fro, you lightning-flicker
  Who give no light, you scaleless fish, you bird
  Who have no coloured plumes, you animal
  Who have no natural instinct, tell me whither
  You lead me stumbling through this labyrinth
  Of naked crags! Stay here upon this peak
  And be a Phaëthon to the brute-creation!
  For I, pathless save only for the track
  The laws of destiny dictate for me,
  Shall, blind and desperate, descend this height
  Whose furrowed brows are frowning at the sun.
  How rudely, Poland, you receive a stranger
  (Hardly arrived, but to be treated hardly)
  And write her entry down in blood with thorns.
  My plight attests this well, but after all,
  Where did the wretchèd ever pity find?

CLARION. Say *two* so wretchèd. Don't you leave me out
  When you complain! If we two sallied out
  From our own country, questing high adventure,
  And after so much madness and misfortune
  Are still two here, and were two when we fell
  Down those rough crags—shall I not be offended
  To share the trouble yet forego the credit?

ROSAURA. I did not give you shares in my complaint
  So as not to rob you of the right to sorrow
  Upon your own account. There's such relief
  In venting grief that a philosopher

Once said that sorrows should not be bemoaned
But sought for pleasure.

CLARION.   Philosopher?
I call him a long-bearded, drunken sot
And would they'd cudgelled him a thousand blows
To give him something worth his while lamenting!
But, madam, what should we do, by ourselves,
On foot and lost at this late hour of day,
Here on this desert mountain far away—
The sun departing after fresh horizons?

ROSAURA. Clarion, how can I answer, being both
The partner of your plight and your dilemma?

CLARION. Would anyone believe such strange events?

ROSAURA. If there my sight is not deceived by fancy,
In the last timid light that yet remains
I seem to see a building.

CLARION.   Either my hopes
Are lying or I see the signs myself.

ROSAURA. Between the towering crags, there stands so small
A royal palace that the lynx-eyed sun
Could scarce perceive it at midday, so rude
In architecture that it seems but one
Rock more down-toppled from the sun-kissed crags
That form the jaggèd crest.

CLARION.   Let's go closer,
For we have stared enough: it would be better
To let the inmates make us welcome.

ROSAURA.   See:
The door, or, rather, that funereal gap,
Is yawning wide—whence night itself seems born,
Flowing out from its black, rugged centre.

A sound of chains is heard.

CLARION. Heavens! What's that I hear?

ROSAURA.   I have become
A block immovable of ice and fire.

CLARION. Was that a little chain? Why, I'll be hanged
If that is not the clanking ghost of some
Past galley-slave—my terror proves it is!

SEGISMUND. Oh, miserable me! Unhappy me!

ROSAURA. How sad a cry that is! I fear new trials
And torments.

CLARION.   It's a fearful sound.

ROSAURA.   Oh, come,
My Clarion, let us fly from suffering!

CLARION. I'm in such sorry trim, I've not the spirit
Even to run away.

ROSAURA.   And if you had,
You'd not have seen that door, not known of it.
When one's in doubt, the common saying goes
One walks between two lights.

CLARION.   I'm the reverse.
It's not that way with me.

ROSAURA.   What then disturbs you?

CLARION. I walk in doubt between two darknesses.

ROSAURA. Is not that feeble exhalation there
A light? That pallid star whose fainting tremors,
Pulsing a doubtful warmth of glimmering rays,
Make even darker with its spectral glow
That gloomy habitation? Yes! because
By its reflection (though so far away)
I recognise a prison, grim and sombre,
The sepulchre of some poor living carcase.
And, more to wonder at, a man lies there
Clothed in the hides of savage beasts, with limbs
Loaded with fetters, and a single lamp
For company. So, since we cannot flee,
Let us stay here and listen to his plaint
And what his sorrows are.

SEGISMUND.   Unhappy me!
Oh, miserable me! You heavens above,
I try to think what crime I've done against you
By being born. Although to have been born,
I know, is an offence, and with just cause
I bear the rigours of your punishment:
Since to be born is man's worst crime. But yet
I long to know (to clarify my doubts)

What greater crime, apart from being born,
Can thus have earned my greater chastisement.
Aren't others born like me? And yet they seem
To boast a freedom that I've never known.
The bird is born, and in the hues of beauty
Clothed with its plumes, yet scarce has it become
A feathered posy—or a flower with wings—
When through ethereal halls it cuts its way,
Refusing the kind shelter of its nest.
And I, who have more soul than any bird,
Must have less liberty?
The beast is born, and with its hide bright-painted,
In lovely tints, has scarce become a spangled
And starry constellation (thanks to the skilful
Brush of the Painter) than its earthly needs
Teach it the cruelty to prowl and kill,
The monster of its labyrinth of flowers.
Yet I, with better instincts than a beast,
Must have less liberty?
The fish is born, the birth of spawn and slime,
That does not even live by breathing air.
No sooner does it feel itself a skiff
Of silver scales upon the wave than swiftly
It roves about in all directions taking
The measure of immensity as far
As its cold blood's capacity allows.
Yet I, with greater freedom of the will,
Must have less liberty?
The brook is born, and like a snake unwinds
Among the flowers. No sooner, silver serpent,
Does it break through the blooms than it regales
And thanks them with its music for their kindness,
Which opens to its course the majesty
Of the wide plain. Yet I, with far more life,
Must have less liberty?
This fills me with such passion, I become
Like the volcano Etna, and could tear
Pieces of my own heart out of my breast!
What law, justice, or reason can decree
That man alone should never know the joys

And be alone excepted from the rights
God grants a fish, a bird, a beast, a brook?

ROSAURA. His words have filled me full of fear and pity.

SEGISMUND. Who is it overheard my speech? Clotaldo?

CLARION. Say "yes!"

ROSAURA. It's only a poor wretch, alas,
Who in these cold ravines has overheard
Your sorrows.

SEGISMUND. Then I'll kill you

Seizes her.

So as to leave no witness of my frailty.
I'll tear you into bits with these strong arms!

CLARION. I'm deaf. I wasn't able to hear that.

ROSAURA. If you were human born, it is enough
That I should kneel to you for you to spare me.

SEGISMUND. Your voice has softened me, your presence halted
me,
And now, confusingly, I feel respect
For you. Who are you? Though here I have learned
So little of the world, since this grim tower
Has been my cradle and my sepulchre;
And though since I was born (if you can say
I really have been born) I've only seen
This rustic desert where in misery
I dwell alone, a living skeleton,
An animated corpse; and though till now,
I never spoke, save to one man who hears
My griefs and through whose converse I have heard
News of the earth and of the sky; and though,
To astound you more, and make you call me
A human monster, I dwell here, and am
A man of the wild animals, a beast
Among the race of men; and though in such
Misfortune, I have studied human laws,
Instructed by the birds, and learned to measure
The circles of the gentle stars, you only
Have curbed my furious rage, amazed my vision,
And filled with wonderment my sense of hearing.

Each time I look at you, I feel new wonder!
The more I see of you, the more I long
To go on seeing more of you. I think
My eyes are dropsical, to go on drinking
What it is death for them to drink, because
They go on drinking that which I am dying
To see and that which, seen, will deal me death.
Yet let me gaze on you and die, since I
Am so bewitched I can no longer think
What not seeing you would do to me—the sight
Itself being fatal! that would be more hard
Than dying, madness, rage, and fiercest grief:
It would be life—worst fate of all because
The gift of life to such a wretchèd man
Would be the gift of death to happiness!

ROSAURA. Astonished as I look, amazed to hear,
I know not what to say nor what to ask.
All I can say is that heaven guided me
Here to be comforted, if it is comfort
To see another sadder than oneself.
They say a sage philosopher of old,
Being so poor and miserable that he
Lived on the few plain herbs he could collect,
One day exclaimed: "Could any man be poorer
Or sadder than myself?"—when, turning round,
He saw the very answer to his words.
For there another sage philosopher
Was picking up the scraps he'd thrown away.
I lived cursing my fortune in this world
And asked within me: "Is there any other
Suffers so hard a fate?" Now out of pity
You've given me the answer. For within me
I find upon reflection that my griefs
Would be as joys to you and you'd receive them
To give you pleasure. So if they perchance
In any measure may afford relief,
Listen attentively to my misfortune
And take what is left over for yourself.
I am . . .

CLOTALDO, *within.* Guards of the tower! You sluggards
  Or cowards, you have let two people pass
  Into the prison bounds . . .

ROSAURA.   Here's more confusion!

SEGISMUND. That is Clotaldo, keeper of my prison.
  Are my misfortunes still not at an end?

CLOTALDO. Come. Be alert, and either seize or slay them
  Before they can resist!

VOICES, *within.*   Treason! Betrayal!

CLARION. Guards of the tower who let us pass unhindered,
  Since there's a choice, to seize us would be simpler.
  Enter CLOTALDO *with soldiers. He holds a pistol and they
  all wear masks.*

CLOTALDO, *aside to the soldiers.*
  Cover your faces, all! It's a precaution
  Imperative that nobody should know us
  While we are here.

CLARION.   What's this? A masquerade?

CLOTALDO. O you, who ignorantly passed the bounds
  And limits of this region, banned to all—
  Against the king's decree which has forbidden
  That any should find out the prodigy
  Hidden in these ravines—yield up your weapons
  Or else this pistol, like a snake of metal,
  Will spit the piercing venom of two shots
  With scandalous assault upon the air.

SEGISMUND. Tyrannic master, ere you harm these people
  Let my life be the spoil of these sad bonds
  In which (I swear it by Almighty God)
  I'll sooner rend myself with hands and teeth
  Amid these rocks than see them harmed and mourn
  Their suffering.

CLOTALDO.   Since you know, Segismund,
  That your misfortunes are so huge that, even
  Before your birth, you died by heaven's decree,
  And since you know these walls and binding chains
  Are but the brakes and curbs to your proud frenzies,
  What use is it to bluster?

To the guards.

> Shut the door
> Of this close prison! Hide him in its depths!

SEGISMUND. Ah, heavens, how justly you denied me freedom!
　　For like a Titan I would rise against you,
　　Pile jasper mountains high on stone foundations
　　And climb to burst the windows of the sun!

CLOTALDO. Perhaps you suffer so much pain today
　　Just to forestall that feat.

ROSAURA. 　　　　　　　Now that I see
　　How angry pride offends you, I'd be foolish
　　Not to plead humbly at your feet for life.
　　Be moved by me to pity. It would be
　　Notoriously harsh that neither pride
　　Nor humbleness found favour in your eyes!

CLARION. And if neither Humility nor Pride
　　Impress you (characters of note who act
　　And motivate a thousand mystery plays)
　　Let me, here, who am neither proud nor humble,
　　But merely something halfway in between,
　　Plead to you both for shelter and for aid.

CLOTALDO. Ho, there!

SOLDIER. 　　　　　Sir?

CLOTALDO. 　　　　　　　Take their weapons. Bind their eyes
　　So that they cannot see the way they're led.

ROSAURA. This is my sword. To nobody but you
　　I yield it, since you're, after all, the chief.
　　I cannot yield to one of meaner rank.

CLARION. My sword is such that I will freely give it
　　To the most mean and wretched.

To one soldier.

> Take it, you!

ROSAURA. And if I have to die, I'll leave it to you
　　In witness of your mercy. It's a pledge
　　Of great worth and may justly be esteemed
　　For someone's sake who wore it long ago.

CLOTALDO, *apart*. Each moment seems to bring me new
     misfortune!

ROSAURA. Because of that, I ask you to preserve
  This sword with care. Since if inconstant Fate
  Consents to the remission of my sentence,
  It has to win me honour. Though I know not
  The secret that it carries, I do know
  It has got one—unless I trick myself—
  And prize it just as the sole legacy
  My father left me.

CLOTALDO.   Who then was your father?

ROSAURA. I never knew.

CLOTALDO.   And why have you come here?

ROSAURA. I came to Poland to avenge a wrong.

CLOTALDO, *apart*.
  Sacred heavens!
  On taking the sword he becomes very perturbed.
                What's this? Still worse and worse.
  I am perplexed and troubled with more fears.
  Aloud.
  Tell me: who gave that sword to you?

ROSAURA.   A woman.

CLOTALDO. Her name?

ROSAURA.   A secret I am forced to keep.

CLOTALDO. What makes you think this sword contains a secret?

ROSAURA. That she who gave it to me said: "Depart
  To Poland. There with subtlety and art
  Display it so that all the leading people
  And noblemen can see you wearing it,
  And I know well that there's a lord among them
  Who will both shelter you and grant you favour."
  But, lest he should be dead, she did not name him.

CLOTALDO, *aside*. Protect me, heavens! What is this I hear?
  I cannot say if real or imagined
  But here's the sword I gave fair Violante
  In token that, whoever in the future
  Should come from her to me wearing this sword,

Would find in me a tender father's love.
Alas, what can I do in such a pass,
When he who brings the sword to win my favour
Brings it to find his own red death instead
Arriving at my feet condemned already?
What strange perplexity! How hard a fate!
What an inconstant fortune to be plagued with!
This is my son not only by all signs
But also by the promptings of my heart,
Since, seeing him, my heart seems to cry out
To him, and beat its wings, and, though unable
To break the locks, behaves as one shut in,
Who, hearing noises in the street outside,
Cranes from the window-ledge. Just so, not knowing
What's really happening, but hearing sounds,
My heart runs to my eyes which are its windows
And out of them flows into bitter tears.
Protect me, heaven! What am I to do?
To take him to the king is certain death.
To hide him is to break my sacred oath
And the strong law of homage. From one side
Love of one's own, and from the other loyalty—
Call me to yield. Loyalty to my king
(Why do I doubt?) comes before life and honour.
Then live my loyalty, and let him die!
When I remember, furthermore, he came
To avenge an injury—a man insulted
And unavenged is in disgrace. My son
Therefore he is not, nor of noble blood.
But if some danger has mischanced, from which
No one escapes, since honour is so fragile
That any act can smash it, and it takes
A stain from any breath of air, what more
Could any nobleman have done than he,
Who, at the cost of so much risk and danger,
Comes to avenge his honour? Since he's so brave
He is my son, and my blood's in his veins.
And so betwixt the one doubt and the other,
The most important mean between extremes
Is to go to the king and tell the truth—

That he's my son, to kill, if so he wishes.
Perhaps my loyalty thus will move his mercy
And if I thus can merit a live son
I'll help him to avenge his injury.
But if the king prove constant in his rigour
And deal him death, he'll die in ignorance
That I'm his father.

Aloud to ROSAURA *and* CLARION.

                    Come then, strangers, come!
And do not fear that you have no companions
In your misfortunes, since, in equal doubt,
Tossed between life and death, I cannot guess
Which is the greater evil or the less.

A hall at the royal palace, in court

Enter ASTOLFO *and soldiers at one side: from the other side*
PRINCESS STELLA *and ladies. Military music and salvos.*

ASTOLFO. To greet your excellent bright beams
As brilliant as a comet's rays,
The drums and brasses mix their praise
With those of fountains, birds, and streams.
With sounds alike, in like amaze,
Your heavenly face each voice salutes,
Which puts them in such lively fettle,
The trumpets sound like birds of metal,
The songbirds play like feathered flutes.
And thus they greet you, fair señora—
The salvos, as their queen, the brasses,
As to Minerva when she passes,
The songbirds to the bright Aurora,
And all the flowers and leaves and grasses
As doing homage unto Flora,
Because you come to cheat the day
Which now the night has covered o'er—
Aurora in your spruce array,

Flora in peace, Pallas in war,
But in my heart the queen of May.

STELLA. If human voice could match with acts
You would have been unwise to say
Hyperboles that a few facts
May well refute some other day
Confounding all this martial fuss
With which I struggle daringly,
Since flatteries you proffer thus
Do not accord with what I see.
Take heed that it's an evil thing
And worthy of a brute accursed,
Loud praises with your mouth to sing
When in your heart you wish the worst.

ASTOLFO. Stella, you have been badly misinformed
If you doubt my good faith. Here let me beg you
To listen to my plea and hear me out.
The third Eugtorgius died, the King of Poland.
Basil, his heir, had two fair sisters who
Bore you, my cousin, and myself. I would not
Tire you with all that happened here. You know
Clorilene was your mother who enjoys,
Under a better reign, her starry throne.
She was the elder. Lovely Recisunda
(Whom may God cherish for a thousand years!)
The younger one, my mother and your aunt,
Was wed in Muscovy. Now to return:
Basil has yielded to the feebleness
Of age, loves learnèd study more than women,
Has lost his wife, is childless, will not marry.
And so it comes that you and I both claim
The heirdom of the realm. You claim that you
Were daughter to the elder daughter. I
Say that my being born a man, although
Son of the younger daughter, gives me title
To be preferred. We've told the king, our uncle,
Of both of our intentions. And he answered
That he would judge between our rival claims,
For which the time and place appointed was

Today and here. For that same reason I
Have left my native Muscovy. With that
Intent I come—not seeking to wage war
But so that you might thus wage war on me!
May Love, wise god, make true what people say
(Your "people" is a wise astrologer)
By settling this through your being chosen queen—
Queen and my consort, sovereign of my will;
My uncle crowning you, for greater honour;
Your courage conquering, as it deserves;
My love applauding you, its emperor!

STELLA. To such chivalrous gallantry, my breast
Cannot hold out. The imperial monarchy
I wish were mine only to make it yours—
Although my love is not quite satisfied
That you are to be trusted since your speech
Is somewhat contradicted by that portrait
You carry in the locket round your neck.

ASTOLFO. I'll give you satisfaction as to that.

Drums.

But these loud instruments will not permit it
That sound the arrival of the king and council.

Enter KING BASIL *with his following.*

STELLA. Wise Thales . . .

ASTOLFO. 　　　　　Learned Euclid . . .

STELLA. Among the signs . . .

ASTOLFO. 　　　　　　　　　Among the stars . . .

STELLA. Where you preside in power . . .

ASTOLFO. 　　　　　　　　Where you reside . . .

STELLA. And plot their paths . . .

ASTOLFO. 　　　　　　And trace their fiery trails . . .

STELLA. Describing . . .

ASTOLFO. 　　　　　. . . Measuring and judging them . . .

STELLA. Please read my stars that I, in humble bonds . . .

ASTOLFO. Please read them, so that I in soft embraces . . .

STELLA. May twine as ivy to this tree!

ASTOLFO.   May find
  Myself upon my knees before these feet!

BASIL. Come and embrace me, niece and nephew. Trust me,
  Since you're both loyal to my loving precepts,
  And come here so affectionately both—
  In nothing shall I leave you cause to cavil,
  And both of you as equals will be treated.
  The gravity of what I have to tell
  Oppresses me, and all I ask of you
  Is silence: the event itself will claim
  Your wonderment. So be attentive now,
  Belovèd niece and nephew, illustrious courtiers,
  Relatives, friends, and subjects! You all know
  That for my learning I have merited
  The surname of The Learnèd, since the brush
  Of great Timanthes, and Lisippus' marbles—
  Stemming oblivion (consequence of time)—
  Proclaimed me to mankind Basil the Great.
  You know the science that I most affect
  And most esteem is subtle mathematics
  (By which I forestall time, cheat fame itself)
  Whose office is to show things gradually.
  For when I look my tables up and see,
  Present before me, all the news and actions
  Of centuries to come, I gain on Time—
  Since Time recounts whatever I have said
  After I say it. Those snowflaking haloes,
  Those canopies of crystal spread on high,
  Lit by the sun, cut by the circling moon,
  Those diamond orbs, those globes of radiant crystal
  Which the bright stars adorn, on which the signs
  Parade in blazing excellence, have been
  My chiefest study all through my long years.
  They are the volumes on whose adamantine
  Pages, bound up in sapphire, heaven writes,
  In lines of burnished gold and vivid letters,
  All that is due to happen, whether adverse
  Or else benign. I read them in a flash,
  So quickly that my spirit tracks their movements—
  Whatever road they take, whatever goal

They aim at. Would to heaven that before
My genius had been the commentary
Writ in their margins, or the index to
Their pages, that my life had been the rubble,
The ruin, and destruction of their wrath,
And that my tragedy in them had ended,
Because, to the unlucky, even their merit
Is like a hostile knife, and he whom knowledge
Injures is but a murderer to himself.
And this I say myself, though my misfortunes
Say it far better, which, to marvel at,
I beg once more for silence from you all.
With my late wife, the queen, I had a son,
Unhappy son, to greet whose birth the heavens
Wore themselves out in prodigies and portents.
Ere the sun's light brought him live burial
Out of the womb (for birth resembles death)
His mother many times, in the delirium
And fancies of her sleep, saw a fierce monster
Bursting her entrails in a human form,
Born spattered with her lifeblood, dealing death,
The human viper of this century!
The day came for his birth, and every presage
Was then fulfilled, for tardily or never
Do the more cruel ones prove false. At birth
His horoscope was such that the bright sun,
Stained in its blood, entered ferociously
Into a duel with the moon above.
The whole earth seemed a rampart for the strife
Of heaven's two lights, who—though not hand-to-hand—
Fought light-to-light to gain the mastery!
The worst eclipse the sun has ever suffered
Since Christ's own death horrified earth and sky.
The whole earth overflowed with conflagrations
So that it seemed the final paroxysm
Of existence. The skies grew dark. Buildings shook.
The clouds rained stones. The rivers ran with blood.
In this delirious frenzy of the sun,
Thus, Segismund was born into the world,
Giving a foretaste of his character

By killing his own mother, seeming to speak thus
By his ferocity: "I am a man,
Because I have begun now to repay
All kindnesses with evil." To my studies
I went forthwith, and saw in all I studied
That Segismund would be the most outrageous
Of all men, the most cruel of all princes,
And impious of all monarchs, by whose acts
The kingdom would be torn up and divided
So as to be a school of treachery
And an academy of vices. He,
Risen in fury, amidst crimes and horrors,
Was born to trample me (with shame I say it)
And make of my grey hairs his very carpet.
Who is there but believes an evil Fate?
And more if he discovers it himself,
For self-love lends its credit to our studies.
So I, believing in the Fates, and in
The havoc that their prophecies predestined,
Determined to cage up this newborn tiger
To see if on the stars we sages have
Some power. I gave out that the prince had died
Stillborn, and, well-forewarned, I built a tower
Amidst the cliffs and boulders of yon mountains
Over whose tops the light scarce finds its way,
So stubbornly their obelisks and crags
Defend the entry to them. The strict laws
And edicts that I published then (declaring
That nobody might enter the forbidden
Part of the range) were passed on that account.
There Segismund lives to this day, a captive,
Poor and in misery, where, save Clotaldo,
His guardian, none have seen or talked to him.
The latter has instructed him in all
Branches of knowledge and in the Catholic faith,
Alone the witness of his misery.
There are three things to be considered now:
Firstly, Poland, that I love you greatly,
So much that I would free you from the oppression
And servitude of such a tyrant king.

He would not be a kindly ruler who
Would put his realm and homeland in such danger.
The second fact that I must bear in mind
Is this: that to deny my flesh and blood
The rights which law, both human and divine,
Concedes, would not accord with Christian charity,
For no law says that, to prevent another
Being a tyrant, I may be one myself,
And if my son's a tyrant, to prevent him
From doing outrage, I myself should do it.
Now here's the third and last point I would speak of,
Namely, how great an error it has been
To give too much belief to things predicted,
Because, even if his inclination should
Dictate some headlong, rash precipitancies,
They may perhaps not conquer him entirely,
For the most accursèd destiny, the most
Violent inclination, the most impious
Planet—all can but influence, not force,
The free will which man holds direct from God.
And so, between one motive and another
Vacillating discursively, I hit
On a solution that will stun you all.
I shall tomorrow, but without his knowing
He is my son—your king—place Segismund
(For that's the name with which he was baptised)
Here on my throne, beneath my canopy,
Yes, in my very place, that he may govern you
And take command. And you must all be here
To swear him fealty as his loyal subjects.
Three things may follow from this test, and these
I'll set against the three which I proposed.
The first is that should the prince prove prudent,
Stable, and benign—thus giving the lie
To all that prophecy reports of him—
Then you'll enjoy in him your rightful ruler
Who was so long a courtier of the mountains
And neighbour to the beasts. Here is the second:
If he prove proud, rash, cruel, and outrageous,
And with a loosened rein gallop unheeding

Across the plains of vice, I shall have done
My duty, and fulfilled my obligation
Of mercy. If I then re-imprison him,
That's incontestably a kingly deed—
Not cruelty but merited chastisement.
The third thing's this: that if the prince should be
As I've described him, then—by the love I feel
For you, my vassals—I shall give you worthier
Rulers to wear the sceptre and the crown;
Because your king and queen will be my nephew
And niece, each with an equal right to rule,
Each gaining the inheritance he merits,
And joined in faith of holy matrimony.
This I command you as a king, I ask you
As a kind father, as a sage I pray you,
As an experienced old man I tell you,
And (if it's true, as Spanish Seneca
Says, that the king is slave unto his nation)
This, as a humble slave, I beg of you.

ASTOLFO. If it behoves me to reply (being
The person most involved in this affair)
Then, in the name of all, let Segismund
Appear! It is enough that he's your son!

ALL. Give us our prince: we want him for our king!

BASIL. Subjects, I thank you for your kindly favour.
Accompany these, my two Atlases,
Back to their rooms. Tomorrow you shall see him.

ALL. Long live the great King Basil! Long live Basil!

Exeunt all, accompanying STELLA *and* ASTOLFO. *The* KING
remains.

Enter CLOTALDO *with* ROSAURA *and* CLARION.

CLOTALDO. May I have leave to speak, sire?

BASIL.　　　　　　　　　　　　　Oh, Clotaldo!
You're very welcome.

CLOTALDO.　　　　　Thus to kneel before you
Is always welcome, sire—yet not today
When sad and evil Fate destroys the joy
Your presence normally concedes.

BASIL.   What's wrong?

CLOTALDO. A great misfortune, sire, has come upon me
Just when I should have met it with rejoicing.

BASIL. Continue.

CLOTALDO.   Sire, this beautiful young man
Who inadvertently and daringly
Came to the tower, wherein he saw the prince,
Is my . . .

BASIL.   Do not afflict yourself, Clotaldo.
Had it not been just now, I should have minded,
I must confess. But I've revealed the secret,
And now it does not matter if he knows it.
Attend me afterwards. I've many things
To tell you. You in turn have many things
To do for me. You'll be my minister,
I warn you, in the most momentous action
The world has ever seen. These prisoners, lest you
Should think I blame your oversight, I'll pardon.

Exit.

CLOTALDO. Long may you live, great sire! A thousand years!
Aside.

Heaven improves our fates. I shall not tell him
Now that he is my son, since it's not needed
Till he's avenged.
Aloud.

Strangers, you may go free.

ROSAURA. Humbly I kiss your feet.

CLARION.   Whilst I'll just *miss* them—
Old friends will hardly quibble at one letter.

ROSAURA. You've granted me my life, sir. I remain
Your servant and eternally your debtor.

CLOTALDO. No! It was not your life I gave you. No!
Since any wellborn man who, unavenged,
Nurses an insult does not live at all.
And seeing you have told me that you came
For that sole reason, it was not life I spared—
Life in disgrace is not a life at all.

Aside.

I see this spurs him.

ROSAURA.   Freely I confess it—
Although you spared my life, it was no life.
But I will wipe my honour's stain so spotless
That after I have vanquished all my dangers
Life well may seem a shining gift from you.

CLOTALDO. Take here your burnished steel: 'twill be enough,
Bathed in your enemies' red blood, to right you.
For steel that once was mine (I mean of course
Just for the time I've had it in my keeping)
Should know how to avenge you.

ROSAURA. Now, in your name I gird it on once more
And on it I will swear to take revenge
Although my foe were even mightier.

CLOTALDO. Is he so powerful?

ROSAURA.   So much so that . . .
Although I have no doubt in your discretion . . .
I say no more because I'd not estrange
Your clemency.

CLOTALDO. You would have won me had you told me, since
That would prevent me helping him.

Aside.

If only I could discover who he is!

ROSAURA. So that you'll not think that I value lightly
Such confidence, know that my adversary
Is no less than Astolfo, Duke of Muscovy.

CLOTALDO, *aside.* (I hardly can withstand the grief it gives me
For it is worse than aught I could imagine!
Let us inquire of him some further facts.)

Aloud.

If you were born a Muscovite, your ruler
Could never have affronted you. Go back
Home to your country. Leave this headstrong valour.
It will destroy you.

ROSAURA.   Though he's been my prince,
I know that he has done me an affront.

CLOTALDO. Even though he slapped your face, that's no affront.
Aside.

O heavens!

ROSAURA.   My insult was far deeper!

CLOTALDO.   Tell it:
Since nothing I imagine could be deeper.

ROSAURA. Yes. I will tell it, yet, I know not why,
With such respect I look upon your face,
I venerate you with such true affection,
With such high estimation do I weigh you,
That I scarce dare to tell you—these men's clothes
Are an enigma, not what they appear.
So now you know. Judge if it's no affront
That here Astolfo comes to wed with Stella
Although betrothed to me. I've said enough.

Exeunt ROSAURA *and* CLARION.

CLOTALDO. Here! Listen! Wait! What mazed confusion!
It is a labyrinth wherein the reason
Can find no clue. My family honour's injured.
The enemy's all powerful. I'm a vassal
And she's a woman. Heavens! Show a path
Although I don't believe there is a way!
There's nought but evil bodings in the sky.
The whole world is a prodigy, say I.

ACT II

A Hall in the Royal Palace

Enter BASIL *and* CLOTALDO.

CLOTALDO. All has been done according to your orders.

BASIL. Tell me, Clotaldo, how it went?

CLOTALDO.   Why, thus:
I took to Segismund a calming drug
Wherein are mixed herbs of especial virtue,
Tyrannous in their overpowering strength,
Which seize and steal and alienate man's gift
Of reasoning, thus making a live corpse
Of him. His violence evaporated
With all his faculties and senses too.
There is no need to prove it's possible
Because experience teaches us that medicine
Is full of natural secrets, that there is no
Animal, plant, or stone that has not got
Appointed properties. If human malice
Explores a thousand poisons which deal death,
Who then can doubt, that being so, that other
Poisons, less violent, cause only sleep?
But (leaving that doubt aside, as proven false
By every evidence) hear then the sequel:
I went down into Segismund's close prison
Bearing the drink wherein, with opium,
Henbane and poppies had been mixed. With him
I talked a little while of the humanities,
In which dumb Nature has instructed him,
The mountains and the heavens and the stars,
In whose divine academies he learned
Rhetoric from the birds and the wild creatures.
To lift his spirit to the enterprise
Which you require of him, I chose for subject
The swiftness of a stalwart eagle, who,

Deriding the base region of the wind,
Rises into the sphere reserved for fire,
A feathered lightning, an untethered comet.
Then I extolled such lofty flight and said:
"After all, he's the king of birds, and so
Takes precedence, by right, over the rest."
No more was needful for, in taking up
Majesty for his subject, he discoursed
With pride and high ambition, as his blood
Naturally moves, incites, and spurs him on
To grand and lofty things, and so he said
That in the restless kingdom of the birds
There should be those who swear obedience, too!
"In this, my miseries console me greatly,
Because if I'm a vassal here, it's only
By force, and not by choice. Of my own will
I would not yield in rank to any man."
Seeing that he grew furious—since this touched
The theme of his own griefs—I gave the potion
And scarcely had it passed from cup to breast
Before he yielded all his strength to slumber.
A chill sweat ran through all his limbs and veins.
Had I not known that this was mere feigned death
I would have thought him dead. Then came the men
To whom you've trusted this experiment,
Who placed him in a coach and brought him here
To your own rooms, where all things were prepared
In royalty and grandeur as befitting
His person. In your own bed they have laid him
Where, when the torpor wanes, they'll do him service
As if he were Your Majesty himself.
All has been done as you have ordered it,
And if I have obeyed you well, my lord,
I'd beg a favour (pardon me this freedom)—
To know what your intention is in thus
Transporting Segismund here to the palace.

BASIL. Your curiosity is just, Clotaldo,
And yours alone I'll satisfy. The star
Which governs Segismund, my son, in life,
Threatens a thousand tragedies and woes.

And now I wish to see whether the stars
(Which never lie—and having shown to us
So many cruel signs seem yet more certain)
May yet be brought to moderate their sentence,
Whether by prudence charmed or valour won,
For man does have the power to rule his stars.
I would examine this, bringing him here
Where he may know he is my son, and make
Trial of his talent. If magnanimously
He conquers and controls himself, he'll reign,
But if he proves a tyrant and is cruel,
Back to his chains he'll go. Now, you will ask,
Why did we bring him sleeping in this manner
For the experiment? I'll satisfy you,
Down to the smallest detail, with my answer.
If he knows that he is my son today,
And if tomorrow he should find himself
Once more reduced to prison, to misery,
He would despair entirely, knowing truly
Who, and whose son, he is. What consolation
Could he derive, then, from his lot? So I
Contrive to leave an exit for such grief,
By making him believe it was a dream.
By these means we may learn two things at once:
First, his character—for he will really be
Awake in all he thinks and all his actions;
Second, his consolation—which would be
(If he should wake in prison on the morrow,
Although he saw himself obeyed today)
That he might understand he had been dreaming,
And he will not be wrong, for in this world,
Clotaldo, all who live are only dreaming.

CLOTALDO. I've proofs enough to doubt of your success,
But now it is too late to remedy it.
From what I can make out, I think he's wakened
And that he's coming this way, by the sound.

BASIL. I shall withdraw. You, as his tutor, go
And guide him through his new bewilderments
By answering his queries with the truth.

CLOTALDO. You give me leave to tell the truth of it?

BASIL. Yes, because knowing all things, he may find
Known perils are the easiest to conquer.

Exit BASIL.

Enter CLARION.

CLARION. It cost me four whacks to get here so quickly.
I caught them from a red-haired halberdier
Sprouting a ginger beard over his livery,
And I've come to see what's going on.
No windows give a better view than those
A man brings with him in his head, not asking
For tickets of admission or paid seats,
Since at all functions, festivals, or feasts
He looks out with the same nice self-composure.

CLOTALDO, *aside.* Here's Clarion who's the servant of that
        person—
That trader in woes, importer from Poland
Of my disgrace.

Aloud.

                    Come, Clarion, what news?

CLARION. Item the first: encouraged by the fact
Your clemency's disposed to venge her insult,
Rosaura has resumed her proper clothing.

CLOTALDO. That's right: it's less indecorous and bold.

CLARION. Item: she's changed her name, and given out
That she's your niece. And now they've made so much
Of her that she's been raised to maid of honour
To the unique and only princess, Stella.

CLOTALDO. That's right: her honour stands to my account.

CLARION. Indeed she merely bides the time till you
Will settle all accounts about her honour.

CLOTALDO. Biding the time is wise, for in the end
It's Time that's going to settle all accounts!

CLARION. Item: that she's attended like a queen,
Because they take her for your niece. Item:
That I, who trudged along with her, am dying
Of hunger. Nobody remembers me,

Nor yet remembers that I'm like my name
And (should I sound my Clarion) could tell
All to the king and Stella and Astolfo.
For I am both a Clarion and a servant—
Two things which ill-accord with secrecy.
If silence should, by chance, let slip my hand,
Then there's a chorus which would fit me well:
"Dawn-breaking Clarion plays no better tune!"

CLOTALDO. You've reason for complaint. I'll satisfy it
If you'll but serve me . . .

CLARION.   Hush, here's Segismund!

Enter musicians, singing, and servants arraying SEGISMUND,
who seems amazed.

SEGISMUND. Heavens above! What's this that I am seeing?
I wonder at it all, with naught of fear!
But with a mighty doubt, I disbelieve it!
I?—in a sumptuous palace? I—encircled
With rich brocades and silks? I—overwhelmed
With servants in such brilliant liveries?
I—to awake in such a gorgeous bed?
I—in the middle of so many footmen
Who clothe me in rich garments? I'm awake:
It would be false to take this for a dream.
Am I not Segismund? Heavens! disabuse me
If I'm mistaken. Say, what could have happened
In my imagination while I slept—
That I should find myself in such a place?
But why should I worry, whatever it was?
I'll let myself be served and entertained—
Befall what may.

FIRST SERVANT, *aside to* SECOND SERVANT *and* CLARION.
              He's very melancholy!

SECOND SERVANT. Who would not be, considering all that's
      happened
To him?

CLARION. I would not be!

SECOND SERVANT.   You, speak to him.

FIRST SERVANT. Shall they begin to sing again?

SEGISMUND.   Why, no,
  I would not have them sing.

SECOND SERVANT.   You're so distraught,
  I wish you entertained.

SEGISMUND.   My griefs are such
  That no mere voices can amuse me now—
  Only the martial music pleased my mind.

CLOTALDO. Your Highness, mighty prince, give me your hand
  To kiss. I'm glad to be the first to offer
  Obedience at your feet.

SEGISMUND, *aside*.   This is Clotaldo.
  How is it he, that tyrannised my thralldom,
  Should now be treating me with such respect?
  Aloud.
  Tell me what's happening all round me here.

CLOTALDO. With the perplexities of your new state,
  Your reason will encounter many doubts,
  But I shall try to free you from them all
  (If that may be) because you now must know
  You are hereditary Prince of Poland.
  If you have been withdrawn from public sight
  Under restraint, it was in strict obedience
  To Fate's inclemency, which will permit
  A thousand woes to fall upon this empire
  The moment that you wear the sovereign's crown.
  But trusting that you'll prudently defeat
  Your own malignant stars (since they can be
  Controlled by magnanimity) you've been
  Brought to this palace from the tower you knew
  Even while your soul was yielded up to sleep.
  My lord the king, your father, will be coming
  To see you, and from him you'll learn the rest.

SEGISMUND. Then, vile, infamous traitor, what have I
  To know more than this fact of who I am,
  To show my pride and power from this day onward?
  How have you played your country such a treason
  As to deny me, against law and right,
  The rank which is my own?

CLOTALDO. Unhappy me!

SEGISMUND. You were a traitor to the law, a flattering liar
To your own king, and cruel to myself.
And so the king, the law, and I condemn you,
After such fierce misfortunes as I've borne,
To die here by my hands.

SECOND SERVANT. My lord!

SEGISMUND. Let none
Get in the way. It is in vain. By God!
If you intrude, I'll throw you through the window.

SECOND SERVANT. Clotaldo, fly!

CLOTALDO. Alas, poor Segismund!
That you should show such pride, all unaware
That you are dreaming this.
Exit.

SECOND SERVANT. Take care! Take care!

SEGISMUND. Get out!

SECOND SERVANT. He was obeying the king's orders.

SEGISMUND. In an injustice, no one should obey
The king, and I'm his prince.

SECOND SERVANT. He had no right
To look into the rights and wrongs of it.

SEGISMUND. You must be mad to answer back at me.

CLARION. The prince is right. It's you who're in the wrong!

SECOND SERVANT. Who gave you right to speak?

CLARION. I simply took it.

SEGISMUND. And who are you?

CLARION. I am the go-between,
And in this art I think I am a master—
Since I'm the greatest jackanapes alive.

SEGISMUND, *to* CLARION.
In all this new world, you're the only one
Of the whole crowd who pleases me.

CLARION. Why, my lord,
I am the best pleaser of Segismunds
That ever was: ask anybody here!

Enter ASTOLFO.

ASTOLFO. Blessèd the day, a thousand times, my prince,
　　On which you landed here on Polish soil
　　To fill with so much splendour and delight
　　Our wide horizons, like the break of day!
　　For you arise as does the rising sun
　　Out of the rugged mountains, far away.
　　Shine forth then! And although so tardily
　　You bind the glittering laurels on your brows,
　　The longer may they last you still unwithered.

SEGISMUND. God save you.

ASTOLFO.　　　　　　　That you do not know me, sir,
　　Is some excuse for greeting me without
　　The honour due to me. I am Astolfo
　　The Duke of Muscovy. You are my cousin.
　　We are of equal rank.

SEGISMUND.　　　　Then if I say,
　　"God save you," do I not display good feeling?
　　But since you take such note of who you are,
　　The next time that I see you, I shall say
　　"God save you *not*," if you would like that better.

SECOND SERVANT, *to* ASTOLFO.
　　Your Highness, make allowance for his breeding
　　Amongst the mountains. So he deals with all.

　　To SEGISMUND.

　　Astolfo does take precedence, Your Highness—

SEGISMUND. I have no patience with the way he came
　　To make his solemn speech, then put his hat on!

SECOND SERVANT. He's a grandee!

SEGISMUND.　　　　　　　　I'm grander than grandees!

SECOND SERVANT. For all that, there should be respect between
　　　　you,
　　More than among the rest.

SEGISMUND.　　　　　And who told you
　　To mix in my affairs?

　　Enter STELLA.

STELLA. Many times welcome to Your Royal Highness,

Now come to grace the dais that receives him
With gratitude and love. Long may you live
August and eminent, despite all snares,
And count your life by centuries, not years!

SEGISMUND, *aside to* CLARION.

Now tell me, who's this sovereign deity
At whose divinest feet Heaven lays down
The fleece of its aurora in the east?

CLARION. Sir, it's your cousin Stella.

SEGISMUND.   She were better
Named "sun" than "star"!

To STELLA.

                                Though your speech was fair,
Just to have seen you and been conquered by you
Suffices for a welcome in itself.
To find myself so blessed beyond my merit
What can I do but thank you, lovely Stella,
For you could add more brilliance and delight
To the most blazing star? When you get up
What work is left the sun to do? O give me
Your hand to kiss, from out whose cup of snow
The solar horses drink the fires of day!

STELLA. Be a more gentle courtier.

ASTOLFO.   I am lost.

SECOND SERVANT. I know Astolfo's hurt. I must divert him.

To SEGISMUND.

Sir, you should know that thus to woo so boldly
Is most improper. And, besides, Astolfo . . .

SEGISMUND. Did I not tell you not to meddle with me?

SECOND SERVANT. I only say what's just.

SEGISMUND.   All this annoys me.
Nothing seems just to me but what I want.

SECOND SERVANT. Why, sir, I heard you say that no obedience
Or service should be lent to what's unjust.

SEGISMUND. You also heard me say that I would throw
Anyone who annoys me from that balcony.

SECOND SERVANT. With men like me you cannot do such things.

SEGISMUND. No? Well, by God, I'll have to prove it then!

He takes him in his arms and rushes out, followed by many,
to return soon after.

ASTOLFO. What on earth have I seen? Can it be true?

STELLA. Go, all, and stop him!

SEGISMUND, *returning.*   From the balcony
He's fallen in the sea. How strange it seems!

ASTOLFO. Measure your acts of violence, my lord:
From crags to palaces, the distance is
As great as that between man and the beasts.

SEGISMUND. Well, since you are for speaking out so boldly,
Perhaps one day you'll find that on your shoulders
You have no head to place your hat upon.

Exit ASTOLFO.

Enter BASIL.

BASIL. What's happened here?

SEGISMUND.   Nothing at all. A man
Wearied me, so I threw him in the sea.

CLARION, *to* SEGISMUND. Be warned. That is the king.

BASIL.   On the first day,
So soon, your coming here has cost a life?

SEGISMUND. He said I couldn't: so I won the bet.

BASIL. It grieves me, Prince, that, when I hoped to see you
Forewarned, and overriding Fate, in triumph
Over your stars, the first thing I should see
Should be such rigour—that your first deed here
Should be a grievous homicide. Alas!
With what love, now, can I offer my arms,
Knowing your own have learned to kill already?
Who sees a dirk, red from a mortal wound,
But does not fear it? Who can see the place
Soaking in blood, where late a man was murdered,
But even the strongest must respond to nature?
So in your arms seeing the instrument
Of death, and looking on a blood-soaked place,
I must withdraw myself from your embrace,
And though I thought in loving bonds to bind
Your neck, yet fear withholds me from your arms.

SEGISMUND. Without your loving arms I can sustain
    Myself as usual. That such a loving father
    Could treat me with such cruelty, could thrust me
    From his side ungratefully, could rear me
    As a wild beast, could hold me for a monster,
    And pray that I were dead, that such a father
    Withholds his arms from winding round my neck,
    Seems unimportant, seeing that he deprives
    Me of my very being as a man.

BASIL. Would to heaven I had never granted it,
    For then I never would have heard your voice,
    Nor seen your outrages.

SEGISMUND.   Had you denied
    Me being, then I would not have complained,
    But that you took it from me when you gave it—
    That is my quarrel with you. Though to give
    Is the most singular and noble action,
    It is the basest action if one gives
    Only to take away.

BASIL.   How well you thank me
    For being raised from pauper to a prince!

SEGISMUND. In this what is there I should thank you for?
    You tyrant of my will! If you are old
    And feeble, and you die, what can you give me
    More than what is my own by right of birth?
    You are my father and my king, therefore
    This grandeur comes to me by natural law.
    Therefore, despite my present state, I'm not
    Indebted to you, rather can I claim
    Account of all those years in which you robbed me
    Of life and being, liberty, and honour.
    You ought to thank me that I press no claim
    Since you're my debtor, even to bankruptcy.

BASIL. Barbarous and outrageous brute! The heavens
    Have now fulfilled their prophecy: I call
    Them to bear witness to your pride. Although
    You know now, disillusioned, who you are,
    And see yourself where you take precedence,
    Take heed of this I say: be kind and humble

Since it may be that you are only dreaming,
Although it seems to you you're wide-awake.

Exit BASIL.

SEGISMUND. Can I perhaps be dreaming, though I seem
So wide-awake? No: I am not asleep,
Since I can touch, and realise what I
Have been before, and what I am today.
And if you even now relented, Father,
There'd be no cure since I know who I am
And you cannot, for all your sighs and groans,
Cheat me of my hereditary crown.
And if I was submissive in my chains
Before, then I was ignorant of what I am,
Which I now know (and likewise know that I
Am partly man but partly beast as well).

Enter ROSAURA *in woman's clothing.*

ROSAURA, *aside.* I came in Stella's train. I am afraid
Of meeting with Astolfo, since Clotaldo
Says he must not know who I am, not see me,
Because (he says) it touches on my honour.
And well I trust Clotaldo since I owe him
The safety of my life and honour both.

CLARION. What pleases you, and what do you admire
Most, of the things you've seen here in the world?

SEGISMUND. Why, nothing that I could not have foreseen—
Except the loveliness of women! Once,
I read among the books I had out there
That who owes God most grateful contemplation
Is Man: who is himself a tiny world.
But I think who owes God more grateful study
Is Woman—since she is a tiny heaven,
Having as much more beauty than a man
As heaven than earth. And even more, I say,
If she's the one that I am looking at.

ROSAURA, *aside.* That is the prince. I'll go.

SEGISMUND.   Stop! Woman! Wait!
Don't join the sunset with the breaking day
By fading out so fast. If east and west

Should clash like that, the day would surely suffer
A syncope. But what is this I see?

ROSAURA. What I am looking at I doubt, and yet
Believe.

SEGISMUND, *aside.* This beauty I have seen before.

ROSAURA, *aside.* This pomp and grandeur I have seen before
Cooped in a narrow dungeon.

SEGISMUND, *aside.*   I have found
My life at last.
Aloud.

    Woman (for that sole word
Outsoars all wooing flattery of speech
From one that is a man), woman, who are you?
If even long before I ever saw you
You owed me adoration as your prince,
How much the more should you be conquered by me
Now I recall I've seen you once before!
Who are you, beauteous woman?

ROSAURA, *aside.*   I'll pretend.
Aloud.

In Stella's train, I am a luckless lady.

SEGISMUND. Say no such thing. You are the sun from which
The minor star that's Stella draws its life,
Since she receives the splendour of your rays.
I've seen how in the kingdom of sweet odours,
Commander of the squadrons of the flowers,
The rose's deity presides, and is
Their empress by divine right of her beauty.
Among the precious stones which can be listed
In the academy of mines, I've seen
The diamond much preferred above the rest,
And crowned their emperor, for shining brightest.
In the revolving empire of the stars
The morning star takes pride among the others.
In their perfected spheres, when the sun calls
The planets to his council, he presides
And is the very oracle of day.
Then if among stars, gems, planet, and flowers

The fairest are exalted, why do you
Wait on a lesser beauty than yourself
Who are, in greater excellence and beauty,
The sun, the morning star, the diamond, and the rose!

Enter CLOTALDO, *who remains by the stage-curtain.*

CLOTALDO, *aside.*

I wish to curb him, since I brought him up.
But, what is this?

ROSAURA.   I reverence your favour,
And yet reply, rhetorical, with silence,
For when one's mind is clumsy and untaught,
He answers best who does not speak at all.

SEGISMUND. Stay! Do not go! How can you wish to go
And leave me darkened by my doubts?

ROSAURA.   Your Highness,
I beg your leave to go.

SEGISMUND.   To go so rudely
Is not to beg my leave but just to take it.

ROSAURA. But if you will not grant it, I must take it.

SEGISMUND. That were to change my courtesy to rudeness.
Resistance is like venom to my patience.

ROSAURA. But even if this deadly, raging venom
Should overcome your patience, yet you dare not
And could not treat me with dishonour, sir.

SEGISMUND. Why, just to see then if I can, and dare to—
You'll make me lose the fear I bear your beauty,
Since the impossible is always tempting
To me. Why, only now I threw a man
Over this balcony who said I couldn't:
And so to find out if I can or not
I'll throw your honour through the window too.

CLOTALDO, *aside.*

He seems determined in this course. Oh, heavens!
What's to be done that for a second time
My honour's threatened by a mad desire?

ROSAURA. Then with good reason it was prophesied
Your tyranny would wreak this kingdom

Outrageous scandals, treasons, crimes, and deaths.
But what can such a creature do as you
Who are not even a man, save in the name—
Inhuman, barbarous, cruel, and unbending
As the wild beasts amongst whom you were nursed?

SEGISMUND. That you should not insult me in this way
I spoke to you most courteously, and thought
I'd thereby get my way; but if you curse me thus
Even when I am speaking gently, why,
By the living God, I'll really give you cause.
Ho there! Clear out, the lot of you, at once!
Leave her to me! Close all the doors upon us.
Let no one enter!

Exeunt CLARION *and other attendants.*

ROSAURA.   I am lost . . . I warn you . . .

SEGISMUND. I am a tyrant and you plead in vain.

CLOTALDO, *aside.*

Oh, what a monstrous thing! I must restrain him
Even if I die for it.
Aloud.

                    Sir! Wait! Look here!

SEGISMUND. A second time you have provoked my anger,
You feeble, mad old man! Do you prize lightly
My wrath and rigour that you've gone so far?

CLOTALDO. Brought by the accents of her voice, I came
To tell you you must be more peaceful
If still you hope to reign, and warn you that
You should not be so cruel, though you rule—
Since this, perhaps, is nothing but a dream.

SEGISMUND. When you refer to disillusionment
You rouse me near to madness. Now you'll see,
Here as I kill you, if it's truth or dreaming!
As he tries to pull out his dagger, CLOTALDO *restrains him
and throws himself on his knees before him.*

CLOTALDO. It's thus I'd save my life: and hope to do so—

SEGISMUND. Take your presumptuous hand from off this steel.

CLOTALDO. Till people come to hold your rage and fury
I shall not let you go.

ROSAURA.   O heavens!

SEGISMUND.   Loose it,

They struggle.

I say, or else—you interfering fool—
I'll crush you to your death in my strong arms!

ROSAURA. Come quickly! Here's Clotaldo being killed!

Exit.

ASTOLFO *appears as* CLOTALDO *falls on the floor, and the
former stands between* SEGISMUND *and* CLOTALDO.

ASTOLFO. Why, what is this, most valiant prince? What?
    Staining
Your doughty steel in such old, frozen blood?
For shame! For shame! Sheathe your illustrious weapon!

SEGISMUND. When it is stained in his infamous blood!

ASTOLFO. At my feet here he has found sanctuary
    And there he's safe, for it will serve him well.

SEGISMUND. Then serve me well by dying, for like this
    I will avenge myself for your behaviour
    In trying to annoy me first of all.

ASTOLFO. To draw in self-defence offends no king,
    Though in his palace.

    ASTOLFO *draws his sword and they fight.*

CLOTALDO, *to* ASTOLFO. Do not anger him!

Enter BASIL, STELLA, *and attendants.*

BASIL. Hold! Hold! What's this? Fighting with naked swords?

STELLA, *aside.* It is Astolfo! How my heart misgives me!

BASIL. Why, what has happened here?

ASTOLFO.   Nothing, my Lord,
    Since you've arrived.

    Both sheathe their swords.

SEGISMUND.   Much, though you *have* arrived.
    I tried to kill the old man.

BASIL.   Had you no
    Respect for those white hairs?

CLOTALDO.   Sire, since they're only
    Mine, as you well can see, it does not matter!

SEGISMUND. It is in vain you'd have me hold white hairs
   In such respect, since one day you may find
   Your own white locks prostrated at my feet
   For still I have not taken vengeance on you
   For the foul way in which you had me reared.
   Exit.

BASIL. Before that happens you will sleep once more
   Where you were reared, and where what's happened may
   Seem just a dream (being mere earthly glory).
   All save ASTOLFO *and* STELLA *leave.*

ASTOLFO. How seldom does prediction fail, when evil!
   How oft, foretelling good! Exact in harm,
   Doubtful in benefit! Oh, what a great
   Astrologer would be one who foretold
   Nothing but harms, since there's no doubt at all
   That they are always due! In Segismund
   And me the case is illustrated clearly.
   In him, crimes, cruelties, deaths, and disasters
   Were well predicted, since they all came true.
   But in my own case, to predict for me
   (As I foresaw beholding rays which cast
   The sun into the shade and outface heaven)
   Triumphs and trophies, happiness and praise,
   Was false—and yet was true: it's only just
   That when predictions start with promised favours
   They should end in disdain.

STELLA.   I do not doubt
   Your protestations are most heartfelt; only
   They're not for me, but for another lady
   Whose portrait you were wearing round your neck
   Slung in a locket when you first arrived.
   Since it is so, she only can deserve
   These wooing flatteries. Let her repay you
   For in affairs of love, flatteries and vows
   Made for another are mere forged credentials.
   ROSAURA *enters but waits by the curtain.*

ROSAURA, *aside.* Thanks be to God, my troubles are near ended!
   To judge from what I see, I've naught to fear.

ASTOLFO. I will expel that portrait from my breast
   To make room for the image of your beauty
   And keep it there. For there where Stella is
   Can be no room for shade, and where the sun is
   No place for any star. I'll fetch the portrait.

   Aside.

   Forgive me, beautiful Rosaura, that,
   When absent, men and women seldom keep
   More faith than this.

   Exit.

   ROSAURA *comes forward.*

ROSAURA, *aside.* I could not hear a word. I was afraid
   That they would see me.

STELLA.   Oh, Astrea!

ROSAURA.   My lady!

STELLA. I am delighted that you came. Because
   To you alone would I confide a secret.

ROSAURA. Thereby you greatly honour me, your servant.

STELLA. Astrea, in the brief time I have known you
   I've given you the latchkey of my will.
   For that, and being who you are, I'll tell you
   A secret which I've very often hidden
   Even from myself.

ROSAURA.   I am your slave.

STELLA.   Then, briefly:
   Astolfo, who's my cousin (the word cousin
   Suffices, since some things are plainly said
   Even by thinking them), is to wed me
   If Fortune thus can wipe so many cares
   Away with one great joy. But I am troubled
   In that, the day he first came here, he carried
   A portrait of a lady round his neck.
   I spoke to him about it courteously.
   He was most amiable, he loves me well,
   And now he's gone for it. I am embarrassed
   That he should give it me himself. Wait here,
   And tell him to deliver it to you.

Do not say more. Since you're discreet and fair:
You'll surely know just what love is.

Exit.

ROSAURA.　　　　　　　　　　　　Great heavens!
How I wish that I did not! For who could be
So prudent or so skilful as would know
What to advise herself in such a case?
Lives there a person on this earth today
Who's more beset by the inclement stars,
Who has more cares besieging him, or fights
So many dire calamities at once?
What can I do in such bewilderment
Wherein it seems impossible to find
Relief or comfort? Since my first misfortune
No other thing has chanced or happened to me
But was a new misfortune. In succession
Inheritors and heirs of their own selves
(Just like the Phoenix, his own son and father)
Misfortunes reproduce themselves, are born,
And live by dying. In their sepulchre
The ashes they consume are hot forever.
A sage once said misfortunes must be cowards
Because they never dare to walk alone
But come in crowds. I say they are most valiant
Because they always charge so bravely on
And never turn their backs. Who charges with them
May dare all things because there is no fear
That they'll ever desert him; and I say it
Because in all my life I never once
Knew them to leave me, nor will they grow tired
Of me till, wounded and shot through and through
By Fate, I fall into the arms of death.
Alas, what can I do in this dilemma?
If I reveal myself, then old Clotaldo,
To whom I owe my life, may take offence,
Because he told me to await the cure
And mending of my honour in concealment.
If I don't tell Astolfo who I am
And he detects me, how can I dissimulate?

Since even if I say I am not I,
The voice, the language, and the eyes will falter,
Because the soul will tell them that they lie.
What shall I do? It is in vain to study
What I should do, when I know very well
That, whatsoever way I choose to act,
When the time comes I'll do as sorrow bids,
For no one has control over his sorrows.
Then since my soul dares not decide its actions
Let sorrow fill my cup and let my grief
Reach its extremity and, out of doubts
And vain appearances, once and for all
Come out into the light—and Heaven shield me!

Enter ASTOLFO.

ASTOLFO. Here, lady, is the portrait . . . but . . . great God!

ROSAURA. Why does Your Highness halt, and stare astonished?

ASTOLFO. Rosaura! Why, to see you here!

ROSAURA.   Rosaura?
Sir, you mistake me for some other lady.
I am Astrea, and my humble station
Deserves no perturbation such as yours.

ASTOLFO. Enough of this pretence, Rosaura, since
The soul can never lie. Though as Astrea
I see you now, I love you as Rosaura.

ROSAURA. Not having understood Your Highness' meaning
I can make no reply except to say
That Stella (who might be the star of Venus)
Told me to wait here and to tell you from her
To give to me the portrait you were fetching
(Which seems a very logical request)
And I myself will take it to my lady.
Thus Stella bids: even the slightest things
Which do me harm are governed by some star.

ASTOLFO. Even if you could make a greater effort
How poorly you dissimulate, Rosaura!
Tell your poor eyes they do not harmonise
With your own voice, because they needs must jangle
When the whole instrument is out of tune.

You cannot match the falsehood of your words
With the sincerity of what you're feeling.

ROSAURA. All I can say is—that I want the portrait.

ASTOLFO. As you require a fiction, with a fiction
I shall reply. Go and tell Stella this:
That I esteem her so, it seems unworthy
Only to send the counterfeit to her
And that I'm sending her the original.
And you, take the original along with you,
Taking yourself to her.

ROSAURA.   When a man starts
Forth on a definite task, resolved and valiant,
Though he be offered a far greater prize
Than what he seeks, yet he returns with failure
If he returns without his task performed.
I came to get that portrait. Though I bear
The original with me, of greater value,
I would return in failure and contempt
Without the copy. Give it me, Your Highness,
Since I cannot return without it.

ASTOLFO.   But
If I don't give it you, how can you do so?

ROSAURA. Like this, ungrateful man! I'll take it from you.

She tries to wrest it from him.

ASTOLFO. It is in vain.

ROSAURA.   By God, it shall not come
Into another woman's hands!

ASTOLFO.   You're terrifying!

ROSAURA. And you're perfidious!

ASTOLFO.   Enough, my dear
Rosaura!

ROSAURA. I, your dear? You lie, you villain!

They are both clutching the portrait.

Enter STELLA.

STELLA. Astrea and Astolfo, what does this mean?

ASTOLFO, *aside*. Here's Stella.

ROSAURA, *aside.*   Love, grant me the strength to win
My portrait.

To STELLA.

If you want to know, my lady,
What this is all about, I will explain.

ASTOLFO, *to* ROSAURA, *aside.* What do you mean?

ROSAURA.   You told me to await
Astolfo here and ask him for a portrait
On your behalf. I waited here alone
And as one thought suggests another thought,
Thinking of portraits, I recalled my own
Was here inside my sleeve. When one's alone,
One is diverted by a foolish trifle
And so I took it out to look at it.
It slipped and fell, just as Astolfo here,
Bringing the portrait of the other lady,
Came to deliver it to you as promised.
He picked my portrait up, and so unwilling
Is he to give away the one you asked for,
Instead of doing so, he seized upon
The other portrait which is mine alone
And will not give it back though I entreated
And begged him to return it. I was angry
And tried to snatch it back. That's it he's holding,
And you can see yourself if it's not mine.

STELLA. Let go the portrait.

She snatches it from him.

ASTOLFO.   Madam!

STELLA.   The draughtsman
Was not unkind to truth.

ROSAURA.   Is it not mine?

STELLA. Why, who could doubt it?

ROSAURA.   Ask him for the other.

STELLA. Here, take your own, Astrea. You may leave us.

ROSAURA, *aside.* Now I have got my portrait, come what will.
Exit.

STELLA. Now give me up the portrait that I asked for

Although I'll see and speak to you no more.
I do not wish to leave it in your power
Having been once so foolish as to beg it.

ASTOLFO, *aside.* Now how can I get out of this foul trap?

To STELLA.

Beautiful Stella, though I would obey you,
And serve you in all ways, I cannot give you
The portrait, since . . .

STELLA.　　　　　　You are a crude, coarse villain
And ruffian of a wooer. For the portrait—
I do not want it now, since, if I had it,
It would remind me I had asked you for it.

Exit.

ASTOLFO. Listen! Look! Wait! Let me explain!

Aside.

　　　　　　　　　　　　　　　　Oh, damn

Rosaura! How the devil did she get
To Poland for my ruin and her own?

The prison of Segismund in the tower

SEGISMUND *lying on the ground loaded with fetters and clothed
in skins as before.* CLOTALDO, *two attendants, and* CLARION

CLOTALDO. Here you must leave him—since his reckless pride
Ends here today where it began.

ATTENDANT.　　　　　　　　His chain
I'll rivet as it used to be before.

CLARION. O Prince, you'd better not awake too soon
To find how lost you are, how changed your fate,
And that your fancied glory of an hour
Was but a shade of life, a flame of death!

CLOTALDO. For one who knows so well to wield his tongue
It's fit a worthy place should be provided
With lots of room and lots of time to argue.

This is the fellow that you have to seize
To the attendants.
And that's the room in which you are to lock him.
Points to the nearest cell.

CLARION. Why me?

CLOTALDO.   Because a Clarion who knows
Too many secrets must be kept in gaol—
A place where even clarions are silent.

CLARION. Have I, by chance, wanted to kill my father
Or thrown an Icarus from a balcony?
Am I asleep or dreaming? To what end
Do you imprison me?

CLOTALDO.   You're Clarion.

CLARION. Well, say I swear to be a cornet now,
A silent one, a wretched instrument . . . ?
They hustle him off.

CLOTALDO *remains.*

Enter BASIL, *wearing a mask.*

BASIL. Clotaldo.

CLOTALDO.   Sire . . . and is it thus alone
Your Majesty has come?

BASIL.   Vain curiosity
To see what happens here to Segismund.

CLOTALDO. See where he lies, reduced to misery!

BASIL. Unhappy prince! Born at a fatal moment!
Come waken him, now he has lost his strength
With all the opium he's drunk.

CLOTALDO.   He's stirring
And talking to himself.

BASIL.   What is he dreaming?
Let's listen now.

SEGISMUND.   He who chastises tyrants
Is a most pious prince . . . Now let Clotaldo
Die by my hand . . . my father kiss my feet . . .

CLOTALDO. He threatens me with death!

BASIL.   And me with insult
And cruelty.

CLOTALDO.   He'd take my life away.

BASIL. And he'd humiliate me at his feet.

SEGISMUND, *still in a dream.*

Throughout the expanse of this world's theatre
I'll show my peerless valour, let my vengeance
Be wreaked, and the Prince Segismund be seen
To triumph—over his father . . . but, alas!

Awakening.

Where am I?

BASIL, *to* CLOTALDO. Since he must not see me here,
I'll listen further off. You know your cue.

Retires to one side.

SEGISMUND. Can this be I? Am I the same who, chained
And long imprisoned, rose to such a state?
Are you not still my sepulchre and grave,
You dismal tower? God! What things I have dreamed!

CLOTALDO, *aside.* Now I must go to him to disenchant him.

Aloud.

Awake already?

SEGISMUND.   Yes: it was high time.

CLOTALDO. What? Do you have to spend all day asleep?
Since I was following the eagle's flight
With tardy discourse, have you still lain here
Without awaking?

SEGISMUND.   No. Nor even now
Am I awake. It seems I've always slept,
Since, if I've dreamed what I've just seen and heard
Palpably and for certain, then I am dreaming
What I see now—nor is it strange I'm tired,
Since what I, sleeping, see, tells me that I
Was dreaming when I thought I was awake.

CLOTALDO. Tell me your dream.

SEGISMUND.   That's if it *was* a dream!
No, I'll not tell you what I dreamed; but what
I lived and saw, Clotaldo, I *will* tell you.

I woke up in a bed that might have been
The cradle of the flowers, woven by Spring.
A thousand nobles, bowing, called me Prince,
Attiring me in jewels, pomp, and splendour.
My equanimity you turned to rapture
Telling me that I was the Prince of Poland.

CLOTALDO. I must have got a fine reward!

SEGISMUND. Not so:
For as a traitor, twice, with rage and fury,
I tried to kill you.

CLOTALDO. Such cruelty to me?

SEGISMUND. I was the lord of all, on all I took revenge,
Except I loved one woman . . . I believe
That *that* was true, though all the rest has faded.

Exit BASIL.

CLOTALDO, *aside*. I see the king was moved, to hear him speak.
Aloud.

Talking of eagles made you dream of empires,
But even in your dreams it's good to honour
Those who have cared for you and brought you up.
For Segismund, even in dreams, I warn you
Nothing is lost by trying to do good.

Exit.

SEGISMUND. That's true, and therefore let us subjugate
The bestial side, this fury and ambition,
Against the time when we may dream once more,
As certainly we shall, for this strange world
Is such that but to live here is to dream.
And now experience shows me that each man
Dreams what he is until he is awakened.
The king dreams he's a king and in this fiction
Lives, rules, administers with royal pomp.
Yet all the borrowed praises that he earns
Are written in the wind, and he is changed
(How sad a fate!) by death to dust and ashes.
What man is there alive who'd seek to reign
Since he must wake into the dream that's death.
The rich man dreams his wealth which is his care

And woe. The poor man dreams his sufferings.
He dreams who thrives and prospers in this life.
He dreams who toils and strives. He dreams who injures,
Offends, and insults. So that in this world
Everyone dreams the thing he is, though no one
Can understand it. I dream I am here,
Chained in these fetters. Yet I dreamed just now
I was in a more flattering, lofty station.
What is this life? A frenzy, an illusion,
A shadow, a delirium, a fiction.
The greatest good's but little, and this life
Is but a dream, and dreams are only dreams.

ACT III

The tower

Enter CLARION.

CLARION. I'm held in an enchanted tower, because
Of all I know. What would they do to me
For all I don't know, since—for all I know—
They're killing me by starving me to death.
O that a man so hungry as myself
Should live to die of hunger while alive!
I am so sorry for myself that others
May well say "I can well believe it," since
This silence ill accords with my name "Clarion",
And I just can't shut up. My fellows here?
Spiders and rats—fine feathered songsters those!
My head's still ringing with a dream of fifes
And trumpets and a lot of noisy humbug
And long processions as of penitents
With crosses, winding up and down, while some
Faint at the sight of blood besmirching others.
But now to tell the truth, I am in prison.
For knowing secrets, I am kept shut in,
Strictly observed as if I were a Sunday,
And feeling sadder than a Tuesday, where
I neither eat nor drink. They say a secret
Is sacred and should be as strictly kept
As any saint's day on the calendar.
Saint Secret's Day for me's a working day
Because I'm never idle then. The penance
I suffer here is merited, I say:
Because being a lackey, I was silent,
Which, in a servant, is a sacrilege.

A noise of drums and trumpets.

FIRST SOLDIER, *within.*

Here is the tower in which he is imprisoned.
Smash in the door and enter, everybody!

CLARION. Great God! They've come to seek me. That is certain
Because they say I'm here. What can they want?

Enter several soldiers.

FIRST SOLDIER. Go in.

SECOND SOLDIER.   He's here!

CLARION.   No, he's not here!

ALL THE SOLDIERS.   Our lord!

CLARION. What, are they drunk?

FIRST SOLDIER.   You are our rightful prince.
We do not want and never shall allow
A stranger to supplant our trueborn prince.
Give us your feet to kiss!

ALL THE SOLDIERS.   Long live the prince!

CLARION. Bless me, if it's not real! In this strange kingdom
It seems the custom, everyday, to take
Some fellow and to make him prince and then
Shut him back in this tower. That *must* be it!
So I must play my role.

ALL THE SOLDIERS.   Give us your feet.

CLARION. I can't. They're necessary. After all
What sort of use would be a footless prince?

SECOND SOLDIER. All of us told your father, as one man,
We want no prince of Muscovy but you!

CLARION. You weren't respectful to my father? Shame!

FIRST SOLDIER. It was our loyalty that made us tell him.

CLARION. If it was loyalty, you have my pardon.

SECOND SOLDIER. Restore your empire. Long live Segismund!

CLARION, *aside.* That is the name they seem to give to all
These counterfeited princes.

Enter SEGISMUND.

SEGISMUND.   Who called Segismund?

CLARION, *aside.* I seem to be a hollow sort of prince.

FIRST SOLDIER. Which of you's Segismund?

SEGISMUND.   I am.

SECOND SOLDIER, *to* CLARION.   Then, why,

Rash fool, did you impersonate the prince
Segismund?

CLARION.   What? I, Segismund? Yourselves
Be-Segismunded me without request.
All yours was both the rashness and the folly.

FIRST SOLDIER. Prince Segismund, whom we acclaim our lord,
Your father, great King Basil, in his fear
That heaven would fulfil a prophecy
That one day he would kneel before your feet
Wishes now to deprive you of the throne
And give it to the Duke of Muscovy.
For this he called a council, but the people
Discovered his design and knowing, now,
They have a native king, will have no stranger.
So scorning the fierce threats of destiny,
We've come to seek you in your very prison,
That aided by the arms of the whole people,
We may restore you to the crown and sceptre,
Taking them from the tyrant's grasp. Come, then:
Assembling here, in this wide desert region,
Hosts of plebeians, bandits, and freebooters,
Acclaim you king. Your liberty awaits you!
Hark to its voice!

Shouts within.

Long life to Segismund!

SEGISMUND. Once more, you heavens will that I should dream
Of grandeur, once again, 'twixt doubts and shades,
Behold the majesty of pomp and power
Vanish into the wind, once more you wish
That I should taste the disillusion and
The risk by which all human power is humbled,
Of which all human power should live aware.
It must not be. I'll not be once again
Put through my paces by my fortune's stars.
And since I know this life is all a dream,
Depart, vain shades, who feign, to my dead senses,
That you have voice and body, having neither!
I want no more feigned majesty, fantastic
Display, nor void illusions, that one gust

Can scatter like the almond tree in flower,
Whose rosy buds, without advice or warning,
Dawn in the air too soon and then, as one,
Are all extinguished, fade, and fall, and wither
In the first gust of wind that comes along!
I know you well. I know you well by now.
I know that all that happens in yourselves
Happens as in a sleeping man. For me
There are no more delusions and deceptions
Since I well know this life is all a dream.

SECOND SOLDIER. If you think we are cheating, just sweep
Your gaze along these towering peaks, and see
The hosts that wait to welcome and obey you.

SEGISMUND. Already once before I've seen such crowds
Distinctly, quite as vividly as these:
And yet it was a dream.

SECOND SOLDIER.   No great event
Can come without forerunners to announce it
And this is the real meaning of your dream.

SEGISMUND. Yes, you say well. It was the fore-announcement
And just in case it was correct, my soul,
(Since life's so short) let's dream the dream anew!
But it must be attentively, aware
That we'll awake from pleasure in the end.
Forewarned of that, the shock's not so abrupt,
The disillusion's less. Evils anticipated
Lose half their sting. And armed with this precaution—
That power, even when we're sure of it, is borrowed
And must be given back to its true owner—
We can risk anything and dare the worst.
Subjects, I thank you for your loyalty.
In me you have a leader who will free you,
Bravely and skilfully, from foreign rule.
Sound now to arms, you'll soon behold my valour.
Against my father I must march and bring
Truth from the stars. Yes: he must kneel to me.
Aside.
But yet, since I may wake before he kneels,
Perhaps I'd better not proclaim what may not happen.

ALL. Long live Segismund!

Enter CLOTALDO.

CLOTALDO.   Gracious heavens! What is
This riot here?

SEGISMUND.   Clotaldo!

CLOTALDO.   Sir!

Aside.

                              He'll prove
His cruelty on me.

CLARION.   I bet he throws him
Over the mountain.

CLOTALDO.   At your royal feet
I kneel, knowing my penalty is death.

SEGISMUND. Rise, rise, my foster father, from the ground,
For you must be the compass and the guide
In which I trust. You brought me up, and I
Know what I owe your loyalty. Embrace me!

CLOTALDO. What's that you say?

SEGISMUND.   I know I'm in a dream,
But I would like to act well, since good actions,
Even in a dream, are not entirely lost.

CLOTALDO. Since doing good is now to be your glory,
You will not be offended that I too
Should do what's right. You march against your father!
I cannot give you help against my king.
Here at your feet, my lord, I plead for death.

SEGISMUND, *aloud.* Villain!

Aside.

                              But let us suffer this annoyance.
Though my rage would slay him, yet he's loyal.
A man does not deserve to die for that.
How many angry passions does this leash
Restrain in me, this curb of knowing well
That I must wake and find myself alone!

SECOND SOLDIER. All this fine talk, Clotaldo, is a cruel
Spurn of the public welfare. We are loyal
Who wish our own prince to reign over us.

CLOTALDO. Such loyalty, after the king were dead,
  Would honour you. But while the king is living
  He is our absolute, unquestioned lord.
  There's no excuse for subjects who oppose
  His sovereignty in arms.

FIRST SOLDIER.   We'll soon see well
  Enough, Clotaldo, what this loyalty
  Is worth.

CLOTALDO. You would be better if you had some.
  It is the greatest prize.

SEGISMUND.   Peace, peace, I pray you.

CLOTALDO. My lord!

SEGISMUND.   Clotaldo, if your feelings
  Are truly thus, go you, and serve the king;
  That's prudence, loyalty, and common sense.
  But do not argue here with anyone
  Whether it's right or wrong, for every man
  Has his own honour.

CLOTALDO.   Humbly I take my leave.
  Exit.

SEGISMUND. Now sound the drums and march in rank and
    order
  Straight to the palace.

ALL.   Long live Segismund!

SEGISMUND. Fortune, we go to reign! Do not awake me
  If I am dreaming! Do not let me fall
  Asleep if it is true! To act with virtue
  Is what matters, since if this proves true,
  That truth's sufficient reason in itself;
  If not, we win us friends against the time
  When we at last awake.

A room in the royal palace

Enter BASIL *and* ASTOLFO.

BASIL. Whose prudence can rein in a bolting horse?
    Who can restrain a river's pride, in spate?
    Whose valour can withstand a crag dislodged
    And hurtling downwards from a mountain peak?
    All these are easier by far than to hold back
    A crowd's proud fury, once it has been roused.
    It has two voices, both proclaiming war,
    And you can hear them echoing through the mountains,
    Some shouting "Segismund," others "Astolfo."
    The scene I set for swearing of allegiance
    Lends but an added horror to this strife:
    It has become the back cloth to a stage
    Where Fortune plays out tragedies in blood.

ASTOLFO. My lord, forget the happiness and wealth
    You promised me from your most blessèd hand.
    If Poland, which I hope to rule, refuses
    Obedience to my right, grudging me honour,
    It is because I've got to earn it first.
    Give me a horse, that I with angry pride
    May match the thunder in my voice and ride
    To strike, like lightning, terror far and wide.

    Exit ASTOLFO.

BASIL. No remedy for what's infallible!
    What is foreseen is perilous indeed!
    If something has to be, there's no way out;
    In trying to evade it, you but court it.
    This law is pitiless and horrible.
    Thinking one can evade the risk, one meets it:
    My own precautions have been my undoing,
    And I myself have quite destroyed my kingdom.

    Enter STELLA.

STELLA. If you, my lord, in person do not try

To curb the vast commotion that has started
In all the streets between the rival factions,
You'll see your kingdom, swamped in waves of crimson,
Swimming in its own blood, with nothing left
But havoc, dire calamity, and woe.
So frightful is the damage to your empire
That, seen, it strikes amazement; heard, despair.
The sun's obscured, the very winds are hindered.
Each stone is a memorial to the dead.
Each flower springs from a grave while every building
Appears a mausoleum, and each soldier
A premature and walking skeleton.

Enter CLOTALDO.

CLOTALDO. Praise be to God, I reach your feet alive!

BASIL. Clotaldo! What's the news of Segismund?

CLOTALDO. The crowd, a headstrong monster blind with rage,
Entered his dungeon tower and set him free.
He, now exalted for the second time,
Conducts himself with valour, boasting how
He will bring down the truth out of the stars.

BASIL. Give me a horse, that I myself, in person,
May vanquish such a base, ungrateful son!
For I, in the defence of my own crown,
Shall do by steel what science failed to do.
Exit.

STELLA. I'll be Bellona to your Sun, and try
To write my name next yours in history.
I'll ride as though I flew on outstretched wings
That I may vie with Pallas.
Exit.

Enter ROSAURA, *holding back* CLOTALDO.

ROSAURA. I know that all is war, Clotaldo, yet
Although your valour calls you to the front,
First hear me out. You know quite well that I
Arrived in Poland poor and miserable,
Where, shielded by your valour, I found mercy.
You told me to conceal myself, and stay
Here in the palace, hiding from Astolfo.

He saw me in the end, and so insulted
My honour that (although he saw me clearly)
He nightly speaks with Stella in the garden.
I have the key to it and I will show you
How you can enter there and end my cares.
Thus bold, resolved, and strong, you can recover
My honour, since you're ready to avenge me
By killing him.

CLOTALDO.   It's true that I intended,
Since first I saw you (having heard your tale)
With my own life to rectify your wrongs.
The first step that I took was bid you dress
According to your sex, for fear Astolfo
Might see you as you were, and deem you wanton.
I was devising how we could recover
Your honour (so much did it weigh on me)
Even though we had to kill him. (A wild plan—
Though since he's not my king, I would not flinch
From killing him.) But then, when suddenly
Segismund tried to kill me, it was he
Who saved my life with his surpassing valour.
Consider: how can I requite Astolfo
With death for giving me my life so bravely,
And when my soul is full of gratitude?
So torn between the two of you I stand—
Rosaura, whose life I saved, and Astolfo,
Who saved my life. What's to be done? Which side
To take, and whom to help, I cannot judge.
What I owe you in that I gave you life
I owe to him in that he gave me life.
And so there is no course that I can take
To satisfy my love. I am a person
Who has to act, yet suffer either way.

ROSAURA. I should not have to tell so brave a man
That if it is nobility to give,
It's baseness to receive. That being so
You owe no gratitude to him, admitting
That it was he who gave you life, and you
Who gave me life, since he forced you to take

A meaner role, and through me you assumed
A generous role. So you should side with me:
My cause is so far worthier than his own
As giving is than taking.

CLOTALDO.   Though nobility
Is with the giver, it is gratitude
That dwells with the receiver. As a giver
I have the name of being generous:
Then grant me that of being grateful too
And let me earn the title and be grateful,
As I am liberal, giving or receiving.

ROSAURA. You granted me my life, at the same time
Telling me it was worthless, since dishonoured,
And therefore was no life. Therefore from you
I have received no life at all. And since
You should be liberal first and grateful after
(Since so you said yourself) I now entreat you
Give me the life, the life you never gave me!
As giving magnifies the most, give first
And then be grateful after, if you will!

CLOTALDO. Won by your argument, I will be liberal.
Rosaura, I shall give you my estate
And you shall seek a convent, there to live.
This measure is a happy thought, for, see,
Fleeing a crime, you find a sanctuary.
For when the empire's threatened with disasters
And is divided thus, I, born a noble,
Am not the man who would augment its woes.
So with this remedy which I have chosen
I remain loyal to the kingdom, generous
To you, and also grateful to Astolfo.
And thus I choose the course that suits you best.
Were I your father, what could I do more?

ROSAURA. Were you my father, then I would accept
The insult. Since you are not, I refuse.

CLOTALDO. What do you hope to do then?

ROSAURA.   Kill the duke!

CLOTALDO. A girl who never even knew her father
Armed with such courage?

ROSAURA.   Yes.

CLOTALDO.   What spurs you on?

ROSAURA. My good name.

CLOTALDO.   In Astolfo you will find . . .

ROSAURA. My honour rides on him and strikes him down!

CLOTALDO. Your king, too, Stella's husband!

ROSAURA.   Never, never
  Shall that be, by almighty God, I swear!

CLOTALDO. Why, this is madness!

ROSAURA.   Yes it is!

CLOTALDO.   Restrain it.

ROSAURA. That I cannot.

CLOTALDO.   Then you are lost forever!

ROSAURA. I know it!

CLOTALDO.   Life and honour both together!

ROSAURA. I well believe it!

CLOTALDO.   What do you intend?

ROSAURA. My death.

CLOTALDO.   This is despair and desperation.

ROSAURA. It's honour.

CLOTALDO.   It is nonsense.

ROSAURA.   It is valour.

CLOTALDO. It's frenzy.

ROSAURA.   Yes, it's anger! Yes, it's fury!

CLOTALDO. In short you cannot moderate your passion?

ROSAURA. No.

CLOTALDO.   Who is there to help you?

ROSAURA.   I, myself.

CLOTALDO. There is no cure?

ROSAURA.   There is no cure!

CLOTALDO.   Think well
  If there's not some way out . . .

ROSAURA.   Some other way
  To do away with me . . .

Exit.

CLOTALDO.   If you are lost,
My daughter, let us both be lost together!

In the country

Enter SEGISMUND *clothed in skins. Soldiers marching.*
CLARION. *Drums beating.*

SEGISMUND. If Rome, today, could see me here, renewing
 Her olden triumphs, she might laugh to see
 A wild beast in command of mighty armies,
 A wild beast, to whose fiery aspirations
 The firmament were all too slight a conquest!
 But stoop your flight, my spirit. Do not thus
 Be puffed to pride by these uncertain plaudits
 Which, when I wake, will turn to bitterness
 In that I won them only to be lost.
 The less I value them, the less I'll miss them.
 A trumpet sounds.

CLARION. Upon a rapid courser (pray excuse me,
 Since if it comes to mind I must describe it)
 In which it seems an atlas was designed
 Since if its body is earth, its soul is fire
 Within its breast, its foam appears the sea,
 The wind its breath, and chaos its condition,
 Since in its soul, its foam, its breath and flesh,
 It seems a monster of fire, earth, sea, and wind,
 Upon the horse, all of a patchwork colour,
 Dappled, and rushing forward at the will
 Of one who plies the spur, so that it flies
 Rather than runs—see how a woman rides
 Boldly into your presence.[1]

SEGISMUND.   Her light blinds me.

CLARION. Good God! Why, here's Rosaura!

---

[1] Clarion's speech is a parody of exaggerated style—including
Calderón's. [R.C.]

SEGISMUND.   It is heaven

  That has restored her to my sight once more.

  Enter ROSAURA *with sword and dagger in riding costume.*

ROSAURA. Generous Segismund, whose majesty

  Heroically rises in the lustre

  Of his great deeds out of his night of shadows,

  And as the greatest planet, in the arms

  Of his aurora, lustrously returns

  To plants and roses, over hills and seas,

  When, crowned with gold, he looks abroad, dispersing

  Radiance, flashing his rays, bathing the summits,

  And broidering the fringes of the foam,

  So may you dawn upon the world, bright sun

  Of Poland, that a poor unhappy woman

  May fall before your feet and beg protection

  Both as a woman and unfortunate—

  Two things that must oblige you, sire, as one

  Who prize yourself as valiant, each of them

  More than suffices for your chivalry.

  Three times you have beheld me now, three times

  Been ignorant of who I am, because

  Three times you saw me in a different clothing.

  The first time you mistook me for a man,

  Within that rigorous prison, where your hardships

  Made mine seem pleasure. Next time, as a woman,

  You saw me, when your pomp and majesty

  Were as a dream, a phantasm, a shade.

  The third time is today when, as a monster

  Of both the sexes, in a woman's costume

  I bear a soldier's arms. But to dispose you

  The better to compassion, hear my story.

  My mother was a noble in the court

  Of Moscow, who, since most unfortunate,

  Must have been beautiful. Then came a traitor

  And cast his eyes on her (I do not name him,

  Not knowing who he is). Yet I deduce

  That he was valiant too from my own valour,

  Since he gave form to me—and I could wish

  I had been born in pagan times, that I might

Persuade myself he was some god of those
Who rain in showers of gold, turn into swans
Or bulls, for Danaës, Ledas, or Europas.
That's strange: I thought I was just rambling on
By telling old perfidious myths, yet find
I've told you how my mother was cajoled.
Oh, she was beautiful as no one else
Has been, but was unfortunate like all.
He swore to wed her (that's an old excuse)
And this trick reached so nearly to her heart
That thought must weep, recalling it today.
The tyrant left her only with his sword
As Aeneas left Troy. I sheathed its blade here
Upon my thigh, and I will bare it too
Before the ending of this history.
Out of this union, this poor link which neither
Could bind the marriage nor handcuff the crime,
Myself was born, her image and her portrait,
Not in her beauty, but in her misfortune,
For mine's the same. That's all I need to say.
The most that I can tell you of myself
Is that the man who robbed me of the spoils
And trophies of my honour is Astolfo.
Alas! to name him my heart rages so
(As hearts will do when men name enemies).
Astolfo was my faithless and ungrateful
Lord, who (quite forgetful of our happiness,
Since of a past love even the memory fades)
Came here to claim the throne and marry Stella
For she's the star who rises as I set.
It's hard to credit that a star should sunder
Lovers the stars had made conformable!
So hurt was I, so villainously cheated,
That I became mad, brokenhearted, sick,
Half wild with grief, and like to die, with all
Hell's own confusion ciphered on my mind
Like Babel's incoherence. Mutely I told
My griefs (since woes and griefs declare themselves
Better than can the mouth, by their effects),
When, with my mother (we were by ourselves),

She broke the prison of my pent-up sorrows
And from my breast they all rushed forth in troops.
I felt no shyness, for in knowing surely
That one to whom one's errors are recounted
Has also been an ally in her own,
One finds relief and rest, since bad example
Can sometimes serve for a good purpose too.
She heard my plaint with pity, and she tried
To palliate my sorrows with her own.
How easily do judges pardon error
When they've offended too! An example,
A warning, in herself, she did not trust
To idleness, or the slow cure of time,
Nor try to find a remedy for her honour
In my misfortunes, but, with better counsel,
She bade me follow him to Poland here
And with prodigious gallantry persuade him
To pay the debt to honour that he owes me.
So that it would be easier to travel,
She bade me don male clothing, and took down
This ancient sword which I am wearing now.
Now it is time that I unsheathe the blade
As I was bid, for, trusting in its sign,
She said: "Depart to Poland, show this sword
That all the nobles may behold it well,
And it may be that one of them will take
Pity on you, and counsel you, and shield you."
I came to Poland and, you will remember,
Entered your cave. You looked at me in wonder.
Clotaldo passionately took my part
To plead for mercy to the king, who spared me,
Then, when he heard my story, bade me change
Into my own clothes and attend on Stella,
There to disturb Astolfo's love and stop
Their marriage. Again you saw me in woman's dress
And were confused by the discrepancy.
But let's pass to what's new: Clotaldo, now
Persuaded that Astolfo must, with Stella,
Come to the throne, dissuades me from my purpose,
Against the interests of my name and honour.

But seeing you, O valiant Segismund,
Are claiming your revenge, now that the heavens
Have burst the prison of your rustic tower,
(Wherein you were the tiger of your sorrows,
The rock of sufferings and direful pains)
And sent you forth against your sire and country,
I come to aid you, mingling Dian's silks
With the hard steel of Pallas. Now, strong Captain,
It well behoves us both to stop this marriage—
Me, lest my promised husband should be wed,
You, lest, when their estates are joined, they weigh
More powerfully against your victory.
I come, as a mere woman, to persuade you
To right my shame; but, as a man, I come
To help you battle for your crown. As woman,
To melt your heart, here at your feet I fall;
But, as a man, I come to serve you bravely
Both with my person and my steel, and thus,
If you today should woo me as a woman,
Then I should have to kill you as a man would
In honourable service of my honour;
Since I must be three things today at once—
Passionate, to persuade you: womanly,
To ply you with my woes: manly, to gain
Honour in battle.

SEGISMUND.   Heavens! If it is true I'm dreaming,
Suspend my memory, for in a dream
So many things could not occur. Great heavens!
If I could only come free of them all!
Or never think of any! Who ever felt
Such grievous doubts? If I but dreamed that triumph
In which I found myself, how can this woman
Refer me to such sure and certain facts?
Then all of it was true and not a dream.
But if it be the truth, why does my past life
Call it a dream? This breeds the same confusion.
Are dreams and glories so alike, that fictions
Are held for truths, realities for lies?
Is there so little difference in them both
That one should question whether what one sees

And tastes is true or false? What? Is the copy
So near to the original that doubt
Exists between them? Then if that is so,
And grandeur, power, majesty, and pomp,
Must all evaporate like shades at morning,
Let's profit by it, this time, to enjoy
That which we only can enjoy in dreams.
Rosaura's in my power: my soul adores her beauty.
Let's take the chance. Let love break every law
On which she has relied in coming here
And kneeling, trustful, prostrate at my feet.
This is a dream. If so, dream pleasures now
Since they must turn to sorrows in the end!
But with my own opinions, I begin
Once again to convince myself. Let's think.
If it is but vainglory and a dream,
Who for mere human vainglory would lose
True glory? What past blessing is not merely
A dream? Who has known heroic glories,
That deep within himself, as he recalls them,
Has never doubted that they might be dreams?
But if this all should end in disenchantment,
Seeing that pleasure is a lovely flame
That's soon converted into dust and ashes
By any wind that blows, then let us seek
That which endures in thrifty, lasting fame
In which no pleasures sleep, nor grandeurs dream.
Rosaura's without honour. In a prince
It's worthier to restore it than to steal it.
I shall restore it, by the living God,
Before I win my throne! Let's shun the danger
And fly from the temptation which is strong!
Then sound to arms!

To a soldier.

Today I must give battle before darkness
Buries the rays of gold in green-black waves!

ROSAURA. My lord! Alas, you stand apart, and offer
No word of pity for my plight. How is it

You neither hear nor see me nor even yet
Have turned your face on me?

SEGISMUND.   Rosaura, for your honour's sake
I must be cruel to you, to be kind.
My voice must not reply to you because
My honour must reply to you. I am silent
Because my deeds must speak to you alone.
I do not look at you since, in such straits,
Having to see your honour is requited,
I must not see your beauty.
Exit with soldiers.

ROSAURA. What strange enigma's this? After such trouble
Still to be treated with more doubtful riddles!
Enter CLARION.

CLARION. Madam, may you be visited just now?

ROSAURA. Why, Clarion, where have you been all this time?

CLARION. Shut in the tower, consulting cards
About my death: "to be or not to be."
And it was a near thing.

ROSAURA.   Why?

CLARION.   Because I know
The secret who you are: in fact, Clotaldo . . .
Drums.

But hush what noise is that?

ROSAURA.   What can it be?

CLARION. From the beleaguered palace a whole squadron
Is charging forth to harry and defeat
That of fierce Segismund.

ROSAURA.   Why, what a coward
Am I, not to be at his side, the terror
And scandal of the world, while such fierce strife
Presses all round in lawless anarchy.
Exit.

VOICES OF SOME. Long live our king!

VOICES OF OTHERS.   Long live our liberty!

CLARION. Long live both king and liberty. Yes, live!
And welcome to them both! I do not worry.
In all this pother, I behave like Nero
Who never grieved at what was going on.
If I had anything to grieve about
It would be me, myself. Well hidden here,
Now, I can watch the sport that's going on.
This place is safe and hidden between crags,
And since death cannot find me here, two figs for death!

He hides. Drums and the clash of arms are heard.

Enter BASIL, CLOTALDO, *and* ASTOLFO, *fleeing.*

BASIL. Was ever king so hapless as myself
Or father more ill used?

CLOTALDO.   Your beaten army
Rush down, in all directions, in disorder.

ASTOLFO. The traitors win!

BASIL.   In battles such as these
Those on the winning side are ever "loyal,"
And traitors the defeated. Come, Clotaldo,
Let's flee from the inhuman cruelty
Of my fierce son!

Shots are fired within. CLARION *falls wounded.*

CLARION.   Heavens, save me!

ASTOLFO.   Who is this
Unhappy soldier bleeding at our feet?

CLARION. I am a most unlucky man who, wishing
To guard myself from death, have sought it out
By fleeing from it. Shunning it, I found it,
Because, to death, no hiding-place is secret.
So you can argue that whoever shuns it
Most carefully runs into it the quickest.
Turn, then, once more into the thick of battle:
There is more safety there amidst the fire
And clash of arms than here on this secluded
Mountain, because no hidden path is safe
From the inclemency of Fate; and so,
Although you flee from death, yet you may find it
Quicker than you expect, if God so wills.

He falls dead.

BASIL. "If God so wills" . . . With what strange eloquence
   This corpse persuades our ignorance and error
   To better knowledge, speaking from the mouth
   Of its fell wound, where the red liquid flowing
   Seems like a bloody tongue which teaches us
   That the activities of man are vain
   When they are pitted against higher powers.
   For I, who wished to liberate my country
   From murder and sedition, gave it up
   To the same ills from which I would have saved it.

CLOTALDO. Though Fate, my lord, knows every path, and finds
   Him whom it seeks even in the midst of crags
   And thickets, it is not a Christian judgment
   To say there is no refuge from its fury.
   A prudent man can conquer Fate itself.
   Though you are not exempted from misfortune,
   Take action to escape it while you can!

ASTOLFO. Clotaldo speaks as one mature in prudence,
   And I as one in valour's youthful prime.
   Among the thickets of this mount is hidden
   A horse, the very birth of the swift wind.
   Flee on him, and I'll guard you in the rear.

BASIL. If it is God's will I should die, or if
   Death waits here for my coming, I will seek
   Him out today, and meet him face to face.

Enter SEGISMUND, STELLA, ROSAURA, *soldiers, and their train.*

A SOLDIER. Amongst the thickets of this mountain
   The king is hiding.

SEGISMUND.   Seek him out at once!
   Leave no foot of the summit unexplored
   But search from stem to stem and branch to branch!

CLOTALDO. Fly, sir!

BASIL.   What for?

ASTOLFO.   What do you mean to do?

BASIL. Astolfo, stand aside!

CLOTALDO.   What is your wish?

BASIL. To take a cure I've needed for sometime.

To SEGISMUND.

If you have come to seek me, here I am.

Kneeling.

Your father, prince, kneels humbly at your feet.
The white snow of my hair is now your carpet.
Tread on my neck and trample on my crown!
Lay low and drag my dignity in dust!
Take vengeance on my honour! Make a slave
Of me and, after all I've done to thwart them,
Let Fate fulfil its edict and claim homage
And Heaven fulfil its oracles at last!

SEGISMUND. Illustrious court of Poland, who have been
The witnesses of such unwonted wonders,
Attend to me, and hear your prince speak out.
What Heaven decrees and God writes with his finger
(Whose prints and ciphers are the azure leaves
Adorned with golden lettering of the stars)
Never deceives nor lies. They only lie
Who seek to penetrate the mystery
And, having reached it, use it to ill purpose.
My father, who is here to evade the fury
Of my proud nature, made me a wild beast:
So, when I, by my birth of gallant stock,
My generous blood, and inbred grace and valour,
Might well have proved both gentle and forbearing,
The very mode of life to which he forced me,
The sort of bringing up I had to bear
Sufficed to make me savage in my passions.
What a strange method of restraining them!
If one were to tell any man: "One day
You will be killed by an inhuman monster,"
Would it be the best method he could choose
To wake that monster when it was asleep?
Or if they told him: "That sword which you're wearing
Will be your death," what sort of cure were it
To draw it forth and aim it at his breast?
Or if they told him: "Deep blue gulfs of water
Will one day be your sepulchre and grave

Beneath a silver monument of foam,"
He would be mad to hurl himself in headlong
When the sea highest heaved its showy mountains
And crystalline sierras plumed with spray.
The same has happened to the king as to him
Who wakes a beast which threatens death, to him
Who draws a naked sword because he fears it,
To him who dives into the stormy breakers.
Though my ferocious nature (hear me now)
Was like a sleeping beast, my inborn rage
A sheathèd sword, my wrath a quiet ripple,
Fate should not be coerced by man's injustice—
This rouses more resentment. So it is
That he who seeks to tame his fortune must
Resort to moderation and to measure.
He who foresees an evil cannot conquer it
Thus in advance, for though humility
Can overcome it, this it can do only
When the occasion's there, for there's no way
To dodge one's fate and thus evade the issue.
Let this strange spectacle serve as example—
This prodigy, this horror, and this wonder,
Because it is no less than one, to see,
After such measures and precautions taken
To thwart it, that a father thus should kneel
At his son's feet, a kingdom thus be shattered.
This was the sentence of the heavens above,
Which he could not evade, much though he tried.
Can I, younger in age, less brave, and less
In science than the king, conquer that fate?

To the KING.

Sire, rise, give me your hand, now that the heavens
Have shown you that you erred as to the method
To vanquish them. Humbly I kneel before you
And offer you my neck to tread upon.

BASIL. Son, such a great and noble act restores you
Straight to my heart. Oh, true and worthy prince!
You have won both the laurel and the palm.
Crown yourself with your deeds! For you *have* conquered!

ALL. Long live Segismund! Long live Segismund!

SEGISMUND. Since I have other victories to win,
   The greatest of them all awaits me now:
   To conquer my own self. Astolfo, give
   Your hand here to Rosaura, for you know
   It is a debt of honour and must be paid.

ASTOLFO. Although, it's true, I owe some obligations—
   She does not know her name or who she is,
   It would be base to wed a woman who . . .

CLOTALDO. Hold! Wait! Rosaura's of as noble stock
   As yours, Astolfo. In the open field
   I'll prove it with my sword. She is my daughter
   And that should be enough.

ASTOLFO.   What do you say?

CLOTALDO. Until I saw her married, righted, honoured,
   I did not wish for it to be discovered.
   It's a long story but she is my daughter.

ASTOLFO. That being so, I'm glad to keep my word.

SEGISMUND. And now, so that the princess Stella here
   Will not remain disconsolate to lose
   A prince of so much valour, here I offer
   My hand to her, no less in birth and rank.
   Give me your hand.

STELLA.   I gain by meriting
   So great a happiness.

SEGISMUND.   And now, Clotaldo,
   So long so loyal to my father, come
   To my arms. Ask me anything you wish.

FIRST SOLDIER. If thus you treat a man who never served you,
   What about me who led the revolution
   And brought you from your dungeon in the tower?
   What will you give me?

SEGISMUND.   That same tower and dungeon
   From which you never shall emerge till death.
   No traitor is of use after his treason.

BASIL. All wonder at your wisdom!

ASTOLFO.   What a change
   Of character!

ROSAURA.   How wise and prudent!

SEGISMUND.   Why
   Do you wonder? Why do you marvel, since
   It was a dream that taught me and I still
   Fear to wake up once more in my close dungeon?
   Though that may never happen, it's enough
   To dream it might, for thus I came to learn
   That all our human happiness must pass
   Away like any dream, and I would here
   Enjoy it fully ere it glide away,
   Asking (for noble hearts are prone to pardon)
   Pardon for faults in the actors or the play.

NOTES

GENERAL. A comprehensive list of Spanish works that have been translated into English has been published under the title: *English Translations from the Spanish, 1484–1943, A Bibliography,* by Remigio Ugo Pane (Rutgers University Press, 1944). A highly readable general history of Spanish literature is now available in paperbacks: *The Literature of the Spanish People* by Gerald Brenan (Meridian Books, 1957). For those who can read a little Spanish, a Spanish collection with English notes is recommended: *Diez Comedias del Siglo de Oro,* edited by Hyman Alpern and José Martel (Harper & Bros., 1939).

CELESTINA (first version published in 1499) has been published in four English translations: James Mabbe's (1631), Lesley Byrd Simpson's (1955), Mack Hendricks Singleton's (1958), and Phyllis Hartnoll's (1959). Mabbe's text stands to the later ones as the King James Bible stands to the several twentieth-century versions of holy writ: modern scholars, as it seems to the present editor, cannot make up in accuracy for what they lose in poetry and wit.

For this reason, Mabbe's text is the basis of the stage version published here. A few obsolete words have been replaced by familiar ones. Brief, bridging passages were written in when the cuts made them necessary. But Mabbe's words were seriously interfered with by the modern adaptor only where Mabbe had replaced the Catholic nomenclature of the Spanish with pagan nomenclature. In order, no doubt, to avoid religious controversy, Mabbe made Rojas' characters visit a "myrtle grove" and pray to "Jove" where the Spanish bluntly said St. Mary Magdalen's Church and God. There was obviously no need to conceal Rojas' anti-clericalism in the year 1959.

A number of English stage versions of *Celestina* have preceded the present one. The most famous of these, an early sixteenth-century "Interlude," was reprinted with the Mabbe text in the Broadway Translations. Another anonymous stage adaptation, this one much closer to the original, was published in London in 1707, a copy being preserved in Columbia University Library. At least two English-language productions of a shortened *Celestina* have been reported in the nineteen-fifties: one in a text prepared by Mack Hendricks Singleton at the University of Wisconsin, the other, based on Mabbe, at Joan Littlewood's Theatre Workshop in East London. Neither of these adaptations has been available for inspection, nor has the recent Spanish adaptation, successfully produced at the Eslava Theatre in Madrid and taken to the International Festival in Paris.

There is one important study of *Celestina* in English: *The Art of La Celestina*, by Stephen Gilman (Madison, Wisconsin, 1956).

Two Victorian translations of THE SIEGE OF NUMANTIA (1585) precede the Campbell version in print. The first was that of G. W. J. Gyll in 1870 (as included in a volume of Cervantes also containing *The Voyage to Parnassus* and *The Commerce of Algiers*), the second that of James Young Gibson (1885), Gibson's translation being dedicated "To the Memory of General Gordon, the Hero of Khartoum, the Modern Paladin," etc. If in the nineteenth century, Cervantes was enlisted in the cause of British Imperialism, in the twentieth he was made to serve Stalinism as represented by Rafael Alberti (who made two different modern versions: one for Madrid in 1937, one for Montevideo in 1943). In the same year as the "realist" Alberti made his first "social" interpretation of the play, a "formalist" of the Paris theatre, Jean-Louis Barrault, used Cervantes' text as the basis for an exploration of the theatrical medium. Today the play is probably better known in Paris than in any other city in the world: when an enterprising publisher started a paperback series called "Répertoire pour un théâtre populaire," *La Numance* was in the first group of plays chosen.

The author of the present translation was a supporter of General Franco in war and peace: what *The Siege of Numantia* would mean to him can be deduced from his poem *Flowering Rifle*.

In his book *Sentido y Forma del Teatro de Cervantes* (Madrid, 1951), Joaquín Casalduero advances the view that the play is essentially unpolitical.

It was in the late eighteenth century that the classic Spanish drama first made a tremendous impact upon European culture, and from then on, for some decades at least, the most favored of the Spanish playwrights was Calderón. The Calderón vogue was challenged before the mid-nineteenth century, however, by George Henry Lewes for one, who preferred Lope de Vega. If Calderón's *Life is a Dream* remained, in the general mind, the Spanish masterpiece par excellence, its position was at least endangered in the twentieth century by Lope's FUENTE OVEJUNA (1619). The reason for this is evident in the first important defence of the play in Spanish, that of Menendez y Pelayo, who wrote: "There is not a more democratic work in all of Castilian theatre . . ." As such the play was taken up by the avant-garde Russian theatre before the Revolution and widely championed by Communists in later decades. An article on "Revolutionary Staging of the Classics" by G. Boyadzhiev, "a prominent Soviet critic," in *Theatre Workshop*, New York, 1938, is all about *Fuente Ovejuna*. In the forties, Erwin Piscator put the "left-wing" interpretation of the play on the stage of his Dramatic Workshop in New York City. And in the late fifties one finds the play recommended for the *théâtre populaire* and *teatro populare* by French and Italian writers of the Communist ambiance.

The limits of the modern, "left-wing" view of the play have been defined by Joaquín Casalduero in his essay "Fuenteovejuna" in *La Revista de Filologia Hispanica*, 1943.

Two translations into English have preceded Roy Campbell's in print: that of John Garrett Underhill in his *Four Plays of Lope de Vega* (1936) and that of Angel Flores and Muriel

Kittel in John Gassner's *Treasury of the Theatre* (New York, 1950–51) and in Mr. Flores' *Masterpieces of the Spanish Golden Age* (New York, 1957).

Even if THE TRICKSTER OF SEVILLE (1630) were not a great play, it would still be a great document of European civilisation, and therefore it is no less than amazing that, through the centuries, it was never translated into English. Pane's bibliography lists only one translation: *The Love-Rogue. A Poetic Drama in Three Acts* (New York, 1923). The translator was Harry Kemp, and his book is neither good writing nor faithful translation.

The play marks the entrance into literature of Don Juan. Though even this fact is often overlooked by non-Spanish writers, it has been known to those who wished to know it; for example, to Bernard Shaw, who once answered as follows the present editor's request for the right to reprint *Man and Superman* alongside Molière's *Festin de Pierre*: "*Le Festin de Pierre* should be preceded by Tirso de Molina's *Burlador de Seville* [sic] not followed by *Man and Superman.*"

The Don Juan literature is surveyed in *La Légende de Don Juan* by Gendarme de Bévotte, Paris, 1911, 2 volumes, and in *The Metamorphoses of Don Juan* by Leo Weinstein, Stanford, California, 1959. There is one good book on Tirso de Molina in English: *Tirso de Molina: Studies in Dramatic Realism* by I. L. McClelland, Liverpool, 1948.

On Tirso's possible model for the now legendary role, see: "Grandeur and Misery of Don Juan," by Gregorio Marañón, in *Partisan Review*, Summer 1957. Of the many speculations on the legendary figure himself, particularly suggestive, though chiefly based on the Mozart-Da Ponte version, is Otto Rank's *Die Don Juan Gestalt* (Leipzig, 1924).

A radio adaptation of the Campbell version of *Trickster of Seville* has already been printed in *Masterpieces of the Spanish Golden Age*, edited by Angel Flores (New York, 1957). Though the radio is not mentioned in this publication, no attempt has been made to delete interpolations made to identify characters for an audience that cannot see them.

LOVE AFTER DEATH (1632–33) was translated by Mac-Carthy (1853) in his (luckily) inimitable Hispano-English. Though it has made less noise in the world than the other plays in this book, it not only presents one of the great themes of Spanish history—the conflict of Moorish and Hispanic culture—but is second to no Spanish play in sheer theatricality.

LIFE IS A DREAM (1635), still perhaps the most celebrated of all Spanish plays, has been translated into English a number of times. The earliest attempt recorded by Pane is that of R. C. Trench (an incomplete translation) in 1856. After Trench came Fitzgerald (1865), though earlier he had written: "Such plays as the *Magico Prodigioso* and the *Vida es Sueño* require another translator"; MacCarthy (1873); William E. Colford (1958). (The foregoing have all been inspected by the present editor. Three others are mentioned in Colford's bibliography: Frank Birch and J. B. Trend in collaboration [1925], C. Morgan [1928], and W. F. Stirling [1942].) Of value to anyone wishing to produce the play is the French stage version by Alexandre Arnoux which was the fruit of a collaboration with Charles Dullin (in Calderón: *Trois Comédies*, Paris, 1955).

The most authoritative recent discussion of the play's meaning is, perhaps, "La vida es sueño," by E. M. Wilson, *Revista de la Universidad de Buenos Aires*, 1947. Along with this article, the following are recommended: the same author's "Gerald Brenan's Calderón," *Bulletin of the Comediantes*, 1952, and A. A. Parker's *The Approach to the Spanish Drama of the Golden Age*, a lecture separately published by The Hispanic & Luso-Brazilian Councils, London, 1957, and reprinted in The Tulane Drama Review, Autumn, 1959.

APPENDIX

THE WONDER-WORKING MAGICIAN, Calderón de la Barca

The poet Shelley was a great pioneer translator of Calderón as he was of Goethe. There follow the scenes Shelley translated from Calderón's *El Magico Prodigioso* (1637), which almost amount to an abridged version of the play.

The time is the third century A.D.; the place Antioch. George Santayana summarises the plot as follows: "This earlier hero, St. Cyprian of Antioch, is like Faust in being a scholar, signing his soul to the devil, practising magic, embracing the ghost of beauty, and being ultimately saved. Here the analogy ends. Cyprian, far from being disgusted with all theory, and particularly with theology, is a pagan philosopher eagerly seeking God, and working his way, with full faith in his method, toward Christian orthodoxy. He floors the devil in scholastic argument about the unity of God, his power, wisdom, and goodness. He falls in love, and sells his soul merely in the hope of satisfying his passion. He studies magic chiefly for the same reason; but magic cannot overrule the free-will of the Christian lady he loves (a modern and very Spanish one, though supposed to adorn ancient Antioch). The devil can supply only a false phantasm of her person, and as Cyprian approaches her and lifts her veil, he finds a hideous death's-head beneath; for God can work miracles to cap those of any magician, and can beat the devil at his own game. Thunderstruck at this portent, Cyprian becomes a Christian. Half-naked, ecstatic, taken for a madman, he bears witness loudly and persistently to the power, wisdom, and goodness of the one true God; and, since the persecution of Decius is then going on, he is hurried away to martyrdom. His lady, sentenced also for the same cause, encourages him by her heroic attitude and words. Their earthly passion is dead; but their souls are united in death and in immortality. In this drama we see magic checkmated by miracles, doubt yielding to faith, purity resisting temptation, passion transformed into zeal, and all the glories of the world collapsing before disillusion and asceticism. These glories are nothing, the poet tells us, but dust, ashes, smoke, and air."

Enter CYPRIAN, *dressed as a student;* CLARIN *and* MOSCON
as poor scholars, with books.

CYPRIAN. In the sweet solitude of this calm place,
This intricate wild wilderness of trees
And flowers and undergrowth of odorous plants,
Leave me; the books you brought out of the house
To me are ever best society.
And while with glorious festival and song,
Antioch now celebrates the consecration
Of a proud temple to great Jupiter,
And bears his image in loud jubilee
To its new shrine, I would consume what still
Lives of the dying day in studious thought,
Far from the throng and turmoil. You, my friends,
Go, and enjoy the festival; it will
Be worth your pains. You may return for me
When the sun seeks its grave among the billows
Which, among dim grey clouds on the horizon,
Dance like white plumes upon a hearse; and here
I shall expect you.

MOSCON.   I cannot bring my mind,
Great as my haste to see the festival
Certainly is, to leave you, sir, without
Just saying some three or four thousand words.
How is it possible that on a day
Of such festivity, you can be content

To come forth to a solitary country
With three or four old books, and turn your back
On all this mirth?

CLARIN.   My master's in the right;
There is not anything more tiresome
Than a procession day, with troops, and priests,
And dances, and all that.

MOSCON.   From first to last,
Clarin, you are a temporising flatterer;
You praise not what you feel but what he does;
Toadeater!

CLARIN.   You lie—under a mistake—
For this is the most civil sort of lie
That can be given to a man's face. I now
Say what I think.

CYPRIAN.   Enough, you foolish fellows!
Puffed up with your own doting ignorance,
You always take the two sides of one question.
Now go; and as I said, return for me
When night falls, veiling in its shadows wide
This glorious fabric of the universe.

MOSCON. How happens it, although you can maintain
The folly of enjoying festivals,
That yet you go there?

CLARIN.   Nay, the consequence
Is clear: who ever did what he advises
Others to do?

MOSCON.   Would that my feet were wings,
So would I fly to Livia.
        Exit.

CLARIN.   To speak truth,
Livia is she who has surprised my heart;
But he is more than halfway there. Soho!
Livia, I come; good sport, Livia, soho!
        Exit.

CYPRIAN. Now, since I am alone, let me examine
The question which has long disturbed my mind
With doubt, since first I read in Plinius

The words of mystic import and deep sense
In which he defines God. My intellect
Can find no God with whom these marks and signs
Fitly agree. It is a hidden truth
Which I must fathom.

CYPRIAN *reads; the* DAEMON, *dressed in a court dress, enters.*

DAEMON.   Search even as thou wilt,
But thou shalt never find what I can hide.

CYPRIAN. What noise is that among the boughs? Who moves?
What art thou?

DAEMON.   'Tis a foreign gentleman.
Even from this morning I have lost my way
In this wild place; and my poor horse at last,
Quite overcome, has stretched himself upon
The enamelled tapestry of this mossy mountain,
And feeds and rests at the same time. I was
Upon my way to Antioch upon business
Of some importance, but wrapped up in cares
(Who is exempt from this inheritance?)
I parted from my company, and lost
My way, and lost my servants and my comrades.

CYPRIAN. 'Tis singular that even within the sight
Of the high towers of Antioch you could lose
Your way. Of all the avenues and green paths
Of this wild wood there is not one but leads,
As to its centre, to the walls of Antioch;
Take which you will, you cannot miss your road.

DAEMON. And such is ignorance! Even in the sight
Of knowledge, it can draw no profit from it.
But as it still is early, and as I
Have no acquaintances in Antioch,
Being a stranger there, I will even wait
The few surviving hours of the day,
Until the night shall conquer it. I see
Both by your dress and by the books in which
You find delight and company, that you
Are a great student; for my part, I feel
Much sympathy in such pursuits.

CYPRIAN.   Have you
Studied much?

DAEMON.   No—and yet I know enough
Not to be wholly ignorant.

CYPRIAN.   Pray, sir,
What science may you know?

DAEMON.   Many.

CYPRIAN.   Alas!
Much pains must we expend on one alone,
And even then attain it not; but you
Have the presumption to assert that you
Know many without study.

DAEMON.   And with truth.
For in the country whence I come the sciences
Require no learning,—they are known.

CYPRIAN.   Oh, would
I were of that bright country! for in this
The more we study, we the more discover
Our ignorance.

DAEMON.   It is so true, that I
Had so much arrogance as to oppose
The chair of the most high Professorship,
And obtained many votes, and, though I lost,
The attempt was still more glorious, than the failure
Could be dishonourable. If you believe not,
Let us refer it to dispute respecting
That which you know the best, and although I
Know not the opinion you maintain, and though
It be the true one, I will take the contrary.

CYPRIAN. The offer gives me pleasure. I am now
Debating with myself upon a passage
Of Plinius, and my mind is racked with doubt
To understand and know who is the God
Of whom he speaks.

DAEMON.   It is a passage, if
I recollect it right, couched in these words:
"God is one supreme goodness, one pure essence,
One substance, and one sense, all sight, all hands."

CYPRIAN. 'Tis true.

DAEMON.   What difficulty find you here?

CYPRIAN. I do not recognize among the gods
The God defined by Plinius; if he must
Be supreme goodness, even Jupiter
Is not supremely good; because we see
His deeds are evil, and his attributes
Tainted with mortal weakness; in what manner
Can supreme goodness be consistent with
The passions of humanity?

DAEMON.   The wisdom
Of the old world masked with the names of gods
The attributes of nature and of man;
A sort of popular philosophy.

CYPRIAN. This reply will not satisfy me, for,
Such awe is due to the high name of God
That ill should never be imputed. Then,
Examining the question with more care,
It follows that the gods would always will
That which is best, were they supremely good.
How then does one will one thing, one another?
And that you may not say that I allege
Poetical or philosophic learning:
Consider the ambiguous responses
Of their oracular statues; from two shrines
Two armies shall obtain the assurance of
One victory. Is it not indisputable
That two contending wills can never lead
To the same end? And, being opposite,
If one be good, is not the other evil?
Evil in God is inconceivable;
But supreme goodness fails among the gods
Without their union.

DAEMON.   I deny your major.
These responses are means towards some end
Unfathomed by our intellectual beam.
They are the work of Providence, and more
The battle's loss may profit those who lose,
Than victory advantage those who win.

CYPRIAN. That I admit; and yet that God should not
   (Falsehood is incompatible with deity)
   Assure the victory; it would be enough
   To have permitted the defeat. If God
   Be all sight—God, who had beheld the truth,
   Would not have given assurance of an end
   Never to be accomplished: thus, although
   The Deity may according to his attributes
   Be well distinguished into persons, yet
   Even in the minutest circumstance
   His essence must be one.

DAEMON.   To attain the end
   The affections of the actors in the scene
   Must have been thus influenced by his voice.

CYPRIAN. But for a purpose thus subordinate
   He might have employed genii, good or evil—
   A sort of spirits called so by the learnèd,
   Who roam about inspiring good or evil,
   And from whose influence and existence we
   May well infer our immortality.
   Thus God might easily, without descent
   To a gross falsehood in his proper person,
   Have moved the affections by this mediation
   To the just point.

DAEMON.   These trifling contradictions
   Do not suffice to impugn the unity
   Of the high gods; in things of great importance
   They still appear unanimous; consider
   That glorious fabric, man,—his workmanship
   Is stamped with one conception.

CYPRIAN.   Who made man
   Must have, methinks, the advantage of the others.
   If they are equal, might they not have risen
   In opposition to the work, and being
   All hands, according to our author here,
   Have still destroyed even as the other made?
   If equal in their power, unequal only
   In opportunity, which of the two
   Will remain conqueror?

DAEMON. On impossible
And false hypothesis there can be built
No argument. Say, what do you infer
From this?

CYPRIAN. That there must be a mighty God
Of supreme goodness and of highest grace,
All sight, all hands, all truth, infallible,
Without an equal and without a rival,
The cause of all things and the effect of nothing,
One power, one will, one substance, and one essence.
And, in whatever persons, one or two,
His attributes may be distinguished, one
Sovereign power, one solitary essence,
One cause of all cause.

They rise.

DAEMON. How can I impugn
So clear a consequence?

CYPRIAN. Do you regret
My victory?

DAEMON. Who but regrets a check
In rivalry of wit? I could reply
And urge new difficulties, but will now
Depart, for I hear steps of men approaching,
And it is time that I should now pursue
My journey to the city.

CYPRIAN. Go in peace!

DAEMON. Remain in peace! *Aside.* Since thus it profits him
To study, I will wrap his senses up
In sweet oblivion of all thought but of
A piece of excellent beauty; and, as I
Have power given me to wage enmity
Against Justina's soul, I will extract
From one effect two vengeances.

Exit.

CYPRIAN. I never
Met a more learnèd person. Let me now
Revolve this doubt again with careful mind.

He reads.

FLORO *and* LELIO, *young gentlemen, enter.*

LELIO. Here stop. These toppling rocks and tangled boughs,
Impenetrable by the noonday beam,
Shall be sole witnesses of what we—

FLORO.   Draw!
If there were words, here is the place for deeds.

LELIO. Thou needest not instruct me; well I know
That in the field, the silent tongue of steel
Speaks thus.
They fight.

CYPRIAN.   Ha! what is this? Lelio—Floro,
Be it enough that Cyprian stands between you,
Although unarmed.

LELIO.   Whence comest thou, to stand
Between me and my vengeance?

FLORO.   From what rocks
And desert cells?
Enter MOSCON *and* CLARIN.

MOSCON.   Run! run! for where we left
My master I now hear the clash of swords.

CLARIN. I never run to approach things of this sort,
But only to avoid them. Sir! Cyprian! Sir!

CYPRIAN. Be silent, fellows! What! Two friends who are
In blood and fame the eyes and hope of Antioch,
One of the noble race of the Colalti,
The other son o' the Governor, adventure
And cast away, on some slight cause no doubt,
Two lives, the honour of their country?

LELIO.   Cyprian!
Although my high respect towards your person
Holds now my sword suspended, thou canst not
Restore it to the slumber of the scabbard:
Thou knowest more of science than the duel;
For when two men of honour take the field,
No counsel nor respect can make them friends
But one must die in the dispute.

FLORO.   I pray
That you depart hence with your people, and

Leave us to finish what we have begun
Without advantage.

CYPRIAN.   Though you may imagine
That I know little of the laws of duel,
Which vanity and valour instituted,
You are in error. By my birth I am
Held no less than yourselves to know the limits
Of honour and of infamy, nor has study
Quenched the free spirit which first ordered them;
And thus to me, as one well experienced
In the false quicksands of the sea of honour,
You may refer the merits of the case;
And if I should perceive in your relation
That either has the right to satisfaction
From the other, I give you my word of honour
To leave you.

LELIO.   Under this condition then
I will relate the cause, and you will cede
And must confess the impossibility
Of compromise; for the same lady is
Beloved by Floro and myself.

FLORO.   It seems
Much to me that the light of day should look
Upon that idol of my heart—but he—
Leave us to fight, according to thy word.

CYPRIAN. Permit one question further: is the lady
Impossible to hope or not?

LELIO.   She is
So excellent, that if the light of day
Should excite Floro's jealousy, it were
Without just cause, for even the light of day
Trembles to gaze on her.

CYPRIAN.   Would you, for your
Part, marry her?

FLORO.   Such is my confidence.

CYPRIAN. And you?

LELIO.   Oh! would that I could lift my hope
So high, for though she is extremely poor,
Her virtue is her dowry.

CYPRIAN.   And if you both
Would marry her, is it not weak and vain,
Culpable and unworthy, thus beforehand
To slur her honour? What would the world say
If one should slay the other, and if she
Should afterwards espouse the murderer?

The rivals agree to refer their quarrel to CYPRIAN, *who in
consequence visits* JUSTINA *and becomes enamoured of her;
she disdains him, and he retires to a solitary seashore.*

SCENE 2

CYPRIAN. O memory! permit it not
That the tyrant of my thought
Be another soul that still
Holds dominion o'er the will,
That would refuse, but can no more,
To bend, to tremble, and adore.
Vain idolatry!—I saw,
    And gazing, became blind with error;
Weak ambition, which the awe
    Of her presence bound to terror!
So beautiful she was—and I,
Between my love and jealousy,
Am so convulsed with hope and fear,
Unworthy as it may appear;
So bitter is the life I live,
That, hear me, Hell! I now would give
To thy most detested spirit
My soul, forever to inherit,
To suffer punishment and pine,
So this woman may be mine.
Hear'st thou, Hell! dost thou reject it?
My soul is offered!

DAEMON, *unseen*.   I accept it.

Tempest, with thunder and lightning.

CYPRIAN. What is this? ye heavens forever pure,

At once intensely radiant and obscure!
　　Athwart the aethereal halls
The lightning's arrow and the thunderballs
　　　The day affright,
　　As from the horizon round,
　　Burst with earthquake sound,
In mighty torrents the electric fountains;
　Clouds quench the sun, and thunder smoke
Strangles the air, and fire eclipses heaven.
　Philosophy, thou canst not even
Compel their causes underneath thy yoke:
From yonder clouds even to the waves below
The fragments of a single ruin choke
　　Imagination's flight;
　For, on flakes of surge, like feathers light,
The ashes of the desolation, cast
　　Upon the gloomy blast,
　Tell of the footsteps of the storm;
And nearer, see, the melancholy form
Of a great ship, the outcast of the sea,
　　　Drives miserably!
And it must fly the pity of the port,
Or perish, and its last and sole resort
　Is its own raging enemy.
　The terror of the thrilling cry
　Was a fatal prophecy
　Of coming death, who hovers now.
　　Upon that shattered prow,
That they who die not may be dying still.
And not alone the insane elements
　　Are populous with wild portents,
But that sad ship is as a miracle
　Of sudden ruin, for it drives so fast
It seems as if it had arrayed its form
　　　With the headlong storm.
　It strikes—I almost feel the shock—
　It stumbles on a jaggèd rock,
Sparkles of blood on the white foam are cast.

A tempest.

ALL, *within*. We are all lost!

DAEMON, *within*.   Now from this plank will I
  Pass to the land and thus fulfil my scheme.

CYPRIAN. As in contempt of the elemental rage
    A man comes forth in safety, while the ship's
    Great form is in a watery eclipse
  Obliterated from the ocean's page,
  And round its wreck the huge sea monsters sit,
  A horrid conclave, and the whistling wave
  Is heaped over its carcase, like a grave.

  The DAEMON *enters, as escaped from the sea.*

DAEMON, *aside*. It was essential to my purposes
  To wake a tumult on the sapphire ocean,
  That in this unknown form I might at length
  Wipe out the blot of the discomfiture
  Sustained upon the mountain, and assail
  With a new war the soul of Cyprian,
  Forging the instruments of his destruction
  Even from his love and from his wisdom. O
  Belovèd earth, dear mother, in thy bosom
  I seek a refuge from the monster who
  Precipitates itself upon me.

CYPRIAN.   Friend,
  Collect thyself; and be the memory
  Of thy late suffering and thy greatest sorrow
  But as a shadow of the past, for nothing
  Beneath the circle of the moon, but flows
  And changes and can never know repose.

DAEMON. And who art thou, before whose feet my fate
  Has prostrated me?

CYPRIAN.   One who, moved with pity,
  Would soothe its stings.

DAEMON.   Oh, that can never be!
  No solace can my lasting sorrows find.

CYPRIAN. Wherefore?

DAEMON.   Because my happiness is lost.
  Yet I lament what has long ceased to be

The object of desire or memory,
And my life is not life.

CYPRIAN.   Now, since the fury
Of this earthquaking hurricane is still,
And the crystàlline heaven has reassumed
Its windless calm so quickly that it seems
As if its heavy wrath had been awakened
Only to overwhelm that vessel, speak,
Who art thou and whence comest thou?

DAEMON.   Far more
My coming hither cost, than thou hast seen
Or I can tell. Among my misadventures
This shipwreck is the least. Wilt thou hear?

CYPRIAN.   Speak.

DAEMON. Since thou desirest, I will then unveil
Myself to thee; for in myself I am
A world of happiness and misery;
This I have lost, and that I must lament
Forever. In my attributes I stood
So high and so heroically great,
In lineage so supreme, and with a genius
Which penetrated with a glance the world
Beneath my feet, that, won by my high merit,
A king—whom I may call the King of kings,
Because all others tremble in their pride
Before the terrors of His countenance,
In His high palace roofed with brightest gems
Of living light—call them the stars of heaven—
Named me His counsellor. But the high praise
Stung me with pride and envy, and I rose
In mighty competition, to ascend
His seat and place my foot triumphantly
Upon His subject thrones. Chastised, I know
The depth to which ambition falls; too mad
Was the attempt, and yet more mad were now
Repentance of the irrevocable deed:
Therefore I chose this ruin, with the glory
Of not to be subdued, before the shame
Of reconciling me with Him who reigns

By coward cession.—Nor was I alone,
Nor am I now, nor shall I be alone;
And there was hope, and there may still be hope,
For many suffrages among His vassals
Hailed me their lord and king, and many still
Are mine, and many more, perchance shall be.
Thus vanquished, though in fact victorious,
I left His seat of empire, from mine eye
Shooting forth poisonous lightning, while my words
With inauspicious thunderings shook heaven,
Proclaiming vengeance, public as my wrong,
And imprecating on His prostrate slaves
Rapine, and death, and outrage. Then I sailed
Over the mighty fabric of the world,
A pirate ambushed in its pathless sands,
A lynx crouched watchfully among its caves
And craggy shores; and I have wandered over
The expanse of these wide wildernesses
In this great ship, whose bulk is now dissolved
In the light breathings of the invisible wind,
And which the sea has made a dustless ruin,
Seeking ever a mountain, through whose forests
I seek a man, whom I must now compel
To keep his word with me. I came arrayed
In tempest, and although my power could well
Bridle the forest winds in their career,
For other causes I forbore to soothe
Their fury to favonian gentleness;
I could and would not: *Aside.* Thus I wake in him
A love of magic art. *Aloud.* Let not this tempest,
Nor the succeeding calm excite thy wonder;
For by my art the sun would turn as pale
As his weak sister with unwonted fear;
And in my wisdom are the orbs of heaven
Written as in a record; I have pierced
The flaming circles of their wondrous spheres
And know them as thou knowest every corner
Of this dim spot. Let it not seem to thee

That I boast vainly; wouldst thou that I work
A charm over this waste and savage wood,
This Babylon of crags and agèd trees,
Filling its leafy coverts with a horror
Thrilling and strange? I am the friendless guest
Of these wild oaks and pines—and as from thee
I have received the hospitality
Of this rude place, I offer thee the fruit
Of years of toil in recompense; whate'er
Thy wildest dream presented to thy thought
As object of desire, that shall be thine.

.   .   .   .   .

And thenceforth shall so firm an amity
'Twixt thee and me be, that neither Fortune,
The monstrous phantom which pursues success,
That careful miser, that free prodigal,
Who ever alternates, with changeful hand,
Evil and good, reproach and fame; nor Time,
That lodestar of the ages, to whose beam
The wingèd years speed o'er the intervals
Of their unequal revolutions; nor
Heaven itself, whose beautiful bright stars
Rule and adorn the world, can ever make
The least division between thee and me,
Since now I find a refuge in thy favour.

SCENE 3

The DAEMON *tempts* JUSTINA, *who is a Christian.*

DAEMON. Abyss of Hell! I call on thee,
　Thou wild misrule of thine own anarchy!
　　From thy prison house set free
　　The spirits of voluptuous death,
　　　That with their mighty breath
　They may destroy a world of virgin thoughts;
　Let her chaste mind with fancies thick as motes

Be peopled from thy shadowy deep,
Till her guiltless fantasy
Full to overflowing be!
And with sweetest harmony,
Let birds, and flowers, and leaves, and all things move
    To love, only to love.
    Let nothing meet her eyes
But signs of love's soft victories;
    Let nothing meet her ear
But sounds of love's sweet sorrow,
So that from faith no succour she may borrow,
    But, guided by my spirit blind
    And in a magic snare entwined,
      She may now seek Cyprian.
    Begin, while I in silence bind
My voice, when thy sweet song thou hast began.

ONE VOICE, *singing within*. What is the glory far above
    All else in human life?

ALL.   Love! love!

While these words are sung, the DAEMON *goes out at one door, and* JUSTINA *enters at another.*

THE VOICE. There is no form in which the fire
    Of love its traces has impressed not.
Man lives far more in love's desire
    Than by life's breath, soon possessed not.
If all that lives must love or die,
All shapes on earth, or sea, or sky,
With one consent to heaven cry
That the glory far above
All else in life is—

ALL.   Love! oh, love!

JUSTINA. Thou melancholy thought which art
    So flattering and so sweet, to thee
    When did I give the liberty
      Thus to afflict my heart?
What is the cause of this new power
    Which doth my fevered being move,
Momently raging more and more?
What subtle pain is kindled now

Which from my heart doth overflow
    Into my senses?—

ALL.   Love! oh, love!

JUSTINA. 'Tis that enamoured nightingale
    Who gives me the reply;
He ever tells the same soft tale
    Of passion and of constancy
To his mate, who rapt and fond,
Listening sits, a bough beyond.

Be silent, nightingale—no more
    Make me think, in hearing thee
Thus tenderly thy love deplore,
    If a bird can feel his so,
    What a man would feel for me.
    And, voluptuous vine, O thou
Who seekest most when least pursuing,
    To the trunk thou interlacest
    Art the verdure which embracest,
And the weight which is its ruin—
No more, with green embraces, vine,
    Make me think on what thou lovest,
For whilst thus thy boughs entwine,
    I fear lest thou shouldst teach me, sophist,
How arms might be entangled too.

Light-enchanted sunflower, thou
Who gazest ever true and tender
On the sun's revolving splendour!
Follow not his faithless glance
With thy faded countenance,
Nor teach my beating heart to fear,
If leaves can mourn without a tear,
How eyes must weep! O nightingale,
Cease from thy enamoured tale—
Leafy vine, unwreathe thy bower,
    Restless sunflower, cease to move,
Or tell me all, what poisonous power
    Ye use against me—

ALL.   Love! Love! Love!

JUSTINA. It cannot be!—Whom have I ever loved?
Trophies of my oblivion and disdain,
Floro and Lelio did I not reject?
And Cyprian?

She becomes troubled at the name of CYPRIAN.

Did I not requite him
With such severity that he has fled
Where none has ever heard of him again?
Alas! I now begin to fear that this
May be the occasion whence desire grows bold,
As if there were no danger. From the moment
That I pronounced to my own listening heart,
"Cyprian is absent!"—O me miserable!
I know not what I feel!

More calmly.

It must be pity
To think that such a man, whom all the world
Admired, should be forgot by all the world,
And I the cause.

She again becomes troubled.

And yet if it were pity,
Floro and Lelio might have equal share,
For they are both imprisoned for my sake.

Calmly.

Alas! what reasonings are these? It is
Enough I pity him, and that, in vain,
Without this ceremonious subtlety.
And, woe is me! I know not where to find him now,
Even should I seek him through this wide world.

Enter DAEMON.

DAEMON. Follow, and I will lead thee where he is.

JUSTINA. And who art thou, who hast found entrance hither,
Into my chamber through the doors and locks?
Art thou a monstrous shadow which my madness
Has formed in the idle air?

DAEMON.   No. I am one
Called by the thought which tyrannizes thee

From his eternal dwelling; who this day
Is pledged to bear thee unto Cyprian.

JUSTINA. So shall thy promise fail. This agony
Of passion which afflicts my heart and soul
May sweep imagination in its storm;
The will is firm.

DAEMON.   Already half is done
In the imagination of an act.
The sin incurred, the pleasure then remains;
Let not the will stop halfway on the road.

JUSTINA. I will not be discouraged, nor despair,
Although I thought it, and although 'tis true
That thought is but a prelude to the deed:
Thought is not in my power, but action is:
I will not move my foot to follow thee.

DAEMON. But a far mightier wisdom than thine own
Exerts itself within thee, with such power
Compelling thee to that which it inclines
That it shall force thy step; how wilt thou then
Resist, Justina?

JUSTINA.   By my free will.

DAEMON.   I
Must force thy will.

JUSTINA.   It is invincible;
It were not free if thou hadst power upon it.
He draws, but cannot move her.

DAEMON. Come, where a pleasure waits thee.

JUSTINA.   It were bought
Too dear.

DAEMON.   'Twill soothe thy heart to softest peace.

JUSTINA. 'Tis dread captivity.

DAEMON.   'Tis joy, 'tis glory.

JUSTINA. 'Tis shame, 'tis torment, 'tis despair.

DAEMON.   But how
Canst thou defend thyself from that or me,
If my power drags thee onward?

JUSTINA.　　　　　　　　　My defence
　Consists in God.
　He vainly endeavours to force her, and at last releases her.

DAEMON.　　　　　Woman, thou hast subdued me,
　Only by not owning thyself subdued.
　But since thou thus findest defence in God,
　I will assume a feignèd form, and thus
　Make thee a victim of my baffled rage.
　For I will mask a spirit in thy form
　Who will betray thy name to infamy,
　And doubly shall I triumph in thy loss,
　First by dishonouring thee, and then by turning
　False pleasure to true ignominy.
　Exit.

JUSTINA.　　　　　　　　　I
　Appeal to Heaven against thee; so that Heaven
　May scatter thy delusions, and the blot
　Upon my fame vanish in idle thought,
　Even as flame dies in the envious air,
　And as the floweret wanes at morning frost;
　And thou shouldst never— But, alas! to whom
　Do I still speak? Did not a man but now
　Stand here before me? No, I am alone,
　And yet I saw him. Is he gone so quickly?
　Or can the heated mind engender shapes
　From its own fear? Some terrible and strange
　Peril is near. Lisander! Father! Lord!
　Livia!
　Enter her father LISANDER *and* LIVIA, *their servant.*

LISANDER. Oh, my daughter! What?

LIVIA.　　　　　　　　　What!

JUSTINA.　　　　　　　　　Saw you
　A man go forth from my apartment now?—
　I scarce contain myself!

LISANDER.　　　　A man here!

JUSTINA. Have you not seen him?

LIVIA.　　　　　　　　No, lady.

JUSTINA. I saw him.

LISANDER.   'Tis impossible; the doors
  Which led to this apartment were all locked.

LIVIA, *aside.* I daresay it was Moscon whom she saw,
  For he was locked up in my room.

LISANDER.   It must
  Have been some image of thy fantasy.
  Such melancholy as thou feedest is
  Skilful in forming such in the vain air
  Out of the motes and atoms of the day.

LIVIA. My master's in the right.

JUSTINA.   Oh, would it were
  Delusion; but I fear some greater ill.
  I feel as if out of my bleeding bosom
  My heart was torn in fragments; ay,
  Some mortal spell is wrought against my frame;
  So potent was the charm that, had not God
  Shielded my humble innocence from wrong,
  I should have sought my sorrow and my shame
  With willing steps. —Livia, quick, bring my cloak,
  For I must seek refuge from these extremes
  Even in the temple of the highest God
  Where secretly the faithful worship.

LIVIA.   Here.

JUSTINA, *putting on her cloak.*
  In this, as in a shroud of snow, may I
  Quench the consuming fire in which I burn,
  Wasting away!

LISANDER.   And I will go with thee.

LIVIA. When I once see them safe out of the house
  I shall breathe freely.

JUSTINA.   So do I confide
  In thy just favour, Heaven!

LISANDER.   Let us go.

JUSTINA. Thine is the cause, great God! Turn for my sake,
  And for Thine own, mercifully to me!

ANCHOR BOOKS

DRAMA

4Ab

DRAMA (cont'd)